Imagining Education

Bold Visions in Educational Research

Series Editors

Kenneth Tobin (*The Graduate Center, City University of New York, USA*)
Carolyne Ali-Khan (*College of Education & Human Services,
University of North Florida, USA*)

Co-founding Editor

Joe Kincheloe (with Kenneth Tobin)

Editorial Board

Daniel L. Dinsmore (*University of North Florida, USA*)
Gene Fellner (*College of Staten Island, City University of New York, USA*)
Alejandro J. Gallard (*Georgia Southern University, USA*)
S. Lizette Ramos de Robles (*University of Guadalajara, Mexico*)
Kashi Raj Pandey (*Kathmandu University, Nepal*)
L. Earle Reybold (*College of Education and Human Development,
George Mason University, USA*)

VOLUME 75

The titles published in this series are listed at *brill.com/bver*

Imagining Education

Taking CHAT Based Transformative Action

By

Sharada Gade

BRILL

LEIDEN | BOSTON

Cover illustration: Qutub Shahi Tombs, Hyderabad, photograph by Sirisha Gade

All chapters in this book have undergone peer review.

The Library of Congress Cataloging-in-Publication Data is available online at https://catalog.loc.gov

Typeface for the Latin, Greek, and Cyrillic scripts: "Brill". See and download: brill.com/brill-typeface.

ISSN 1879-4262
ISBN 978-90-04-51214-6 (paperback)
ISBN 978-90-04-51215-3 (hardback)
ISBN 978-90-04-51216-0 (e-book)

Copyright 2022 by Koninklijke Brill NV, Leiden, The Netherlands.
Koninklijke Brill NV incorporates the imprints Brill, Brill Nijhoff, Brill Hotei, Brill Schöningh, Brill Fink, Brill mentis, Vandenhoeck & Ruprecht, Böhlau Verlag and V&R Unipress.
All rights reserved. No part of this publication may be reproduced, translated, stored in a retrieval system, or transmitted in any form or by any means, electronic, mechanical, photocopying, recording or otherwise, without prior written permission from the publisher. Requests for re-use and/or translations must be addressed to Koninklijke Brill NV via brill.com or copyright.com.

This book is printed on acid-free paper and produced in a sustainable manner.

For fellow practitioners,
both teachers and researchers

For my students,
my friends and my family

∵

Contents

Preface XI

List of Figures and Tables XII

1   Introducing This Book: Arts-and-Science-in-the-Making 1
- 1 Preamble 1
- 2 Human Action 2
- 3 Cultivating Humanity 6
- 4 Human Transformation 9
- 5 Artistic Imagination 12
- 6 Humanistic Mathematics 16
- 7 Arts-and-Science-in-the-Making: Coda 18

2   Classroom Teaching: Schools Are for Teachers Too 23
- 1 Preamble 23
- 2 Where the Mind Is without Fear 24
- 3 Human Beings Who Are Integrated 26
- 4 The Rollercoaster of Teaching 29
- 5 Personal Practical Knowledge 32
- 6 Vygotsky in *Educational Psychology* 35
- 7 Schools Are for Teachers Too: Coda 38

3   Doctoral Research: Ascending to the Concrete 41
- 1 Preamble 41
- 2 Cooperative Learning | zpd 42
- 3 Collaborative Classroom Practice 48
- 4 Cultural Tools | Development | Methodology 54
- 5 Artefacts | Mediated Action | Mediated Agency 61
- 6 Activity | as Unit of Analysis 66
- 7 Ascending to the Concrete: Coda 71

4   Wider CHAT Research: From Activity to Directivity 76
- 1 Preamble 76
- 2 Making Human Beings Human 79
- 3 Situated Learning 82
- 4 Functional Approach to Literacy 87
- 5 Funds of Knowledge 92

VIII CONTENTS

6   Rousing Minds to Life   96
7   From Activity to Directivity: Coda   100

5   Practitioner Research: Art and Life Are Not One   105
1   Preamble   105
2   Narrative Research   107
3   Action Research   112
4   Teacher Research   116
5   Life History Research   121
6   Person Centric Research   125
7   Art and Life Are Not One: Coda   130

6   Pedagogical Perspectives: The Tone of Teaching   137
1   Preamble   137
2   Contexts for Local Change   140
3   Lads and Ear'oles   144
4   Socio-Institutional Pedagogy   147
5   Pedagogical Categories   151
6   Leading Activity across Ages   154
7   The Tone of Teaching: Coda   160

7   Critical Perspectives: Dialectical Inquiry   165
1   Preamble   165
2   Critical Consciousness   169
3   Critical Ontology for Teachers   173
4   Hidden Curriculum of Work   178
5   Research as Praxis   181
6   Research as Bricolage   184
7   Dialectical Inquiry: Coda   188

8   Curriculum Studies: Schooling Is a Bold and Risky Means   197
1   Preamble   197
2   Teacher as Artist Is Researcher   202
3   Deliberating the Practical   207
4   Arts in Education   210
5   Cases – Portfolios – Tasks   215
6   Taking Intelligent Action   219
7   Schooling Is a Bold and Risky Means: Coda   223

CONTENTS IX

9 Taking Transformative Action: Gaining from Triangulation 229
   1   Preamble   229
   2   Relational Knowing | The Equal to Sign   234
   3   Relational Agency | Problem Posing   241
   4   Cogenerative Dialogue | Making Measurements   247
   5   Expansive Learning | Meaningful Activities   253
   6   Forests and Trees | A Multilectic   259
   7   Gaining from Triangulation: Coda   264

10 Epilogue: Practitioner-as-Artist-and-Scientist 272
   1   Preamble   272
   2   Promising CHAT Avenues   273
   3   Short Summary of Key Findings   278
   4   Nature of Action, Theory and Dialectic at Play   282
   5   Practitioner-as-Artist-and-Scientist: Coda   287

   Subject Index   293
   Author Index   296

Preface

This writing is about a researcher-practitioner collaborating with teacher-practitioners and conducting instructional interventions in their ongoing mathematics classrooms. In an impressionist manner this also traces my intellectual journey from growing up and teaching middle school grades in India, my doctoral training in Norway, an extended post doctoral in Sweden which funded visiting fellowships in the US and UK, before returning to teach Bachelor and Master students in India.

Such a travelogue is rooted in perspectives of human development put forth by the Vygotsky, Luria and Leont'ev branch of Soviet psychology, termed cultural historical activity theory and/or CHAT in present times. Explicit attention to the concrete practical makes this effort, integrative – across time, continents and institutions, and interdisciplinary – braiding practitioner, pedagogical, critical and curriculum genres of inquiry.

In doing the above I draw on the arts as well as the sciences to present my case of arts-and-science-in-the-making, one that positions the taking of practitioner action and attention to human development as central to educational theory and practice. Three features singular to CHAT are realised (1) adopting a tool-and-result approach, (2) ascending from the conceptual abstract to the practical concrete and (3) conceiving the cultural-historical development of students and practitioners, besides their agency and becoming human, in a dialectical manner.

All chapters in this book begin with a preamble and end with a coda, offering thematic sections in-between that serve as insightful lenses with which to both grasp and take transformative action. The epilogue gathers aspects from across my writing that qualify the nature of action, nature of theory and nature of dialectic at play in various concrete practicals. I also forward a wholistic practitioner-as-artist-and-scientist as analytical unit, deployable across educational practices of different grain size.

The notion of taste as forwarded by the Russian literary philosopher Bakhtin, underpins my citing scholarship from diverse fields compatible with CHAT throughout my writing. Also germane is his counsel that art and life are not one and need to become united, as we answer our lifelong calling as practitioners. May our tribe flourish and ever increase.

Figures and Tables

Figures

1   TASK 1 of the group-task as in Gade (2006).   45
2   *When together* as in Gade (2006).   48
3   Five group solutions to *When together* as in Gade (2006).   49
4   *How heavy* as in Gade (2006).   49
5   Three kinds of group solutions to *How heavy* as in Gade (2006).   50
6   Rules of cooperation that were adhered to as in Gade (2006).   51
7   Engeström's triangular construct of activity as unit of analysis.   70
8   Students' inscriptions in the four-stage action cycle as in Gade (2012).   240
9   Students graphs as in Gade and Forsgren (2019).   259

Tables

1   Progression of students' learning within instruction as in Gade (2014).   51
2   Classification of artefacts in Olaf and Knut's instruction as in Gade (2006).   63
3   Leont'ev's construct of activity as unit of analysis, with farming as example.   68
4   The activity of conducting two group-tasks as unit of analysis.   69
5   Comparison of the practices of teaching and research, conceived as activity systems, in the study of teacher-researcher collaboration as in Gade and Blomqvist (2016).   247

CHAPTER 1

Introducing This Book
Arts-and-Science-in-the-Making

1 Preamble

For more than a decade I was classroom teacher at middle school grades in India. For more than a decade that followed I became classroom researcher at similar grades, by conducting doctoral work in Norway and an extended post-doctoral work in Sweden. This latter enabled me to pursue my research interests in US and UK as well. Now back in India, I find myself teaching students pursuing their Bachelors in Social Sciences and their Masters in Education at the Tata Institute of Social Sciences (TISS hereafter), Hyderabad. In this writing I thus attempt to capture the journey that was possible for me to make and gather many an invaluable notion which enabled me to understand the practice of school education, as well as the practice of educational research at large.

Five specific notions elaborated in sections that follow, guide such consolidated efforts (1) human action, (2) cultivating humanity, (3) human transformation, (4) artistic imagination and (5) humanistic mathematics. I conclude this chapter with a coda, wherein I argue for my pursuing an arts-and-science-in-the-making. Herein I broadly ask, what collective of theoretical, concrete-practical as well as methodological perspectives inform a productive practice of school education and educational research. In doing so and towards Chapter 9, I gravitate towards specific ways in which researchers and teachers can collaborate productively with one another as practitioners and take transformative action that is found necessary in ongoing classrooms.

I began classroom teaching after attaining a Masters degree in Physics. Such training was basis for teaching mathematics and science at middle school grades. This was also basis for continued reading in these subject areas, enabling me to spend time on aspects college courses allowed little time for back then. In doing so I freely navigated the expanse that lies between popular writing on one hand and philosophical commentaries on the other. While I enjoyed school teaching and reflected on many an intricate aspect that constituted its wider practice, such efforts were enormously time consuming as well. Even as I did not see myself pursing a doctorate at that time, I began writing short articles for *Teacher Plus*, a teacher's journal, about the elliptical shape

© KONINKLIJKE BRILL NV, LEIDEN, 2022 | DOI:10.1163/9789004512160_001

of an egg, fruits arranged on a push cart or Pythagoras' theorem say and later compiled a handbook for practicing teachers. Titled *Creativity: Modern school mathematics* (Gade, 2004/2018), I considered the ideas suggested therein to be worthy of trying out by teachers in ongoing mathematics classrooms.

Personal circumstances led me to leave classroom teaching and pursue doctoral work in Mathematics Education in due course. A program for pursuing doctoral work by practicing teachers was not available in India back then and still eludes many teachers the world over. One is expected to make the transition to full time doctoral work, with most programs geared for graduates straight out of college, so that the training imparted would presumably be of service for the longest duration ahead in society. Yet, I wanted to carry forward my experiences as classroom teacher and found a program that allowed me to pursue my own interests. Both in my doctoral program and many post doctoral fellowships which followed, I have had the freedom to seek notions that shed light on my experiences with teaching and my reflective understanding of the same. Such a focus has allowed me to also cast aside a lot of research that has little potential of enriching ongoing instruction in everyday schools.

Clearly empowering myself as teacher and researcher in such efforts, I have also worked to explicitly empower practitioners at large. Matching my free wheeling nature of reading, such a stance led my efforts to be interdisciplinary in spirit and lie at the intersection of four overlapping areas in educational research – mathematics education, cultural historical activity theory or CHAT perspectives, practitioner inquiry/research and classroom based curriculum studies. Greater exploring these fields in chapters that follow, I begin with the notion of human action and use the pronoun she in my writing even as I include all practitioners. Elaborating as I proceed on specific actions practitioners can take in their classrooms, I presently examine the political dimension of taking action for which I turn to writings of Hannah Arendt and Mahatma Gandhi.

2 Human Action

I was introduced to Hannah Arendt by Ken Tobin when in New York. My emerging from The Graduate Centre building of the City University of New York where he worked, to encounter eager tourists lined right across the street to reach the top of The Empire State building, offered a surreal backdrop to my reading Arendt's (1958) *The Human Condition*. Arendt's writings spring from a phenomenological tradition in Western philosophy and draw attention to our very being in the world. Holding lessons for how we practitioners could empower ourselves, Arendt points out that our intellect or thinking, identity or who we

INTRODUCING THIS BOOK 3

are, and ontology or the reality we live in, are primarily political. Dwelling on three key ideas grounded in this premise, I turn *first* to her notion of *plurality*,

> Plurality is the condition of human action because we are all the same, that is, human, in such a way that nobody is ever the same as anyone else who ever lived, lives, or will live. (Arendt, 1958, p. 8)

I find Arendt above to recognise each of us to be positioned differently as practitioners in the societal practice of education. She also acknowledges that the actions we take are bound to be plural in nature and different from one another's. Following Arendt, John McGowan *next* explains how taking diverse actions is also revealing of our *identity*,

> To act is to be human – in other words, only those who are free, who initiate something in the world, and who 'distinguishing themselves' as 'unique' count as human. ...
>
> Action in Arendt can be best defined as an activity staged in front of others that reveals the agent's identity. ... In political action one achieves one's identity, one doesn't lose it. Only that which creates identity counts as action in Arendt – .... (McGowan, 1997, p. 63)

Arendt allows me to view practitioner action taken in response to ongoing events in classroom scenarios, to be an activity by means of which we distinguish ourselves as unique. Given that our role as educators is a combination of the moral, intellectual and political, as practitioners we might also acknowledge that such revelation of individual identity is far from problem free. While we may find it necessary to justify the actions we take on occasion, at other times we are left interpreting the response of others to the actions we take. It is towards partial resolution of this predicament that I turn one *last* time to Arendt, on *education*,

> Education is the point at which we decide whether we love the world enough to assume responsibility for it and by the same token save it from that ruin which, except for renewal, except for the coming of the new and young, would be inevitable. And education, too, is where we decide whether we love our children enough to expel them from our world and leave them to their own devices, nor to strike from their hands their chance of undertaking something new, something unforeseen by us, but to prepare them in advance for the task of renewing a common world. (Arendt, 1968, p. 196)

Arendt above highlights for me, the authority laden role of practitioners in preparing our young and for renewing the world we share with them. Such a view implies that our young take action too, developing identities via taking shared responsibility towards our combined renewal. My drawing on Arendt is with intention of shedding light on the politically charged nature of our being and the political nature of actions we take everyday, as practitioners. For insight from someone who took political action that enabled a people to envision and renew their collective future in India, I turn to Mahatma Gandhi.

Unlike being introduced to Arendt by means of a single book, I came to Gandhi's thought in more ways than one. Growing up in the 1970s in India, amongst fellow beings grasping the significance of their struggle for Indian independence, meant tales of a past filled with sacrifice and a future yet to be realised. Amongst these inspiring anecdotes lay a quiet reverence for Gandhi coupled with the challenge of grasping his uniquely transformative views. Appearing ascetic on one hand and human on the other, English novelist E M Foster is believed to have said of him – He is with the great artists, though art was not his medium. In Arendt's view, I find Gandhi's actions to reveal his identity and deep humanity.

A cohort of four ideas seem key to understanding Gandhi's thoughts on human action – *swaraj, satyagraha, ahimsa* and *sarvodaya*. While the roots of these ideas lie in an older Indian philosophical tradition, it was their conceptualisation by Gandhi for political purposes that bore fruit in our collective movement for independence. Even as Gandhi engaged with wider international thought, Dennis Dalton (2012) argues that it was Gandhi's formulation of these ideas in local Indian languages that made them gain local currency. Speaking to the reality of colonisation of his people and recognising that change must come from within individuals, Gandhi spoke about the need for *swaraj*, self-rule or self-governing autonomy. Unlike independence, Gandhi argued *swaraj* to be achievable by self-knowledge, self-restraint and self-realisation. As a version of what may be referred to nowadays as one's empowerment, Gandhi's *swaraj* promised liberation from fear and ensured self-esteem. *Swaraj* in addition was achievable via the practice of *satyagraha* or holding firmly to truth, or achieving inner strength by exercising compassion and non-violence. Such authority had a greater power than brute force.

Gandhi's arguments for practicing non-violence and/or *ahimsa* holds enduring charm in that its practice recognises that the social realities in which action is taken can only be known in a partial, incomplete manner. It is thus imperative for individuals to not exercise violence in any form and strive collaboratively for greater truth in one's pursuits. Gene Sharp (2013) views Gandhi's concept of nonviolence to be neither inaction nor passive, but action

INTRODUCING THIS BOOK

bound by a dogged pursuit for truth. It was these very principles that galvanised a vast expanse of people in pre-independent India, whose self and collective sacrifice led to achieving their political freedom. Such achievements exemplify how the aims of *satyagraha* were also *sarvodaya* or upliftment for all. Far from being limited to individual freedom alone, the braiding and practice of *swaraj, satyagraha, ahimsa* and *sarvodaya* proclaimed social welfare for all, by definition.

I find Gandhi's call to action to have interesting parallels with the lives we practitioners lead. In the *first* is the manner in which we are given to forge connections between existing theory and practice. In contrast to using concepts which seem distant and as with Gandhi, practitioners are also asked to make connections between the two in circumstances where they have little option but to succeed. *Second*, Gandhi's *satyagraha* and *ahimsa* are values practitioners seem to implicitly follow in organising instructional scenarios, where constant negotiation seeks neither enemies nor losers. *Third* is the effort practitioners put into their everyday lives to gain some modicum of professional independence, a kind of effort which *swaraj* also demands. As Gandhi noted,

> *swaraj* will not drop from heaven, all of a sudden, one fine morning. But it has to be built up brick by brick by corporate self-effort. (Gandhi as quoted in Dalton, 2012, p. 17)

I find it significant to note here that Gandhi conceived means and ends in interchangeable terms. In recognising this very dialectic Joan Bondurant *finally* highlights a feature of utmost significance, that such manner of pursuing truth is end-creating as well. She points out,

> The claim for *satyagraha* is that through the operation of non-violent action the truth as judged by the fulfilment of human needs will emerge in the form of a mutually satisfactory and agreed-upon solution. (Bondurant, 1988, p. 195)

I wish to underscore the end-creating function that *satyagraha* promotes to be of immense methodological worth, one quite often neglected in mainstream educational research. I argue that in taking political action while (1) pursuing greater truth than is acknowledged at any one point of time, (2) towards ends that can be co-determined in agreement with those being researched, besides (3) adopting an end-creating stance, these aspects help steer and guide the conduct of one's research in terms of democratic and equitable forms of educational inquiry. Towards these holistic aims and by viewing Arendt's plurality alongside Gandhi's political action, I have striven over the years to free my own evolving professional thinking in line with tenets of liberal education. I now turn to Martha Nussbaum, who speaks insightfully to this very issue.

3 Cultivating Humanity

I came to Martha Nussbaum's writings via those of John Elliott, while conducting independent post doctoral research. I found Elliott's (1978/2007) distinction between research on education and educational research, useful in informing the kind of research I was myself contemplating. Following CHAT perspectives which I soon introduce, my collaborating with a teacher in her classroom led me to Elliott's writings within the area of action research. I presently discuss two points Elliott makes, before two which Nussbaum makes. Elliott *first* sees the conduct of *research on education* as viewing classrooms to be beyond the sphere of practitioner action and seeking to develop formal theory, like cognitive dissonance of students, by making use of a priori concepts. In contrast, *educational research* views classrooms from the perspective of action which practitioners can take to develop a substantive theory of action so as to bring about change, using a posteriori concepts. While the former views participants as objects of research, in the latter the meaning of actions taken by teachers and students is subject to interpretation. One also does not deploy definitive concepts common to an abstract class of objects in the latter, but sensitising concepts that are heuristic and guide action. It was my preference for conducting educational research that guided my design of many a classroom intervention from then on.

Extending the distinction just made between research on education and educational research, Elliott *second* makes a parallel distinction between teacher effectiveness research and research based teaching, with regards to research involving teachers. It is here that Elliott directs attention to the distinction Nussbaum makes between a search for general rules versus universal rules in research. While *general rules* emerge from and cover many studies by virtue of non-concrete characteristics often abstracted from processes of time and circumstance, *universal rules* on the contrary attend to concrete characteristics that apply across numerous cases which are similar. About the latter Elliott observes,

> As such they are useful guides to perception, to discerning the practically/ethically relevant features of particular concrete and complex situations that tend to repeat themselves from one situation to another. This

INTRODUCING THIS BOOK

is quite different from the normative function of *general rules* as 'the ultimate authorities against which the correctness of particular choices is assessed.' *Universal rules*, captured in summaries of good concrete judgements in similar cases, represent the 'voice of concrete practical experience.' (Elliott, 2009, p. 177)

Following Nussbaum and Elliott, the above distinction brought clarity to my own need to search for universal rules in my forthcoming conduct of educational research. My taking such a stand in turn directed my attention to the importance of practitioner perception in being able to discern the many concrete aspects that would likely yield universal rules. Even as I greater examine these aspects in relation to practitioners in Chapter 5, I presently turn to Nussbaum's own writings on this issue.

Breathing fresh life into ancient Greek literature, Nussbaum at *first* discusses perception in relation to the Aristotelian conception of a human being and how to live a good life. She explains *human perception* to be a form of responsiveness or ability to read concrete situations and single out what is relevant for thought and action. The intention here is not to transcend any given situation, but see life as a story worth embracing, filled in its entirety with its pains, surprises and joys. Nussbaum thus views an agentive person as one who deals with a complex situation by not missing out on concrete details, but be able to deal with aspects of both emotional and practical relevance. She argues,

> But this means that the person of practical wisdom lies surprisingly close to the artist and/or the perceiver of art, not in the sense that this conception reduces moral value to aesthetic value or makes moral judgement a matter of taste, but in the sense that we are asked *to see morality as a high type of vision of and response to the particular*, an ability that we seek and value in our greatest artists, and especially our novelists, whose value for us is above all practical and never detached from our questions about how to live. (Nussbaum, 1990, p. 84, emphasis added)

Just as Nussbaum views human perception in terms of the complexities of life itself, she conceives practical wisdom too in terms of a highly artistic vision of and a response to the particular. In addition, I find Nussbaum arguing literature to be vital means for cultivating such perception and wisdom life-long. Such a view follows Aristotle's key observation that each of us would have never lived enough, so that without reading our lives would remain confined and parochial. The underlying aim then is for each citizen to become a person with potential for practical wisdom, based on cultivating a practical perception that can be put to use on behalf of the entire group one belongs to. Nussbaum explains,

> Aristotelian education is aimed at producing citizens who are perceivers. ... As both Aristotle and Periclean Athens insist, the core of this education will be found in the studies we now call 'the humanities' – in the qualitatively rich study of human life, through works of art and literature, through the study of history, and through humanistic forms of social inquiry. (Nussbaum, 1990, p. 103)

Nussbaum's perception based view of education, allows me to *second* introduce her notion of *liberal education*. Here she draws on philosopher Seneca's notion of 'liberalis' as being connected to freedom, encouraging students to liberate their minds from any form of bondage and also take charge of one's thinking. Towards this she quotes Seneca from the end of his treatise on the destructive effects of anger and hatred saying,

> Soon we shall breathe our last. Meanwhile, while we live, while we are among human beings, let us cultivate our humanity. (Seneca, as quoted in Nussbaum, 1997, p. 301)

Nussbaum thus offers three ways by which one could liberate our minds and cultivate our humanity. *First* by developing a capacity for critically examining the impact on one's thinking, of one's traditions. This would enable us to live a well examined life as proclaimed by Socrates, whose student Plato was in turn Aristotle's tutor. *Second* by viewing oneself as belonging not to one's local group alone but also as citizens of the wider world order. This implies being a human being who is bound to very many others by ties of recognition and concern. *Finally*, by developing *a narrative imagination* or as she explains, the ability to think and place oneself in the shoes of a person different from oneself. This positions one to understand the myriad social circumstances that could be shaping the wishes and desires of others we encounter.

Where Aristotelian education sought to produce citizens as perceivers, Nussbaum's notion of liberal education extends the same onto the world stage. The aim of personal responsiveness is nonetheless central to both, geared towards well informed thought and action. I find the notions of being thoughtful, responsive and liberal, central to our everyday work as practitioners, guiding how we as well as our young can be nurtured. With the role of humanities recognised as key is such preparation, I now turn to introduce psychological neo-Vygotskian perspectives of CHAT whose pursuit is geared towards a key

INTRODUCING THIS BOOK

organising premise – that of determining what is distinctively human, in us human beings.

4　　Human Transformation

I was introduced to Lev Vygotsky, whose pioneering ideas form basis for cultural historical activity theory or CHAT perspectives of developmental psychology, during doctoral work by Roger Säljö. This proved a turning point in my search for notions that could both shed light and inform the manner in which ongoing instruction could be viewed and organised in everyday classrooms. Even as I exemplify the use of many a CHAT notion throughout this book, I presently discuss four ideas which sketch their singular view of human development. Representative of the branch of Soviet psychology that was steered primarily by Lev Vygotsky, Alexander Luria, Aleksei Leont'ev and their many collaborators in the 1930s, I draw from *Mind in society,* a work in English which caught world wide attention when first published in 1978.

Differentiating us humans from our closest relatives the apes, the *first* idea relates to the *role of speech* in carrying out practical activity with cultural tools and signs. Drawing on research comparing the development of apes and children, Vygotsky observed the latter's use of practical tools during their preverbal stage as being comparable to that of the apes. However, as soon as speech became part of practical activity, the actions of children stand transformed and become organised in their development as a single complex psychological function. Vygotsky argued,

> The specifically human capacity for language enables children to provide for auxiliary tools in the solution of difficult tasks, to overcome impulsive action, to plan a solution to a problem prior to its execution and to master their own behaviour. Signs and words serve children first and foremost as a means of social contact with other people. The cognitive and communicative functions of language then become the basis of a new and superior form of activity in children, distinguishing them from animals. (Vygotsky, 1978, pp. 28–29)

The study of the distinctive nature of human behaviour, mediated by tools such as speech in communication, to overcome impulsiveness and to master one's own behaviour has since became leitmotif of Vygotskian research. The *second* related idea which Vygotsky introduced pertains to human *perception of real objects*, about which he argued,

A special feature of human perception – which arises at a very young age – is the *perception of real objects*. This is something for which there is no analogy in animal perception. By this term I mean I do not see the world simply in color and shape but also as a world with sense and meaning. I do not merely see something round and black with two hands; I see a clock and I can distinguish one hand from the other. (Vygotsky, 1978, p. 33)

In human beings engaging with the external world by drawing upon personal sense and meaning, Vygotsky *third* drew attention to our ability to solve problems by voluntarily establishing connections with relevant tools available in our sociocultural or even sociohistorical milieu. For example the clock above could be used as means by us to bide time while waiting to catch one's train. This manner of restructuring and mastering one's own psychological activity in a voluntarily manner, represented for Vygotsky a fundamental break of human behaviour from that observed in animals. Far from being driven by innate biology, Vygotsky termed such behaviour as *higher psychological activity* and recognised the vital ability of human beings to control their behaviour from their outside. In human development making such manner of qualitative leap in relation to that which animals display, Vygotsky went on to proclaim,

The internalisation of socially rooted and historically developed activities is the distinguishing feature of human psychology, the basis of the qualitative leap from animal to human psychology. As yet, the barest outline of this process is known. (Vygotsky, 1978, p. 57)

In highlighting the uniqueness of human behaviour in its ability to use tools and signs to master oneself from the outside, Vygotskian premise opened up the scope for developmental research worldwide. Yet and at the same time, in tracing the path of internalisation or the manner in which culturally, socially and historically rooted forms of human activity grew inwards, Vygotsky foresaw the methodological challenges his line of thinking proposed and recognised *fourth* that,

The search for method becomes one of the most important problems of the entire enterprise of understanding the uniquely human forms of psychological activity. In this case, the method is simultaneously prerequisite and product, the tool and the result of the study. (Vygotsky, 1978, p. 65, emphasis in original)

The brief outline of ideas just offered, forming basis for what could be perceived as a theory of human development within cultural-historical besides

INTRODUCING THIS BOOK

practical activity, directs attention to the myriad ways in which Vygotskian research could be carried out. Having bearing on forms of activity that could be educational, I now draw attention to two specific aspects, (1) how CHAT perspectives could inform instruction, besides (2) the kind of transformative potential their perspectives portend.

As to the manner in which ongoing instruction can be organised in everyday classrooms, I mention two premise in brief. *First* is Vygotsky's (1997) recognition that any educational process needs to be active at three levels, that of the teacher, the student and the environment between them. *Second* is his radical view that when enabling students to master cultural tools to steer their psychological or cultural-historical development, instruction needs to proceed *ahead of* and/or *lead* development (Stetsenko & Arievitch, 2002). Having implications for how practitioners could orchestrate instruction and as elaborated in greater detail in chapters that follow, these premise next direct attention to the nature of human transformation which the CHAT enterprise envisages. It is to explore these very aspects that I turn to Anna Stetsenko who guided my post-doctoral work, once again at The Graduate Center, City University of New York. I had come across Anna's writings during doctoral work and sought her consent for this opportunity when I met her at The Vatican, which we both happened to visit on sidelines of attending the International Society for Cultural and Activity Research or ISCAR conference at Rome.

Clarifying Vygotsky's contribution to psychology and psychology's contribution to society, Stetsenko underscores human development to be transformative in two respects. *First* is the very transformation of existing environments towards creation of new ones. Knowledge is here viewed as a practical act, brought to fruition while producing and deploying tools in collaborative material practices. Such actions are geared towards setting individuals free and creating newer forms of social life. Together with Igor Arievitch she finds such seamless flow of knowledge and practice to not only represent transformation, but also a unity of its theoretical and practical dimensions. Alluding to Kurt Lewin's dictum well known in the field of action research, they offer the following key insight,

> Kurt Lewin's famous expression that there is nothing more practical than a good theory could thus be expanded, in the spirit of Vygotskian approach, by the mirror expression – that there is nothing more theoretically rich than a good practice. The works by Vygotsky and his colleagues are a living embodiment of *such a two-fold view*, suggesting an alternative to psychology's outdated image and dubious social role in perpetuating the status quo in society. Instead, they help to open this discipline to the challenges of creating a new, free and equal, society for all – .... (Stetsenko & Arievitch, 2004, p. 78, emphasis added)

Stetsenko *second* articulates a *transformative activist stance* as central to individuals contributing to and changing their world. According to this view, human transformation is a unified process of knowing, being, doing and becoming human. Not surprisingly she identifies teaching/learning to be at the heart of this process and explains the enterprise of education to not be about acquiring knowledge for the sake of knowing,

> but *an active project of becoming human,* a process that drives develop-ment and makes it possible ... Learning then appears as the pathway to creating one's identity by finding one's place among other people and, ultimately, finding a way to contribute to the continuous flow of sociocul-tural practices. That is, learning appears as a project of constantly striving to join in with historically evolving, transformative practices of humanity and, through this, of becoming oneself – a unique human being who rep-resents a distinctive and irreplaceable instantiation of humanness and a unique contribution to it. (Stetsenko, 2008, p. 487)

While in the first view of transformation presented above, Stetsenko and Arievitch make explicit the ideological quest in CHAT of creating a free and equal society by challenging the status quo; in the second, Stetsenko views the enterprise of education in terms of our becoming human while contributing to historical sociocultural practices in society. I argue either view to be valuable encapsulation not only of Vygotsky's own efforts in laying the foundation of contemporary CHAT, but also of providing direction to how we practitioners could conceive ongoing practices of instruction within everyday schooling. In doing so I find Stetsenko to conceptually parallel Arendt's creation of one's identity in taking human action that is political by nature, besides Nussbaum's use of a narrative imagination in terms of which practitioners could conceive educational experiences of the many social others we encounter. It is to exam-ine the role of artistic imagination towards these very ends, that I now turn to writings of Elliot Eisner and Maxine Greene.

5 Artistic Imagination

I came across Elliot Eisner's (2002) *What can education learn from the arts about the practice of education?* as part of wider literature search during doc-toral work and was keen to acquaint myself with his arguments for two reasons. *First* and as I discuss in the next chapter, the school I taught at was founded by an artist whose approach to many an issue provided an alternative worldview

INTRODUCING THIS BOOK

to the one my own scientific training brought forward. *Second* and as with Aristotle's arguments which favour the practical, I was thankful that there were well thought through answers to such a question at all. I have since asked my Master students to draw on Eisner's writings for their take home assignments.

I find Eisner's arguments compelling on many fronts, from which I presently discuss four. It is appropriate to clarify here that by arts Eisner does not refer to fine arts or painting and music alone but arts as a distinct field of human inquiry, just as the pursuit of science also is. *First* and unlike the situation faced by students in many instructional scenarios, where there is a single answer to a question, one which the teacher alone seems to know, in practicing arts Eisner points out that,

> Not all problems have single correct answers. One of the important lessons that arts teach is that solutions to problems can take many forms. This lesson from the arts would not be so important were it not for the fact that so much of what is taught in school teaches just the opposite lesson. ...
>
> The arts teach a different lesson. They celebrate imagination, multiple perspectives and the importance of personal interpretation. (Eisner, 1992, p. 594)

Opening the pursuit of content in any curricular subject to the personal and the imaginative, Eisner *second* points out that in practicing the arts, ends may follow means. This implies that in carrying out various artistic acts, our work may suggest ends to which ongoing work surrenders itself. Since ends need not precede but could follow artistic acts, unlike in a deductive stance, Eisner uses John Dewey's term *flexible purposing* to describe such a shift in one's educational objectives,

> Flexible purposing is opportunistic; it capitalizes on the emergent features appearing within a field of relationships. It is not rigidly attached to predefined aims when the possibility of better ones emerge. The kind of thinking that flexible purposing requires thrives best in an environment in which the rigid adherence to a plan is not a necessity. As experienced teachers well know, the surest road to hell in a classroom is to stick to the lesson plan no matter what. (Eisner, 2002, p. 10)

In line with both arguments cited above, Eisner *third* draws attention to the cultivation of dispositions in students along with their acquisition of curricular skills. Laying emphasis on exploration, the metaphorical and the very journey in education, he seeks a culture of schooling, in which more importance is placed on exploration than on discovery, more value is assigned to surprise than to control, more attention is devoted to what is distinctive than to what is standard, more interest is related to what is metaphorical than to what is literal. It is an educational culture that has a greater focus on becoming than on being, places more value on the imaginative than on the factual, assigns greater priority to valuing than to measuring, and regards the quality of the journey as more educationally significant than the speed at which the destination is reached. (Eisner, 2002, p. 16)

Even as I examine various intricacies of the above outlined stand while dwelling on curricular studies in Chapter 8, I turn to Eisner one *last* time in relation to the importance he places upon artistic imagination. In doing so I find him recall poet Robert Browning as saying 'a man's reach should exceed his grasp or what's a heaven for?' Arguing against a directive of simply following procedures within instruction, Eisner sides once again with Dewey in utilising imagination to outrun evidence and become an instrument for the good. In clear echo to both Aristotle and Nussbaum discussed previously, Eisner concludes,

Imagination is no mere ornament; nor is art. Together they can liberate us from our indurated habits. They might help us restore decent purpose to our efforts and help us create the kind of schools our children deserve and our culture needs. Those aspirations, my friends, are stars worth stretching for. (Eisner, 2002, p. 16)

Eisner's arguments and emphasis on artistic imagination bring me to Maxine Greene who speaks in explicit terms about its role for our very existence. In particular she makes four points about the dangers that lurk when students and teachers are governed by an alienated, technocratised vision of education. Speaking in favour of imagined realities and looking at situations as if they could be otherwise, Greene at *first* argues,

Imagination, as is well known, is the capacity that enables us to move through the barriers of the taken-for-granted and summon up alternative possibilities for living, for being in the world. It permits us to set aside (at least for a while) the stiflingly familiar and the banal. It opens us to visions of the possible rather than the predictable; it permits us, if we choose to give our imaginations free play, to look at things as if they could be otherwise. (Greene, 1994, pp. 494–495)

INTRODUCING THIS BOOK   15

As with Eisner, Greene *second* points to the dangers of an enterprise of school-ing being at odds with the experience of the arts. She finds policy documents in the USA, to often focus on the manageable, competitive, predictable and measurable, resulting in both students and teachers to not define themselves but be defined by others. Greene observes,

> They have also helped support the dominant arguments for the devel-opment of 'higher-level skills,' academic achievement, standards, and preparation for the workplace.
>   The danger afflicting both teachers and students because of such emphases is, in part, the danger of feeling locked in to existing circum-stances defined by others. Young people find themselves described as 'human resources' rather than as persons who are centers of choice and evaluation. ... Perhaps it is no wonder that the dominant mood in many classrooms is one of passive reception. (Greene, 1995, p. 379)

About the dangers of teachers experiencing a sense of alienation arising out of the scenario portrayed above, I have myself cited Greene while examining the nature of relationship my collaborating teacher and I were able to realise while conducting an intervention in her classroom. Herein by drawing on our own selves, our shared intersubjectivity as well as the subjectivity of our students, we remained alive to ongoing educational demands and needs. In this regard Greene *third* argues,

> Alienated teachers, out of touch with their own existential reality, may contribute to the distancing and even to the manipulating that pre-sumably takes place in many schools. This is because, estranged from themselves as they are, they may well treat whatever they imagine to be selfhood as a kind of commodity, a possession they carry within, imper-vious to organizational demand and impervious to control. Such people are not personally present to others or in the situations of their lives. They can, even without intending it, treat others as objects or things. (Greene, 1979, as in Gade, 2015, pp. 607–608)

In line with her above outlined stance, I find Greene to *finally* dispute the notion that knowledge is antecedent and independent of knowers. Greene perceives the relationship between knower and known as co-present in dia-lectical terms, each modifying and shaping the other. Clearly echoing Nuss-baum's views on the subtle qualities of human perception, I argue it prudent to recognise this aspect to hold true for students as well as teachers alike. About the resulting quest for individual freedom by the knower, I find her arguments parallel the dialectic at play between theory and practice besides being and becoming human, which Stetsenko draws attention to. Greene argues,

> a teacher in search of his/her own freedom may be the only kind of teacher who can arouse young persons to go in search of their own. It will be argued as well that children who have been provoked to reach beyond themselves, to wonder, to imagine, to pose their own questions are the ones most likely to learn to learn. (Greene, 1988, p. 14)

Having traced a running thread in relation to the nature of being human in preceding sections by dwelling on human action, cultivating humanity, human transformation and artistic imagination, I now turn to examine and outline a philosophy of mathematics that is argued as humanistic.

6   Humanistic Mathematics

I first became familiar with writings of Ruben Hersh and Imre Lakatos during doctoral work. I found time to revisit these again only recently, while teaching a course titled *Appreciation of Mathematics* to Bachelor of Arts students in the Social Sciences. There was thus occasion to examine Hersh's arguments from his book *What is mathematics really?*,

> Repudiating Platonism and formalism, while recognising the reasons that make them (alternatively) seem plausible, I show that *from the viewpoint of philosophy* mathematics must be understood as a human activity, a social phenomena, part of human culture, historically evolved, and intelligible only in a social context. I call this viewpoint 'humanist.' (Hersh, 1997, p. XI)

With respect to the societal practice of education, I argue Hersh's view proposing a humanistic philosophy of mathematics to be both subtle and profound. He is able to draw attention to an issue oft neglected in relation to the everyday instruction of mathematics – that of the meaninglessness which a vast majority of students encounter while doing mathematics in everyday classrooms. The incessant dialectic between the knower and the known, each shaping the other which Greene draws our attention to, is missing in its everyday instruction for the most part. The causes for this may lie in a lack of personal familiarity or confidence with subscribing to a humanistic view of mathematics, by the spectrum of professionals from curriculum developers on one hand and classroom teachers on the other. As a result the subject of mathematics risks being presented as an activity far removed from the very activity of human living.

In *Proofs and refutations: the logic of mathematical discovery,* Lakatos (1976) examines the principal ways in which the body of mathematics progresses – by rigorous proofs and critical refutations. He argues in addition that far too much emphasis is placed in present day instruction of the subject of mathematics, upon what he calls meta-mathematics or the formal aspects of the overall discipline. There is hardly any attention as a consequence to its informal and heuristic nature, one that contributes to its situational logic of growth and personal exploration. While the field of mathematics education research and its societal practice have made considerable gains to redress such a view in contemporary times, the causes for insufficient attainment in the subject of mathematics by a vast majority of students may well have to do with how its nature is far from seen from a humanistic point of view, in line with Hersh.

I find arguments of Hersh and Lakatos above particularly relevant to those made by Anne Watson (2008) in her writing *School mathematics as a special kind of mathematics*. Describing school mathematics as the institutionalisation of mathematical knowledge for student novices in wider society, Watson argues that the kind of mathematical activity which takes place in this sphere of education to be quite removed from the kind of activity in which mathematicians themselves take part. Contending school mathematics to not be a subset of the discipline of mathematics, Watson argues that the major goals of school mathematics are to prepare students for future study and employment. Towards these aims students are required to explicitly recall ways of working in mathematics, with fluency and accuracy. Yet Watson points out, that coming to know mathematics involves guiding everyday thinking of students, in ways that conform to modes of inquiry and critique intrinsic to the discipline of mathematics itself. This latter, she argues, requires school teachers to gain from their personal experience of doing mathematics over time, as a result of which they could explore first hand the kind of questions which have intellectual and mathematical purpose, beyond pedagogic purpose alone. Watson goes on to argue,

> Limited time slots, curricular pressures, and assessment regimes constrain or prevent the development of the kinds of questions and ways of working which characterise the discipline. Authority in school mathematics lies with teachers, textbooks and assessment regimes, not with mathematical argument.
>
> It is not only ways of working and goals that are different between school and disciplinary maths; it is the way that these shape the available

forms of mathematical enquiry that makes school mathematics a different discipline, with its own rules, purposes, authorities and warrants. (Watson, 2008, p. 7)

My own efforts in attempting to address the problematic Watson refers to has been to collaborate with teachers in their classrooms at middle school grades and initiate transformative action focused on promoting students' cultural-historical development in line with CHAT. Such an effort has meant conducting interventions which not only challenge prior status quo in instruction, but also bring about the unity of knowing, being, becoming and doing for students and teachers, in line with Stetsenko.

While our drawing on CHAT has been productive, as I greater describe in Chapter 9, the viability of our interventions also drew on our ability to focus on instructional activities we orchestrated for students in our care. Serving as unit of analysis for gauging the cultural-historial development of students and teachers, two key features of such activities have been identified by Wolff-Michael Roth and Luis Radford (2011) in *A cultural-historical perspective on mathematics teaching and learning*. *First*, such instructional activities are the smallest unit which allow practitioners to understand human thought, consciousness, emotions, personality and subjectivity within a system of societal relations, outside of which there is no activity per se. As greater dwelt in Chapter 3, the notion of activity here is holistic and human in terms of Hersh. *Second*, in practical activity that is instructional in its objectives, the conscious, the sensual and the concrete are irreducible moments of the very same phenomena. Herein teachers as well as students are subjects of the social world they are taking part and where in the process, both are reproduced and changed. I argue such a stance to echo Stetsenko's views discussed earlier, that education is an active project of becoming human while contributing to practices that are historical and collaborative, whereby existing environments are transformed to create new ones. Such processes drive, lead and/or make human development possible. The underlying Marxian premise in either of these views is that it is not consciousness that gives rise to human life, but human life that gives rise to our consciousness and thought. In other words, as Vygotsky recognised, material, practical and meaningful life determines human consciousness and not vice versa.

7   Arts-and-Science-in-the-Making: Coda

The collective of arguments forwarded by scholars whom I allude to in preceding sections, prepares a broad, yet rich canvas in terms of which I intend to

INTRODUCING THIS BOOK

build my arguments in chapters that follow. This might thus be appropriate occasion to ponder about what manner of study I conduct, especially when in the problematic I examine, the material and practical, individual and collective, ideal and real, besides animal and human come together in dialectic flux. Is my underlying rubric artistic in enterprise or scientific in endeavour? Even as I argue for a productive blend of both, I presently turn to Jacob Bronowski and Yehuda Elkana to help shed light and nuance various aspects of such an effort.

In *Science and human values,* Bronowski (1965) views our collective pursuit of science as human progress itself and argues,

> Science is not a mechanism but a human progress, and not a set of findings but a search for them. Those who think science is ethically neutral confuse the findings of science, which are, with the activity of science, which is not. ... But human search and research is a learning by steps of which none is final, and the mistakes of one generation are rungs in the ladder, no less than their correction by the next. This is why the values of science turn out to be recognisable human values: ... (Bronowski, 1965, pp. 63–64)

In line with Bronowski, my arguments in previous sections and those I present in sections that follow, are points of valuable departure for my purpose at hand in two distinct ways. In the *first* they serve as rungs in the ladder of the activity of science which are far from final or finished in substance or thought. While invaluable as stepping stones for carrying out further explorations, they are just as fallible as we humans also are. *Second,* as Bronowski does not fail to reiterate, science just as with art, is not a copy of nature but its human recreation. It is thus that in Chapters 5 through 8, I examine writings in areas that complement CHAT research – practitioner research, pedagogical perspectives, critical perspectives, besides curriculum studies. Such a stance is intentional and is designed to serve our collective ability to envision what is possible, as well as take transformative action as practitioners. For the tentative and value laden nature of such efforts, be they conceived as science or art, I now turn to Elkana whose notion of science-in-the-making I extend for my purposes as arts-and-science-in-the-making.

As philosopher of science, in his writing titled *Science, philosophy of science and science teaching*, Yehuda Elkana (2000) makes two points I consider valuable in understanding how science is recreated to make the human progress Bronowski views to be the natuure of science. *First* is the distinction Elkana makes between science and science-in-the-making. This allows him to distinguish the public language of science from its private language. The student of science, Elkana argues, must know that there is no one language of science in which discoveries are made. By recognising the presence of a language of science that is prevalent in its public discourse, one we participate in accordance with convention, he also points to a language utilised when science is in the making or in flux. Arguing science-in-flux to not be ambiguous, but private science which can be approached through individual cases, he maintains,

> The logic of science is only the description of the axiomatically formulated, polished, ideal science; logic cannot account for science-in-the-making, for science-in-flux. In order to understand what science-in-flux looks like, we have to forgo the elegance and clearness of logical description. Science-in-flux is not unambiguous, it is not public science, but private science. It can be approached only through individual cases and not through generalisations. That is the reason why the psychological and the historical argument are preferable to the logical one. (Elkana, 2000, pp. 472–473)

Belying a singular logic of scientific discovery and acknowledging the presence of vagueness in the personal conduct of any scientific study, Elkana thus seeks case studies which present historical and psychological aspects of any individual's efforts.

Following Elkana, I view the pursuit of CHAT research and its wider enterprise to currently be in a science-in-flux stage. Demanding a two-fold practical-theoretical approach as argued by Stetsenko and Arievitch, in an endeavour that is no doubt time consuming as well, the ability of its use to bring about cultural-historical development on one hand and newer forms of social life to live by on the other, holds much promise. It is towards my ability to evidence these very aspects that I consider my present writing as a case history, one for which I draw on my artistic instincts as practitioner and scientific training as researcher. My practice of educational research by drawing upon CHAT perspectives, thus has me view my combined efforts as an arts-and-science-in-the-making. In continued pursuit of such a personal science, with every intention of contributing to its public manifestation as well, I turn next to classroom teaching where my extended journey in this direction all began.

References

Arendt, H. (1958). *The human condition.* University of Chicago Press.
Arendt, H. (1968). The crisis in education. In H. Arendt (Ed.), *Between past and future: Eight exercises in political thought* (pp. 173–196). Penguin Books.

Bondurant, J. (1988). *Conquest of violence: The Gandhian philosophy of conflict*. Princeton University Press.

Bronowski, J. (1965). *Science and human values*. Harper and Row.

Dalton, D. (2012). *Mahatma Gandhi: Nonviolent power in action*. Columbia University Press.

Eisner, E. (1992). The misunderstood role of the arts in human development. *The Phi Delta Kappan, 73*(8), 591–595.

Eisner, E. (2002). What can education learn from the arts about the practice of education? *Journal of Curriculum and Supervision, 18*(1), 4–16.

Elkana, Y. (2000). Science, philosophy of science and science teaching. *Science and Education, 9*(5), 463–485.

Elliott, J. (2007). Classroom research: Science or commonsense. In J. Elliot (Ed.), *Reflecting where the action is: The selected works of John Elliott* (pp. 91–98). Routledge. (Original work published 1978)

Elliott, J. (2009). Research-based teaching. In S. Gewirtz, P. Mahony, I. Hextall, & A. Cribb (Eds.), *Changing teacher professionalism: International trends, challenges and ways forward* (pp. 170–183). Routledge.

Gade, S. (2015). Unpacking teacher-researcher collaboration with three theoretical frameworks – A case of expansive learning activity? *Cultural Studies of Science Education, 10*(3), 603–619.

Gade, S. (2018). *Creativity: Modern school mathematics – A resource book for mathematics teachers*. Orient Blackswan. (Original work published 2004)

Greene, M. (1979). Teaching as personal reality. In A. Liberman & L. Miller (Eds.), *New perspectives of staff development* (pp. 23–35). Teacher College Press.

Greene, M. (1988). *The dialectic of freedom*. Teachers College Press.

Greene, M. (1994). Carpe diem: The arts and school restructuring. *Teachers College Record, 95*(4), 494–507.

Greene, M. (1995). Art and imagination: Reclaiming the sense of possibility. *The Phi Delta Kappan, 76*(5), 378–382.

Hersh, R. (1997). *What is mathematics really?* Oxford University Press.

Lakatos, I. (1976). *Proofs and refutations: The logic of mathematical discovery*. Cambridge University Press.

McGowan, J. (1997). *Hannah Arendt: An introduction*. University of Minnesota Press.

Nussbaum, M. (1990). *Love's knowledge: Essays on philosophy and literature*. Oxford University Press.

Nussbaum, M. (1997). *Cultivating humanity: A classical defense of reform in liberal education*. Harvard University Press.

Roth, W.-M., & Radford, L. (2011). *A cultural-historical perspective on mathematics teaching and learning*. Sense.

Sharp, G. (2013). *How non-violent struggle works*. The Albert Einstein Institution.

Stetsenko, A. (2008). From relational ontology to transformative activist stance on development and learning: Expanding Vygotsky's (CHAT) project. *Cultural Studies of Science Education, 3*(2), 471–491.

Stetsenko, A., & Arievitch, I. (2002). Teaching, learning, and development: A post-Vygotskian perspective. In G. Wells & G. Claxton (Eds.), *Learning for life in the 21st century* (pp. 84–96). Blackwell Publishers.

Stetsenko, A., & Arievitch, I. M. (2004). Vygotskian collaborative project of social transformation: History, politics, and practice in knowledge construction. *The International Journal of Critical Psychology, 12*(4), 58–80.

Vygotsky, L. S. (1978). *Mind in society: The development of higher psychological processes.* Harvard University Press.

Vygotsky, L. S. (1997). *Educational psychology.* St. Lucie Press.

Watson, A. (2008). School mathematics as a special kind of mathematics. *For the Learning of Mathematics, 28*(3), 3–7.

CHAPTER 2

Classroom Teaching

Schools Are for Teachers Too

1 Preamble

My history as a school student saw me attend a round the corner *Blue Bells Nursery*, a girls only *Mater Dei Convent School* and a privately run *Delhi Public School* in India's capital of New Delhi. This was followed by attending a central government run *Kendriya Vidyalaya* in Patna, the capital city of the Indian state of Bihar. My experiences with teaching later on were at the privately run *Vidyaranya High School* in Hyderabad, capital of the Indian state of Telangana. My journey as a student prior to teaching was not eventful, except for dealing with expectations built into various school systems. A liking for the sciences however took root, accompanied by an appreciation for societal progress that its pursuit brings. Watching the Apollo mission land on the moon in 1969 as a nine year old was by all means inspiring. Yet, there was less attention back then to issues facing the girl child, as she, while privileged to attend school had to navigate a society wanting of many a civic solution. While the ideal of working towards a better country was omnipresent, the means for making relevant contributions were meagre. It was against such a backdrop that I completed a Masters and took to classroom teaching.

In portraying teaching and the central role this had in my professional journey to date, I take a broad view and dwell on five significant aspects. *First*, I engage with writings of Indian poet laureate Rabindranath Tagore to exemplify the kind of idealism that was commonplace while growing up in Independent India. *Second*, I engage with Indian philosopher Jiddu Krishnamurti whose original thoughts I had opportunity to examine and read while teaching middle school grades. *Third*, I attempt to sketch classroom teaching as I have myself experienced, viewed from personal reflections on the same in later life. Leading from this and *fourth* I outline the notion of personal practical knowledge which stemming from a narrative perspective allows one to capture teaching. I engage *finally* with Vygotsky's own writings with regards to teaching and engage with Seymour Sarason in my coda, in relation to how teaching could be a lonely profession and that schools are for teachers too.

© KONINKLIJKE BRILL NV, LEIDEN, 2022 | DOI:10.1163/9789004512160_002

24 CHAPTER 2

2   Where the Mind Is without Fear

Rabindranath Tagore wrote at a time of social upheaval, national unrest, political strife and instability in India, one which demanded considerable personal sacrifice and thoughtful action from us all. I engage with three of his writings in this section which help portray my own transition from a school student to a young adult in such turbulent times. Yet, I preface these with his reflections on the timeless spirit behind the binary of *sukh-dukh* or happiness-sadness of mortal human life,

> The essence of the matter is this: that men are small and their lives are fleeting, yet the stream of life, with its good and bad and its happiness and sadness, flows and will eternally flow with its ancient solemn murmur. On the edge of the town and in the darkness of the evening that constant murmuring sound can be heard. (Tagore, as cited in Radice, 1994, p. 17)

The ancient murmur which Tagore writes about, helps me place my life while growing up in a historical, as well as philosophical perspective. As argued by Nussbaum and exemplifying the role that literature can play in creating a reality larger than one's own, I remember Tagore's writings to prevent us children in a newly formed country from being parochial and become world citizens. As the *first* of his writings that called for such an outlook, is a poem from his collection *Gitanjali,*

> Where the mind is without fear and the head is held high;
> Where knowledge is free;
> Where the world has not been broken up into fragments by narrow domestic walls;
> Where words come out from the depth of truth;
> Where tireless striving stretches its arms towards perfection;
> Where the clear stream of reason has not lost its way into the dreary desert sand of dead habit;
> Where the mind is led forward by thee into ever-widening thought and action;
> Into that heaven of freedom, my Father, let my country awake. (Tagore, 1971, pp. 49–50)

Recited by many of us across our country both then and today, Tagore's idealism offered wise counsel to take on an uncertain future – a mind without fear, a sense of personal pride, a world conceived as a whole, a scorn for dead habit, a search for deep seated truths and an individual striving for expansive thought

CLASSROOM TEACHING   25

and action. All these ideas were penned for people of an ancient land yet fledgling country, to dream and pursue a heaven conceived in terms of our freedom.

I turn *second* to Tagore's understanding about our human condition as portrayed in his story titled *Kabuliwallah* or simply, vendor from Kabul. In this writing Tagore narrates the deep bond of friendship his very young daughter Mini strikes with Rahamat, who sold nuts, apricots and raisins. Wanting to make his annual trip home to Afghanistan, one year Rahamat ventures to collect debts that customers owe him. He however ends up quarrelling and is convicted of assaulting one of them. Rahamat serves time in prison and returns the day after his release, to offer Mini his customary box of raisins. By this time however he finds Mini to have grown and to be married. This reminds Rahamat of his own daughter Parvati whose soot stained hand print on a piece of paper, he always carried with him. Rahamat and Tagore both realise that Parvati like Mini would be old enough to be married as well. As Rahamat refuses money for the box of raisins he brings, Tagore ends his story thus,

> I took out a banknote and gave it to him. 'Rahamat,' I said, 'go back to your homeland and your daughter; by your blessed reunion, Mini will be blessed.'
>
> By giving him this money, I had to trim certain items from the wedding-festivities. I wasn't able to afford the electric illuminations I had planned, nor did the trumpet-and-drum band come. The womenfolk were very displeased with this; but for me, the ceremony was lit by a kinder, more gracious light. (Tagore, 1994, p. 120)

Tagore's *Kabuliwallah* nuances many as aspect of the times we lived by in my childhood – friendships with strangers we became acquainted with, the need to care for the growing girl child, our collective vulnerability as a people and our sharing in the joys and sorrows of one another, even of those who came from a neighbouring land. Just as Tagore's poem cited earlier instilled idealism, his poignant and well known *Kabuliwallah* was evocative about what it meant to live life as a human being, especially in adverse times that were not entirely of our own making.

Where Tagore's poem dealt with idealism and his story with humanity, his *third* writing is a dance drama titled *Chandalika*, one I saw staged by my seniors while still at school. Not completely understood by me as a 15 year old back then, the play however sensitised me to the divide that lay in society between man and woman, entitled and marginalised, besides desire and convention, the complexities of which I continue to learn even to this present day. In the play Tagore heightens the encounter between a Buddhist monk Ananda and Prakriti, a girl born to the lowest rung of castes in our society. Against convention

Ananda asks Prakriti for water, offering which she becomes conscious of her desire as a woman that is denied to her, also by convention. Asking her mother to intervene with a spell, followed by The Buddha himself intervening to break the same, Ananda's accepting of water enables Prakriti to be conscious of her own self not in terms of the restrictions that society imposes on her, but in terms of her ability to judge herself and be of service to others.

My recent reflection on Tagore for the last two summaries above, one paralleling my own passing into adulthood, helped me refocus on the manner in which Tagore positions the girl child in these writings. While he makes himself and Rahamat rally around and care for a very young Mini and Parvati in *Kabuliwallah*, in *Chandalika* I find him asking much more from the girl child – in terms of her need to be conscious of her own personal dignity. Introducing *Chandalika* in a collection titled *Three plays*, K R Kripalani, a Gandhian and Tagore scholar, goes on to observe that without human rights there can be no obligations towards society. Similarly one's service to others, when forced and not offered in a voluntary manner is a version of slavery. He points out,

> *Chandalika* is a tragedy of self-consciousness over-reaching its limit. Self-consciousness up to a point, is necessary to self-development, for without an awareness of the dignity of one's own role and function, one cannot give one's best to the world. (Kripalani, 1953, p. 135)

For me Tagore's writings not only evidence his mastery across literary forms, but also help me sketch the backdrop of struggles the girl child in my generation had to contend with. Herein for most times the dignity of our role and function in society was and still remains our only armour. Such fortitude is however excellent preparation for practitioners to take up teaching which demands its own share of self consciousness and self development, while pursuing the wider call of educating others in society. Keeping such a mission alive and not being relegated to a lesser purpose, sought genuine compassion for others, a sharp and practical intellect, a sense of idealism to work towards – one also demanding much personal sacrifice, human courage and professional integrity. It is to dwell upon aspects such as these, which are both phenomenological and existential in nature, that I now turn to Jiddu Krishnamurti's philosophy.

3 Human Beings Who Are Integrated

A writer of children's literature, Shanta Rameshwar Rao, the founder of the school I taught at drew inspiration from Jiddu Krishnamurti amongst others.

As with Gandhi, my own encounter with Krishnamurti's thinking was thus by way of teaching at her school, before I came to read and reflect on the larger dialogue he initiated. While I portray my experiences with classroom teaching in the next section, I presently engage with four excerpts from his writings. As with Tagore, the *first* of these articulates Krishnamurti's view of education as not being one of training our young in specific techniques and narrow specialisations, but one of awakening within them an *integrated intelligence*,

> The function of education is to create human beings who are integrated and therefore intelligent. ... We have made examinations and degrees the criterion of intelligence and have developed cunning minds that avoid vital human issues. Intelligence is the capacity to perceive the essential, the what is; and to awaken this capacity, in oneself and in others, is education. (Krishnamurti, 1953, p. 14)

With one stroke in the above passage, Krishnamurti draws our attention to the creation of thoughtful human beings, who would not avoid but vitally address critical issues facing humankind at large. The intelligence with which this was possible, he argues, was not something mere results at examinations and completion of university degrees could deliver. In practice and at the school I taught, we thus held examinations for students only from their grade eight onwards and thereby reduced to a large extant the vexed issue recognised as teaching to test.

Placing any manner of change both in oneself and society, at the behest of the individual, Krishanmurti *next* talked about *human freedom* in terms of removing or doing away with fear by means of understanding one's own psychological process. About such an examination he argued,

> Freedom comes only when one understands the ways of the self, the experiencer. It is only when the self, with its accumulated reactions, is not the experiencer, that experience takes on an entirely different significance and becomes creation. (Krishnamurti, 1953, p. 28)

In the parlance of mainstream educational research, I found Krishnamurti to lay central emphasis on one's self or ontology. At school Shanta would remind us teachers too that the presence of fear in us and/or our students, had the ability to destroy our capacity to think and take any action in an intelligent manner. In my years of attending a variety of schools while growing up as a student, I never encountered the issue of addressing fear in our personal selves being discussed at all. Examinations, the issue of not earning adequate credits in them and constantly being ranked ahead or behind fellow students was the unquestioned norm. Not denying the benefits that otherwise came with attending those institutions, such a narrow and reductionist emphasis was presumably to sort out students with a specific set of skills, one bestowed on schools by society.

In contrast to the competitive norm which she would consider as jungle law, Shanta stressed on collaborative efforts amongst teachers, students and respective peers. This brings me to Krishnamurti's *third* writing which conceives human existence as an interconnected whole, wherein the pursuit of truth, human freedom besides the *what is* he lay emphasis on, had no particular route and was a pathless journey which one had to embark upon. Asking individuals to work towards a harmony between reason and love and in a sermon dissolving the *Order of the Star* of which he was head, Krishnamurti offered the following anecdote,

> You may remember the story of how the devil and a friend of his were walking down the street, when they saw ahead of them a man stoop down and pick up something from the ground, look at it, and put it away in his pocket. The friend said to the devil, 'What did that man pick up?' 'He picked up a piece of Truth,' said the devil. 'That is a very bad business for you, then,' said his friend. 'Oh, not at all,' the devil replied, 'I am going to let him organize it.' (Krishnamurti, 1929)

Predisposing my professional development as a practitioner to qualities which Nussbaum attributed to liberal education, Krishnamurti's assertion that *truth is a pathless land*, one that could not be arrived at in a specific manner, directed my attention to the human in our lives, be observant of one's own phenomenological experience and attend to ways in which we could take on life as a whole. He *finally* proclaimed,

> When we train our children according to a system of thought or a particular discipline, when we teach them to think within departmental divisions, we prevent them from growing into integrated men and women, and therefore they are incapable of thinking intelligently, which is to meet life as a whole. (Krishnamurti, 1953, p. 24)

Taken together, the integrated intelligence Krishnamurti spoke in favour of in his writings and one we strove towards in many ways at our school, sensitised my journey in educational research to three particular aspects (1) view education in terms of the social reality in which each of us lived our lives, (2) adopt a critical stance in relation to such reality in terms of grasping the *what is* of any situation, and (3) adopt a stance that was plural in a methodological sense in one's personal ongoing inquiry. With intelligent thinking sought in terms of meeting life as a whole, I now turn to dwell on my experiences as a classroom teacher for over a decade at our relatively small school of about five hundred pupils.

4 The Rollercoaster of Teaching

Armed with a Masters in Physics, I approached *Vidyaranya High School* to ask if I could teach the sciences and possibly mathematics. Nestled in the heart of the city, I found the school environment to be both informal and welcoming. A class teacher was on leave for a year's time and the office thought I might fill in as a replacement. To my surprise they welcomed my not having a Bachelors training in Education, as the programs offered back then were of rather poor quality. The experience I would gain by teaching under guidance of its founder, it was argued, would be of greater value and relevance. The ability to keep an open mind and learn as one taught, was what was expected. I returned the following day to meet Shanta, the founder. Apart from questions about my interests and education till then, Shanta inquired about where I stayed in the city and surmised me as an individual.

Shanta's invitation to teaching was unmistakable, full of humanism and grace, beaming like sunshine. While she did not discuss educational philosophy, I began teaching under her watch and guidance which she looked forward to and enjoyed as well. Little did I know how significant her role as mentor would be in my professional life. From drawing my attention to childhood as a special period of human development and to counselling parents of students, her guidance explicated the intricacies of teaching in particular and schooling at large. 'It must pain in the stomach' she would say, reminding us teachers that neither was teaching for the faint hearted nor our lives as teachers commonplace.

I started as class teacher at grade five and taught mathematics, science, geography and english. I managed to establish rapport with the students and took interest in their ideas and lives, like their visit to the local fair or their grandmother's cooking. We co-created living history as it were and wove a web of belonging. The fact that this was easy to do was because of the way in which our school functioned, laying emphasis on students speaking up for what they believed in and view their learning as being creative, imaginative and fun, both inside and outside the classroom and school. Insisting on even representation of boys and girls, the larger effort at school was also to have students cooperate and not compete with one another. Instilling fear in oneself or others was out of the question. How else, Shanta would stress, were children to learn, grasp and comprehend the *what is* which Krishnamurti drew attention to.

I taught math with relative ease, with knowledge of how various topics were interconnected with one another. I drew the attention of students to mathematical relationships in various aspects of their lives, had them engage with its feature of abstraction and paid attention to technique that was needed to master. In subjects less familiar I relied upon textbooks, though we were not expected to use these alone. Newspaper cuttings of events which lent educational value were often incorporated, as were guest lectures by parents of students, or acquaintances who could share valuable expertise. The use of the television or a video player was not commonplace and in an old worldly manner we made imaginative use of whatever was available to enrich the purpose we had at hand.

I stayed on to teach for over a decade, teaching science, physics and mathematics largely at middle school grades. In wider reading that I spent during this time, I searched for new content, new ways to present content besides new connections between existing content. Such preparation led to innovative teaching, though I returned to the textbook to keep the pace I set with students evenly grounded. Such experiences led me to initially carry out project work with children, whose results I went on to discuss in a teachers journal titled *Teacher Plus.* It was only much later that I went on to compile a handbook of implementable ideas for practicing teachers titled *Creativity: Modern school mathematics*, wherein I argued that one never quite learnt as a teacher until one went on to teach.

The trajectory of my teaching was also enhanced by my sharing what it meant to teach with fellow teachers and borrowing useful ideas in right earnest. This was particularly valuable in a thirty year old school, which remained experimental and stood outside the norm. We were ready to take on society and discuss what teaching meant with parents of students and interested public at large. In addressing questions on why we did things differently, our very fabric of classroom teaching was up for lively scrutiny and debate. In research parlance, we teachers were reflective and examined ongoing teaching, the classroom and schooling, both personally on our own as well as collectively together.

The canvass I portray thus far was in addition under constant critique and continuous revival by Shanta. Maintaining direct contact with parents and observing how individual children were experiencing school, Shanta monitored its pulse and brought her cumulative thoughts to bear by laying focus on

CLASSROOM TEACHING 31

our teaching. She was clear about founding and leading a school *for* teachers. Even as she gauged the expectations of stakeholders at large, she was vocal about the right of teachers to teach as well. She encouraged us to try out new ideas, taking personal interest in most of them, knowing only too well that some of these might also not materialise as we would have intended. Many of us thus experienced the highs and lows that came with such efforts to be like a roller-coaster ride. Shanta in addition had the ability to not use academic terms like neo-liberalism or critical theory, but put their essence into concrete practice at appropriate occasion. In such a holistic manner and as recognised in contemporary literature within teacher preparation, the invaluable role of a guru, guide or mentor was carried out by Shanta with great elan.

Classroom teaching against such a backdrop was an alert enterprise to the drama that was life itself, the needs of students, besides the buzz that both sympathetic and adversarial colleagues created. One became alert to wider trends in society too, as they would pervade the classroom by the onset of various channels brought home by the newly introduced satellite TV. This meant students trading WWF playing cards or trying to dance like Michael Jackson. In some ways our performance as teachers was under pressure to match the palpable excitement created outside its four walls. Yet the kind of satisfaction one derived in teaching was intrinsic and far from extrinsic, carried out for its own sake. The one constant that accompanied this experience were the stories we teachers were able to take home. As Frank McCourt reveals in *Teacher Man*,

> At the end of a school day you leave with a head filled with adolescent noises, their worries, their dreams. They follow you to dinner, to the movies, to the bathroom, to the bed. You try to put them out of your mind. Go away. Go away. I'm reading a book, the paper, the writing on the wall. Go away. (McCourt, 2005, pp. 217–218)

My experiences with classroom teaching seeded four key ideas that I carry with me to this day. *First* is my approach to arriving at the *what is* of ongoing practice in a pathless manner, an aspect one might recognise as being intuitive. Despite keeping abreast with existing research, I tend to ask anew about what could be really going on in any local context. *Second* is my being on the lookout for the joy and fun that I experienced as inseparable from the goings on of everyday teaching and learning. While reference to this aspect is elusive in most research, I have found mention of aspects relating to one's emotions within feminist literature. Shanta being a writer leads me to a *third* issue, which is my ability to juxtapose the arts and the sciences as the yin and yang in human inquiry. Trained as I was in the sciences and teaching at a school led by an artist, the subtext of ongoing dialogue between her and me was underpinned by these two distinct, yet equally insightful avenues of educational inquiry. My arriving at some conclusion or the other in teaching in line with a scientific outlook, was on more than one occasion met with an alternative that seemed equally valid and true. My interest of understanding the arts as a methodology which decidedly rivals the sciences springs from these encounters. Such a quest leads me to my *final* idea, which is my search for perspectives in educational research that have potential to explain and grasp ongoing teaching and learning in everyday classrooms and schools. Such a search was probably my parting yet defining contribution, that would accompany my transition from teaching to research.

5 Personal Practical Knowledge

My search for perspectives that made sense to me as a practitioner led me to two sets of writings which I found particularly relevant. I explore those which came with my interests in narrative perspectives in this section and examine those forwarded by Vygotsky himself in the next. I trace my interests in narrative forms to four aspects, ending with recognition of the knowledge teachers have in terms of personal practical knowledge. In the *first*, was my experience of becoming a teacher under the guidance of a writer-educator. This alerted me to the vast potential a storied approach had for education, besides life itself. *Second* was my being immersed in a wider culture of orality in India. In many of us conversing in dialects and languages without scripts in parallel with mainstream languages, our immersion in multiple linguistic forms necessitates us to develop a keen ear for unique narrative qualities which the spoken word exercises. *Third* was the ability I found of narratives to speak to the kind of experiences that schooling provides, at times in conflict with everyday lives being led by students and their families. As example I often recall is one narrated by Mary-Lynn Lindstone in relation to how an African-American grandmother of one of her students responded, when Mary handed out an assessment report with her granddaughter's failing marks. Speaking to the misgivings Mary herself had as a teacher about standardised tests and how students could be evaluated via alternative means, Mary recounts the grandmother's response as follows,

> What does this say about my child – that she's a moron, she's stupid and slow? ... Does it say that her mother's in jail and her daddy died just last year? Does it tell you that's she's getting her life together, slowly? ... What

CLASSROOM TEACHING

> does this piece of paper say about my baby? I don't want it near her. She needs good things. She's had enough in her life telling her that she's no good. She doesn't need this and I won't have it. I refuse to sign a piece of paper that says my child is no good. (African-American grandmother as narrated by Mary-Lynn Lindstone in Hollingsworth, 1992, p. 391)

While the above narrative helped Mary reflect on how the grandmother spoke from her heart and a very sound mind, in my reading of the same I was taken up by the ability of the grandmother's response besides Mary's reflection, to ably convey what it meant for education to meet life as a whole in line with Krishnamurti. My *fourth* turn to narratives extends the above outlined ability to encapsulate experience and recognises the personal practical knowledge of teachers as articulated by Jean Clandinin. Recognising the kind of experience Mary and teachers at large are able to grasp and know, one they build over many years of teaching, Clandinin's construct of *personal practical knowledge* argues,

> Teachers develop and use a special kind of knowledge. This knowledge is neither theoretical, in the sense of theories of learning, teaching, and curriculum, nor merely practical, in the sense of knowing children. If either of these were the essential ingredient of what teachers know, then it would be that others have a better knowledge of both; academics with better knowledge of the theoretical and parents and others with better knowledge of the practical. A teacher's special knowledge is composed of both kinds of knowledge, blended by the personal background and characteristics of the teacher and by her in particular situations. (Clandinin, 1985, p. 361)

Found embodied in teachers and revealed in their narrative of teaching in ongoing practice, I find Clandinin to highlight four key features as she unpacks the above construct. In doing so she not only speaks to me as a practitioner but also brakes new ground in terms of coining an elusive site of knowledge in theoretical research. *First*, she gives credence to the body of knowledge which practitioners gain by way of experience, which they become conscious of while taking action in classrooms. Today I will ask students to work at question 7 and not 9. Such actions, she *next* suggests makes up the practice of any teacher, one inclusive of planning, judgment and norms of appraisal she would use. Discuss the first three paragraphs of the text in groups and then draw up a time line of events that unfold, on the sheet of paper given. Clandinin *third* points to the manner in which personal practical knowledge is closely intertwined with one's being, wherein the personal and professional elements of teaching remain quite inseparable, often surprising the practitioner herself. I have no idea what got into me and made me ask them to draw today? *Finally* Clandinin recognises that the taking of action and display of such manner of holistic knowledge to not only unfold with personal experience but also be interpretative in nature. Its detailed study is thus best revealed in the narrative of experience in which any practitioner's teaching unfolds. Watch how she gets her students to be conscious of their spelling as they read together! Given that so much of what I learnt about teaching, was by teaching under Shanta's guidance and as school life abounded, I have found Clandinin's construct of personal practical knowledge useful in recognising teachers as knowledgable people. Such a stance brings me to two other constructs she argues with her mentor Michael Connelly – knowledge as narrative and professional knowledge landscapes.

In relation to teachers and teaching, Clandinin and Connelly make a vital distinction between knowledge as attribute and knowledge as narrative. Based on their conviction that school reform is closely bound to an epistemological stance, they argue *knowledge as attribute* as that which teachers are made familiar with and/or given in a theoretical manner in teacher preparation programs. Such knowledge can be added to or modified but does not alter the way practitioners come to know their classrooms. It is to rectify this predicament that they suggest focusing on *knowledge as narrative*, one that becomes narratively embodied in them as they take a required stand, while experiencing ongoing teaching in their everyday classrooms. Clandinin and Connelly thus argue that while knowledge as attribute can be handed out as written material in teacher preparation programs, knowledge as narrative comes from teaching and needs to be experienced by teachers in various local contexts.

Via *professional knowledge landscapes* Clandinin and Connelly argue that any teacher's personal practical knowledge emerges and is bound by the local context of the school in which they teach. Exemplified by my own experiences with teaching, they maintain,

> The professional knowledge context shapes effective teaching, what teachers know, what knowledge is seen as essential for teaching, and who is warranted to produce knowledge about teaching. ...
>
> Conceptualizing the professional knowledge context as a landscape is particularly well-suited to our purpose. It allows us to talk about space, time, and place. It has a sense of expansiveness and the possibility of being filled with diverse people, things, and events in different relationships. Because we see the professional knowledge landscape as

composed of relationships among people, places, and things, we see it as both an intellectual and a moral landscape. (Clandinin & Connelly, 1996, pp. 24–25)

My intention of dwelling on personal practical knowledge, knowledge as narrative and professional knowledge landscapes close on the heels of recounting my own narrative of classroom teaching, is to highlight the manner in which the personal, professional and contextual elements of one's teaching combine in incessant dialectic. Since theory and practice become inseparable in the actions we practitioners take, practice here can also be seen as theory in action. Even as I elaborate on principles of a dialectical methodology at work herein in Chapter 7, I turn to Vygotsky's own writing for teacher practitioners, one that became foundational to his personal development as a theorist, besides present day CHAT which also adopts a distinctly dialectic approach.

6 Vygotsky in *Educational Psychology*

While my use of narrative perspectives in research had to wait till I began conducting independent research after completing my doctoral work, my doctoral thesis itself drew on neo-Vygotskian CHAT perspectives, for which his book *Mind in Society* was introductory reading in our course. To engage further with the underlying rationale of his thinking I turned to *Educational Psychology* a handbook he wrote for teachers, one which lay the foundation for a cultural-historical psychology that was yet to come. In this section I shed light on this effort by drawing on two chapters, (1) the role of a child's social environment, and (2) the psychological aspects of any teacher's instruction.

In a chapter titled *Biological and social factors in education*, Vygotsky demanded a shift away from the biological factors of children and drew attention to the key role of the social environment in relation to a child's cultural-historical development. Laying emphasis on children's personal experience, Vygotsky argued that the teacher needed to direct or organise the social environment in such a manner that the student would educate himself or herself. He viewed the plasticity of the social environment as the most flexible of all tools within education. On the dynamic role of the teacher in such a process he emphasised,

This is also why an active role is the lot of the teacher in the course of education. The teacher fashions, takes apart and puts together, shreds, and carves out elements of the environment, and combines them together in the most diverse ways in order to reach whatever goal he has to reach. Thus is the educational process an active one on three levels: the student is active, the teacher is active, and the environment created between them is an active one. (Vygotsky, 1997a, p. 54)

Conceiving the educational process to be active at three levels, Vygotsky also sought attention to the kind of psychological relations adults needed to enter with children, resulting in their development,

> If, upon leaving home, I arrange with my child where I'm going to leave the key for him, there can be no doubt that I am thereby forming a new relation with my child. But if this reaction does not have any purpose other than help him find the key, from the psychological point of view it cannot be termed educational. Consequently, not everything we do with children is education, in the scientific understanding of this term. (Vygotsky, 1997a, p. 58)

The two passages above draw attention to the manner in which Vygotsky wanted any child's social environment to be orchestrated, so that (s)he could realise her own cultural-historical development. In fact, Vygotsky saw children to be maladjusted to their immediate environment in their childhood, necessitating grown-ups to steady and carefully assist their development over time. Viewing their transformation into adulthood as one of the greatest dramas in life, he even compared such long drawn out efforts to that of a tooth breaking through its protective gums.

In his chapter titled *Psychology and the teacher*, Vygotsky underscored three vital aspects. *First* is the kind of relationship any teacher needed to bring about for her to realise instruction. He argued,

> the very method of instruction demands of the teacher that same sense of activity, that same sense of group spirit, with which the soul of the school must be infused with. The teacher must live within the school collective, as if an integral part of it. It is in this sense that the relationship between teacher and student can attain a force, a transparency, and a depth without equal in the entire social scale of human relationships. (Vygotsky, 1997b, p. 345)

My own experience as a teacher testifies to the importance of being an integral part of school and attempting to gain transparency in purpose and deed, besides a depth without equal in human to human relationships that I strove

CLASSROOM TEACHING

to initiate and nurture with my students. As I found Krishnamurti to also argue, Vygotsky *second* gave credence to the importance of life at large for realising education, by arguing,

> Ultimately, only life educates, and the deeper that life, the real world, burrows into the school, the more dynamic and the more robust will be the educational process. That the school has been locked away and walled in as if by a tall fence from life has been its greatest failing. Education is just as meaningless outside the real world as is a fire without oxygen, or as is breathing in a vacuum. The teacher's educational work, therefore, must inevitably be connected with his creative, social and life work. (Vygotsky, 1997b, p. 345)

In line with the above and as mentioned in the previous section there was opportunity for us teachers at the school I taught, to bring various aspects of life at large up for discussion within our classrooms. As I mentioned earlier, our students too were encouraged to express their views without fear and draw upon *their* integrated intelligence.

Vygotsky further recognised students' learning at school in terms of their ability to bridge their unstructured knowledge of *everyday concepts* with those structured in a scientific manner as *academic concepts*. Even as I greater dwell upon this aspect in the next chapter, I presently turn to Vygotsky's *third* contention which argues the psychological development of children and human beings to lie largely in their own hands,

> Man has set himself the goal of becoming master of his own feelings, of lifting the instincts to the heights of consciousnesses and making them transparent, of stretching the thread of will into what is concealed and into the underground, and to thereby lift himself up to a new stage, to create a 'higher' sociobiological type, a, so to speak, super-man. (Vygotsky, 1997b, p. 351)

I find Vygotsky to make two points above. *First* and as introduced in the previous Chapter, Vygotsky prepares ground for his construct of higher psychological activity, one which he pointed out enabled human beings to regulate their behaviour from their outside. *Second* and in concluding his treatise cited above, I find Vygotsky asking us practitioners to examine the manner in which each of us and our students are able to master our biological selves and become the sociobiological super-being, which he argued we could become. It is towards attempting an overview of my doctoral study in which I wrestle with a collective of such radical ideas in the next chapter, that I presently turn to Sarason who discusses the role of schools themselves in education at large.

7   Schools Are for Teachers Too: Coda

I came across insightful reference to American psychologist Seymour Sarason while reading Tharp and Gallimore's (1988) *Rousing minds to life: Teaching, learning, and schooling in social context*, whose writings I greater engage with in Chapter 4. Sarason's writings, reporting work he conducted in the late 19th century in the US, echo Kurt Lewin's advocacy for action research, altering existing power relationships if necessary. Yet I found Sarason to highlight two central issues, which seemed to ring true with my own teaching experiences. Sarason argued,

> The *first* is the assumption that schools exist primarily for the growth and development of children. That assumption is invalid because teachers cannot create and sustain the conditions for productive development of children if those conditions do not exist for teachers. The *second* issue is that there is now an almost unbridgeable gulf that students perceive between the world of the school and the world outside it. ... Teachers continue to teach subject matter, not children. Any reform effort that does not confront these two issues and the changes they suggest is doomed. (Sarason, 1990, p. XIV, emphasis added)

In clear echo to my reading of both Krishnamurti and Vygotsky who lay emphasis on the need for school to be relevant to life at large, Sarason found schools to be geared solely for children and not for the professional development of teachers. Sarason also pointed to the complex ways in which schools were structured, along with a lack of their having any self-correcting mechanism in their day to day workings which would help bring about necessary and timely reform. In arguing for schools to be key sites for individuals to become teachers, he also viewed teachers as key to bringing about reform and change. Four themes emerged from Sarason's interviews with teachers then (1) their acute sensitivity to the here-and-now, (2) the importance they gave to informality and freedom, (3) their interest in the well being of each of their students, and (4) their resistance to inflexible curriculum and administrative evaluation. It is against such a backdrop that he pointed to the very *isolation of the teacher*,

> It has been pointed out that although a school is one of the most densely populated settings on earth, 'teaching is a lonely profession' ... It is not

CLASSROOM TEACHING

the loneliness of solitude but a feeling compounded of isolation, frustration and the pressure to appear competent to any and all problems. It is a sense of loneliness that gnaws, debilitates, feeds on itself, and frequently leads to a sense of stagnation. The reasons for this are many, but chief among them is the traditional way of defining roles and resources. (Sarason, 1982, pp. 276–278)

In pointing out the loneliness, solitude and isolation that teachers most often experience, Sarason drew attention to the equally important fact that children too felt powerless to bring about any manner of change in their school. He thus keenly sought alternative models and ways of perceiving educational phenomena and taking action in the form of *theory*,

Theory is a necessary myth that we construct to understand something we know we understand incompletely. Theory is a deliberate attempt to go beyond what we know or to correct what we think are the erroneous explanations of others. It is intended to make a difference not only on the level of theory but on the level of action, be it a laboratory, a classroom, or a school. ... Educational reform rarely derives from whatever we mean by theory but rather from opinion, anecdote, an uncritical acceptance of research, or a desperation. (Sarason, 1990, p. 123)

In the first of many explorations of what theory could come to mean for us practitioners throughout this writing, in chapters that follow I also attempt to work at many an aspect Sarason draws attention to (1) the need for teachers and students to not only initiate but also contribute to change, (2) the ability of teachers to overcome isolation and work collaboratively with fellow teachers and/or researchers, besides (3) understand as well as deploy CHAT theory with intention of going beyond the here and now in altering existing status quo. Such an inviting canvass was mine to embark upon, while transitioning to doctoral research.

References

Clandinin, D. J. (1985). Personal practical knowledge: A study of teachers' classroom images. *Curriculum Inquiry, 15*(4), 361–385.

Clandinin, D. J., & Connelly, F. M. (1996). Teachers' professional knowledge landscapes: Teacher stories – stories of teachers – school stories – stories of schools. *Educational Researcher, 25*(3), 24–30.

Hollingsworth, S. (1992). Learning to teach through collaborative conversation: A feminist approach. *American Educational Research Journal, 29*(2), 373–404.

Kripalani, K. R. (1953). Introduction. In R. Tagore (Ed.), *Three plays: Muktadhara, Natir puja, Chandalika* (pp. 133–135). Oxford University Press.

Krishnamurti, J. (1929). *Truth is a pathless land.* Retrieved September 1, 2019, from https://jkrishnamurti.org/about-dissolution-speech

Krishnamurti, J. (1953). *Education and the significance of life.* Krishnamurti Foundation of India.

McCourt, F. (2005). *Teacher man: A memoir.* Scribner.

Radice, W. (1994). Introduction. In R. Tagore (Ed.), *Rabindranath Tagore: Selected short stories* (pp. 1–30). Penguin.

Sarason, S. (1982). *The culture of school and the problem of change.* Allyn and Bacon Inc.

Sarason, S. (1990). *The predictable failure of educational reform: Can we change the course before it's too late.* Jossey-Bass Publishers.

Tagore, R. (1971). *Gitanjali: A collection of Indian songs.* Macmillan.

Tagore, R. (1994). Kabuliwallah. In R. Tagore (Ed.), *Rabindranath Tagore: Selected short stories* (pp. 113–120). Penguin.

Tharp, R., & Gallimore, R. (1988). *Rousing minds to life: Teaching, learning, and schooling in social context.* Cambridge University Press.

Vygotsky, L. S. (1997a). Biological and social factors in education. In L. S. Vygotsky (Ed.), *Educational psychology* (pp. 47–58). St. Lucie Press.

Vygotsky, L. S. (1997b). Psychology and the teacher. In L. S. Vygotsky (Ed.), *Educational psychology* (pp. 337–351). St. Lucie Press.

CHAPTER 3

Doctoral Research

Ascending to the Concrete

1 Preamble

Many aspects related to my transition from the practice of teaching to the practice of research need mentioning, as I attempt to capture some salient features of my doctoral research in this chapter. To begin with was the need I personally felt for a theoretical framework that would be able to explain and underpin the actions I could take as a practitioner. Alluding to the dense language in which most theory was expressed, the parting caution I received from Shanta was 'Now nobody will understand you.' My transitioning to doctoral work by this time was however facilitated by Barbara Jaworski, whom I wrote to when she was at the University of Oxford. Even as I applied to some universities in the US, I accepted her invitation to doctoral work as this was accompanied by her own move to Norway. This latter helped satisfy my wanting to become familiar with diverse traditions of educating our young. Upon seeking guidance, she suggested three writings which I read before embarking on my doctoral journey. *First*, was her book titled *Investigating mathematics teaching: A constructivist inquiry* (Jaworski, 1996) which detailed her own conduct of classroom research. *Next* was Richard Pring's (2000) *Philosophy of educational research*, which elaborated the underlying aims and goals of our conducting educational research. *Finally* was Margaret Donaldson's (1978) *Children's minds* which not only countered Piaget's model of intellectual development in children, but introduced me to key notions forwarded by Vygotsky. Not familiar with the methodological notion of triangulation as yet, these readings however gave me enough confidence to leave home for another country and doctoral research.

My working under Barbara's doctoral supervision at the University of Agder in Norway, brought two fortunate coincidences. First, I received guidance from Roger Säljö with regards to conducting neo-Vygotskian CHAT research, whose perspectives I drew largely upon in my doctoral study. Second was doctoral co-supervision by Hans Erik Borgersen a mathematician, who introduced me to two teachers of mathematics at an upper secondary school located nearby our university. It was teaching in Norwegian and English by these two teachers that made it possible for me to conduct a year long classroom study. I provide

© KONINKLIJKE BRILL NV, LEIDEN, 2022 | DOI:10.1163/9789004512160_003

extracts from this study in five sections that follow and portray (1) the rubric of cooperative learning by students in small groups, in terms of which teachers carried out everyday instruction and (2) the collaborative classroom practice they established together with their students. Following these I move on to discuss three central CHAT notions (3) the role of cultural tools in human development, (4) mediated action and mediated agency, besides (5) activity as unit of analysis. In my coda I dwell on the strange sounding principle of ascending to the concrete in CHAT research.

2 Cooperative Learning | zpd

I met the two teachers in whose classroom I conducted my doctoral study, prior to the academic year in which I took observational field notes and collected empirical data. Identifying the two teachers as Olaf and Knut, I availed of their opportunity to sit beside and observe students take part in designated group work. I anonymised each of the students as well, whose active consent I obtained in compliance with guidelines of the Norwegian Data Protection Authority or the *Datatilsynet*. I began my year long study with attempting to understand how Olaf and Knut organised day to day instruction, besides how their students took part in the same in terms of CHAT perspectives. In making these efforts I strove to infer students' actions as they cooperated with one another in small groups. The nature of engagement between Olaf and Knut as practitioners, a theme I have pursued in post doctoral work, was not an explicit goal in my doctoral study. I had not come across Clandinin and Connelly's writings at that time, but argue the manner in which Olaf and Knut organised instruction aimed at having students cooperate in small groups to exemplify their professional knowledge landscape, one driven by the personal practical knowledge they had each developed over time. Embodied in each of them this latter was externalised in the many instructional actions they each took. Yet, beyond arguing for the relevance of Clandinin and Connelly's constructs, I refrain from making greater claims. To do so I would require empirical data in the form of in-depth interviews, both individually and as a team, in relation to instructional events which transpired.

Taking a wide-angle view of Olaf and Knut's instruction, my study led to a doctoral thesis titled, *The micro-culture of a mathematics classroom: artefacts and activity in meaning making and problem solving* (Gade, 2006). In my attempts to unpack this micro-culture, in this section I *first* discuss the notion of zone of proximal development or zpd followed by the relation Vygotsky underscores between processes of learning and a child's psychological development. I *second* dwell on the role of cultural tools in mediating learning and development before *finally* describing the nature of cooperative learning that was possible for me to observe.

The Vygotskian construct of zpd, centrally focuses on the role of social interaction in the development of higher psychological functions. Unlike *lower psychological functions* which are biological and unmediated, Vygotsky argued *higher psychological functions* to be sociocultural in origin and mediated, permitting individuals to control their behaviour or psychological functions from the outside. Speaking one's particular dialect, using a spoon to feed oneself or applying relevant mathematical formula are examples of psychological functions which are not only sociocultural in origin but also mediated and guided initially by others. The underlying Marxian premise is that in transforming the world via utilising these functions, children transform themselves as well. Vygotsky observed,

> Every function in the child's cultural development appears twice: first, on the social level, and later on the individual level; first, *between* people (*interpsychological*), and then *inside* the child (*intrapsychological*). This applies equally to voluntary attention, to logical memory and to the formation of concepts. All the higher functions originate as actual relations between human individuals. (Vygotsky, 1978, p. 57)

Drawing attention to how social relations lie at the root of psychological development, enabling children to in turn accomplish more than they might be able to do so on their own accord, Vygotsky conceived the *zone of proximal development* or *zpd* in the following manner,

> *It is the distance between the actual developmental level as determined by independent problem solving and the level of potential development as determined through problem solving under adult guidance or in collaboration with more capable peers.* ...
>
> The zone of proximal development defines those functions that have not yet matured but are in the process of maturation, functions that will mature tomorrow but are currently in an embryonic state. ... The actual developmental level characterises mental development retrospectively, while the zone of proximal development characterises mental development prospectively. (Vygotsky, 1978, pp. 86–87, emphasis in original)

I find the two quotes cited above to highlight four important aspects, (1) that psychological activity of children is preceded by their social interaction with others, (2) that a child's propensity to take assistance is by no means a sign of weakness but indicative of his or her prospective mental development, (3) that psychological functions which are in an embryonic stage gain maturity on the formation of a zpd, and (4) that unlike psychological functions which have matured prior to a child's social and collaborative activity, those in a nascent state within them gain from appropriate assistance in a zpd and have potential to attain maturity in the proximal future. Vygotsky thus explained,

> We propose that an essential feature of learning is that it creates the zone of proximal development; that is, learning awakens a variety of internal developmental processes that are able to operate only when the child is interacting with people in his environment and in cooperation with his peers. Once these processes are *internalised*, they become part of the child's independent developmental achievement. (Vygotsky, 1978, p. 90, emphasis added)

Following the above, it is vital to note that in processes of *internalisation* or the turning inwards of social relations and/or actual relations between human individuals, Vygotsky distinguished processes of learning from those of a child's psychological development and reiterated,

> From this point of view, learning is not development; however, properly organised learning results in mental development and sets in motion a variety of developmental processes that would be impossible apart from learning. Thus, *learning is a necessary and universal aspect of the process of developing culturally organised, specifically human, psychological functions*. (Vygotsky, 1978, p. 90, emphasis added)

Vygotsky argued the above to have four specific implications for carrying out instruction, (1) that developmental processes lag behind learning processes, (2) that learning and children's development can become united, (3) that while learning and development are related they are neither parallel nor accomplished in equal measure, and (4) that good learning lies in advance of children's psychological development.

Our understanding of the nature of social and collaborative interaction that creates a zpd, is next enhanced by attending to the role of *cultural tools* which mediate children's learning and subsequent development. In a mathematics classroom these cultural tools could be a measuring tape, a calculator, a protractor, a mathematical formula or specific terminology. In this regard Stetsenko extends Vygotskian arguments and highlights two aspects with regards to the manner in which cultural tools mediate higher psychological functions. At *first* she points out that cultural tools can be conceived as types of activities, which encapsulate templates of human action. Their use and meaning is gained by children acting upon them under the guidance of knowledgable others in collaborative activity. As such cultural tools can also be seen as *objects-that-can-be-used-for-a-certain-purpose* in human practices at large, within which these tools are encountered. Stetsenko *second* ties together social interaction, cultural tools and the very realisation of a zpd, in turn explaining how processes of learning *lead* children's development,

> When one looks at the links that bridge social interaction, cultural tools, and ZPD then – and only then – does it become possible to understand why learning plays a leading role in development, why it constitutes the very essence of development rather than merely following or supporting development. *Learning leads development because it is through learning that the child comes to be able to master – through and within interactions with an adult – the new cultural tools*; this mastery constitutes the very cornerstone of mental functioning and human development. (Stetsenko, 1999, p. 248, emphasis added)

The above discussion however brief summarises how CHAT perspectives (1) distinguish higher psychological functions which are cultural and mediated from biological lower psychological functions, (2) identify the internalisation or growing inwards of actual relations between people as central to the formation of a child's zpd, (3) conceive cultural tools as templates of action or objects-that-can-be-used-for-a-certain-purpose in respective social practices, besides (4) view instructional activity as lying in advance and able to lead a child's psychological development.

It is against the above theoretical backdrop that I turn to describe the manner of cooperative learning that took place in a group of students made up of three boys Kim, Levi and Thor besides a girl Nora, whom I observed by sitting beside them. An extract of the group-task that Olaf and Knut handed to them as well as all other student groups in their classroom, is given in Figure 1.

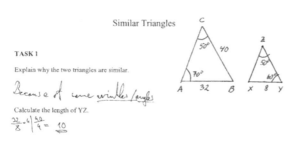

FIGURE 1

TASK 1 of the group-task as in Gade (2006)

46   CHAPTER 3

A transcript of events which took place in this small group evidences the kind of *social interaction* that ensued in their cooperative learning. I found Olaf give instructions in relation to the group-task while stationed at the blackboard besides facing all other student groups as well. This was followed by Knut's visiting the group of students I was sitting beside, to supervise their efforts. Olaf and Knut's instructions for group work and their visiting each of the student groups at their tables subsequently, was a routine they followed throughout their instruction. Audible to the whole class, Olaf guided all student groups as follows,

Olaf   The angles of triangle ABC are similar to ...
Levi   Those of XYZ

Seated at their table, I recorded the following events and discussion to be audible only to students within their small group,

Thor   The angles of the two triangles are similar
Thor   They are similar
Kim   The reason is they add up to 180 degrees
Thor   Values? [addressing me]
Myself   [agreeing with his use of the word values and offering him a pen to
          write with]
Levi   [speaks with Knut in relation to the third question in TASK 1]
Olaf   *Omvendt!* [inverse in the Norwegian language and referring to the
          inverse of the nature of relationship which he had thought between
          the corresponding sides of triangles ABC and XYZ]
Myself   [observe Kim to take guidance form his textbook, Thor to use the cal-
          culator briefly, besides Levi and Nora to discuss how to approach the
          next question in the group-task]
Thor   Are angles and values the same as vinkles? [addressing me and ask-
          ing for confirmation which I give, before him responding to the first
          question of the group-task. His use of the word vinkles is a modifica-
          tion of the word vinkler in Norwegian and refers to angles of both
          triangles in the plural]

The above transcript allows me to shed light on the nature of social interaction and zpd formed in Kim, Levi, Thor and Nora's group, besides the manner in which Olaf and Knut's instruction was able to lead their development. *First* is Olaf's drawing attention of all his students to the relationship of similarity between the two triangles given. On asking students about which triangle ABC was similar to, Levi responded by saying XYZ. While this response may seem obvious, since XYZ was the only other triangle given in TASK 1, the rhetorical

DOCTORAL RESEARCH

sounding question seemed to have *led* Thor's psychological activity, making him wonder why the triangles were similar. *Second,* one can infer following Kim's reasoning. which referred to the fact that the sum of angles of any triangle added up to 180 degrees, that the students in his group came to find the magnitudes of the angles not mentioned or missing in each triangle. Taken together, these events directed the attention of the student group to the underlying relationship of equivalence between corresponding angles, and their conclusion that triangles ABC and XYZ were similar.

Following Vygotsky, one can argue that the concept of similarity was in an embryonic stage in Thor's psychological development at the time of his attempting TASK 1. One can also argue that the group-task along with Olaf's rhetorical questioning provided opportunity for Thor's thinking to be *led* within instruction and develop. The other aspect that strengthens this claim is Thor's use of words in English and Norwegian to articulate the underlying mathematical concept of equivalence and explain how the two triangles were similar. Such usage may have been embryonic and in the process of maturing in his zpd. The concepts of angles and triangles were however not embryonic, since their usage was evident by the time the four students attempted their group-task.

Following Stetsenko, the triangles were prior cultural tools known to students which bore the mathematical relationship that Kim went on to articulate. As objects-that-could-be-used-for-a-certain-purpose their angle sum measure of 180 degrees, was acted upon by Levi, Kim and Thor in the interaction that transpired within their social group. Such manner of interaction exemplifies how Olaf and Knut's instruction *led* individual development of at least Levi, Kim and Thor. The *cooperative learning* that was organised around TASK 1, was thus opportunity for students to learn from the guidance that was available to them and master the use of cultural tools besides their own psychological activity. As pointed out by Stetsenko again, it was only when social interaction, cultural and zpd of students in the group was bridged together, that one could appreciate how students' learning constituted their psychological functioning and played a leading role in their individual development.

In addition to reporting the formation of the above manner of zpd in my thesis, in Gade (2010) I extended such reporting by evidencing the formation of a zpd, both for students within the group outlined above as well as for students from groups across Olaf and Knut's classroom. Here, a mnemonic introduced by a student in one group was put to skilful use by a student in another, after Olaf explicitly highlighted for all students the uses the said mnemonic could be put to. The creation of a zpd across student groups was in turn facilitated by the formation of a collaborative classroom practice, that Olaf and Knut went on to establish with their students. As elaborated in the next section, this practice was consciously participated in and explicitly recognised by all.

3 Collaborative Classroom Practice

Olaf and Knut's ability to realise a zpd both within and across student groups, marked my introduction to the central notion of a *practice* within CHAT. Following pioneering arguments by Vygotsky himself and methodological in scope, this notion however remains programmatic and seeks further theoretical investigation in a variety of concrete practices – an aspect I greater dwell upon in Chapter 4. Nonetheless my engagement with CHAT perspectives both in this and successive chapters has a two fold purpose in my writing – to showcase their ability to grasp everyday instruction besides facilitate the conduct of interventions found necessary. In line with these aims, my study of Olaf and Knut's classroom allows me to *first* evidence how they met with their goal of having students take part in cooperative learning in small groups. I *second* focus on the nature of psychological development that was possible, as their students took part in the collaborative practice they together established.

At the commencement of the academic year Olaf taught by stationing himself at the blackboard, even as his students were seated around groups of tables. A shift to their working in groups took place when Knut joined teaching upon his return from parental leave. Olaf and Knut signalled this shift by conducting two group-tasks titled *When together* and *How heavy* on consecutive days. The first group-task was presented as in Figure 2, with inscriptions by students from different groups appearing in Figure 3.

When Together
- In the pentagon alongside are two dots, black and white, on the move.
- The black moves two corners counter clockwise. The white moves three corners clockwise.
- After how many moves are the two dots together?

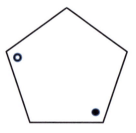

FIGURE 2 *When together* as in Gade (2006)

I observed the conduct of *When together* to arouse student interest and bring forth student cooperation with one another in respective groups, in a brisk manner. The task itself did not ask for any particular mathematical knowledge on behalf of students. On their part Olaf and Knut observed the emergence of various group solutions on their routine visits. It was also the case that by the time of conducting the next group-task, the topic followed in the textbook being used was of simple equations in algebra. Titled *How heavy*,

DOCTORAL RESEARCH 49

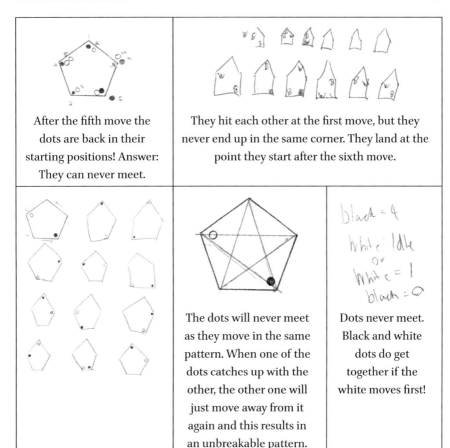

FIGURE 3   Five group solutions to *When together* as in Gade (2006)

Olaf and Knut's second group-task lent itself to this topic and was introduced as in Figure 4. Inscriptions of a selection of solutions, showing increasing use of algebra in attempts made by student groups appear in Figure 5.

How heavy?

If a brick balances with three-quarters of a brick and three quarters of a pound, then how much does the brick weigh?

FIGURE 4   *How heavy* as in Gade (2006)

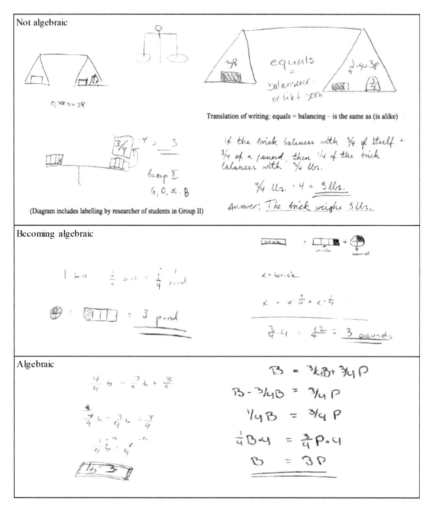

FIGURE 5   Three kinds of group solutions to *How heavy* as in Gade (2006)

The outcome of Olaf and Knut's conduct of *When together* and *How heavy* as outlined above on successive days, helped their actions establish cooperative learning by students in small groups as classroom norm. The rules governing such cooperation were discussed by Olaf, Knut and each of the eight student groups after completion of three cycles of textbook instruction. When agreed upon and with guidance from Olaf and Knut, these were put up in bold letters on chart paper on one of the display boards in the classroom. I enclose a list of these rules in Figure 6 and mention these rules to be adhered to by Olaf, Knut and their students through the academic year. As different from students taking part in cooperative learning in small groups, in my doctoral thesis I went on to identify such manner of classroom wide practice of teaching and learning mathematics as a distinctive *collaborative classroom practice*.

Cooperative learning in mathematics

Everyone must be treated with respect
Everyone must contribute
All ideas must be considered by the group
Everyone must be aware of what transpires before the group moves ahead
Everyone must be able to present the work of the group
Everyone must ask the others in the group before seeking help from teachers

FIGURE 6 Rules of cooperation that were adhered to as in Gade (2006)

At a PME mathematics education conference subsequent to doctoral work, I adopted a longitudinal person-in-practice perspective and argued the above collaborative classroom practice to be an artefact of Olaf and Knut's instruction. Herein students had opportunity to both take part in learning mathematics that led their development and make meaning of the mathematics being learnt (Gade, 2011). The four themes in terms of which I understood the participation of students, was an aspect I was able to categorise in relation to instruction of the first three chapters of the textbook. Table 1 outlines the manner in which students' learning besides their subjectivity evidenced discernible changes as instruction progressed, and the manner in which the practice itself

TABLE 1 Progression of students' learning within instruction as in Gade (2014)

Theme → ——— Chapter ↓	The collaborative practice	The consolidation of meaning	Problem solving know-how	Cooperation in problem solving
Number understanding	Establishment by the teacher of his intentions	Building of meaning in teacher-driven practice	Discussion by turning rules into questions	Cooperation established, consolidated
Equations and proportionality	Participation by students in their and other's intentions	Building upon of students meaning making	Building up solutions for application	Students conjecture reality with given graphs
Scale factor in similar figures	Participation by students with independent intention	Building upon of students intuitive knowing	Questions become problems that students can solve	Students question reality with given model

was consolidated over time. I have engaged with smaller sections of this very table, in papers presented at two other mathematics education conferences as well (Gade, 2013, 2014).

The progression of students' participation in terms of the collaborative classroom practice, is opportunity to observe how the social interaction brought about by adhering to the same within classroom instruction, gave rise to the psychological development of students. As example the very ability of students to (1) display different states of intention, (2) make meaning towards greater knowing, (3) develop skills to solve problems, and (4) question reality in relation to mathematical models that came up in group discussion, were a result of the formation of a zpd which the collaborative classroom practice provided opportunity for. While similar outcomes can be found in relation to social practices teachers organise in their classrooms the world over, I presently turn to examine the construct of *practice* within CHAT research.

To begin with I allude to Vygotsky's own deliberation on the manner in which a child's social environment can help foster the development of his or her higher psychological functions. Towards these ends and while arguing for a new science of psychology in his times, in a seminal paper titled *The crisis of psychology*, Vygotsky sought scientific analysis of events encountered in concrete reality by offering an example,

> Any concrete phenomena is completely inexhaustible and infinite in its separate features. We must always search in the phenomenon what makes it a scientific fact. Exactly this distinguishes the observation of a solar eclipse by the astronomer from the observation of the same phenomenon by a person who is simply curious. The former discerns in the phenomenon what makes it an astronomical fact. The latter observes the accidental features which happen to catch his attention. (Vygotsky, 1997, p. 238)

Drawing methodological attention to the network of theoretical concepts in which any event becomes a scientific fact, Vygotsky argued the notion of practice as foundational to such an endeavour and pointed out,

> *Practice sets the task and serves as the supreme judge of theory, as its truth criterion. It dictates how to construct the concepts and how to formulate the laws.* ... The most complex contradictions of psychological methodology are transferred to the ground of practice and only there can they be solved. There the debate stops being fruitless, it comes to an end. 'Method' means 'way,' we view it as a means of knowledge acquisition. But in all its

points, the way is determined by the goal to which it leads. That is why practice reforms the whole methodology of science. (Vygotsky, 1997, pp. 305–306, emphasis added)

In line with Vygotsky, the development of higher psychological functions in Olaf and Knut's students was a result of their actively participating in the collaborative classroom practice they had also helped established. The progression of students' development evidenced, stands in relation to the four themes in terms of which I understood ongoing instruction. As such the dialectic between classroom practice and theoretical themes are both criteria and arbiter of the truth of my claims. Far from being adopted in an a priori manner, my choice of themes elicits the interplay between the objectification of students' learning on one hand and subjectification of higher psychological functions in them on the other. In terms of CHAT, my adopting such a stance facilitated my understanding of how students came to master themselves, in mastering their world.

Three recent arguments aid appreciation of the notion of practice. In a chapter titled *The role of practice in cultural-historical science,* Seth Chaiklin whose course I had opportunity to attend during doctoral work, *first* articulates the objective of CHAT research as follows,

> Cultural-historical science is the general science of the origins, development, and transformations of practices, both from individual and collective perspectives. It is directed at studying practice as an ideal, expressed in historically developed traditions of action organised to produce products that satisfy collective needs. The aim is to understand the structural dynamics that organise these actions (e.g., the needs and products around which a practice is organised; the traditions of action used to realise these needs; the processes by which individuals acquire the ability to work within a practice). (Chaiklin, 2011, pp. 235–236)

My ability to grasp the manner in which Olaf and Knut's collaborative classroom practice was able to transform students' learning and cultural-historical development, follows Chaiklin's arguments. In continuation to the above, Chaiklin *second* points to how practices produce objects that are both meaningful and satisfy our collective needs in society. Olaf and Knut's classroom practice can thus be seen as satisfying the societal need of teaching children mathematics. Following Marx's well known thesis that problems in the world can be solved not merely by interpreting them but by changing them, Chaiklin *finally* argues that it is in our ability to intervene, engage with and sustain

54 CHAPTER 3

the growth of any practice over time that we can obtain significant knowledge about the same. While my doctoral study was observational, I trace my collaborating with teachers in post-doctoral work to have its roots in Chaiklin's notion of the role of practice within CHAT. Herein we jointly intervened, sustained and took transformative action in ongoing classrooms as was found necessary.

4 Cultural Tools | Development | Methodology

Having dwelt on the constructs of zpd and practice in previous sections, in this section I revisit a key CHAT notion – that of *cultural tools*. While my discussion of the role of cultural tools was less explicit while viewing the formation of a zpd and the sustenance of a practice, understanding its role in human development is key to grasping various actions students take and the agency they acquire while taking part in any practice. This is relevant to also grasp the manner in which a collective of students jointly work towards the aims or objectives of another CHAT construct termed *activity*. Greater discussed in a later section, such analytical basis has enabled me to at times engage with, sustain and study the changes that take place over time within instructional practices.

While holding off discussion on the interchangeable manner in which (1) cultural tools, signs and artefacts are conceived within CHAT and (2) the methodology advocated for studying their role in the development of higher psychological functions until later in this section, I presently turn again to how Vygotsky himself drew attention to children's use *speech as a cultural tool*, in solving practical tasks. Arguing children's perception and speech to become united when they take practical action and as introduced in Chapter 1, he said,

> *children solve practical tasks with the help of their speech, as well as their eyes and hands.* This unity of perception, speech and action which ultimately produces internalisation of the visual field, constitutes the central subject matter for any analysis of the origin of the uniquely human forms of behaviour. (Vygotsky, 1978, p. 26, emphasis in original)

In addition to conceiving psychological functions in a unified manner and in line with his other advise to practitioners that any social environment has immense plasticity, Vygotsky drew attention to the manner in which social origins direct the development of such functions,

> From the very first days of the child's development his activities acquire a meaning of their own in a system of social behaviour and, being directed towards a definite purpose, are refracted through the prism of the child's

DOCTORAL RESEARCH

environment. The path from object to child and from child to object passes through another person. This complex human structure is a product of a development process deeply rooted in the links between individual and *social history*. (Vygotsky, 1978, p. 30, emphasis added)

In addition to conceiving the unity of cultural tools, perception and action in higher psychological functions, Vygotsky above draws attention to how these functions are deeply rooted in links between individuals and human history at large. Cited from *Mind in society*, the above quotes are drawn from his writing titled *Tool and sign*, whose significance Stetsenko elaborates upon by making four insightful points. *First* she argues that the underlying principle of Vygotskian or CHAT driven higher psychological development is that of *human freedom*,

> that is, the human ability to act purposefully according to socially meaningful goals and with the help of socially developed tools, thus overcoming the dictates and constraints of nature and environment. ... and put to use knowledge about specific conditions that are necessary for individuals to develop into fully responsible, free, and competent members of a human community. (Stetsenko, 2004, p. 504)

Stetsenko explains that in psychological development aimed at human freedom, human beings use signs, symbols, language or cultural tools to transform the world, rather than passively adapt to its dictates. As vital constituents of human culture, one each child is born into and has to acquire in order to participate in social life, she finds our working with cultural tools as something that is *quintessentially human*,

> Cultural tools represent humankind's greatest invention, and they arguably form the very basis of a specifically human way of life, creating everything that is human in humans. Cultural tools allow people to embody their collective experience (e.g. skills, knowledge, beliefs) in external forms such as material objects (e.g. words, pictures, books, houses), patterns of behaviour organised in space and time (e.g. rituals) and modes of acting, thinking, and communicating in everyday life. Such external (or reified) forms that embody collective social knowledge and experience constitute a unique dimension of existence – *human culture*, into which each child is born .... (Stetsenko, 2004, p. 505)

The ability of cultural tools to realise freedom besides development in ways that are uniquely human, directs any CHAT study to grasp the ways in which

56 CHAPTER 3

cultural tools at times facilitate or at times even constrain these characteristic human aspects of freedom and development. It is thus not surprising that engaging with how children work with cultural tools in everyday practices is vital to grasp how they act, think, gain agency and communicate or even fail to do so. This leads Stetsenko to *second* argue that *collaborative activities* lie at the root of development, whereby each individual's behaviour is dependent on fellow others. She maintains,

> The child never acts alone but is intimately related to and dependent on other people. In this sense, the human infant, according to Vygotsky, is paradoxically the ultimate social being because of its complete dependency on other people. These collaborative behaviors, the primary forms of which is the parent-child interaction, always entail tools and symbols carried out from previous generations ... to facilitate collective efforts aimed at solving present tasks. The child gradually appropriates these tools, as well as the modes of action embodied in them, through internalisation, whereby the tools are converted into resources of each child's individual behaviour. (Stetsenko, 2004, p. 506)

In stressing the social and collaborative manner in which children come to use cultural tools and realise individual behaviour, Stetsenko makes a *third* vital point, which is that one needs to understand students' mental activity as part and parcel of larger, unified wholes she calls *together-systems*. Extending Vygotsky's earlier argument in relation to the unity of speech, perception and action, Stetsenko explains,

> As Vygotsky points out in several places, there is always a *unity of processes* such as voluntary attention, logical memory, perception, movement, as well as practical intellect and action. Human development entails the emergence of unified systems that combine symbolic, affective, practical, social, motor, and intellectual processes, together-systems that constitute, in Vygotsky's words, 'the only actual object of psychology.' (Stetsenko, 2004, p. 506)

Beyond being part of unified together-systems, Stetsenko points out that our mental processes associated with cognition and mind, are embedded in *larger meaningful activity*. Far from being purely mental and solitary, in activities like playing, writing and drawing, the mental and physical are blended, since we humans never think, act or relate to one another and the world, outside these activities. Demanding CHAT research adopt a historical, collaborative and unified view of psychological development in meaningful activities that we take part, in her *final* point Stetsenko draws attention to the far from logical manner in which such development takes place by offering a simple yet compelling example,

> The process of development goes beyond training and intellectual discovery and instead involves sequential changes in, and reorganisation of, the process of practical activity ... and the contradictions in activities that arise in life, that engender transformations of activity and constitute the development of its new forms, including 'mental' activities.
> ... Vygotsky states: 'The child does not invent new forms of behaviour and he does not derive them logically, but forms them by the same means as walking displaces crawling and speech displaces babbling.' (Stetsenko, 2004, pp. 509–510)

Stetsenko's explanation of our cultural-historical development in terms of freedom, human culture, social collaboration and unity of processes that take place in larger meaningful activity takes me next to the numerous ways in which cultural tools are recognised within CHAT.

Vygotsky's own writing in relation to *cultural tools*, was in terms of tools, signs and artefacts or artificial adaptations. Four arguments are particularly insightful. To discuss the role of tools and signs Vygotsky *first* argued that signs act as instruments in psychological activity, in a manner analogous to the way tools assist human labour. In addition, both tools as means of mastering nature, and signs or language as means of mastering social intercourse could be viewed in terms of the same general concept of *artefacts*. His *second* point is that both tools and signs allow psychological activity to not be in direct response to external stimuli, but to exhibit an indirect or mediated character. As example, a knot is tied in one's handkerchief to remember something later on. This leads to a *third* point of significance in which Vygotsky points out,

> The tools' function is to serve as the conductor of human influence on the object of activity; it is *externally* oriented; it must lead to changes in objects. It is a means by which human external activity is aimed at mastering and triumphing over nature. The sign on the other hand changes nothing in the object of a psychological operation. It is a means of internal activity aimed at mastering oneself, the sign is *internally* oriented. (Vygotsky, 1978, p. 55)

It is the above distinction which led Vygotsky to proclaim that mastering nature and mastering one's own behaviour were mutually linked, or that it is by altering nature, that human beings alter their own nature as well. Pointing to the manner in which cultural tools come to alter the course of psychological development, Vygotsky *finally* argued,

> The use of artificial means, the transition to mediated activity fundamentally changes all psychological operations just as the use of tools limitlessly broadens the range of activities within which the new psychological functions may operate. In this context, we can use the term *higher* psychological function, or *higher behavior* as referring to the combination of tool and sign in psychological activity. (Vygotsky, 1978, p. 55)

The foregoing discussion highlights the many ways in which the use of cultural tools alter the trajectory of human development. Leading to the formation of higher psychological functions in students, the challenge in my doctoral study was to examine the manner in which such tools were deployed and made use of in Olaf and Knut's instructional practice. My grasping their role was however guided by a *dialectical methodology* that Vygotsky also advocated. Far from being formulaic in application and demanding renewed deliberation in every concrete examination, five aspects guided my carrying out such manner of study. In the *first* Vygotsky drew a stark contrast between a naturalistic and a dialectical study. While the former admits that only nature affects human beings and their historical development, he pointed out that,

> The dialectical approach, while admitting the influence of nature on man, asserts that man, in turn, affects nature and creates through his changes in nature new natural conditions for his existence. This position is the keystone of our approach to the study and interpretation of man's higher psychological functions and serves as the basis for the new methods of experimentation and analysis that we advocate. (Vygotsky, 1978, pp. 60–61)

Elaborating upon this very approach Stetsenko and Arievitch argue,

> people not only constantly transform and create their environment; they also create and constantly transform their very life, consequently changing themselves in fundamental ways and, in the process, gaining self-knowledge and knowledge about the world. Therefore, human activity – material, practical, and always, by necessity, social collaborative processes

aimed at transforming the world and people themselves – is the basic form of human life that lies at the very foundation and is formative of everything that is human in humans, including knowledge produced by them. (Stetsenko & Arievitch, 2004, p. 65)

Vygotsky *second* suggested using *the experimental-genetic method,* to examine the development of higher psychological activity in children. Markedly different from experiments aimed at controlling behaviour, his aim was to map the genesis of psychological activity, as this underwent changes in a historical manner. Laying emphasis on how development could be studied as a process, Michael Cole and Sylvia Scribner argue,

> the experiment must provide maximum opportunity for the subject to engage in a variety of activities that can be observed, not just rigidly controlled. One technique Vygotsky effectively used for this purpose was to introduce obstacles or difficulties ... Another method was to provide alternative routes of problem solving ... A third technique was to set a task before a child that exceeded his knowledge and abilities ...
>
> With all these procedures the critical data furnished by the experiment is not performance level as such but *the methods by which the performance is achieved.* (Cole & Scribner, 1978, pp. 12–13, emphasis added)

A *third* point about how cultural tools *mediate* the development of higher psychological functions is once again made by Cole and Scribner. Against a backdrop of stimulus-response theories widely prevalent within American psychology in the 1930s-50s, they point to the role played by individuals in realising their own behaviour,

> It is important to keep in mind that Vygotsky was *not* a S-R learning theorist and did not intend his idea of mediated behavior to be thought of in this context. What he did intend to convey by this notion was that in higher forms of human behavior, the individual actively modifies the stimulus situation as a part of the process of responding to it. It was the entire structure of this activity which produced the behavior that Vygotsky attempted to denote by the term 'mediating'. (Cole & Scribner, 1978, pp. 13–14)

In line with the above it is not difficult to view Vygotsky's methodology as embedded in practical or concrete activities which students attempt. In adopting a dialectical stance and deploying an experimental-genetic method, three aspects bear repeating (1) that in any practical task it is the performance of students that is under study, (2) that the manner in which any student modifies a task situation transforms not only the task itself but the student as well, and (3) that the outcome being observed is indicative of his or her higher psychological functions.

Vygotsky's *fourth* point provides *a rationale for methods* or the ways by which the developmental performance of students could be grasped. The essential features of such manner of analysis is in terms of,

> (1) process analysis as opposed to object analysis, (2) analyses that reveals real, causal or dynamic relations as opposed to enumeration of a process's outer features, that is, explanatory, not descriptive analysis, and (3) developmental analysis that returns to the source and reconstructs all the points in the development of a given structure. The result of development will be neither a purely psychological structure such as descriptive psychology considers the result to be, nor a simple sum of elementary processes such as associationistic psychology saw it, but *a qualitatively new form that appears in the process of development.* (Vygotsky, 1978, p. 65, emphasis added)

In emphasising the qualitatively new in psychological behaviour which students develop in any practical task, Vygotsky viewed any psychologist to act like a detective, bringing to light a crime one never witnessed.

For the *fifth* and final aspect, I turn to Vygotsky's classic text *Thought and language*, first published in English in 1962. In line with the non-dualistic nature of psychology he was building, Vygotsky distinguishes two methods of investigation and argues,

> The first method analyzes complex psychological wholes into *elements.* It may be compared to the chemical analysis of water into hydrogen and oxygen, neither of which possesses the properties of the whole and each of which possesses properties not present in the whole. ... Nothing is left to the investigator but to search out the mechanical interaction of the two elements in the hope of reconstructing, in a purely speculative way, the vanished properties of the whole. (Vygotsky, 1962, p. 3)

Vygotsky however seeks *analysis into units* as method, and argues,

> In our opinion the right course to follow is to use the other type of analysis, which may be called *analysis into units.*

DOCTORAL RESEARCH 61

> By *unit* we mean a product of analysis which, unlike elements, retains all the basic properties of the whole and which cannot be further divided without losing them. Not the chemical composition of water but its molecules and their behavior are the key to the understanding of the properties of water. (Vygotsky, 1962, p. 4)

Consistent with the kind of dialectical methodology argued in favour of all along, in relation to *thought and word* Vygotsky concludes,

> The relation between thought and word is a living process; thought is born through words. A word devoid of thought is a dead thing, and a thought unembodied in words remains a shadow. The connection between them, however, is not a preformed and constant one. *It emerges in the course of development, and itself evolves.* (Vygotsky, 1962, p. 153, emphasis added)

Towards my attempts at studying the role of cultural tools in developing higher psychological functions, the above arguments provide rationale for carrying out my analysis of Olaf and Knut's instructional practice into smaller, yet holistic units. Vitally such analysis is concerned with how development itself emerges. Needless to say I employed a combination of units in my doctoral study of which I greater discuss *mediated action* and *mediated agency*, besides *activity* in sections that follow. As Vladimir Zinchenko (1985) argues, these units were selected in terms of their being a living part of Olaf and Knut's ongoing instruction. The progression of development offered in Table 1 is a summary of such analysis.

5 Artefacts | Mediated Action | Mediated Agency

To discuss instances of mediated action and mediated agency, I begin by treating cultural tools as *artefacts*, a tactic that allows me to borrow from cultural psychology as well as educational theory, following which I identify artefacts found prevalent in Olaf and Kunt's classroom. For the notion of artefacts within cultural psychology I draw upon Cole's neo-Vygotskian arguments as point of departure. Cole views artefacts as a way of building a theory about culture, which in my doctoral study was the micro-culture which Olaf and Knut helped nurture. Cole adds,

> By virtue of the changes wrought in the process of their creation and use, artefacts are simultaneously *ideal* (conceptual) and *material*. They are

62   CHAPTER 3

ideal in that their material form has been shaped by their participation
in the interactions of which they were previously a part and which they
mediate in the present. (Cole, 1996, p. 117)

Beyond pointing to their dual nature, Cole argues artefacts and systems of artefacts to exist only in relation to something else, like an instructional situation,
context, practice or activity. Both Cole and Gordon Wells, whom I shall soon
draw upon, allude to Marx Wartofsky's (1979) three-tier classification of artefacts (1) *primary* artefacts or those directly used in production, (2) *secondary*
artefacts like norms or recipes which are modes of action with which primary
artefacts are used, and (3) *tertiary* artefacts which constitute imaginary worlds
with conventions and outcomes that could exist independently of actual, practical realities. Cole considers the way in which the three tiers of artefacts outlined above and interwoven in any culture, to be worthy of in-depth study.

Wells' approach to building a theory of education based on dialogue and
co-construction of knowledge is also neo-Vygotskian. Wells draws in addition
on writings of linguist Michael Halliday and focuses upon any *activity of know-*
ing, one I take to instantiate the experimental-genetic method which Vygotsky
proposed. Wells points out,

knowing is not an activity that can be undertaken in isolation, either from
other people or from the culturally produced artefacts that provide the
mediational means. Knowing can thus be most adequately understood
as *the intentional activity of individuals who, as members of a community,*
make use of and produce representations in the collaborative attempt to
better understand and transform their shared world. (Wells, 1999, p. 76,
emphasis in original)

Explicating how Wells' activity of knowing is connected to the creation of
knowledge artefacts, in my doctoral thesis I argued,

Knowing, as substantive knowledge, is thus embedded in practical activity and becomes material for a more detached, context-independent form
of knowledge building as *knowledge artefacts*. Created in one cycle these
mediate the next cycle of knowledge building activity, and mark the beginning of theoretical knowing. The activity of knowing and creating knowledge artefacts preserve the outcomes of knowing, which illuminates both
current and prospective practice of teaching-learning. (Gade, 2006, p. 40)

In line with his interests on students' activity of knowing, Wells goes on to
identify six distinctive ways – instrumental, procedural, substantive, aesthetic,

DOCTORAL RESEARCH

theoretical and meta knowing. With potential for practitioners to identify the kind of knowing being realised within instruction, Wells also helps distinguish the more commonly sought *instrumental knowing* from the more abstract *theoretical knowing* as follows,

> In case of instrumental knowing, for example, knowledge inheres in the skillful use of an artifact as tool and in the associated practices: such knowledge is in no sense detachable from the enactment of that mediated action. In the case of theoretical knowing, on the other hand, the construction of knowledge is the main motive or purpose of the activity, and the resulting artifacts, such as the theories and models that are the outcome of this mode of knowing, take on an existence that seems to be independent of the practical situations to which they might apply. (Wells, 1999, p. 67)

I now turn to categorise various artefacts in Olaf and Knut's instruction in Table 2 and mention two aspects which guided my attempts. *First*, I drew broadly upon Wartofsky's three-tier classification. *Second*, I further classified primary artefacts into two kinds based on the manner of activity they brought about (1) those directing the actions of students outwards and resulting in physical activity as *physical artefacts*, besides (2) those directing actions of students inwards and resulting in intellectual activity as *intellectual artefacts*. This latter were the same as what Vygotsky described as psychological tools below,

> language; various systems of counting, mnemonic techniques, algebraic symbol systems, works of art, writing, schemes, diagrams, maps and mechanical drawings, all sort of conventional signs etc. (Vygotsky, 1981, p. 137)

TABLE 2   Classification of artefacts in Olaf and Knut's instruction as in Gade (2006)

Category	Description with example
Primary	*Having a representation and meant for production* (1) *Physical*: Textbook, blackboard, calculator, notebook (2) *Intellectual*: Language, mnemonic techniques, algebraic symbol systems, writing, diagrams, maps, conventional signs
Secondary	*Ways of working with primary artefacts*: Ways of using the calculator, ways of plotting graphs
Tertiary	*Derived and constituted with primary and secondary artefacts*: Models in reasoning, problem solving strategies, knowledge artefacts

My deploying *mediated action* as one of many units of analysis in my study follows earlier arguments of grasping Olaf and Knut's instruction in living units. In relation to actions of their students with respect to various artefacts, I am guided by arguments by James Wertsch in his book *Mind as action*. Unlike viewing human action in the philosophical sense as with Arendt, Wertsch's analytical aims are,

> to explicate the relationships between human *action*, on the one hand, and the cultural, institutional and historical contexts in which this action occurs, on the other. (Wertsch, 1998, p. 24)

Exemplifying mediated action with help of numerous examples, Wertsch makes ten basic claims in relation to its nature as follows,

> (1) mediated action is characterized by an irreducible tension between agent and mediational means; (2) mediational means are material; (3) mediated action typically has multiple simultaneous goals; (4) mediated action is situated on one or more developmental paths; (5) mediational means constrain as well as enable action; (6) new mediational means transform mediated action; (7) the relationship of agents toward mediational means can be characterized in terms of mastery; (8) ... in terms of appropriation; (9) mediational means are often produced for reasons other than to facilitate mediated action; and (10) mediational means are associated with power and authority. (Wertsch, 1998, p. 25)

Each of the claims put forth above allows research to nuance the nature of action that transpires, when students utilise various artefacts in classroom instruction. As Cole and Scribner point out, this also means that students actively modify the situation mediated by artefacts as part of responding to them. In this connection I find Wertsch, Tulviste and Hagstrom (1996) to formulate another insightful unit of analysis, *individual(s)-operating-with-mediational-means* or simply *mediated agency*. Via such a unit, they assign the agency exhibited by students to not be their individual attribute alone, but one distributed across them and the artefacts they utilise. Since access of students to various artefacts is dictated by instructional norms, those exhibited by Olaf and Knut's students was far from unencumbered but situated in their collaborative classroom practice.

Though not published by the time of writing up my doctoral thesis, I found Wertsch (2007) to shed valuable light on two kinds of mediation that artefacts help realise – explicit and implicit. *Mediation is explicit* when artefacts are visible and intentionally introduced in ongoing activity of individuals, like using a measuring tape for instance. *Mediation is implicit* when the role of artefacts is not visible, though their mediational effects are nonetheless discernible like when the use of inner speech directs human action. While I have drawn on this very distinction when conducting many a classroom intervention which I describe in Chapter 9, for now I consider it adequate to mention that the distinction between explicit and implicit mediation also sheds light on the notion of *double stimulation* which Vygotsky saw at play in carrying out the experimental-genetic method. Such a construct recognises that in any experimental situation two stimuli are simultaneously at play (1) the visible artefact mediating the activity as a neutral stimulus, like a graph or a pencil, and (2) the verbal instructions that a student receives as subject while working at any instructional task. While I offer many examples of mediated action and mediated agency in my thesis, with artefacts I enlist in Table 2, I presently choose to deploy these units to grasp Olaf and Knut's conduct of *When together* and *How heavy* once more.

As group-tasks which were experimental-genetic, the conduct of *When together* and *How heavy* presented different kinds of opportunities for Olaf and Knut's students to develop their higher psychological functions. Towards attempting *When together*, students were given a pentagonal diagram with two dots. As given artefact, this diagram mediated the psychological activity of students and was modified by each group in different ways to solve the problem at hand. Some drew lines to convey the paths which the black and white dots would take, some numbered the successive locations the dots would be positioned at, while some redrew many pentagons to replicate successive arrangements. In one case their relative positions were outlined in written text. As in Figure 3, students' inscriptions exemplified the development in student groups of respective higher psychological functions. The given pentagon not only mediated the actions of students but also did so in a variety of ways. This last was therefore indicative of student-groups-operating-with-the-given-pentagon or their mediated agency. As argued by Wertsch et al. such manner of mediated agency did not belong to students alone, but was distributed across students in each group and the given pentagon.

The attempts of student groups at *How heavy* was different in that the group-task conducted was not accompanied by any given artefact that would explicitly mediate the psychological activity of students. Figure 5 thus evidences various ways in which the given task was mediated by students themselves in an explicit and implicit manner. The diagrams representing a physical weighing scale, fractional representations in relation to the brick and more formal algebraic equations were explicit ways in which they externalised their implicit psychological activity. The diagrams drawn by students in respective groups, helped communicate individual thinking with one another so that they could work together as a group towards a shared solution to the problem. The actions of students were mediated this time by the written text of the task, and their agency was evidenced by the diverse ways and means in which they arrived at distinct group solutions. In line with Wertsch et al. this last exemplified student-groups-operating-with-respective-strategies. In demonstrating the use of mediated action and mediated agency as units to analyse two living wholes of Olaf and Knut's instruction, I now move on to another unit of analysis, that of activity for which I shall draw on two different structural conceptions of the same within CHAT research.

6   Activity | as Unit of Analysis

The term *activity* in CHAT research could indicate one of two conceptual aspects. *First* is the psychological theory of activity, alluded to by the letters AT in CHAT. *Second* are two kinds of units of analysis, useful in grasping the many elements at play within any experimental-genetic task or practical activity under study. In this section I dwell briefly on the theory of activity, before elaborating on both kinds of units which allow me to examine instructional activities – the *first* following the writings of Aleksei Leont'ev and the *second* following those of Yrjö Engeström. I shall demonstrate the use of these units to once again grasp Olaf and Knut's conduct of *When together* and *How heavy* evidenced earlier.

The conceptual underpinning to the *psychological theory of activity* flows from Vygotsky's dialectical approach discussed earlier on, as basis for studying higher psychological activity of human beings. While tracing the *Philosophical roots of activity theory*, which incidentally was the topic of my trial lecture during my doctoral defence, Wertsch alludes to Engels and Marx. Unlike others in their time, these two philosophers held that the nature of human consciousness was inseparable from practical, sensuous activity in the living world. Wertsch argues,

> Based on Marx and Engels's approach to the relationship between humans and reality, Soviet psychology stresses the importance of active subjects whose knowledge of preexisting material reality is founded on their interactions with it. Soviet authors constantly stress that no progress can be expected from a psychology based on a framework in which the human being is viewed as passively receiving input from the physical

and social environment. They emphasise that *only by interacting with the material world and with other humans can we develop a knowledge of reality*. (Wertsch, 1981, pp. 10–11, emphasis added)

Two aspects salient to CHAT methodology emerge from the above. *First* and as pointed out by others in this chapter, human beings collaborate with one another and modify the activity they encounter to produce human knowledge. *Second* and of no insignificant consequence is that the aims of such attempts are to develop our knowledge of reality. I recognise this last to be an undeniable strength of CHAT research, one that can inform the attempts of practitioners to conceive and conduct interventions found necessary in material, practical, lived in scenarios. It is such kind of simultaneous theoretical and practical emphasis in any activity, that explains my preference for referring to higher psychological functions in wider literature, as *higher psychological activity*.

Wertsch also argues that Vygotsky himself never made any theoretical contribution to the analytical construct of activity. This effort was carried out by his collaborator Aleksei Leont'ev in his twin writings *Activity, consciousness and personality* (1978) and *Problems in the development of mind* (1981). Assisting the development of present day Activity Theory in its many formulations, Wertsch encapsulates the chief characteristics of this approach in terms of six distinguishing features,

> (1) Activity is analysed in various levels (2) Activity involves the notion of goals and goal-directedness (3) Activity is mediated (4) Activity lays emphasis on developmental or genetic explanation (5) Human activity and the means that mediate it arise through social interaction (6) Activities initially carried out on the external plane are then internalised. (summarised from Wertsch, 1981, pp. 18–32)

Wertsch's features listed above, prepare ground for research to appreciate Leont'ev's explanation of activity as unit of analysis. In these attempts we gain by his acknowledging that any collaborative practical activity in the social world, has a well defined purpose, goal or object – like say producing food via farming, educating young via schooling or caring for one another in one's family. On the psychological consequences of taking part in such manner of activity, Leont'ev argues,

> In activity the object is transformed into its subjective form or image. At the same time, activity is converted into objective results and products. Viewed from this perspective, activity emerges as a process of reciprocal

68   CHAPTER 3

transformations between subject and object poles. According to Marx *in production the individual is objectivized, and in the individual the object is subjectivized.* (Leont'ev, 1981, p. 46, emphasis added)

Elaborating upon his theoretical arguments, Leont'ev continues,

Activity necessarily brings the human into practical contact with objects that deflect, change, and enrich this activity. In other words, it is precisely in external activity that the circle of internal mental processes is broken. It is as if the so-called objective world imperiously penetrated this circle.

Thus, activity becomes an object for psychology not as a special 'part' or 'element' but as a fundamental, inherent function. *It is the function of placing the subject in objective reality and transforming this into a subjective form.* (Leont'ev, 1981, pp. 52–53, emphasis added)

The above quotes provide valuable insight into the psychological theory of activity, explaining *how* human beings interact with the material and social world to develop knowledge of their reality. These arguments in turn prepare ground to discuss Leont'ev's construct of activity, one I implement as unit of analysis in relation to Olaf and Knut's conduct of *When together* and *How heavy*. As detailed earlier on, it was the conduct of both in quick succession by Olaf and Knut that transformed the reality of instruction in their classroom, which began with Olaf teaching at the blackboard to students cooperating in small groups.

Leont'ev's construct of activity which serves as useful unit of analysis consists of three structural levels. I encapsulate these in Table 3 giving relevant examples in relation to the societal activity of farming. At each of the structural levels, one can observe ways in which reciprocal transformations take place

TABLE 3   Leont'ev's construct of activity as unit of analysis, with farming as example

Activity – motive	The overall activity and the object or purpose that motivates its production. e.g. the motive of farming is food production
Actions – goals	The many actions that are undertaken to satisfy many smaller goals which together constitute the overall activity e.g. ploughing for planting seeds as well as sorting the produce for storing and sale
Operations – instrumental conditions	The psychological operations carried out with artefacts related to the many tasks that together constitute the actions taken e.g. using a ploughshare to prepare the earth and weighing the produce after harvesting

DOCTORAL RESEARCH

between subject and object poles i.e. between individuals taking part in farming and the objective conditions which those individuals encounter, leading to change and transformation of their reality and themselves. Such a dialectical conception as Vygotsky and Leont'ev following him would argue, are means by which human beings develop their higher psychological activity.

I now deploy Leont'ev's construct to analyse Olaf and Knut's conduct of the two group-tasks as one composite *activity*, whose *motive* was to transform classroom instruction from blackboard teaching to students cooperating in small groups. Olaf and Knut took two *actions* in terms of *goals* inbuilt within the design and conduct of the two group-tasks. While in the first, students groups began to cooperate, in the second they were able to consolidate their ability to cooperate and began to use algebra which was the next topic in the textbook they were going to engage with. The *operations* in the first group-task involved students using the given pentagon and dots as *instrumental conditions*. In the second group-task and based on their personal understanding, students used diagrams and/or equations to communicate their thoughts with one another.

Following Leont'ev one can view the object and subject poles of the activity of transforming the ongoing reality in Olaf and Knut's classroom instruction, to be in dynamic dialectic at three different levels. By deploying various instruments available in service of goals within each group-task and these exemplifying the objective pole, the actions and operations carried out by student groups in terms of higher psychological activity exemplified the subjective pole. As summarised in Table 4, these aspects qualify the nature of dialectical, reciprocal and qualitative transformations that Leont'ev envisaged, something Olaf and Knut were able to realise via conducting the group-tasks.

TABLE 4   The activity of conducting two group-tasks as unit of analysis

Activity – motive	Having students attempt *When together* and *How heavy* in succession – To establish and consolidate cooperation by students in groups
Actions – goals	(1) Have students attempt *When together* – To initiate cooperation (2) Have students attempt *How heavy* – To consolidate cooperation
Operations – instrumental conditions	(1) Students follow rules outlined in the task – They use the given pentagon and two dots to communicate their thinking to one another (2) Students develop ways to accomplish the task – They draw their own diagrams and equations to to communicate their thinking to one another

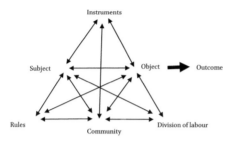

Subject	– who is involved
Instruments	– tools which mediate
Object	– goal motivating participation
Outcome	– of the activity system
Rules	– norms and regulations
Community	– wider environment
Division of labour	– distribution of responsibilities

FIGURE 7   Engeström's triangular construct of activity as unit of analysis

I now turn to the second conception of activity as unit of analysis, one outlined by Yrjö Engeström. Drawing on Leont'ev though also on other scholarship in more recent times, *Engeström's triangular construct* draws attention to seven components at play in a simultaneous manner in any practical activity, namely – subject, instruments, object, outcome, rules, community and division of labour. I deploy this construct as in Figure 7 to each of the group-tasks Olaf and Knut conducted, to grasp both similarities and differences in their functioning.

As reported in Gade (2014), four of seven components in Engeström's unit of analysis were the same for both group-tasks (1) the *Subject* or those taking part in either group-task, namely Olaf and Knut's students seated in respective small groups, (2) the *Rules* or norms followed as students cooperated in small groups, i.e. students worked towards goals specified in each, (3) the *Community* or wider social environment or the collaborative class practice, in which the group-tasks were carried out, and (4) the *Division of labour* or the distribution of responsibilities among Olaf and Knut's students in either group-task, as they cooperated with one another to arrive at a solution to the problem at hand.

The three remaining components of either group-task when analysed with the triangular construct were however different. As evidenced, the material artefacts that were handed out in either group-task which acted as *Instruments* or tools that mediated the attempts of students were quite different. While in the first the given pentagon with two dots mediated students' attempts, in the second it was various diagrams or algebraic equations offered by students in their groups which communicated their personal understanding of the task at hand. The *Object* or goal of each group-task which motivated students to participate was also different. While the first asked students to ascertain a particular condition i.e. if the two dots would meet, the second asked students to ascertain the unknown weight of the brick in question. Finally the *Outcomes* of the group-tasks were different as well. While Olaf and Knut's students cooperated in *When Together* for the first time within instruction, in *How Heavy* they consolidated their prior group cooperation. In such conduct Olaf and Knut's explicit direction for students to cooperate in the first group-task, had become implicit by their attempts at the second.

DOCTORAL RESEARCH

Just as with Leontev's construct of activity, Engeström's construct too offers insight into the kind of dialectical and reciprocal interactions which took place between subject and object poles of either group-task. The larger activity of altering the reality of classroom instruction as a whole was satisfied by the conduct of these in quick succession. While the kind of insight into the nature of students' higher psychological activity was different in my using either construct as unit of analysis, I argue one is fortunate to have two insightful versions to choose from, when wanting to study developmental change that is transformative as well.

My treating either group-task as unit of analysis not only enabled me to understand Olaf and Knut's instruction as a whole, but also allowed me to grasp their thinking, objective and subjectivity as teachers, besides those of their student groups, in relation to the social relations that their collaborative classroom practice came to bring about. In line with Roth and Radford's arguments in Chapter 1, there was no activity outside these two group-tasks as well. While more can also be said about both Leont'ev and Engeström's constructs of activity, my dwelling upon them in a brief manner does allow me to conclude a ring side tour of my doctoral efforts. Before turning to how other scholars have drawn on the neo-Vygotskian CHAT oeuvre to conduct research into other kinds of material realities in the next chapter, I turn presently to the manner in which CHAT privileges the material concrete in its very conduct.

7   Ascending to the Concrete: Coda

Alexander Luria, the other principal collaborator who worked with Vygotsky besides Aleksei Leont'ev, argued the antecedents of present day CHAT to be a *romantic science* and not a classical one. Luria drew upon Max Verwon who thought scientists belonged to one of two categories, classical or romantic. Luria went on to explain,

> Classical scholars are those who look upon events in terms of their constituent parts. Step by step they single out important units and elements until they can formulate abstract, general laws. ... The properties of the living whole are lost, which provoked Goethe to pen, '*Grey is every theory, but evergreen is the tree of life.*'
>
> Romantic scholars' traits, attitudes, and strategies are just the opposite. They do not follow the path of reductionism, ... It is of utmost importance to romantics to preserve the wealth of living reality, and they aspire to a science that retains this richness. (Luria, 1979, p. 174, emphasis added)

I quote Luria above to shed light on the kind of non-classical science that he, Vygotsky and their many collaborators were arduously attempting to build. In doing so I allude to two other people who likely influenced their thought – Johann Wolfgang von Goethe and Georg Wilhelm Friedrich Hegel. Andy Blunden explains that for Goethe, the study of nature was a *holistic practice* in a Buddhist sense, pursued diligently throughout one's life. On the nature of such pursuit I have myself argued,

> First, Goethe asked phenomena to be explained in terms of experience and not in terms of constructs which made any study metaphysical. Second, he sought scientific studies to be collaborative, participated by all and not by an elitist group with specialised training. Finally, he sought nourishment of human imagination, beyond use of instruments and training of intellect alone. (Gade, 2016, p. 405)

Blunden elaborates on Hegel's use of the terms *abstract* and *concrete*,

> By 'abstract' Hegel means underdeveloped, lacking in connections with other things, thin in content, formal; as opposed to 'concrete' which means mature, developed, having many nuances and connections with other concepts, rich in content. (Blunden, 2010, p. 62)

Both Goethe and Hegel allow me to appreciate Luria's view of what constitutes *scientific observation,* whereby one attempts to ascertain how any observational event is far from an isolated event but connected with so many other living events as well. Luria maintains,

> Scientific observation is not merely pure description of separate facts. Its main goal is to view an event from as many perspectives as possible. ...
> The more we single out important relations during our description, the closer we come to the essence of the object, to an understanding of its qualities and the rules of its existence. And the more we preserve the whole wealth of its qualities, the closer we come to the inner laws that determine its existence. It was this perspective which led Karl Marx to describe the process of scientific description with the strange-sounding expression, 'ascending to the concrete.' (Luria, 1979, pp. 177–178)

Four key aspects about the kind of research I wanted to pursue as an erstwhile teacher and the kind of research CHAT perspectives allowed me to carry out in my doctoral study seem to coalesce in the discussion above. *First* is the

DOCTORAL RESEARCH

notion of a romantic science, one which is far from reductionist and one that enabled my study to preserve the richness of lived in reality within Olaf and Knut's classroom. While going against mainstream efforts which whittles down complexity and adopts a narrow focus to conduct its disciplined inquiry, I associated my efforts with the needs of practitioners who had to engage with complex realities within ongoing instruction. The potential of a cultural-historical and activity or CHAT approach to both grasp and engage with knowledge in relation to such realities has thus been personally inviting and rewarding.

Second is the wisdom of Goethe's inputs which recognise the colour of life as green and colour of any theory as a grey portrayal at best. The wider pursuit of science too is a democratic enterprise for the many and not a guarded province of an elite few. As practitioners would appreciate, such manner of pursuit is inviting in addition of imaginative elements beyond those forwarded solely by deductive reasoning say.

Third is Hegel's point that a lack of connections in relation to any observation or event makes its content abstract, while the presence of nuanced connections within these in concrete reality that are lived, is indicative of the mature nature of its content. One will probably find wide agreement among practitioners in line with Hegel's arguments, that many a theoretical notion presented to them in teacher preparation programs are abstract, found quite unsuitable for use in one's educational concrete. It is thus that Luria drew attention to Marx's strange sounding expression of ascending to the concrete, which is the object, purpose or motive of the psychological theory of activity being pursued in CHAT.

Finally and as Vygotsky and his many collaborators have pointed out, it can only be a non-reductionist and holistic account of the lived in world, that research could lay any claim to understanding processes of change and transformation which good education can bring about i.e. by leading the development of students' higher psychological functions or higher psychological activity. I argue such a stance to be sturdy basis that holds promise for conducting interventions, which are found necessary in the interests of students, teachers, schools and research.

References

Blunden, A. (2010). *Interdisciplinary theory of activity*. Brill.
Chaiklin, S. (2011). The role of practice in cultural-historical science. In M. Kontopodis, C. Wul, & B. Fichtner (Eds.), *Children, development and education: Cultural, historical, anthropological perspectives* (pp. 227–246). Springer.

Cole, M. (1996). *Cultural psychology: A once and future discipline*. The Belknap Press of Harvard University Press.

Cole, M., & Scribner, S. (1978). Introduction. In L. S. Vygotsky (Ed.), *Mind in society: The development of higher psychological processes* (pp. 1–14). Harvard University Press.

Donaldson, M. (1978). *Children's minds*. W.W. Norton.

Gade, S. (2006). *The micro-culture of a mathematics classroom: Artefacts and activity in meaning making and problem solving* [Doctoral dissertation]. Agder University College.

Gade, S. (2010). Cooperation and collaboration as zones of proximal development within the mathematics classroom. *Nordic Studies in Mathematics Education, 15*(2), 49–68.

Gade, S. (2011). Students' meaning making in a collaborative classroom practice as initiated by two teachers. In B. Ubuz (Ed.), *Proceedings of the 35th conference of the International Group of the Psychology of Mathematics Education (PME)* (Vol. 2, pp. 361–368). PME.

Gade, S. (2013). Surface area to volume ratio and metabolism: Analysing small group-task as Vygotskian activity. In C. Smith (Ed.), *Proceedings of the British Society for Research into Learning Mathematics (BSRLM), 33*(3), 25–30.

Gade, S. (2014). Analysing two group-tasks and a collaborative classroom practice with Engeström's activity theory. In P. Barmby (Ed.), *Proceedings of the British Society for Research into Learning Mathematics (BSRLM), 34*(1), 43–48.

Gade, S. (2016). Oneself in practitioner research, with Vygotsky and Bakhtin. *Reflective Practice, 17*(4), 403–414.

Jaworski, B. (1996). *Investigating mathematics teaching: A constructivist inquiry*. Routledge Falmer.

Leont'ev, A. N. (1978). *Activity, consciousness, and personality*. Prentice-Hall.

Leont'ev, A. N. (1981). *Problems of the development of the mind*. Progress Publishers.

Luria, A. R. (1979). *The making of mind: A personal account of Soviet psychology*. Harvard University Press.

Pring, R. (2000). *Philosophy of educational research*. Continuum.

Stetsenko, A. P. (1999). Social interaction, cultural tools and the zone of proximal development: in search of a synthesis. In S. Chaiklin, M. Hedegaard, & U. Juul Jensen (Eds.), *Activity theory and social practice: cultural historical approaches* (pp. 235–252). Aarhus University Press.

Stetsenko, A. P. (2004). Introduction to Scientific legacy: Tool and sign in the development of the child. In R. W. Rieber & D. K. Robinson (Eds.), *The essential Vygotsky* (pp. 501–512). Kluwer Academic/Plenum Publishers.

Stetsenko, A. P., & Arievitch, I. M. (2004). Vygotskian collaborative project of social transformation: History, politics, and practice in knowledge construction. *The International Journal of Critical Psychology, 12*(4), 58–80.

Vygotsky, L. S. (1962). *Thought and language*. The MIT Press.

Vygotsky, L. S. (1978). *Mind in society: The development of higher psychological processes*. Harvard University Press.

Vygotsky, L. S. (1981). The instrumental method in psychology. In J. V. Wertsch (Ed.), *The concept of activity in Soviet psychology* (pp. 134–143). M.E. Sharpe.

Vygotsky, L. S. (1997). *The collected works of L. S. Vygotsky: Volume 3 – Problems of the theory and history of psychology*. Plenum Press.

Wartofsky, M. W. (1979). *Models: Representation and the scientific understanding*. D. Reidel Publishing Co.

Wells, C. G. (1999). *Dialogic inquiry: Towards a sociocultural practice and theory of education*. Cambridge University Press.

Wertsch, J. V. (1981). The conception of activity in Soviet psychology: An introduction. In J. V. Wertsch (Ed.), *The concept of activity in Soviet psychology* (pp. 3–36). M.E. Sharpe.

Wertsch, J. V. (1998). *Mind as action*. Oxford University Press.

Wertsch, J. V. (2007). Mediation. In H. Daniels, M. Cole, & J. V. Wertsch (Eds.), *The Cambridge Companion to Vygotsky* (pp. 178–192). Cambridge University Press.

Wertsch, J. V., Tulviste, P., & Hagstrom, F. (1996). A sociocultural approach to agency. In E. A. Forman, N. Minick, & C. A. Stone (Eds.), *Contexts for learning: Sociocultural dynamics in children's development* (pp. 336–356). Oxford University Press.

Zinchenko, V. P. (1985). Vygotsky's ideas about units for the analysis of mind. In J. V. Wertsch (Ed.), *Culture, communication and cognition: Vygotskian perspectives* (pp. 94–118). Cambridge University Press.

CHAPTER 4

Wider CHAT Research

From Activity to Directivity

1   Preamble

One disconcerting aspect that I experienced during doctoral work was my inability to give adequate attention to penetrating ideas, in the writings of scholars whom I did not quite draw upon in my thesis. Scant time, frugal funding and focused supervision directed my attention to the imminent goal of thesis writing and a forthcoming public defence. Yet on clearing these goal posts, even with uncertainty looming about where one might be employed next, I began to appreciate how data was collected and theory built in relation to diverse concrete realities encountered in these writings. Such an effort is particularly relevant to CHAT research, where intervening and developing as a human being is intrinsic to knowing one's reality. While pursuing such an agenda is both challenging and time consuming, it is nonetheless inviting and rewarding. It is also the case that CHAT has still some distance to cover in terms of becoming more unified and accepted as a mainstream framework, amenable for use in educational research. With issues of accurate translation from Russian originals remain, new research tools continue to bring fresh insight and make the overall enterprise worth pursuing however. Greater delving into exemplars of work done by one another is thus a prudent way of finding imaginative ways with which to move forward. In any case attention to the concrete practical remains central focus, in line with Vygotsky's dictum that practice is supreme judge of theory and its truth criterion. It is against such a backdrop that in this chapter I engage with wider CHAT research and presently dwell on five salient features recognised by many a scholar with regards to its unique and radical methodology.

I *begin* with Luria, who points out that if research into higher forms of conscious behaviour were to be found in any individual's social relations with the external world, the key to grasping such forms was to step outside the human body. Luria maintained,

> But man is not only a product of his environment, he is also an active agent in creating that environment. The chasm between natural scientific explanations of elementary processes and mentalist descriptions of

complex processes could not be bridged until we could discover the way natural processes such as physical maturation and sensory mechanisms become intertwined with culturally determined processes to produce the psychological functions of adults. We needed, as it were, *to step outside the organism to discover the sources of specifically human forms of psycho-logical activity*. (Luria, 1979, p. 43, emphasis added)

I turn *next* to Rene van der Veer and Jaan Valsiner who point out that while making observations in any study, Vygotsky recognised our very observations to be couched in the concepts we bring to bear in making them. They explain such a theory laden stance as follows,

> The natural sciences are only seemingly of a pure empirical nature. One reason for this is that we make a selection from the stream of experiences and another is the fact that scientific facts are presented in verbal or symbolic form. … Every so-called purely empirical observation is a mixture of perception and thought. There is no way to separate our conceptual knowledge couched in language from our perceptions. This line of thought leads Vygotsky to the thesis that in the scientific enterprise 'in the beginning was the word' and that the word is theory or science in embryonic form …. (Veer & Valsiner, 1988, p. 75)

As greater engaged with in a later section I find Vygotsky's above cited emphasis on the word, to have bearing on his view about the kind of instruction schools need to engage with – in terms of enabling students to bridge concepts they are aware of in their everyday lives with those that are interconnected with one another in a scientific manner.

Turning greater attention to the dialectical manner in which CHAT research is conducted, Fred Newman and Lois Holzman *third* underscore that any Vygotskian study is not cognition driven but activity based in its conduct. They thus view Vygotsky's dialectical methodology to amount to one's deploying a *tool-and-result approach* rather than a tool-for-result approach, which is often the norm in mainstream research. About the key significance of adopting such a stance they argue,

> Practice, for Vygotsky, does not derive from theory. Rather, it is practice that restructures science 'from beginning to end,' that 'poses the task and is the supreme judge of theory' … *Practicing method* simultaneously creates the object of knowledge and the tool by which that knowledge might be known. Tool and result come into existence together; their relationship is

one of *dialectical unit*, not instrumental duality .... (Newman & Holzman, 1997, pp. 78–79, emphasis in original)

In decided echo with my own reading of Gandhi's end creating practice of *satyagraha* in society, the stance outlined by Newman and Holzman recognises that the outcome of any intended inquiry is one that emerges towards the end of its conduct, by which time interim contradictions are overcome and a dialectical unity arrived at.

While I greater outline my deploying a tool-and-result approach in the interventions I conducted with teachers in Chapter 9, I mention adopting such a stance in this writing as well. Alluding to Vygotsky's own notes and extensive writings, Chris Sinha *fourth* observes,

Vygotsky's texts do not illustrate or propound his method and theory: they *are* his method and his theory, inasmuch as they are the vehicle for his engagement with the complex of problems which he saw as simultaneously a 'crisis' of psychology and an imperative to social action. ...

... His texts are not the *result* of his project, but the *record* of his translation of it into practice. His writing, in this practice, becomes both the means and the material of his investigations. (Sinha, 1989, pp. 310–313, emphasis in original)

An imperative to reflecting upon and engaging with social action brings me *finally* to the kind of cultural-historical psychology Vygotsky was attempting to lay foundations for. His plea for practice being the arbiter for theory, even with respect to his own writing, led him to the vital importance of being a practitioner alongside being a thinker in one's efforts. As Luria and Leont'ev together point out,

Vygotskii demanded that psychology become more than a scientific study of education and go beyond abstract theoretical knowledge and intervene in human life and actively help in shaping it. Psychology, he said, must cast off indifference and become 'partial' (not impartial); it must not bypass either the great ethical problems of personal life, or the little day-to-day problems. A psychologist cannot but be a thinker, but he has to be a practitioner too. 'I am for practicing psychologists,' Vygotskii wrote, 'for practical work, and so in the broad sense for boldness and the advance of our branch of science into life.' (Leontiev & Luria, 1968, p. 367)

Towards examining the boldness with which fellow CHAT researchers have intervened and advanced wider understanding of everyday social life, in a variety of concrete realms, I turn to their work as exemplars and beacon. Besides the ones I engage with in this chapter, I am aware of many others still left to be acquainted with.

2 Making Human Beings Human

Having migrated along with his parents as a child from Soviet Russia to the United States, Urie Bronfenbrenner received his doctoral training in developmental psychology. Among others, he conducted a comparative study between the two countries which while industrialised in a similar manner, differed substantially with respect to their child rearing practices. He found the primary responsibility for socialising children in American society or *making human beings human*, rested with the family. Yet it is Bronfenbrenner's methodological arguments that I now examine, which incorporate existing social settings as units of analysis in the Vygotskian sense. I dwell also on his rationale of transforming experiment, ecological validity, besides what makes schools alienated settings.

Bronfenbrenner modelled children's development in terms of their *social settings or ecologies* in which they took part. He argued,

> Whether and how people learn in educational settings is a function of sets of forces, or systems, at two levels:
> (a) The first comprises the relations between the characteristics of learners and the surroundings in which they live out their lives (e.g., home, school, peer group, work place, neighborhood, community).
> (b) The second encompasses the relations and interconnections that exist between these environments.
> The scientific study of both sets of relations as they affect learning constitutes the *ecology of education* and represents a major and necessary focus for educational research. (Bronfenbrenner, 1976, p. 5, emphasis in original)

Seeking research in real-life settings towards understanding relationships between children and their environment and those between environments, Bronfenbrenner conceived any educational environment in terms of four ecological structures, each nested within the other namely micro-, meso-, exo- and macro-systems. His premise was that a comprehensive grasp of child behaviour must take into account the environment beyond the immediate setting the child is in. For learners, (1) the *micro-system* was their immediate setting like home, day-care facility or their classroom. Here children spent considerable time in activities, wherein they engaged in and with particular roles like daughter, father, student and teacher. (2) The *meso-system* was a system of micro-systems and thus comprised of social interactions among families like schools, nature camps or activities led by places of worship. (3) The *exo-system* was an extension of the meso-system, which in formal and informal ways could determine what went on in the micro-system. Operating at the local community level and evolving in real time, this included one's neighbourhood, mass media, means of transportation, local government and community libraries. (4) The *macro-system* was the overarching structure of culture at large in which learners resided, whose norms were fleshed out in terms of economic, educational, political and legal activities prevailing therein. Carriers of ideology and individual agency, this system mandated say if learners could speak up in a democratic manner or were given equal opportunity for participation irrespective of their gender.

In seeking research that recognises interactions of learners in the above systems, Bronfenbrenner infused developmental research with *ecological validity*. The limitation of mainstream research he pointed out,

> derives from the fact that many of these experiments involve situations that are unfamiliar, artificial, and short-lived and that call for unusual behaviors that are difficult to generalize to other settings. From this perspective, it can be said that much of contemporary development psychology is *the science of the strange behavior of children in strange situations with strange adults for the briefest possible periods of time.* (Bronfenbrenner, 1977, p. 513, emphasis in original)

Bronfenbrenner thus argued for an approach he called the transforming experiment, an early frontrunner for Formative Interventions in CHAT research (Engeström et al. 2014), greater discussed in Chapter 9. In doing so he drew on arguments made by two scholars, Walter Dearborn and Aleksei Leont'ev. As first mentor in his graduate school, Dearborn offered Bronfenbrenner the following advice,

> *If you wish to understand the relation between the developing person and some aspect of his or her environment, try to budge the one, and see what happens to the other.* (Bronfenbrenner, 1977, p. 518, emphasis in original)

As exchange scholar to the USSR, he met with Leont'ev who compared developmental psychology in either country and concluded,

> It seems to me that American researchers are constantly seeking to explain how the child came to be what he is; we in the USSR are striving

to discover not how the child came to be what he is, but how he can become what he not yet is. (Leont'ev in Bronfenbrenner, 1977, p. 528)

Leont'ev's observation above reminded Bronfenbrenner of Dearborn's earlier advice of altering learners environment to observe developmental changes. This thus led him to the notion in Soviet psychology of the *transforming experiment* – one that did not perpetuate the status quo in any social reality and was able to radically restructure the environment. By way of conducting transforming experiments, previously unrealised behavioural potentials of the subject could be activated and observed. With reference to his own interest in ecologies, he argued,

> *Research on the ecology of education requires experiments involving the innovative restructuring of prevailing ecological systems in ways that depart from existing institutional ideologies and structures by redefining goals, roles, and activities, and providing interconnections between systems previously isolated from each other.* (Bronfenbrenner, 1977, p. 528, emphasis in original)

Acknowledging such experiments to be rare, Bronfenbrenner provided examples. For example (1) have students provide care for children of working mothers, assist families in emergencies, visit the old and lonely, (2) facilitate transition of children from home to school, by introducing their family members with personnel of their school, and (3) introduce flexible work timings for families with children, enabling parents to look after their young especially when they fell ill. The underlying intention in Bronfenbrenner's examples was to make pedagogical transitions possible between eco-systems he identified. In taking the ecosystems of students into account, there was opportunity to expand the repertoire of actions students could then take. Bronfenbrenner's objective was for scientists to work from different perspectives in different ways to alter ecologies that were existing, so as to better understand human development in a variety of transformed contexts. His lucid conclusion was – experiments created as real, are real in their consequences.

Following the above Bronfenbrenner argued that more was presently known by society about children, than was known about environments that affected the course of children's development. As a consequence, he found public policy to be very limited in scope. As example, he found that *schools had become increasingly isolated* from children's homes besides society as a whole, and maintained,

> As neighborhood schools disappear, the school buildings are farther away, larger, and more impersonal. The staff, too, increase in number, are

drawn from a larger area, and often commute rather than live in the local community. As a result, parents and teachers are less likely to know each other, let alone to engage in joint activities or become friends.

... As schools are moved to the outskirts of town, they become compounds, physically and socially insulated from the life of the community, neighborhood, and families, as well as from the life for which they are supposedly preparing the children. (Bronfenbrenner, 1979, p. 848)

Bronfenbrenner's article from which the above quote is cited, also points to the problem of segregating students in age based classes, resulting in a lack of social identity and feeling of common community for children to share an active sense of responsibility.

Read with other writings discussed previously, I find Bronfenbrenner to make two invaluable contributions, (1) offer a framework with which to grasp wider environments we live in, and (2) offer a cautionary tale about the consequences of not knowing enough about various ecosystems which our students inhabit. In line with Vygotsky, Bronfenbrenner's unit of analysis is wide-angled, one that is easy to ignore by the sheer weight of minutiae that we practitioners deal with in our day to day lives. As a result, it may be deceptively easy for us to underestimate the role of four nested ecological environments and the significance of their interrelationships as singled out by Bronfenbrenner. For it is not only classrooms and families, but these ecologies too which need to be intervened with and understood, for the sake of students' learning and subsequent development.

3　Situated Learning

As part of post-doctoral work I had opportunity to travel to conferences, present my work and meet with scholars whose work I had in turn read. It was in this manner that I had occasion to meet with Jean Lave at the ISCAR conference in Rome. As doctoral students we read her book with Etienne Wenger during course work titled, *Situated learning: Legitimate peripheral participation*. Reading this book for the first time, transposed me to my childhood experience of making pickles in my grandmother's large kitchen, with a glistening maroon floor and its black border. This room was packed with her, my mother, my aunts and us grandchildren. In the anteroom, her sons and grandsons would cut raw mangoes to pieces with a knife blade as a lever, on a block of wood. On one side lay cleaned and dry, white and brown coloured ceramic jars to store the variety of pickles we were together going to make.

WIDER CHAT RESEARCH

Over many summers we took part in the many intricate processes that pickle making involved, so that one day when I ran my own kitchen I was able to make pickles with great ease. Years of careful observation, the ability to keep the whole process as dry as possible, measuring out salt, mustard powder, chilli powder and other spices in proportion by weight to one another, and this weighed out mixture in volume to the raw mango pieces wiped clean on the other was a rewarding experience. One also felt triumphant when we savoured the pickles after they were well seasoned. Such an experience helped us tweak our own pickle making process later in life, by the memories we had by then embodied. The theory outlined by Lave and Wenger seemed to explain how we together came to learn my grandmother's pickle making expertise with ease. I became aware too that my experience of learning to make pickles stood in stark contrast with the isolated, disembodied and far from triumphant experience many a student had with learning mathematics in classrooms and schools. I turn to examine this wider problematic by (1) dwelling on Lave and Wenger's perspectives on situated learning, before (2) engaging with the contrast Lave draws between a practice of understanding and a culture of acquisition, one that often prevails in classrooms.

To begin with, the brief portrayal of my grandmother's pickle making practice, exemplifies the premise of ascending to the concrete, discussed in the previous chapter. This means that my analysis of her pickle making practice takes into account how things, events and people were related, both with one another as well as the pickles we produced. Our division of labour, distribution of responsibilities besides quality of relationships we nurtured testifies not only to how we collectively apprenticed over time to my grandmother's mastery, but also how such *apprenticeship* allowed the practice of pickle making to survive across generations. As an educator I am led to ask how such participation brought about learning and the kind of learning our collective participation brought about. Lave and Wenger's theory of situated learning draws on their study of similar apprenticeships in midwifery, meat cutting and tailoring say. About the nature of *situated learning* William Hanks' preface points to research that explores situated ways of human understanding and communication and argues,

> It takes as its focus the relationship between learning and social situations in which it occurs. Rather than defining it as the acquisition of propositional knowledge, Lave and Wenger situate learning in certain forms of co-participation. Rather than asking what kinds of cognitive processes and conceptual structures are involved, they ask what kinds of social engagements provide the proper context for learning to take place.

... The common element here is the premise that meaning, under-standing, and learning are all defined relative to actional contexts, not to self-contained structures. (Hanks, as cited in Lave & Wenger, 1991, pp. 14–15)

Several aspects of situated learning are exemplified in my portrayal of pickle making. For a start is the actional context in which pickle making was carried out. Neither did any of us sit idle nor did anyone of us fail to contribute. If one was not able to dice mangoes, one volunteered to wipe the jars clean, or weigh out spices that were to be mixed. Social relations were integral to this exercise. There was opportunity for us to bond with our aunts and rank uncles in jest according to their abilities of dicing mangoes. While I still take pride in following my grandmother's recipe, it is just as well that some of my cousins now choose recipes that have been handed down in families they are now married into. Such opportunities for comparison and innovation however remain part and parcel of our propensity to talk about pickle making in the first place. As Lave and Wenger would argue, co-participation and learning were integral to our being and becoming part of the pickle making practice. Yet two aspects also stand out, the importance of our personal identities as consummate pickle makers and the personal confidence gained from our being and becoming experienced practitioners. Both are visible markers also of the current stage of learning any one of us in my grandmother's family is at, in our pickle making journey today. Such efforts are of course dependent on personal agency, motivation and material circumstances, which each of us in the next generation are lucky to have or not.

Lave and Wenger term the above manner of participation as *legitimate peripheral participation* whose underlying premise they argue is,

> not a simple participation structure in which an apprentice occupies a particular role at the edge of a larger process. It is rather an interactive process in which the apprentice engages by simultaneously performing in *several roles* – status subordinate, learning practitioner, sole responsible agent in minor parts of the performance, aspiring expert and so forth – each implying a different sort of responsibility, a different set of role relations, and a different interactive involvement. (Lave & Wenger, 1991, p. 23)

Legitimate peripheral participation as a concept, Lave and Wenger point out in addition, is not associated with clarity, precision and maximum definition as concepts are in conventional used. Rather such a concept re-conceives the manner in which persons, activities, knowing and their world are interconnected. They explain,

> We have tried, in reflective consonance with our theoretical perspective, to re-conceive it in interconnected, relational terms. Thus the concept of legitimate peripheral participation obtains its meaning, not in a concise definition of its boundaries, but in its multiple, theoretically generative interconnections with persons, activities, knowing, and world. Exploring these interconnections in specific cases has provided a way to *engage in the practice-theory project that insists on participation in the lived-in world as a key unit of analysis in a theory of social practice* (which includes learning), and to develop our thinking in the spirit of this theoretically integrative enterprise. (Lave & Wenger, 1991, p. 121, emphasis added)

In echo with Vygotsky's attention to practice as arbiter of truth, Lave and Wenger's analysis of legitimate peripheral participation highlights two aspects worthy of note (1) that participation in the lived-in, concrete, material world is unit of analysis, and (2) that such analysis favours the spirit of potential theoretical integration. In parallel with CHAT's ability to engage with social reality, I argue these aspects to be another of its theoretical as well as practical strengths.

I now turn to grasp how the demands made on learners in everyday mathematics classrooms are different from those made while apprenticing to a master in a situated learning social practice. Lave discusses these two views in terms of a culture of acquisition and a practice of understanding. By a *culture of acquisition*, Lave refers to the more commonly held view of schooling, where knowledge is decontextualised, presented in abstract and generalisable forms with intention of transfer to real world situations. Culture here is something to be acquired by students and transmitted in teaching. A *practice of understanding* on the other hand assumes,

> that processes of learning and understanding are socially and culturally constituted, and that what is to be learned is integrally implicated in the forms in which it is appropriated, so that, for example, *how* math is learned in school depends on its being learned *there*. Apprenticeship forms of learning are likely to be based on assumptions that knowing, thinking, and understanding are generated in practice, in situations whose specific characteristics are part of practice as it unfolds. (Lave, 1990, pp. 310–311, emphasis in original)

86 CHAPTER 4

Lave contrasts the two models above by drawing on her study of Vai and Gola tailors in Liberia and makes two significant points. *First*, that the curriculum of learning for novices in tailoring practice is a repertoire of whole garments like hats, children's underwear, trousers, women's dresses, prayer gowns, and suits. She notes in particular that,

> The curriculum of tailoring differs sharply in intentions and organisation from school curricula. The curriculum of tailoring is more a set of landmarks *for* learners than specific procedures to be taught *to* learners. It shapes opportunities for tailoring activity and hence the processes of learning to tailor. (Lave, 1990, p. 314)

She *second* points to the underlying order in the process of overall production and points out that the preliminary steps taken by novice tailors to be that of ironing clothes, sewing by hand and using the treadle sewing machine. It is only on gaining required expertise that apprentices learn how to cut out and sew each garment. She explains,

> Reversing production steps has the effect of focusing the apprentices' attention first on the broad outlines of garment construction as they handle garments while attaching buttons and hemming cuffs. Next, sewing turns their attention to the logic (order, orientation) by which different pieces are sewn together, which in turn explains why they are cut out the way they are. Each step offers the unstated opportunity to consider how the previous step contributes to the present one. (Lave, 1990, p. 313)

Lave's portrayal of learning in such a situated social practice has many noteworthy implications. The *first* is that the above manner of production minimises failure. Sewing can be redone whereas cutting cannot. As an educator I find this aspect to take into account the relevance of actions that apprentices take every step of the way. Ironing clothes makes them suitable for delivery, lining garments is a prerequisite for making hats and skills like hemming are required for finishing trousers. These aspects are understood by inference and not taught in a pedantic manner. The *why* question in relation to the actions taken by novices is obvious to them as they participate in the social practice to which they belong. Lave *second* records a high percentage of apprentices becoming masters themselves, with attrition not posing a problem in relation to material resources spent. Such manner of learning is also beneficial is minimising uncertainty, as novices can view the lives they would eventually lead.

Following the above, Lave is in a position to point to the kind of issues that are problematic in mathematics classrooms. For instance she finds learning herein to be highly compartmentalised and reductionist in spirit, spending months on mastering algorithmic procedures without knowing their need or efficacy in everyday lives. Having little opportunity to deal with holistic situations in classrooms, many students don't get to see how mathematics could contribute to their overall functioning. She adds too that dilemmas in mathematics classrooms are not mathematical in nature, but those of performance. As learners try to succeed in terms of situated hidden curricula, they often times go along with only an appearance of understanding. On problem solving in schools, Lave thus argues,

> Ongoing activity in school appears to be shaped by, and shapes in turn, whatever issues are lively and problematic for learners. Teachers cannot make math the central ongoing activity by decree (or lesson plans); math will be problematic in substantive ways only when the central dilemmas of ongoing activity are mathematical ones. Where mathematics learning is consistently the official activity but not the central dilemma, then learners in most U.S. schools should be expected to generate a veneer of accomplishment through activity of a dependable and effective kind, in ways teachers do not teach or intend. (Lave, 1990, pp. 322–323)

Lave's observation of performance and not mathematics being central to the subject being taught in school reminds me of Watson's arguments in Chapter 1 that school mathematics is a special kind of mathematics, with its own rules, purposes, authorities and warrants. As greater detailed in Chapter 9, I came to draw upon Lave's above outlined arguments while jointly conducting an intervention with a teacher at grade eight, whose students displayed minimal relationship with the mathematics that was expected of them. By designing and conducting five successive tasks we were able to change their manner of participation in *their* lived-in world. This led to our being able to observe how adolescent identities of a few at least, were noticeably transformed. Our tasks came to follow guidelines of meaningful practical activity forwarded by del Rio and Alvarez, whose arguments I discuss in the coda of this chapter. I now turn to examine Scribner's functional approach to thinking and cognition.

4 Functional Approach to Literacy

I encountered Sylvia Scribner for the first time by way of her introduction with Michael Cole of *Mind in Society*. Years later when I visited CUNY where she was faculty, I came across a conference hall in the psychology department named after her. Running my fingers on the plaque outside, I couldn't help think of the person whose study of practical thinking at a dairy farm captivated me. Besides being empirically rich, Scribner also engaged explicitly with issues of methodology as well. My dwelling on Scribner's work, follows that of Bronfenbrenner and Lave who show how to greater grasp human minds at work in everyday homes and tailoring shops. In so doing they hold up a mirror to research that understands the human mind working at isolated tasks, often mentalistic, confined too in conduct to a secluded laboratory. As Scribner points out,

> Memory and thinking in daily life are not separate from, but part of doing. We understand cognitive tasks, not merely as ends in themselves but as means for achieving larger objectives and goals; and we carry out these tasks in constant interaction with social and material resources and constraints. ...
>
> ... In the workplace, tasks must be accomplished which require selection and retention of information, accumulation of knowledge, mastery of new symbol systems and on-line problem solving – *all in the service of getting other things done*. (Scribner, 1997, p. 335, emphasis added)

Before detailing Scribner's study of practical thinking at a dairy farm, I begin with lessons from her study of literacy with Cole of the Vai people in Liberia who were triliterate – acquiring English in government schools, the indigenous Vai script from tutors and Quarnic literacy via group study with a teacher but without any schooling. In this study Scribner and Cole were able to question generalisations made about the consequences of literacy, by contrasting two models of literacy – *literacy as development* and *literacy as practice*. The first model came to view a literate person's capacities as being higher-order, one inevitably exhibited upon having acquired skills that were necessary and requisite. They argued,

> A defining characteristic of the developmental perspective is that it specifies literacy's effects as the emergence of general mental capacities – abstract thinking, for example, or logical operations – rather than specific skills. These abilities are presumed to characterize the individual's intellectual functioning across a wide range of tasks. ...
>
> ... It assumes that various components of literacy – say, an alphabetic script or an essayist text – are likely to have the same psychological consequences in all cultures irrespective of the contexts of use or of the social institutions in which literacy is embedded. (Scribner & Cole, 1978, pp. 451–452)

Not to be confused with human development, the literacy as development of general mental capacities however did not find empirical ratification in

Scribner and Cole's study of the Vai in Liberia. They failed to find that abstract thinking or logical reasoning depended on mastery of the written language by the Vai. Specific cognitive skills showed little signs of generalisability across experimental tasks as well. What they did find was that literacy practices among them, produced intellectual outcomes that were closely tied to the functional use they put their literacy to. In other words their *literacy was a practice*. Scribner and Cole clarify,

> *A practice may be considered to be the carrying out of a goal-directed sequence of activities, using particular technologies and applying particular systems of knowledge.* It is a usual mode or method of doing something – playing the piano, sewing trousers, writing letters. This definition shares certain features with the notion of practice in educational psychology – repeated performance of an act in order to acquire proficiency or skill. (Scribner & Cole, 1978, p. 457, emphasis added)

The above working definition of the notion of practice, one which could grasp the kinds of use the Vai put their literary to, provides decided echo to Vygotsky's contention that any practice serves also as truth criteria. It also echos many of the characteristics that Chaiklin argues in Chapter 3, in relation to the notion of a practice in cultural-historical science. The above findings led Scribner and Cole to a methodological point,

> Although we do not advocate a single approach to the complex issues of the psychology of literacy, we believe that the strategy of functional analysis emerging from the Vai research may have particularly useful implications for educational research in our own society. It suggests that different literacy activities need to be analyzed independently. If, as we have demonstrated, particular skills are promoted by particular kinds of literacy practices, we need to know a great deal more about just how literacy is practiced. (Scribner & Cole, 1978, p. 459)

Hampered by her ability to work in an unfamiliar culture, Scribner's next study was conducted at the dairy farm I mention, in Baltimore, USA. Her intention was to ascertain empirical models of cognition at work, by studying workers carrying out ongoing activities. Towards these ends she adopted *a functional approach to cognition* as follows,

> A functional approach to cognition implies a methodological principle. If skill systems are activity- or practice-dependent, one way to determine their characteristics and course of acquisition is to study them as they

function in these practices. To put it somewhat differently, *the practices themselves need to become the objects of study.* (Scribner, 1997, pp. 357–358, emphasis added)

In line with the above, Scribner approached her study of the industrial practice of dairy farming by viewing various tasks within, as her units of analysis. With colleagues she studied four of these (1) product assembly by pre-loaders, (2) product arrays by inventory people, (3) pricing delivery tickets, and (4) computerised inventory. I presently discuss the manner in which pre-loaders computed their arithmetic and went about assembling bottles that had to be sent out for delivery.

In her writing titled *Studying working intelligence*, Scribner describes product assembly by pre-loaders as a warehouse job carried out by them at 6 pm every evening, so that load-out orders that were placed on the dairy trucks were ready for delivery the next day. Working in an icebox maintained at 38 degrees Fahrenheit, the job of pre-loaders involved assembling orders from a range of products like skimmed milk, chocolate milk etc. Scribner begins by explaining 16 quart bottles to make up a case and that the pre-loaders used the representation of 1 + 3 for a delivery of one case and 3 bottles. Understandably this inscription was not a literal mathematical expression, but an interpretive one which got things done. Orders for 17 to 24 quarts for example, thus ranged from 1 + 1 to 1 + 8. Likewise those from 25 to 31 quarts, ranged from 2 − 7 to 2 − 1.

Scribner and her colleagues found pre-loaders to have a repertoire of solution strategies in addition. When an order of 1 − 6 or 10 quarts came up for delivery six times, on two occasions the pre-loader removed six quart bottles from a case of 16. On two other occasions the solution took advantage of cases that were partially full e.g. 4 quarts were removed from a case of 14, just as 1 was removed from a case containing 11. In two more solutions, the take-away problem was transformed to an add-to problem i.e. 2 units were added to 8 and 4 added to 6. Such solutions were neither product specific nor restricted to particular quantities. The pre-loader transformed the original information in load-out orders, into an action sequence that could be mapped onto different cases. About the manner in which *practical thinking* was displayed, Scribner argued,

This is one of the advantages of taking actual occurrences of practical thinking as a starting point for cognitive analysis. They make it possible to say what 'intelligent' practical thinking actually is in a particular setting, not merely what, according to existing theories, it ought to be. In product assembly, we have a suggestion as to one possible defining characteristic of practical thinking which might warrant the use of the qualifier 'intelligent,' that is, the extent to which thinking serves to organise and make more economical the operational components of tasks. (Scribner, 1984, p. 26)

My brief summary of only one of the tasks Scribner observed, does little justice to the meticulous manner in which she lays out many examples of intelligent, practical and working mechanisms, which workers at the dairy exhibited. In the thoughtful and insightful analysis that she presents, one can see Scribner return time and again to demonstrate how thinking in daily life is functional and accomplished in inventive ways, with respect to the specific goals of tasks at hand. In other words human cognition or thinking in daily life in any material practice, be it literacy or preloading in a dairy farm, is what gets the job at hand done.

In continued pursuit of a functional approach to thinking, cognition and literacy, I turn to Scribner one last time to grasp how she argues the *notion of history* could be modified to account for the sociohistorical formation of the human mind. Towards this she points out in *Vygotsky's uses of history*, that Vygotsky himself deployed three levels to offer an explanatory account of what is uniquely human, about human beings – general history, child history, and the history of mental functions. Scribner (1985) argues that this model can be modified by inserting the history of individual societies, at a level between general history and child history. The advantage of doing so she says, is to recognise that the existence of individuals is neither independent nor reducible to ongoing world history. By taking the history of individual societies into account, it is possible to anchor social and psychological change of people in the present. Adopting such a stance leads me to some family history, this time in relation to the literacy of my father's mother.

To begin with, my grandparents' generation became parents at a time when we as a people were struggling for our country's independence. The story of literacy of my mother's and father's mothers is set against this backdrop. The literacy of my mother's mother was at the hands of her father, a math teacher of repute in his town. Trained in law, her husband who was her father's able student, went on to became a High Court judge. His material well being in later life enabled my grandmother to indulge in the social practice of pickle making, which I described at length in the previous section. While literate in Telugu, she taught herself to read headlines in the English newspaper later on in life.

The literacy for my father's mother was in contrast, at her husband's behest, whom she married when very young. Besides owning small land holdings, this grandfather was a school teacher in his town as well as a freedom fighter. This last landed him in jail at least thrice. My father's mother had thus to put her literacy to good use following the values he instilled in her, that the sacrifices they were making was decidedly for a better future for their children and grandchildren. With my grandfather dying in jail due to a neglected diabetic condition, the demands made on my grandmother's literacy changed dramatically. With the assistance of those who valued her independence she stood her ground, maintained her house, kept an eye on the farm yield, besides educated and settled her children in their marriages as well. In so doing she kept her children and step-children from wives my grandfather had previously lost as a tightly knit family, one that survives till today. The scenario I portray came into play when my grandmother was barely in her twenties and lived all those years against a backdrop of people fighting for their independence.

I often wondered what kept my grandmother going despite so many odds in her life. Her literacy restricted to Telugu, included her reading Indian mythology besides philosophical and metaphysical literature. On many an occasion I found her doubled over her books, laughing in jest at what some character in these, caught up in some predicament, said or did. In a Vygotskian sense her texts and literacy, mediated her understanding of the tumultuous history and personal challenges she lived through. She said she followed a simple mantra in life, of placing her belief in the benevolence of the Almighty. Her passing away was the first mail I read when I reached Oxford for post-doctoral work. She and I had travelled far I thought and recollected the most profound story she told me when I was all but ten years old. This related to the Hindu belief of incarnations of the Almighty, visiting others for alms in guise of a human being. It was for us, she said, to recognise the Almighty in that person.

5 Funds of Knowledge

My students pursuing their *Masters in Education* at TISS, Hyderabad, were thankful that we discussed Luis Moll's writings as part of one of my courses. These students who come from across India have fascinating backgrounds which match the eagerness with which they come to learn, in order to return and teach diverse populations. Their resolve to greater understand their own lives and those they intended to in turn educate, is hard to ignore. I found them viewing Moll's writings as not only relevant but also easy to take cue from. Moll's point of departure in Vygotskian perspectives is his recognition that education can contribute to *a theory of psychological development*. Towards building such manner of theory Moll views zpd as a connecting concept which,

> embodies or integrates key elements of the theory: the emphasis on social
> activity and cultural practices as sources of thinking, the importance of

mediation in human psychological functioning, the centrality of pedagogy in development, and the inseparability of the individual from the
social. ...

... The construct of the zpd reminds us that there is nothing 'natural'
about educational settings (and about educational practices such as ability groupings, tracking, and other forms of stratification). *These settings
are social creations, they are socially constituted, and they can be socially
changed.* (Moll, 1990, p. 15, emphasis added)

Viewing the Vygotskian zpd as a theory of possibilities and arguing there was
nothing natural in any educational setting, Moll also points out how easy it is
to underestimate the abilities of students and teachers when these are examined in isolation, whereas by drawing on existing social and cultural resources
one could mediate learning and promote change.

Moll's work with bilingual students, speaking Spanish at home and being
judged for their performance in English at school, is his starting point for questioning normative perceptions held against such students. He goes on to use his
construct of funds of knowledge to wisely draw upon what is already available
at hand in these very educational settings. The disconcerting issue with respect
to the education of these students, Moll points out, is the problematic assumption that by learning English these students would easily assimilate into mainstream society in the US. Little attention is paid however to the social dynamics
these students contend with, or their academic development. Moll points out,

In comparison with the schooling of peers from higher-income families,
instruction for working-class students, be it in bilingual or monolingual
classrooms, can be characterized as rote, drill and practice, and intellec-
tually limited, with an emphasis on low-level literacy and computational
skills. ... This reduction of the curriculum is not only in terms of content,
but in terms of limited and constrained uses of literacy and mathematics,
the primary instructional means. (Moll, 1992, p. 20)

Moll thus turns rightful attention to the households of these very children.
Even as they face the vagaries of a changing economy since they come from
working class families, he recognises the underlying strengths of such households in terms of the social networks they belong to which have strategic educational value besides. He elaborates,

For families with limited incomes, these networks can be a matter of
survival because they facilitate different forms of economic assistance

and labor cooperation that help families avoid the expenses involved in using secondary institutions, such as plumbing companies or automobile repair shops. These networks can also serve other important functions, including finding jobs and providing assistance with child care, releasing mothers, if need be, to enter the labor market. In brief, these networks form social contexts for the acquisition of knowledge, skills, and information, as well as cultural values and norms. (Moll, 1992, p. 21)

The collective of labour driven practices prevalent in households, which constitute bodies of cultural knowledge and are socially networked, is what Moll terms as *funds of knowledge*. His study shows this collective to include invaluable skills related for example to agriculture and mining, appliance repairs, medicine as well as building construction. Moll and his colleagues go on to argue that these kinds of funds of knowledge, which are distributed across people and their respective tools of trade can be fruitfully accessed by teachers for education. In addition to being situated in line with Lave's arguments and manifested through events or activities, they go on to maintain that these funds of knowledge are,

> not possessions or traits of people in the family but characteristics of people-in-an-activity. Our household observations suggest the importance of taking into account not only visible, apparent knowledge, where contexts of application, such as cooking a meal, are ubiquitous, but more latent, hidden knowledge, displayed in helping or teaching others or as part of the families' production. Within these activities, much of the teaching and learning is initiated by the children's interests and their questions. That is children are active in creating their own activities or are active within the structure of the tasks created by the adults. (Moll & Greenberg, 1990, p. 326)

In contrast to the possibility of students learning knowledge that could be abstract, decontextualised, many a time irrelevant and imposed on them by teachers, Moll's approach highlights the opportunities children have in obtaining knowledge that is of interest to them, from adults they have affinity and familiarity with. The very presence and distribution of funds of knowledge around students' households, led teachers working with Moll to invite parents and others who were skilled, to contribute to students' intellectual and academic development. Once such interventions became a regular feature, teachers took on the role of facilitators looking out for future possibilities, a role Moll envisaged for researchers as well to interrogate the naturalness of existing educational settings.

Working with funds of knowledge as basis, Moll (2000) moves on to re-interpret three key elements that contribute significantly to educational theory. *First* is the very concept of *literacy*. His approach above allowed students to read texts in English and discuss the same in Spanish, an aspect which enabled them to amplify personal experiences and interests without hesitation. It was thereby possible for students and their teachers to confront hegemonic interests that were implicit in the instruction they would receive in English. *Second*, is the notion of *community*, for which he intentionally brought in social networks of working class families and households into students' classroom. This enabled their education to draw on locally prevalent resources besides people who were invested in their education as well. Such attention also promoted democratic participation by those who were concerned. *Finally* Moll was able to conceive culture as grounded in lives actually lived by children in their concrete everyday. Being able to counter a notion of culture that seemed handed down in an academic manner, such engagement enabled children to come into their own amongst the very social relations that constituted them. They could thus construct the central mediating creation in Vygotskian development, which is the child's development by the child.

One can summarise Moll's exercise in re-interpretation of education, to highlight *how* the zpd is far from a natural occurrence, but one that is socially created, socially constituted and socially changed. On grasping the *social* in Vygotskian theory, Scribner whom I discuss in the previous section, seeks multiple units of analysis with regards to meaning made in face-to-face encounters with people, their relationships and their projects. Moll cites Scribner, whose observations I too cite below,

> Vygotsky's special genius was in grasping the significance of the social in things as well as people. The world in which we live in is humanized, full of material and symbolic objects (signs, knowledge systems) that are culturally constructed, historical in origin and social in content. Since all human actions, including acts of thought, involve the mediation of such objects (tools and signs) they are, on this score alone, social in essence. Thus is the case, whether acts are initiated by single agents or a collective and whether they are performed individually or with others. (Scribner, 1990, p. 92)

Having dwelt on a resourceful manner in which Moll and his colleagues worked with concrete particulars and built educational theory in often neglected local practices, I now turn to building of theory in institutional settings such as conventionally conceived everyday schools.

6 Rousing Minds to Life

Roland Tharp and Ronald Gallimore greater contextulaise Vygotskian perspectives for schooling, in their book *Rousing minds to life*. Like Moll in the previous section they too respond to Sarason's call in Chapter 1, of creating educational settings *for* teaching. Tharp and Gallimore envision a theory of education in terms of a unified trio of *a theory of teaching*, *a theory of schooling* and *a theory of literacy*. In my continued engagement with Vygotskian premise, I unpack one particular aspect of each of these three theories in this section. My point of departure for such manner of exploration is two key features of any zpd, explored in greater detail in Chapter 3. The *first* recognises that a zpd deals with the development of psychological functions that are currently in an embryonic state and in the process of maturation in any individual. The *second* recognises properly organised learning, involving social interaction with more capable others in a zpd, *leads* development. This is because through learning, individuals master cultural tools besides their own psychological functioning. In line with these arguments, Tharp and Gallimore conceive teaching as assisting the performance of students in the latter's zpd, wherein social interactions are internalised and become their mind. They go on to argue,

> Students cannot be left to learn on their own; teachers cannot be content to provide opportunities to learn and then assess outcomes; recitation must be deemphasized; responsive, assisting interactions must become commonplace in the classroom. *Minds must be roused to life.* (Tharp & Gallimore, 1988, p. 21, emphasis added)

Tharp and Gallimore underscore that until internalisation occurs i.e. until students master their own psychological functioning by means of social interaction, their performance must be assisted. It is via this path that the interpsychological becomes their intrapsychological. This premise leads them to *first* redefine teaching as assisting the performance of students. In fact teaching occurs, they argue, only when the performance of students is achieved with the assistance of teachers. Such performances on part of students evidence the maturation of those psychological functions which are in an embryonic stage and which would likely remain dormant if not for the assistance of teachers. Tharp and Gallimore conclude,

> Distinguishing the *proximal zone* from the *developmental level* by contrasting assisted versus unassisted performance has profound implications for educational practice. It is in the proximal zone that teaching may be defined in terms of child development. ...

... We can therefore derive this general definition of teaching: *Teaching consists in assisting performance through the ZPD. Teaching can be said to occur when assistance is offered at points in the ZPD at which performance requires assistance.* (Tharp & Gallimore, 1988, p. 31, emphasis in original)

Tharp and Gallimore in addition observe that unlike parents who assist the performance of their children, the pedagogical skills which teachers need go far beyond those exercised in their day-to-day. Having important implications for teacher professional development, they insist that the performance of teachers also needs assistance,

> For pedagogical skills to be acquired, there must be training and development experiences that few teachers encounter – opportunity to observe effective examples and effective practitioners of assisted performance, and opportunities to practice nascent skills, to receive video and audio feedback, and to have gentle, competent 'coaching' of a skilled consultant. Teachers themselves must have their performance assisted if they are to acquire the ability to assist the performance of their students. (Tharp & Gallimore, 1988, p. 43)

From attempts at theorising teaching, Tharp and Gallimore *next* direct attention to the social organisation of school in which teachers can assist the performance of students as well as their colleagues. They find school cultures to often hamper the development of teaching and argue,

> Teaching will not be reformed until schools are reformed. Schools will not be reformed until it is understood that schools must be a context for teaching and that context must itself be a teaching context. To demand that teachers truly teach in existing schools is like demanding that a surgeon achieve asepsis under water in a stagnant pond. (Tharp and Gallimore, 1988, p. 6)

In making the above observation, Tharp and Gallimore seek a redefinition of schooling in two ways. *First*, they seek every level in the bureaucratic set up of a school to not merely be assessing and controlling, but geared in particular towards assisting the performance of the other person. They *second* forward the construct of *activity settings*, which are not random but geared towards specific goals. They point out,

> Contexts in which collaborative interaction, intersubjectivity, and assisted performance occur – in which *teaching* occurs – are referred to as *activity*

settings. What are these activity settings, and how can they be considered, evaluated and designed? Although activity settings can be subject to abstract theoretical analysis ... they are homely and familiar as old shoes and the front porch. ... They are the events and people of our work and relations to one another. They are the who, what, when, where, and why, the small recurrent dramas of everyday life, played on the stages of home, school, community, and workplace .... (Tharp & Gallimore, 1988, p. 72)

In pointing to the commonplace occurrence of activity settings, Tharp and Gallimore argue activity settings to be driven by motivation and meaning they offer for those involved, besides the outcomes they produce when individuals assist one another. One can deploy the criteria Tharp and Gallimore outline to the two group-tasks Olaf and Knut conducted, as in Chapter 3. By this is meant that as unit of analysis, the construct of activity setting can help identify the who, what, when, where, and why of their conduct. The social interaction that Olaf, Knut and student groups realised in ongoing instruction, also produced a collaborative classroom practice as tangible outcome. In line with Tharp and Gallimore the two group-tasks were a context in which social interaction, intersubjectivity and assisted performance or *teaching* occurred.

My *final* take on Tharp and Gallimore's writing draws on one specific aspect of their overall focus on the development of language and literacy, which is the transition that schooling could assist students to make, in terms of the Vygotskian distinction between everyday or spontaneous concepts on one hand and academic, scientific or schooled concepts on the other. Tied to social contexts lived in our everyday lives, Tharp and Gallimore describe *everyday concepts* as

closely tied to reality and to the objects and conditions that their names represent. A word that represents an everyday concept is seen as an integral part of the object, an attribute such as color, smell, or size. Words, in the realm of the everyday, can no more be detached from their designata than colors can be detached from the rainbow. Therefore, though the word 'rainbow' has the everyday meaning of the sky's color curve, the word cannot be detached and manipulated in the young child's mind separate from the image of the sky phenomenon. (Tharp & Gallimore, 1988, p. 105)

About *academic concepts* which they term *schooled concepts*, they argue,

In schooled concepts, words are wrested from their designata and manipulated in the mind independent of their images. Many of these new

schooled words are themselves imageless and serve to link and manipulate other words. The child's attention shifts from sign-object relationship
to sign-sign relationships ... A system of words develops, and this system –
with its units of detached, decontextualised words, with its rules of use
and transformation, with its emphasis on internal relationships – floats
free of its sensory moorings and rides over the world, parsing and discussing. (Tharp & Gallimore, 1988, pp. 105–106)

With respect to the concept of rainbow which Tharp and Gallimore offer
above, at some point of time schooling helps students become acquainted
with the optical phenomenon of refraction. It is terms of the latter that not just
rainbows but the apparent bending of a spoon when placed in a glass of water
or honey, are specific instances of the same general scientific phenomena. It
is then that the colours of a rainbow are free for students' understanding of
the same in their everyday. To greater understand how the distinction between
everyday and academic concepts plays out, I turn also to Yuriy Karpov, who forwards the acquisition of academic concepts which he calls scientific concepts
to create a zpd *for* everyday concepts which he calls spontaneous concepts and
explains,

> Spontaneous concepts are the result of generalization of everyday per-
> sonal experience in the absence of systematic instruction. Therefore,
> such concepts are unsystematic, not conscious, and often wrong. ...
> ... In contrast to spontaneous concepts, scientific concepts represent
> the generalization of the experience of humankind that is fixed in sci-
> ence, understood in the broadest sense of the term ... Students are taught
> scientific concepts in the course of systematic instruction and acquire
> them consciously and according to a certain system. *Once scientific con-
> cepts have been acquired, they transform students' everyday life knowledge:
> The students' spontaneous concepts become structured and conscious.*
> (Karpov, 2003, pp. 65–66, emphasis added)

With reference to the example of a rainbow again, for a child its colours
gain prominence in primary personal experience, whose appearance is then
grasped differently when subsequent instruction introduces them to refraction. Identifying the acquisition of academic or scientific concepts to be a conscious activity, Karpov goes on to explain that such acquisition mediates the
thinking and problem solving of students. In being able to consciously reflect
upon their learning while making the transition from everyday to academic
concepts, Karpov echos the very point Tharp and Gallimore also make above,

which is that in learning academic concepts students' thinking becomes much more independent from their personal experience in their everyday lives. The ability of students to so acquire a conscious and mediated manner of thinking enables them to operate at the level of formal-logical thought, an aspect Karpov argues, to result in their transiting from being practitioners initially to becoming theorists later on. Having outlined Tharp and Gallimore's focus on literacy, activity settings in schooling and their redefinition of teaching, I now turn to del Rio and Alvarez' notion of meaningful practical activity.

7   From Activity to Directivity: Coda

I had read Pablo del Rio and Amelia Alvarez's chapter with title *From activity to directivity: The question of involvement in education*, the day before my ninety percent seminar during doctoral work. At this seminar we students presented our ongoing work to others at our university and got feedback on how to consolidate what we had and finalise our thesis. I had submitted my draft chapters for others to read beforehand and was looking to keep my mind occupied, before publicly facing my fellow students, faculty and discussant together. I immediately recognised the importance of the issues being raised by del Rio and Alvarez and knew too that my present study did not factor these in. Reporting from their research in Portugal, Spain and Latin America, del Rio and Alvarez articulate a problematic that could be highly relevant the world over – of students not enjoying school and being disappointed with its functioning. I have since come to act on issues del Rio and Alvarez raised in my post-doctoral work in two ways. *First* and as more elaborated in Chapter 9, I deployed their notion of meaningful practical activity while conducting an intervention with adolescent students at their grade eight. *Second*, I had also discussed their writing with students pursuing their *Bachelors in Social Science* at TISS, Hyderabad, as part of their *Appreciation of mathematics* course. Herein we examined the role of meaningful practical activity as a way to address the larger issue of how so few succeeded at mathematics while a vast majority fall woefully short.

del Rio and Alvarez begin by alluding to the work of political and economic scientist Francis Fukuyama, who sees loss of meaning and moral collapse as two major crisis in late 20th century society. The result of these crisis Fukuyama adds, is symptoms like a demand for immediate satisfaction, an inability for self-sacrifice and a dwindling of trust amongst fellow people. Against such a backdrop del Rio and Alvarez point out that influenced by mass media, the experience of most students is episodic and fragmentary, one not having sufficient influence to create solidarity amongst students, bring about involvement and have them take on responsibility in society. Yet del Rio and Alvarez also found Spanish speaking people in traditional cultures to achieve integrated psychic development, find happiness and display passion in their daily routines, within meaningful activities in their communities. This transpired despite the harshness of their lives and its apparent intellectual poverty. Based on the above del Rio and Alvarez observe,

> In many educational practices, it is true, activity is claimed to be important, but it frequently serves as no more than a means of generating motivation to acquire some item of knowledge, *rather than being central to students' lives and providing the goal of actions for which the knowledge is relevant.* The reduction of higher feelings to superficial emotion, of sense to information, of activity to tasks, risks causing the disintegration of children's minds. If psychological development requires the dynamic integrity of personality, education should be no less integrated. (del Rio & Alvarez, 2002, p. 63, emphasis added)

Offering an alternative to tasks which are fragmentary and reductionist in approach, often times adopted in school instruction, del Rio and Alvarez offer a CHAT based alternative called *meaningful activity* which seeks a goal towards which students' actions are relevant,

> Meaningful activity refers to that real (practical, motor) activity that establishes strong connections with the systems of consciousness developed so far and drives them to new levels of development in their ability to inspire and control real activity. In Vygotsky's view, meaningful activity reorganises the connections between feelings and thought through mental actions (action + emotion + intellect). ... From a CHAT perspective, however, only knowledge that is embedded in a meaningful activity produces these effects. (del Rio & Alvarez, 2002, p. 63)

Underscoring the holistic approach which CHAT adopts with respect to children's action, emotion, intellect and meaning, del Rio and Alvarez outline features of meaningful activities, (1) to be active, (2) emotionally charged, (3) instrumentally mediated, (4) shared and socially mediated, and (5) directive. del Rio and Alvarez go on to clarify *directive functions* as those which include psychological aspects such as self control and self discipline, decision and will, motives, values and morality, conscience and self-knowledge that are brought about in any culture.

As outlined in greater detail in Chapter 9, while conducting an intervention at grade eight my collaborating teacher and I deployed the following notion of *meaningful practical activity* as unit of analysis as well,

> In meaningful practical activities, the object and purpose of the activity are apparent, the result of the action is contingent and feedback is immediate. When the activities are also productive, the results merge into a product that strengthens participants' identity and sense of self-efficacy. The produced artifact also becomes an external, stable symbol of the processes involved in producing it. (del Rio & Alvarez, 2002, p. 64)

My successful utilisation of the above unit and notion, leads me to relate favourably to suggestions del Rio and Alvarez forward towards directive functions being implementable in everyday classrooms and include, (1) designing educational activities to be real activities, neither in place of nor even as preparation for real activities, (2) subordinate science and technology to life-sense, besides knowledge to moral and effective doing, (3) prioritise the development of strong, integrated student identities, without which there is no sense and directivity in life, (4) design activities that integrate school culture with everyday culture and balance cognitive with directive higher mental functions, which are two dimensions of the same cultural-historical trajectory of development.

In forwarding the above, del Rio and Alvarez highlight two aspects which CHAT perspectives advocate. *First*, that being more informed is not necessarily the only goal of education, but vitally thoughtful means of becoming wiser, better and more integrated individuals. *Second*, that an overemphasis of skills and information must be balanced by asserting the relevance of individual narratives which orient students in their lives. In distinct echo to arguments made by Krishnamurti, Vygotsky, Stetsenko and Sarason in Chapter 1, del Rio and Alvarez thus conceive teachers as architects of meaning and not merely working with 'teacher-proof' materials. Their call for teachers to be capable of rousing students minds to consciousness and life, thus prepares ground for my next sojourn into practitioner research.

References

Bronfenbrenner, U. (1976). The experimental ecology of education. *Educational Researcher, 5*(9), 5–15.

Bronfenbrenner, U. (1977). Toward an experimental ecology of human development. *American Psychologist, 32*(7), 513–531.

Bronfenbrenner, U. (1979). Contexts of child rearing: Problems and prospects. *American Psychologist, 34*(10), 844–850.

Engeström, Y., Sannino, A., & Virkkunen, J. (2014). On the methodological demands of formative interventions. *Mind, Culture and Activity, 21*(2), 118–128.

del Rio, P., & Alvarez, A. (2002). From activity to directivity: The question of involvement in education. In G. Wells & G. Claxton (Eds.), *Learning for life in the 21st century: Sociocultural perspectives on the future of education* (pp. 59–72). Blackwell Publishers Limited.

Karpov, Y. (2003). Vygotsky's doctrine of scientific concepts: Its role for contemporary education. In A. Kozulin, B. Gidnis, V. Agayev, & S. Miller (Eds.), *Vygotsky's educational theory in cultural context* (pp. 65–82). Cambridge University Press.

Lave, J. (1990). The culture of acquisition and the practice of understanding. In J. W. Stigler, R. A. Shweder, & G. H. Herdt (Eds.), *Cultural psychology: Essays on comparative human development* (pp. 309–329). Cambridge University Press.

Lave, J., & Wenger, E. (1991). *Situated learning: Legitimate peripheral participation.* Cambridge University Press.

Leontiev, A. N., & Luria, A. R. (1968). The psychological ideas of L. S. Vygotskii. In B. B. Wolman (Ed.), *Historical roots of contemporary psychology* (pp. 338–357). Harper & Row.

Luria, A. R. (1979). *The making of mind: A personal account of Soviet psychology.* Harvard University Press.

Moll, L. C. (1990). Introduction. In L. C. Moll (Ed.), *Vygotsky and education: instructional implications and applications of sociohistorical psychology* (pp. 1–27). Cambridge University Press.

Moll, L. C. (1992). Bilingual classroom studies and community analysis: Some recent trends. *Educational Researcher, 21*(2), 20–24.

Moll, L. C. (2000). Inspired by Vygotsky: Ethnographic experiments in education. In C. D. Lee & P. Smagorinsky (Eds.), *Vygotskian perspectives on literacy research: Constructing meaning through collaborative inquiry* (pp. 256–268). Cambridge University Press.

Moll, L. C., & Greenberg, J. B. (1990). Creating zones of possibilities: Combining social contexts for instruction. In L. C. Moll (Ed.), *Vygotsky and education: Instructional implications and applications of sociohistorical psychology* (pp. 319–348). Cambridge University Press.

Newman, F., & Holzman, L. (1997). *End of knowing: New developmental way of learning.* Routledge.

Scribner, S. (1984). Studying working intelligence. In B. Rogoff & J. Lave (Eds.), *Everyday cognition: Its development in social context* (pp. 9–40). Harvard University Press.

Scribner, S. (1985). Vygotsky's uses of history. In J. V. Wertsch (Ed.), *Culture, communication and cognition: Vygotskian perspectives* (pp. 119–145). Cambridge University Press.

Scribner, S. (1990). Reflections on a model. *The Quarterly Newsletter of the Laboratory of Comparative Human Cognition, 12*(2), 90–94.

Scribner, S. (1997). Mind in action. A functional approach to thinking. In M. Cole, Y. Engeström, & O. Vasquez (Eds.), *Mind, culture and activity: Seminal papers from the Laboratory of Comparative Human Cognition* (pp. 354–368). Cambridge University Press.

Scribner, S., & Cole, M. (1978). Literacy without schooling: Testing for intellectual effects. *Harvard Educational Review, 48*(4), 448–461.

Sinha, C. (1989). Reading Vygotsky. *History of the Human Sciences, 2*(3), 309–331.

Tharp, R., & Gallimore, R. (1988). *Rousing minds to life: Teaching, learning, and schooling in social context.* Cambridge University Press.

Veer, R. v. d., & Valsiner, J. (1988). Vygotskij as a philosopher of science. In M. Hildebrand-Nilshon & G. Rückriem (Eds.), *Proceedings of the 1st international congress on activity theory* (Vol. 1, pp. 73–81). Druck und Verlag System Druck.

CHAPTER 5

Practitioner Research

Art and Life Are Not One

1 Preamble

As with the centrality of practitioners be they teachers and/or researchers with regards to teaching-learning and schooling at large, I position this chapter at the centre of this book. While the first four chapters were foundational to my beginnings with CHAT research, the last five dwell on issues related to my conducting independent, post-doctoral research in line with their perspectives. It has also been the case that while not part of my doctoral study, issues related to practitioners became central to my post doctoral work for many a reason. *First,* was my wanting to engage with CHAT in instructional practices led by teachers in their classrooms. *Second,* with teachers providing invaluable insights to ongoing research, I began to actively collaborate with them and conduct interventions found necessary. Alongside detailing four interventions we were able to so carry out, I outline four frameworks of teacher-researcher collaboration that we realised in tandem in Chapter 9. *Finally,* in having been a teacher myself, I wanted to ascertain how teachers could position themselves as subjects in their own research, as opposed to their being positioned as objects in studies conducted by others. The politics underlying this last, is key to the issue of freedom that Greene drew attention to in Chapter 1.

I also wondered how educational research would recognise and speak to the many contradictions practitioners face in their everyday, with units of grain size as small as classrooms on one hand and societal education on the other. At the same time, my becoming familiar with literature in practitioner research amounted to taking a course as broad in scope as methodology during doctoral work. It was for me to quickly decide how to sharpen my immediate focus. While CHAT perspectives enabled me to have greater control on aspects related to students' development, I was not inclined to delve into action research at that time since I experienced the freedom of trying out new ideas at the school I taught. I was also not inclined to focus upon college based teacher preparation that would be embedded in institutional aspects which would be much harder to tackle. I decidedly wanted to engage with perspectives that would be

---

© KONINKLIJKE BRILL NV, LEIDEN, 2022 | DOI:10.1163/9789004512160_005

viable in ongoing classrooms. My keenness to empower practitioners in this process led me to writings wherein practitioners had agency. The confidence I gained from years of teaching was thus my guide to such manner of efforts. Herein I found quiet echo in Iris Murdoch's words on the importance of education. In a film titled *Iris* she says,

> Education doesn't make you happy, and nor does freedom. We don't become happy just because we are free – if we are, or because we have been educated – if we have, but because education may be the means by which we realise we are happy. It opens our eyes, our ears, tells us where delights are lurking, convinces us that there is only one freedom, of any importance whatsoever, that of the mind, and gives us the assurance, the confidence to walk the path our mind, our educated mind offers. (As noted from viewing the film)

Just as Murdoch directed my search for the many notions I engage with throughout this writing, three perspectives alluded to earlier on direct those within practitioner research – that of human perception, human development and scientific observation. It is by drawing on these notions that I find practitioner agency to be enriched. As discussed in Chapter 1, Nussbaum's view of *human perception* speaks to one's ability to read and respond to concrete situations. The aim here, is not to transcend any situation, but view the same as a story worth embracing, filled with its pains, surprises and joys. As dwelt upon in Chapter 3, Stetsenko draws attention to the unity of processes in *human development* in line with Vygotsky. The aim here is to bring about the emergence of together-systems that unify symbolic, affective, practical, social, motor and intellectual processes. I argue such pursuit to be of relevance to both students and practitioners. In recognising human perception to be theory laden as acknowledged in Chapter 3, Luria details the goals of *scientific observation* in non-classical or romantic psychology in terms of which CHAT is perceived. The aim here is to view an event or phenomena from as many perspectives as possible to consider how they are interconnected. In line with Marx the objective is to ascend from abstract principles to concrete practice. It is towards examining many a tradition in practitioner research, while keeping such a combined stance in mind, that I turn first to narrative research. The content and premise of this area, has not only enabled me to examine many educational concrete in an empirical sense, but also complement scientific rigour with much needed human voice. Allowing me to keep my ear close to the ground, I have found such a linguistic form to literally create educational realities.

PRACTITIONER RESEARCH 107

2 Narrative Research

The first turn I took after my CHAT based doctoral study was to look into narratives we indulge with, in our everyday. As practitioners instinctively know, each of the stories told by our fellow teachers, our students or their parents tend to have their own linguistic flavour and existential concerns. No two appear the same. If setting up time to meet with friends for kite flying over the weekend is of prime concern to a student at one place, driving out to ski when the snow is firm and light just right has rightful immediacy for a teacher in another. As data, narratives are everywhere and I took great pleasure in trying to grasp their significance in our lives, unencumbered by any course work this time. Even as such reading was extensive, I wished to examine *how* ongoing practices could be engaged with, whose importance Vygotsky had been unequivocal about.

While many scholars have examined human narratives, I take Jerome Bruner's writings as point of departure. In distinct echo to Vygotsky's cultural-historical school, Bruner's psycho-cultural approach finds culture to provide a toolkit with which we not only construct our own worlds, but conceptions about our own selves as well. Viewing *narratives* as a mode of thought and a vehicle of making meaning, Bruner points out,

> There appear two broad ways in which human beings organise and manage their knowledge of the world, indeed structure even their immediate experience: one seems more specialised for treating of physical 'things,' the other for treating of people and their plights. These are conventionally known as *logical-scientific* thinking and *narrative* thinking. ... They have varied modes of expression in different cultures, which also cultivate them differently. No culture is without both of them, though different cultures privilege them differently. (Bruner, 1996, pp. 39–40)

Long arguing for greater attention to narrative modes in addition to the logical-scientific alone, Bruner argues schooling to play a defining role in inducting our young into culture's canonical ways. The means of doing so, he points out, is stories or narratives in which we externalise the many plights schooling puts us through. Bruner maintains,

> Obviously, if narrative is to be made an instrument of mind on behalf of meaning making, it requires work on our part – reading it, making it, analysing it, understanding its craft, sensing its uses, discussing it. ...

108 CHAPTER 5

> ... A system of education must help those growing up in a culture find an identity within that culture. Without it, they stumble in their effort after meaning. *It is only in the narrative mode that one can construct an identity and find a place in one's culture.* Schools must cultivate it, nurture it, cease taking it for granted. (Bruner, 1996, pp. 41–42, emphasis added)

The two passages above, allow me to underscore how Bruner conceives culture at large, the world we perceive, account for the version of events we live by, besides our selves and identity, as narratively interconnected. It is not surprising then, that he sees the need for instruction in school to lay emphasis on students grasping narratives and making sense of their uses. On the *structure of a narrative* Bruner clarifies,

> Narrative requires ... four crucial grammatical constituents if it is to be effectively carried out. It requires, first, a means for emphasising human action or 'agentivity' – action directed toward goals controlled by agents. It requires, secondly that a sequential order be established and maintained – that events and states be 'linearized' in a standard way. Narrative, thirdly also requires a sensitivity to what is canonical and what violates canonicality in human interaction. Finally, narrative requires something approximating a narrator's perspective: it cannot, in the jargon of narratology, be 'voiceless.' (Bruner, 1990, p. 77)

I have found the four elements highlighted by Bruner to enable me to understand narratives encountered during field work as a deployable unit of analysis. While I borrowed from other scholars who use elements at variance with the above, I have found it useful to develop a keen ear for listening to narratives that people share as part of making meaning in instructional landscapes we orchestrate (Gade, 2011). Taking behavioural cues into consideration I got better at interpreting narratives over time, in turn allowing me to surmise experiences which others might be going through. Even as I shortly examine the notion of teacher voice, a key outcome of such a process, I turn once last time to Bruner who explains how the notion of *voice* is means for any narrator to achieve coherence in one's own life. This aspect applies to my writing this book as well, where my attempting to narrate my intellectual journey allows me to achieve coherence even if this could be partial, in Bruner's view,

> No autobiography is completed, only ended. No autobiography is free from questions about which self his autobiography is about, composed from what perspective, for whom. The one we write is only one *version*, one way of achieving coherence. (Bruner, 2002, p. 74)

PRACTITIONER RESEARCH

In line with recounting my own journey, I now turn to the opportunity I had during my time at CUNY, to audit Collete Daiute's doctoral course titled *Human Development and Globalisation*. I herein acquainted myself with how the two aspects in the course title were closely intertwined, forcing me to think about how political contexts lying outside the comfort of classroom walls could impinge everyday instruction that was ongoing within them. This in turn made me wonder how teachers dealt with societal forces that lay beyond their individual control. Surely these would lead to demands on their personal selves and their professional integrity. What drew me to Collete's course was a narrative study she herself conducted with youth growing up in social changes that resulted from the political upheaval which arose in former Yugoslavia. Geared towards studying cultural-historical development, the narratives of young people were tools in Daiute's (2010) study titled *Human development and political violence.* Herein via narratives, her subjects inquired about the world at large and their own place within the same. All this despite the grim and divisive uncertainties which they faced. My conceptual image of a functioning classroom became more fragile as a result. Yet, the ability of being able to use narratives to rethink our own psyche, our self and our world was never more evident to me as well.

In narrative research on teaching, I next found Sigrun Gudmundsdottir to discuss how narratives were a central feature of classroom life and also a researchable unit of analysis that could be used in educational contexts. She however finds narratives to be a slippery phenomena to categorise, since the meanings and interpretations they are built upon are in turn based on other people's meanings and interpretations. Gudmundsdottir goes on to conceive *teaching as school practice*, to separate what is being analysed via the notions of teaching and practice. Viewing teaching as much more that what a teacher does, Gudmundsdottir argues,

> I am using 'school practice,' because I am uncomfortable with the word *teaching.* By using 'school practice,' I am widening the unit of analysis to include not just what the teacher does but also what students learn as a result of experiencing school practice. ... Teaching in my mind, focuses too much on what the teacher does. (Gudmundsdottir, 2001, p. 226)

Like all situated human activity, school practice Gudmundsdottir adds is mediated by the larger culture in which it resides. Instances of these could include the way classrooms are arranged, the manner in which teachers are addressed and the way opportunities are made available to boys as well as girls. Yet, to draw attention to the social language that is situated within school practices, Gudmundsdottir forwards the notion of *language of school practice.* Parallel to

Bakhtin's notion of genre, whose writings I discuss in the coda of this chapter, she elaborates,

> The language of school practice is more than just words. It is a cultural reservoir of beliefs, ideas, ways of doing and seeing, all embedded in distinct social activity ...
>
> ... Through the language of practice, social organisations and relationships are defined and tried out, and the language of practice becomes the place where our identity as teachers and researchers, our subjectivity, is conceived.
>
> ... learning the language of practice can also be an instrument for claiming one's own voice, not just repeating someone else's narrative, and for developing one's own language of practice. (Gudmundsdottir, 2001, p. 234)

In forwarding the above, Gudmundsdottir regards the language of school practice as a privileged mode of talking about one's schooling, where a high degree of intersubjectivity leads participants to speak at times in incomplete sentences, express incomplete thoughts and at times engage in conversation wherein partners fill in missing words and infuse them with appropriate expression. A language of practice thus does not reflect social reality, but produces meaning and *creates* reality. As a practitioner, one can identify with many an aspect Gudmundsdottir portrays about such a form of speech, its transient quality and the authority invested in a speech that is locally privileged besides. Vitally, it is also amongst the language of practice in any school that Gudmundsdottir sees an opportunity for practitioners to claim one's individual voice – one's language of practice that is distinct from those of others in terms of which one speaks about one's teaching. While applicable to students and found evident in stands either takes in events that transpire within schooling, the individual voice of the teacher informs teacher knowledge in particular.

It is this last that makes me revisit Clandinin and Connelly's notion of personal practical knowledge, introduced in Chapter 2. Viewing school reform to be an epistemological matter, Clandinin extends the view of voice above and highlights its *dialectical underpinnings*,

> Personal practical knowledge as a concept embodies a dialectical view of theory and practice. In the dialectical view ... theory and practice are viewed as inseparable; practice is seen as theory in action. In this view theory is assumed to change and modify according to the shifting exigencies of the practical world. The essential task of the dialectical is to

resolve oppositions in theory, oppositions in practice, and oppositions between theory and practice. (Clandinin, 1985, p. 364)

Extending Gudmundsdottir's argument that a practitioner can claim one's voice in dialectic with the voices of many others, Clandinin allows us to view any teacher's knowledge as born of a dialectic that is able to resolve oppositions between theoretical perspectives, between kinds of practice, as well as between theory and practice. From Gudmundsdottir's point of view this would mean practitioners claiming their individual voice *as* knowledge, in the language of practice within any school.

I turn finally to Donald Polkinghorne who points out how carrying out and reporting narrative research is different from conventional research. Just as Gudmundsdottir's language of school practice and teacher voice reflect epistemological commitments of teachers, Polkinghorne points out that research reports too reflect epistemological commitments of authors. Narrative research, he argues, does not adhere to any prescribed method of being synchronic, but is *diachronic* as a result of actions researchers take over time in any given context. He maintains,

> The diachronic research report is based on the understanding that *research is a practice, a product of human action*. Research practice shares with other human practices movement through time. Researchers are the protagonists in the drama for understanding. The drama consists of a sequential composition of decisions, actions, chance occurrences, and interactions with subjects and colleagues. Values, desires, inadequacies, skills, and personal characteristics make their appearance at various points in the researcher's performance. (Polkinghorne, 1997, p. 9, emphasis added)

Polkinghorne in addition highlights the value of *practitioner judgement*, an aspect given scant attention in wider research, and argues,

> Practice situations are fluid. They occur over time and usually involve multiple decisions, one after another, to guide a process toward achieving a goal. People can respond differently to the practitioner's actions. The person's response to an action taken early in process can be a different response to the same action taken later in the process. ... The practitioner her or himself undergoes change. ... Practitioner judgment is based on consideration of what action at this time, in this place, with these students, in this situation, and with these resources will help accomplish the goal. (Polkinghorne, 2010, p. 394)

For me the above outlined arguments exemplify the many ways narrative research has potential to inform the work practitioners carry out. Not only does narrative thinking offer an alternative to the more prestigious and normative logical-scientific thinking with regards to schooling, but its perspectives enable practitioners in addition, to greater examine and re-conceive important notions like self making, teaching as school practice, developing one's unique voice, teacher knowledge, reporting research in a diachronic manner, besides the centrality of practitioner judgement. While my present writing is my way of achieving coherence in line with Bruner, my narrative of historical events also enables me to re-examine various interventions conducted in post doctoral work. The first of these was a study of students' narratives in relation to learning mathematics at grade six, led by Charlotta or Lotta, in Umeå (Gade, 2010). Doubling up as a pilot, this study paved way for Lotta and me to collaborate as teacher and researcher and conduct three of four interventions I greater discuss in Chapter 9. The first of these drew upon perspectives of action research, whose premise and insights I now turn to.

3 Action Research

After my pilot study of students' narratives and before conducting action research with Lotta mentioned above, I had begun a routine of visiting Lotta's mathematics classroom once every week. While I kept an open mind on what both of us and her students might together achieve, one day I received the following email from Lotta,

> We worked today at multiplication of numbers that combined addition and subtraction. For example $5 \times 7 + 3 + 9 =$. I discovered that many students have not understood the meaning of the = sign. We discussed a lot that the two sides of the equality sign must be equal. (Gade, 2012, p. 553)

I surmised the content of Lotta's email to not only share a problem she was facing, but implicitly ask if we could intervene in some way and address the issue at hand. As a university based researcher I viewed her mail as a call to take action, for which I took recourse to perspectives of action research. Besides offering articles on how action research had been conducted by various others, I considered the journal *Educational Action Research* to be a prospective platform for reporting our work as well. Towards rectifying the faulty use of the equal to sign which Lotta brought to my notice, we conceived and implemented an action cycle based on Wertsch's notion of explicit mediation. Such

PRACTITIONER RESEARCH

conduct was brought to a close when as teacher, Lotta was satisfied with its outcomes. Two aspects are worthy of note here. *First*, our conduct laid foundations for what was to become a leitmotch in my future research – collaborating with teachers to conduct interventions found necessary in their classrooms. *Second*, my becoming familiar with action research shed greater light for me on how practitioners could direct action in their own classrooms. I presently explore the latter and take Elliott's notion of educational research dwelt in Chapter 1, as point of departure. In his book titled *Action research for educational change*, Elliott defines *action research* as follows,

> Action research may be defined as '*the Study of a social situation with a view to improving the quality of action within it.*' It aims to feed practical judgement in concrete situations, and the validity of the 'theories' or hypothesis it generates depends not so much on 'scientific' tests of truth, as on their usefulness in helping people to act more intelligently and skilfully ... In action-research 'theories' are not validated independently and then applied to practice. They are validated through practice. (Elliott, 1991, p. 69, emphasis in original)

In their book *Teachers investigate their work: An introduction to the methods of action research*, Herbert Altrichter, Peter Posch and Bridget Somekh (1993) also cite Elliott above and elaborate upon features that distinguish action research in terms of (1) its being carried out by people directly concerned with the social situation, (2) by starting from questions that arise from everyday educational work, (3) whose scope is compatible with educational values of the school and work conditions of teachers, (4) wherein methods are tailored to what is seen achievable without overly disrupting practice, and (5) where the overall project has a character of its own. Treated as the green bible in European action research circles, the authors sketch a four stage process that outlines action cycle in terms of (a) finding a starting point, (b) clarifying the situation, (c) developing action strategies and putting them into practice, one feeding back to the previous stage, and (d) making teachers' knowledge public.

Constituting a basic action sequence, which practitioners could modify to meet their demands in local contexts, I consider it pertinent to greater dwell on Altrichter et al.'s reasons for *making teachers knowledge public*. The significance of doing so includes (1) preventing teacher knowledge from being forgotten, (2) allowing teachers to reflect on the quality of their instruction, (3) allow teachers opportunity to clarify their own position and influence policy, (4) become professionally accountable, (5) take a proactive role in their own professional development, (6) reinforce their personal self-confidence, and (7) strengthen the reputation of the profession of teaching at large.

I however acknowledge that the conduct of the four stage process in action research and the making public of knowledge obtained by teachers to be in many instances easier said than done. One needs to be lucky with many conducive circumstances within one's school to make the taking of action by a practitioner possible. *First* is the culture of the school itself within which teachers feel confident to take action that is both necessary and well informed. *Second*, the conduct of action research which needs teachers to act and reflect takes time, an aspect at the mercy of issues like mandated syllabi to be adhered to, school tests to be conducted besides views of staff room colleagues to be contended with. *Third*, making public the knowledge one has come upon is demanding, in that teachers would need to become adept at publishing quality research in addition to their primary responsibility of teaching. Even as I argue that teachers and researchers could collaborate towards these aims, there is a *final* need for an environment of mutual trust in which such work is welcomed and bears fruit. At times teachers need to act on their own, besides encourage others to do so as well. In *My story is my living educational theory*, Jean McNiff speaks to this very issue and concludes,

> My story is that I use my educational influence to encourage others to tell their stories of practice, explain how they give meaning to their work as thoughtful and caring people, and show how they hold themselves accountable for their own stories of educational intent. (McNiff, 2007, p. 326)

The questions McNiff addresses to account for herself while taking such manner of action include the following,

> What is my concern? Why am I concerned? What kind of experiences can I describe to show the reasons for my concern? What can I do about it? What will I do about it? How do I evaluate the educational influences of my actions? How do I demonstrate the validity of the account of my educational influence in learning? How do I modify my concerns, ideas, and actions in the light of my evaluation? (McNiff, 2007, pp. 309–310)

The above overview, however brief, details the *why* as well as *how* of conducting action research in educational contexts. While the scope for taking such action is vast, it is not difficult to surmise that the potential for teacher theorising is equally immense. Summarising the achievements of action research, which has gained acceptance amongst practitioners world wide, Susan Noffke (2009) draws attention to three key dimensions in relation to its manner of theorising – the professional, the personal and the political. With regards to *the professional dimension*, Noffke speaks to rich possibilities that could arise when methodologies and underlying epistemologies in action research are not seen as fixed or predetermined. Rather, by engaging with local contexts and the implicit assumptions which relate to both teaching and research, there is scope for reaping rich dividends. My drawing upon CHAT perspectives in conducting action research stands testimony to this very wisdom. Speaking to *the personal dimension*, Noffke alludes to McNiff and sees wisdom in practitioners wanting to improve practice by seeking to do things differently, give an account of actions they take and develop their own voice. As discussed in the previous section, I argue personal narratives of practitioners are well placed to offer diachronic accounts of actions that are taken. My own reporting gained confidence in this direction and evolved with experience I came to gain over time. About *the political dimension*, Noffke points out that working to improve educational quality and bringing about change means practitioners working through and against existing power structures. Yet, various projects do evidence how practitioners develop a sense of personal agency in dealing with life's issues over the long haul. Such a disposition results in developing civic participation and nurturing democratically based social and political relations. Collaboration is seen as key in such work, one that reaches out and allows others to work for change as well. That I write so centrally about ways in which teachers and researchers could collaborate in this book, would in Noffke's view be seen as taking a political stand, one which I find both personally and professionally rewarding in addition. Over the years my interests have however remain focused on the cultural-historical development of students in line with CHAT perspectives. Designing and conducting the kind of instructional activities which could lead such development in students, has evolved as my abiding and continued interest.

I turn finally to Alfred Marrow's (1969) biography titled *The practical theorist: The life and work of Kurt Lewin*. As a social psychologist and someone who was an early pioneer of action research, Lewin was keen to balance rival interests of employer and employee, or management and factory hand, by seeking the cooperation of both in the enhancement of life's values. Marrow summarises Lewin's position,

> Lewin summed up his views by stressing that man does not live to produce but produces to live. Improving the psychological components of man's work will thus accomplish far more for the worker's well-being

than merely cutting down his hours on the job. What is important, what must always be sought, is an improvement in the *inner value* of the work as experienced by the man performing it. (Marrow, 1969, pp. 16–17, emphasis in original)

My interest in Lewin in twofold, *First* his search for inner value reflected in practitioners wanting to improve the quality of action they would like to take in any social situation. *Second* is his well known dictum that there is nothing as practical as a good theory. As Stetsenko and Arievitch argue in Chapter 1, the dialectical equivalent of this very dictum in line with CHAT perspectives reads – there is nothing as theoretically rich as good practice. This last satisfies Lewin's own asking that any theory not only account for what is known but also point the way forward to the new.

Lewin was in addition keen to move from a static view of contrasting pairs of phenomena as in Aristotelian science, to a dynamic one that surmised how contrasting parts of a pair were unified in a continuum, as with Galilean science. In line with a relational view of phenomena as they interact in their concrete, Lewin advocated that psychology move from an aggregate of many cases to a single case and argued,

the single case was valid only if it were grasped in its totality; that is, only if both the total concrete situation and its specific properties are understood. The concrete single case had to be described, then, in its phenotypical and its genotypical aspects. It was not the frequency of a case's occurrence that was decisive, but the exact description of *all* the forces operating in and upon it at a given moment, including the inner forces (needs) as well as the external ones (environment). (Marrow, 1969, pp. 58–59)

Lewin's aims outlined above offer a striking parallel to attempts within CHAT of ascending to the concrete, as drawn attention to by Luria in Chapter 3. It is to exemplify the kind of insight that such a relational view can offer that I turn to writings of Marilyn Cochran-Smith and colleagues in relation to a robust tradition of practitioner inquiry in the USA.

4   Teacher Research

I came across Marilyn Cochran-Smith and Susan Lytle's (2009) chapter titled *Teacher research as stance*, in *The Sage Handbook of Educational Action*

Research edited by Susan Noffke and Bridget Somekh (2009). I also had occasion to take part in a Discussion Group they together led at the annual meeting of the *American Educational Research Association* or AERA. While both have writings in relation to teacher education and teacher research, I dwell on the latter in this section. In parallel with Elliott's distinction between research on education and educational research, Cochran-Smith and Lytle (1993) distinguish *research on teaching* from *teacher research*. This latter they view as systematic and intentional inquiry by teachers, in which teachers generate local as well as public knowledge of teaching. Such dedicated efforts are geared to making contributions to both university and school communities.

By 2006, I find Cochran-Smith and Kelly Donnell to term teacher research as *practitioner inquiry*, wherein the practitioner is the researcher, her professional context the research site and her practice itself the focus of her study. Both teacher research and practitioner inquiry are however recognised as umbrella terms which draw on different research traditions and social movements. Cochran-Smith and Donnell point out too that most research conducted with K-12 schooling is not conducted by K-12 teachers themselves, leading to the issue of whose knowledge is given official sanction and authority in these classrooms, and whose knowledge is ignored and disenfranchised. They point out,

> Either explicitly or implicitly, practitioner inquiry raises questions and interrupts expectations about the relations of inquiry, knowledge, and practice. This kind of research raises questions about who legitimately can do research and what kind of relationships should exist between researchers and the people and processes they study. ... Finally practitioner inquiry raises many questions about whether it is possible or desirable to do research that privileges the role of neither practitioner nor researcher, but instead forges a new role out of their intersections. (Cochran-Smith & Donnell, 2006, p. 514)

While my own work with teacher-researcher collaboration typifies the role of new intersections highlighted in the quote above, I turn to two key notions which Cochran-Smith and her colleagues forge in their writings favouring teacher research – working the dialectic and inquiry as stance. In dwelling on *working the dialectic*, Cochran-Smith and Lytle recognise that teachers theorise all the time. By this they underscore how teachers constantly negotiate between their classrooms and school life on one hand and their daily work and social movements of change on the other. On working this manner of dialectic they argue,

> By 'dialectic,' we refer to the reciprocal, recursive, and symbiotic relationships of research and practice, analysis and action, inquiry and experience, theorizing and doing, conceptual and empirical scholarship, and being researchers as well as practitioners. We also mean the dialectic of generating local knowledge of practice while at the same time making that knowledge accessible and usable in other contexts and thus helping to transform it into public knowledge. When we 'work the dialectic,' there are not distinct moments when we are only theorizers or only practitioners. Rather these activities and roles are intentionally blurred. (Cochran-Smith & Lytle, 2009a, p. 43)

In working the dialectic Cochran-Smith and Lytle view teacher research as a collective effort to realise productive school cultures, in pursuit of which they discuss *inquiry as stance,* to emphasise teacher research to not be an activity bound to one's own education,

> but rather a larger epistemological stance, or a way of knowing about teaching, learning and schooling that is neither topic- nor project-dependent. Theorized in this way, the notion of inquiry stance talks back to, and challenges, many of the assumptions that define teaching and research on teaching in the current era of acute educational accountability with its singular emphasis on test scores at the expense of other educational purposes, the resultant narrowing of the school curriculum and reduction of the roles of both teachers and students, and increased surveillance of teachers' day-to-day work. (Cochran-Smith & Lytle, 2009a, p. 44)

In *Inquiry as stance: Practitioner research for the next generation,* Cochran-Smith and Lytle (2009b) see inquiry as stance to be a powerful means of affirmative action and educational transformation. Clarifying the stance as being social and political and far from instrumental, they nuance the deliberation that accompanies inquiry in terms of what needs to get done, why anything gets done, who decides what gets done and whose interests are served. As such they articulate its four dimensions in terms of (1) a perspective of knowledge that rejects the dualism of formal and practical knowledge, by forwarding one based on local forms located in global contexts, (2) an expanded view of practice and practitioner as teaching, learning and leading, (3) practitioner communities as primary means for enacting any theory of action, and (4) positioning practitioner inquiry as key to bringing about a more just and democratic society.

PRACTITIONER RESEARCH

I now discuss the kind of relational understanding which practitioner inquiry has potential to bring to light with two studies, in which Cochran-Smith demonstrates how different sets of teachers worked with dialectical relationships and were able to adopt inquiry as stance or not. In Cochran-Smith's (2011) paper *Does learning to teacher ever end?* we meet three teachers Robin Hennessy, Gary McPhail and Erin Hashimoto-Martell. Each of these teachers raise questions from within their instruction and use data they collect to steer personal investigations.

Teaching English to students of colour, as a white woman Robin was unsure if she did or did not know, how to go about her teaching. To examine this issue she asked her ninth-grade students to bring their cultural, linguistic, and experiential knowledge to her English classroom. She honoured their requests of expressing themselves in forms other than Standard English, and found this decision to enable students to believe in their abilities and participate socially in school tasks. They also began to deal with topics like race and ethnicity that were formerly taboo. Her decisions impacted her students' learning of literacy.

Having taught first and second graders for more than a decade, as a male teacher Gary wondered whether female students were more interested and proficient than his male students. He then changed his year-long curriculum to include specific genres of writing which he thought would appeal to only boys, only girls and both combined. On evaluation of their writing, Gary found girls and boys to have differing interests. Yet and importantly, he also found out that they performed at higher levels when they wrote in genres that interested them.

Being an Asian-American woman, Erin's experience of teaching environmental literacy and appreciation to students who were ethnically, socioeconomically and linguistically diverse, made her seek the relation that might exist between science and equity. She wanted to increase the low numbers of students of colour who pursued science in higher education. She then studied four students who showed evidence of developing science identities and asked for additional science learning opportunities. Erin's study led her to greater connect teaching in her classroom with students' lived experiences with science outside school.

Offering the above insights Cochran-Smith draws her arguments to a close and points out that learning to teach never ends, arguing,

> The point is that these teachers, like all teachers in the changing world of schools, had to deal with new questions and new problems all the time. They could not know all the answers prior to entering teaching. *What they needed to know was how to keep on learning over time* – how to pose

important questions, how to develop new ways of seeing, how to unpack deeply held assumptions, and how to work with colleagues to transform students' learning opportunities and outcomes. To do this work, taking an inquiry stance is critical. (Cochran-Smith, 2011, p. 24, emphasis added)

In her article *A tale of two teachers*, Cochran-Smith (2012) contrasts the experiences of two new teachers at K-12 schools in the US, which allows her to identify four key factors, including inquiry as stance, that make a significant difference to a practitioner's failure or success in establishing oneself as a teacher. The teachers we meet here are Gill Maimon and Elsie Reynolds. With a liberal arts and interdisciplinary background in education, good academic scores and teacher certification, Gill joined teaching at the first grade of an urban school. Trained to teach against the grain, Gill wanted to teach for a few years before moving to educational policy. On her part Elsie too had a liberal arts background, excellent scores at graduate entrance tests besides teacher certification. With training in inquiry and classroom research, Elsie joined teaching to make it her lifetime's work. Despite many similarities in their prior trajectories, both Gill and Elsie struggled as new teachers. Even as both were assigned mentors, by the time of Cochran-Smith's reporting Gill had completed seventeen years of classroom teaching while Elsie was not rehired after the first year and left teaching altogether.

Offering relevant details, Cochran-Smith's analysis of Gill and Elsie enabled her to identify four factors which each played a key role in the differences either experienced with teaching. *First*, is *deprivatisation of practice*. By this she means a cessation of viewing teaching as a private act behind closed doors and an acceptance of collegial support for the joint construction of knowledge. *Second*, is *having high expectations* for students and for oneself as a teacher. This in turn means providing opportunities for students that will enable them to learn academically challenging knowledge and skills. Similarly this means working towards efficacy in decision making, being change agents and working to generate knowledge for teachers. *Third*, is conceiving *inquiry as stance* as a world view and critical habit of mind, and not a reductionist time and classroom bound research. *Fourth* is opportunities for teachers to not look inwards with feelings of inadequacy, but with confidence to take part in *multiple overlapping communities*. The presence and participation in this latter lets teachers question their assumptions and replace singular notions of best practice with those that draw on exemplars from histories and cultures of others as well. Cochran-Smith fleshes out Gill and Elsie's teaching with respect to each of the above factors and urges that we look at teaching as much more than raising students' test scores. She argues,

PRACTITIONER RESEARCH

> Learning to teach is something that happens over time, and it happens when new teachers work in the company of more experienced teachers who are also continuing to learn to teach.
>
> This position contrasts dramatically with the ideas of some current policy makers and others involved in alternate approaches to teacher education, who believe that teachers should know how to teach effectively the minute they enter the classroom. ... This kind of thinking fails to acknowledge that *learning to teach takes time, and it is never finished.* (Cochran-Smith, 2012, p. 122, emphasis added)

While I find perspectives of both teacher research and action research, to show how teachers can empower themselves and their own practices, the two papers outlined above help focus on the importance of relationships that underpin a teacher's ability to teach or not in personal terms, besides the kind of support and concrete contexts that are endemic to schools as institutions. With invaluable insights from teacher research as backdrop, I now turn to a third and equally powerful perspective in practitioner research, that of life history research.

5   Life History Research

My coming across teacher voice as articulated by Gudmundsdottir, led me in due course to its conception in Ivor Goodson's writings. Where Gudmundsdottir saw voice as a teacher's coming into her own beliefs and interpretations besides ways of doing and seeing prevalent in a language of practice, Goodson sees teacher voice as autobiographical in nature, one that draws upon one's personal life history. My present writing could thus be seen as my voice in line with perspectives of both scholars. By this I mean the personal flavour I developed an affinity for from amongst the perspectives I came across while conducting research, besides numerous experiences that were seeded in my life history over time.

Goodson argues in addition that to improve school practice one must *not* immediately focus upon a teacher's practice as this exposes the most vulnerable part of the teacher's instruction, placing her work to external scrutiny and negotiation. He instead argues,

> A more valuable and less vulnerable entry point would be to examine teachers' work in the context of the teacher's life. What is needed is a focus that listens above all to the person at whom 'development' is aimed.

122   CHAPTER 5

This means strategies should be developed which facilitate, maximize and in a real sense legislate the capturing of the teacher's voice. What I am asserting here is that, particularly in the world of teacher development, the central ingredient so far missing is the *teacher's voice.* Primarily the focus has been on the teacher's practice, almost the teacher *as* practice. (Goodson, 1991, p. 38, emphasis in original)

Even as I dwelt on the potential of action research and teacher research in the previous two sections, to not only examine but also change existing educational practices, Goodson above points to the kind of error that can be made in focusing on teachers' practices alone. While pointing to the vulnerability of teachers here, he underscores the accompanying risk of viewing teachers *as* their practice. In tracing the sociological origins of life history research, I find Goodson to thus argue,

> *In understanding something so intensely personal as teaching, it is critical that we know about the person the teacher is.* Our paucity of knowledge in this area is manifest indictment of the range of our sociological imagination. The life historian pursues the job from his own perspective, a perspective which emphasizes the value of the person's 'own story.' By tracing this person's life over time, it becomes possible to view the changes and underlying forces which influence that person at work to estimate the part which teaching plays within the overall life of the teacher. (Goodson, 1981, p. 69, emphasis in original)

Quoting sociologist Howard Becker, Goodson expands on the promise of *a well documented life history* as one able to give details of,

> that process whose character we would otherwise only be able to speculate about, and the process to which our data must ultimately be referred if they are to have theoretical and not just an operational and predictive significance. It will describe those crucial interactive episodes in which new lines of individual and collective activity are forged, in which new aspects of the self are brought into being. It is by thus giving a realistic basis to our imagery of the underlying process that the life history serves the purposes of checking assumptions, illuminating, organisation and re-orienting stagnant fields. (Becker, 1970, p. 70, as in Goodson, 1981, p 67)

Grasping teaching via a teacher's life history, Goodson next argues, can help remedy two kinds of problematic aspects found with accounts of teachers

PRACTITIONER RESEARCH

123

in literature. *First* is that of a depersonalised and neutral teacher, portrayed as the same teacher everyone ought to immediately recognise and be familiar with. With the personal nature of teaching not given due attention, such a stance makes teachers *interchangeable*. Any teacher would thus do, to deal with the job at hand. *Second* is the assumption of *timelessness*. As with being interchangeable, teachers are portrayed as responding to educational scenarios in the same manner, whatever the time, irrespective of who the individual is, and how she is positioned. Goodson thus views biographical data across a range of teachers and contexts, to have potential to challenge the notion of interchangeability. In fact the wisdom, tact or sense of humour of teachers, is indeed quite irreplaceable. Similarly, tracing how teachers develop and evolve over time in multi-faceted ways can challenge the assumption of timelessness e.g. an early career teacher may find that her commitment is consuming her personal life, whereas one in her later years might use an approach less personally exhausting and more hands on.

On the nature of data in life history research, Goodson (1991) points to the importance of (1) preventing the treatment of teachers' accounts as irrelevant data, (2) understanding the uniqueness and idiosyncrasies of teachers in all their complexity, (3) identifying how the life-style of teachers both in and out of school and their latent identities impacts their teaching, (4) taking cognisance of decisions teachers make at various stages of their life, (5) grasping how critical incidents in a teacher's life could affect her perception and practice of teaching. A collection of such perspectives, Goodson says, may also help analyse individual teachers in relation to the historical times they have lived through.

Given that the kind of data one collects in life history interviews is narrative in texture and scope, Scherto Gill and Goodson elaborate how narrative accounts of individuals differ from their life history renderings. Unlike temporality, social encounters, structure and organisation of a plot which lends value to a narrative, they point out,

> Closely linked to the notion of narrative, life history is a collection of individuals' or groups' lived experience in the past and present which is analysed by researchers who then place the narrative accounts within the social, political, economic and historical contexts where these experiences took place. *The focus of life history is to understand the interplay between social change, individual (and group) lives and agency.* (Gill & Goodson, 2011, p. 157, emphasis added)

The importance of life history as not just a historical narrative of a teacher's life but a deeper examination of her agency against a backdrop of social, political, economic and historical changes she encounters, allows Goodson to alert us to how any *teachers' voice* could be framed or even closed as it were. He argues,

> Teachers' lives are subject to degrees of closure because they take place in one of the most historically circumscribed of social spaces. Schools are subject to a battery of government regulations, edicts, tests, accountabilities, and assessments – these provide parameters for the actions of teachers. Further, teachers are subject to systematic and invasive socialization during their education as well as pre-service and in-service training. The circumscription of space and the systemic nature of socialization are what predominantly 'frame' and 'close' teachers' lives. (Goodson, 2014, p. 44)

Taken together, Goodson's pursuit of life history seems invaluable to examining the dialectical interplay between the teacher as an individual and the societal matrix of events that the teacher encounters in her life. An example of such a dialectic at play is evidenced by the life history of a teacher Goodson himself had, whom he considered to be not only radical but also academically brilliant. As a teacher Goodson found him to be open, humorous, engaging as well as stimulating. But as the structure of schooling changed from grammar school to a comprehensive one, so as to appeal to wider social groups, he found this teacher to oppose curriculum reform. On Goodson's probing he at first stonewalled responses, giving non committal answers till on Goodson's persistence he opened up one day over a beer. Goodson recounts this interaction as follows,

> Yes, of course he was mainly concerned with disadvantaged pupils; yes, of course that's why he'd come to the factory to drag me back to school. Yes, he was politically radical and yes, he had always voted Labour. But, and here I quote: 'you don't understand my relationship to the school and to teaching. My centre of gravity is not here at all. It's in the community, in the home – that's where I exist, that's where I put my effort now. For me the school is nine to five, I go through the motions.' (Goodson, 1991, pp. 35–36)

With the above illustration I find Goodson to portray how there was more to the life of his teacher than was apparent to him in his study. Goodson thus argues any attempt to grasp teacher development and development of teaching at large, needs to draw vital inspiration on the life histories of teachers themselves. It is thus that I find it appropriate to turn to a final genre of practitioner

PRACTITIONER RESEARCH

research, wherein practitioners can contribute to research as the persons they themselves are.

6   Person Centric Research

Four approaches in practitioner research serve as points of departure to means I term person centric. The issues and mechanisms these highlight, contribute significantly to professional development of teachers as well as practitioner research at large. While the first two focus on the individual teacher, the latter two explore teacher collectives. I turn *first* to Deborah Britzman who allows us to examine the concerns Goodson had raised, in relation to how teachers' lives and voice could be circumscribed, framed or even closed. Britzman draws attention to the autonomy of the self of any practitioner, given normative expectations of professionalism and the need to adhere to mandated curricula in one's teaching. She argues,

> We do know more about what holds education and teacher education back. There is the force of governmental interdictions, censoring both ideas and the personal lives of teachers and students. Our own definitions of professionalism preclude complications of selves and then ask for compliance and conformity. *We have made great strides in emptying the curriculum from debating itself.* (Britzman, 2000, p. 200, emphasis added)

Drawing upon scholars including Arendt to address the crisis being faced in teacher education, Britzman queries the obligations practitioners have not just in getting things done but also about what needs to be done in responding ethically to people whose lives and histories are unknown. If teacher education is to join the wider world and participate in its making, then, Britzman argues, we must rethink norms that exist and prevail in the name of teacher professionalism. She thus argues it wise for teachers to not have to be bound by compliance, fear, controversy and be ignorant of the experiences of others. Drawing upon one's personal self as a means for world making, Britzman points out,

> World making requires self-knowledge of what the world might symbolize or represent for the self. It is both our earliest and oldest technology. ... The work of knowing the self entails acknowledging not just what one would like to know about the self but also what is difficult to know about

> the self, including features we tend to project to others: aggression, self aggrandizement, destructive wishes, and helplessness. These are the devastating qualities of psychical life. And yet, there is also something about education that resists self-knowledge. (Britzman, 2000, pp. 202–203)

Drawing on a psychoanalytic framework, Britzman points to the vital role self-making can play not only for one's own self as a practitioner but also as a prime source *for* world making. In doing so she underscores what it may mean to know about one's own self and also highlights what may be difficult to know about ourselves, if at all.

Alluding to the breadth and unfinished agenda that lies embedded in practitioner research, Britzman's arguments prepare ground for me to *second* introduce Robert Bullough and Stephanie Pinnegar's writings in relation to a rapidly growing field called *self study research*, which offers guidelines on its systematic pursuit. Bullough and Pinnegar (2001) view such research to arise out of four developments which in no particular order are (1) the introduction of naturalistic and qualitative methods in educational research, combined with viewing validity of their outcomes in terms of trustworthiness, (2) a movement in curriculum studies which legitimises understanding of education in terms of studying one's own self, (3) growing involvement of researchers located across the world, enabling diverse intellectual traditions to come together, besides drawing on the humanities beyond the social sciences, and (4) a shift in focus in conducting action research, leading to the blurring of boundaries between research and thoughtful practice, besides researchers and practitioners. Self-study research acknowledges a simple truth, they argue, that to study educational practice is to simultaneously study one's own professional and personal self in relation to another.

The guidelines Bullough and Pinnegar offer, to achieve quality in self study research include the ability of autobiographical accounts of teachers to (1) ring true and enable an educational connection, (2) promote insight as well as interpretation, (3) take an honest stand in one's authorship and engage with history in a forthright manner, (4) deal with problems that relate to making one an educator, (5) uncover deeper truths about human behaviour in addition to offering an authentic voice, (6) seek to improve ongoing learning not only for one's self but also for the other, (7) portray character development and include dramatic action, one which evidences that something genuine is at stake in the story being told, (8) attend to persons in their settings with great care, and (9) offer fresh perspectives on previously established truths. Yet, Bullough and Pinnegar recognise self study research to still be in its infancy. Its durability as

PRACTITIONER RESEARCH

a movement they argue, depends on how its collective findings inform practice and move conversations within research forward. They conclude,

> Like all research, the burden of proof is on those who would conduct and hope to publish autobiographical self-studies. As we have said, articles need to be readable and engaging, themes should be evident and identifiable across the conversation represented or the narrative presented, the connection between autobiography and history must be apparent, the issues attended to need to be central to teaching and teacher education, and sufficient evidence must be garnered that readers will have no difficulty recognizing the authority of the scholarly voice, not just its authenticity. (Bullough & Pinnegar, 2001, p. 20)

In line with Bullough and Pinnegar and in light of conducting many an intervention with teachers I collaborated with, I conducted a self study in relation to the benefits of deploying a theory/practice stance intrinsic to CHAT research (Gade, 2017). Elaborated in greater detail in Chapter 7 and in doing so I had opportunity to unpack many a methodological approach – understanding instructional practices by intervening and transforming them, creating the object of knowledge and tool for its investigation as part of my inquiry, grasping theory and practice in terms of practitioner reflexivity, besides recognise that I was taking political action in dialectic with developmental perspectives of CHAT.

The *third* framework I discuss, which relates to how teacher collectives can engage in self study began during my first post-doctoral in Mumbai, where I worked with a cohort of middle school teachers in a newly established school. My shift to Umeå delayed this search as I had by now begun to make regular visits to Lotta's classroom. On one such occasion I found her class to be led by a substitute teacher, wherein students were working at questions related to subtraction and had to be helped with grasping the need to *carry over* and its algorithmic ways. On introducing myself to this teacher and exchanging notes, she mentioned not having understood the need for carry over as a child and admitted 'I was thirty when I understood carry over for the first time.' In terms of CHAT I found this teacher's lament to speak for many others too whose learning of mathematics, may never have been *led* by knowledgeable others in a zpd. Reminiscent of Sarason's view that teaching was a lonely enterprise, my search for frameworks that could be relevant led me to Jennifer Nias' *Why teachers need their colleagues: A developmental perspective.*

While not conceiving development in line with CHAT, Nias reports from extensive empirical work with primary teachers in which she adopts a humanistic view. She finds primary teachers to make little distinction between personal and professional identities and invest their,

> self-defining values, aspirations, personality, talents, interests, emotions in the job; and, all too often for the comfort of their friends and families, take their work into their private lives, literally, mentally and emotionally. Three things follow from this merging of identities: individuals' personal development influences the work that they do in school and may even in part account for it; private problems and preoccupations ... are not left at the school gate; and for both these reasons individuals may therefore look, consciously or unconsciously, to their colleagues for the satisfaction of personal needs through work. (Nias, 2005, p. 233)

Highlighting the lived consequences of teachers making little distinction between personal and professional selves, Nias points to the importance of schools as workplaces for adults, even if their primary ongoing work is to help students learn and develop. In distinct echo with Sarason, she too argues the need for school environments to nurture the development of teachers as whole persons. Nias goes on to explain,

> Teachers enter the profession preoccupied first with survival and then with a sense of fit between self and choice of occupation. If both of these concerns are satisfied, they look for ways of becoming better practitioners. Some then move into a phase where they want to exercise a wider or more lasting influence upon others, to leave their footprints in the sands of time. Throughout, however, their concerns are self-referential. (Nias, 2005, p. 235)

Suggesting personal development to materialise after teachers achieve personal survival and professional fit, Nias seeks a social setting where sharing their lives with one another and collaboration are the norm. She recognises that such an environment may also result in teachers accepting or rejecting their own views, not only about teaching but also about their selves as practitioners. There is a fine line too she says, between teachers wanting to preserve self-esteem and being dependent on others. Self-preserving strategies she therefore concludes, are key to furthering the professional growth of teachers. Nias ends with a note of caution too, one that sees the development of teachers to be at odds with the development of the school. *Collegially assisted teacher development* needs a nose to the ground engagement she argues, one that ensures, compatibility in teachers' moral and educational beliefs and values. So, different sub-cultures within a school may enhance their members' growth, but may in the process obstruct or stalemate that of others. Put another way, the professional development of some individuals may be achieved only by inhibiting the development of the school as a whole. Resolving this dilemma is a formidable task. Under the 'soft-centred,' humanistic view of teacher development presented here, lies a hard-edged awareness of the power of individual values and of the need for political and micropolitical processes which may help to reconcile them. (Nias, 2005, p. 236)

Nias' study portrays the kind of micro-politics I have known first hand as a teacher, where personal development and professional collegiality could work and remain at visible odds, unless experienced teachers intervene with wisdom drawn from having seen many a day and year pass in living their lives as teachers. The ability of teacher groups to obstruct others is also something that cannot be ignored and may even be key indicator to the lack of collegiality any school is striving hard to achieve. While shedding light on the potential as well as problems of teacher collectives, Nias' framework is however silent on how specific issues such as 'carry over' could be looked into and dealt with. I examine the ability to deal with this manner of support in my *final* framework.

I came to give more attention to the Japanese *Lesson study framework* after attending Konrad Krainer's (2011) keynote at the PME mathematics education conference. Speaking from experience of widespread conduct of action research in Austria, he was commenting on the salient features of this valuable tradition. Among other points Krainer viewed the benefits of teachers and researchers gaining trust and becoming stakeholders in each other's professional practice. Such a stance, he argued, could speak to knowledge bases of both teaching and research. In line with Altrichter et al. cited earlier, he highlighted the vital difference between *technical rationality* and *reflective rationality*. The former, he said, was geared to finding general solutions to practical problems. Developed outside practical situations, these were then applied to practical situations by decree. The latter however recognised that practical problems need particular solutions, developed in the context of which problems arise. These solutions are then proposed as hypothesis for practitioners to carry out in other contexts. I thus found the Lesson study framework to not only allow for reflective rationality, but also for such rationality to be carried out by teacher collectives at their own schools.

By now a world wide movement accompanied by many publications, in the lesson study framework teachers not only plan the instruction of particular lessons together, but also observe teaching of these in actual classrooms. At times subject experts are invited to join the whole process, wherein teachers exchange notes and raise questions as practitioners. Clea Fernandez and Makato Yoshida (2009) trace a six step process that teachers follow (1) collaborative planning of the study lesson, (2) seeing the study lesson in action, (3) discuss the study lesson, (4) revise the study lesson if needed, (5) teach the revised study lesson, if needed, and (6) share reflections about the study lesson. Elaborating on the Japanese terminology they explain lesson study to be a direct translation for,

> the Japanese term *jugyokenkyu*, which is composed of two words: *jugyo*, which means lesson, and *kenkyu*, which means study or research. As denoted by this term, lesson study consists of the study or examination of teaching practice. How do Japanese teachers examine their teaching through lesson study? They engage in a well-defined process that involves discussing lessons that they have first planned and observed together. These lessons are called *kenkyujugyo*, which is simply a reversal of the term *jugyokenkyu* and thus literally means study or research lessons, more specifically lessons that are the object of one's study. (Fernandez & Yoshida, 2009, p. 7)

I argue the lesson study framework to have many benefits for teachers. As recognised by Nias there is basis for collegiality, with added benefit of dealing with curricular content. Following Clandinin and Connelly, there is opportunity to observe personal practical knowledge on display in another teacher's practice, an experience that could be instructive and confidence providing for novice teachers. There is opportunity for asking questions that could be examined further via drawing upon premise in action research, teacher research or practitioner inquiry traditions. While the objective of lesson study is not developmental in the CHAT sense, the object of any study lesson could be an activity setting that could motivate teachers, wherein those experienced could *lead* others less familiar. The formation of a zpd is not difficult to envisage either, one allowing for the interpsychological to become intrapsychological.

7   Art and Life Are Not One: Coda

In my central coda of this book I draw upon Mikhail Bakhtin, Russian literary theorist and philosopher, whose writings shed much light on how we practitioners could view our own role as teachers in our ongoing lives. To begin with and informing how we humans speak with and relate to one another and our students, Bakhtin argues human language to lie at the border between one's self and the self of another. Its nature, he argues, exhibits multiple viewpoints or *heteroglossia*,

> The word in language is half someone else's. It becomes 'one's own' only when the speaker populates it with his own intention, his own accent, when he appropriates the word, adapting it to his semantic and expressive intention. Prior to this moment of appropriation, the word does not exist in a neutral and impersonal language (it is not, after all, out of a dictionary that the speaker gets his words!), but rather it exists in other people's mouths, in other people's contexts, serving other people's intentions: it is from there that one must take the word, and make it one's own. (Bakhtin, 1981, pp. 293–294)

Recognising language to be far from a neutral medium but something that passes with great ease from one person to another, Bakhtin recognises the need for each one of us to populate its use with our own intention and make the word specifically our own. In fact he finds everyday words to be overpopulated with the intentions of others. Bakhtin speaks to the core of any instructional process at two levels. *First* and as practitioners know only too well, the language we use and intend for our students is home to multiple meanings. For example our students might say 'But teacher, isn't a map, what we see in an atlas' when we might speak about mapping elements of a set of square numbers to the corresponding set of natural numbers in mathematics. It is only on further discussion that we teachers can surmise our students to be on their way to grasping the word map in a fresh context of use. *Second* and given the way words are populated with multiple meanings, students would probably arrive at the underlying notion of mapping two entities in a two-dimensional map in their atlas and that of genome sequences in their future study of biology. Words then, can be populated differently within instruction between teacher and students, as well as across the trajectory of learning for any one of us over time. Till such time the word 'map' for eight year olds is overpopulated by colourful images they are accustomed to in their atlas.

My alluding to instructional scenarios leads me next to the distinction Bakhtin makes between two kinds of discourse in any spoken language, in terms of *authoritative discourse* and *internally persuasive discourse*. Discourse or words which are authoritative, Bakhtin argues, are distanced and felt hierarchically higher. Their authority is already acknowledged in the past, prior to their acceptance in the present. Akin to unquestioned words by the head of

132   CHAPTER 5

any family, the authoritative word is distinct from internally persuasive discourse, one that is able to convince the person being spoken with and not spoken to. With words being half ours and half someone else's, its productiveness Bakhtin argues consists,

> precisely in the fact that such a word awakens new and independent words, that it organises masses of our words from within and does not remain in an isolated and static condition. It is not so much interpreted by us as it is further, that is, freely developed, applied to new material, new conditions; it enters into interanimating relationships with new contexts. ... The semantic structure of an internally persuasive discourse is *not finite*, it is *open*; in each of the new contexts that dialogise it, this discourse is able to reveal ever newer *ways to mean*. (Bakhtin, 1981, pp. 345–346, emphasis in original)

In line with Bakhtin, we practitioners use both authoritative and internally persuasive discourse in orchestrating ongoing instruction. Via the former we position ourselves as well as our students in various roles, in order to realise instructional objectives we have in mind in the immediate. We encounter such discourse again say in curricula, policy documents and institutional guidelines, with respect to which we may even have personal misgivings. It is in terms of the latter that our students become willing participants in our instructional efforts. Such discourse is at play while introducing a new concept to our students say, who in turn share with us the meanings they go on to surmise on being internally persuaded by our arguments. It is also the case that at times we are persuaded by what our colleagues tell us about some incident that transpired in school, where at other times we read the situation quite differently from them.

In any of the scenarios portrayed above, Bakhtin would argue, that our ontology or our self does not stand on its own but in relation to others. Such relations are also basis for our coming to know or our epistemology. Although not coined by Bakhtin himself, Michael Holquist uses the term *dialogism* to describe such a philosophy, to be founded on a loophole. By this latter is meant the possibility of our viewing a future that is obscured by a discourse prevailing in the present. Reiterating there is neither a first word nor last which allows for this, he cites Bakhtin as follows,

> The contexts of dialogue are without limit. They extend into the deepest past and the most distant future. Even meanings born in dialogues of the remotest past will never be finally grasped once and for all, for

PRACTITIONER RESEARCH

they will always be renewed in later dialogue. At any present moment of the dialogue there are great masses of forgotten meanings, but these will be recalled again at a given moment in the dialogue's later course when it will be given new life. For nothing is absolutely dead: every meaning will someday have its homecoming festival. (Bakhtin, 1979, p. 373, as in Holquist, 2002, p. 39)

Bakhtin's theorisation of language, one already put to use by others, besides whose meanings are forgotten if only for the time being, is joined by another feature he highlights – the kind of language we use in specific social contexts. Referring to the kind spoken within a hospital say or at a music conservatory, Bakhtin points to the quality of speech which unifies and stratifies language within localised concrete situations as a *genre*. It is thus that Gudmundsdottir recognised the language of practice spoken in any particular school as a genre. Such a language is found laden with meaning and enables practitioners to develop ways of doing things in the everyday as well as realise one's unique voice. Yet since meanings never die and always have a homecoming, Goodson's notion of practitioner voice as born from life histories, bears just as much significance.

The above brings me to two final notions. The *first* of these asks that we practitioners act, since as Bakhtin argues we human beings have *no alibi*. In each of us occupying a unique time and place in life writ large, our very existence is not conceived as a passive stasis, but as a human activity for which we are responsible and vitally *answerable*. Placed in a position to serve and not rest as it were, Bakhtin reiterates,

The centre of gravity in this world is located in the future, in what is desired, in what ought to be, and *not* in the self-sufficient givenness of an object, in its being-on-hand, *not* in its present, its wholeness, its being-already-realised. My relationship to each object within my horizon is never a consummated relationship; rather, it is a relationship which is imposed on me as a task-to-be-accomplished, for the event of being, taken as a whole, is an open event; my situation must change at every moment – I cannot tarry and come to rest. (Bakhtin, 1990, p. 98, emphasis in original)

In the above quote, Bakhtin helps us view the lives of practitioners as those having a task to accomplish, besides realisation of their own being in addition to those of our students. It is in this way that we practitioners may be unable to stay or even find the time to rest for a while as well.

Yet Bakhtin's *second* notion offers wise counsel on how to accomplish such a demanding task, by using our ability to draw upon *art*. Any purity of art divorced from life and life divorced from art, Bakhtin goes on to argue, makes the task of each easier to achieve as such a task would be relieved of any sense of answerability. Since we have no alibi and in what I think is thoughtful consideration about the lasting quality of any practitioner's answerability, Bakhtin argues,

> For it is certainly easier to create without answering for life, and easier to live without any consideration for art.
>
> Art and life are not one, but they must become united in myself – in the unity of my answerability. (Bakhtin, 1990, p. 2)

Following the above I find Bakhtin inform our work as practitioners in three specific directions – the present and the future, the mundane and the profound, as well as the practical and the theoretical. His insights make each of us sensitive to the notion that we must make the words we speak our own, besides exercise authority when needed and internally persuade others in our instructional care. He draws our attention to genres that flourish in various concrete contexts and to our answerability, or even our vulnerability, since we have no alibi. He reminds us too that we cannot encounter life on its own terms alone, but must take recourse to art in doing our life's bidding. In so doing Bakhtin prepares me to examine the very nature of our pedagogy, an aspect I turn to next.

References

Altrichter, H., Posch, P., & Somekh, B. (1993). *Teachers investigate their work: An introduction to the methods of action research*. Routledge.

Bakhtin, M. M. (1979). *Estetika solvesnogo tvorcestva* [*Aesthetics of verbal creativity*]. Moscow.

Bakhtin, M. M. (1981). *The dialogic imagination: Four essays*. University of Texas Press.

Bakhtin, M. M. (1990). *Art and answerability: early philosophical essays*. University of Texas Press.

Becker, H. S. (1970). The career of the Chicago schoolmaster. In H. Becker (Ed.), *Sociological work: Method and substance*. Aldine.

Britzman, D. (2000). Teacher education in the confusion of our times, *Journal of Teacher Education, 51*(3), 200–205.

Bruner, J. (1990). *Acts of meaning*. Harvard University Press.

Bruner, J. (1996). *The culture of education*. Harvard University Press.

Bruner, J. (2002). *Making stories: Law, literature, life*. Harvard University Press.

Bullough Jr., R. V., & Pinnegar, S. (2001). Guidelines for quality in autobiographical forms of self-study research. *Educational Researcher, 30*(3), 13–21.

Cochran-Smith, M. (2011). Does learning to teach ever end? *Kappa Delta Pi Record, 47*(1), 22–24.

Cochran-Smith, M. (2012). A tale of two teachers: Learning to teach over time, *Kappa Delta Pi Record, 48*(3), 108–122.

Cochran-Smith, M., & Donnell, K. (2006). Practitioner inquiry: Blurring the boundaries of research and practice. In J. L. Green, G. Camilli, & P. B. Elmore (Eds.), *Handbook of complementary methods in education research* (pp. 503–518). Lawrence Erlbaum Associates.

Cochran-Smith, M., & Lytle, S. (1993). *Inside/Outside: Teacher research and knowledge*. Teachers College Press.

Cochran-Smith, M., & Lytle, S. (2009a). Teacher research as stance. In S. Noffke & B Somekh (Eds.), *The Sage handbook of educational action research* (pp. 39–50). Sage Publications.

Cochran-Smith, M., & Lytle, S. (2009b). *Inquiry as stance: Practitioner research for the next generation*. Teachers College Press.

Clandinin, J. (1985). Personal practical knowledge: A study of teachers' classroom images. *Curriculum Inquiry, 15*(4), 361–385.

Daiute, C. (2010). *Human development and political violence*. Cambridge University Press.

Elliott, J. (1991). *Action research for educational change*. Open University Press.

Fernandez, C., & Yoshida, M. (2009). *Lesson study: A Japanese approach to improve mathematics teaching and learning*. Routledge.

Gade, S. (2010). Narratives of students learning mathematics: Plurality of strategies and a strategy for practice? In C. Bergsten, E. Jablonka, & T. Wedege (Eds.), *Mathematics and mathematics education: Cultural and social dimensions. Proceedings of the seventh mathematics education research seminar MADIF7* (pp. 102–112). Stockholm University.

Gade, S. (2011). Narrative as unit of analysis for teaching-learning praxis and action: Tracing the personal growth of a professional voice. *Reflective Practice, 12*(1), 35–45.

Gade, S. (2012). Teacher researcher collaboration at a grade four mathematics classroom: Restoring equality to students usage of the '=' sign. *Educational Action Research, 20*(4), 553–570.

Gade, S. (2017). Research as praxis, en route theory/practice teacher-researcher collaboration: A self-study. *Nordic Studies in Mathematics Education, 22*(3), 5–23.

Gill, S., & Goodson, I. (2011). Life history and narrative methods. In B. Somekh & C. Lewin (Eds.), *Theory and methods in social research* (2nd ed., pp. 157–165). Sage.

Goodson, I. F. (1981). Life histories and the study of schooling. *Interchange, 11*(4), 62–76.

Goodson, I. F. (1991). Sponsoring the teacher's voice: Teachers' lives and teacher development. *Cambridge Journal of Education, 21*(1), 35–45.

Goodson, I. F. (2014). Investigating the life and work of teachers. *Eesti Haridusteaduste Ajakiri (Estonian Journal of Education), 2*(2), 28–47.

Gudmundsdottir, S. (2001). Narrative research on school practice. In V. Richardson (Ed.), *Handbook of research on teaching* (4th ed., pp. 226–240). American Education Research Association.

Holquist, M. (2002). *Dialogism: Bakhtin and his world.* Routledge.

Krainer, K. (2011). Teachers as stakeholders in mathematics education research. In B. Ubuz (Ed.), *Proceedings of the International Group of Psychology of Mathematics Education* (PME) (Vol. 1, pp. 47–62). PME.

Marrow, A. J. (1969). *The practical theorist: The life and work of Kurt Lewin.* Basic Books.

McNiff, J. (2007). My story is my living educational theory In J. D. Clandinin (Ed.), *Handbook of narrative inquiry: mapping a methodology* (pp. 308–329). Sage Publications.

Nias, J. (2005). Why teachers need their colleagues: A developmental perspective. In D. Hopkins (Ed.), *The practice and theory of school improvement* (pp. 223–237). Springer.

Noffke, S. E. (2009). Revisiting the professional, personal and political dimensions of action research. In S. Noffke & B. Somekh (Eds.), *The Sage handbook of educational action research* (pp. 6–23). Sage.

Noffke, S. E., & Somekh, B. (Eds.). (2009). *The Sage handbook of educational action research.* Sage.

Polkinghorne, D. E. (1997). Reporting qualitative research as practice. In W. G. Tierney & Y. S. Lincoln (Eds.), *Representation and the text: Reframing the narrative voice* (pp. 3–21). State University of New York Press.

Polkinghorne, D. E. (2010). The practice of narrative. *Narrative Inquiry, 20*(2), 392–396.

CHAPTER 6

Pedagogical Perspectives
The Tone of Teaching

1 Preamble

Beyond outlining my journey till I conducted doctoral work, followed by a brief overview of wider CHAT and practitioner research, I now turn to experiences had from conducting independent research. After a brief stint with Homi Bhabha Centre for Science Education (TIFR), Mumbai, India, this corresponds to my shift to Umeå University, Umeå, Sweden, where I was post-doctoral researcher for two years and Assistant Professor for the next six. Viewed as an extended post-doctoral opportunity, this latter not only allowed me to spend hundred percent of my time pursuing research interests for eight years, but also provided for visiting fellowships of one year duration each at relevant centres at the City University of New York, USA and the University of Oxford, UK. While I did miss out on the kind of critique students so ably provide if I had taught during this period, my engagement with institutional work was also down to a minimum. This last enabled me to conduct and report on interventions with Lotta at grade four and Tomas at grade eight, more elaborated in Chapter 9. While Swedish was used at grades four and eight for instruction, I also had occasion to engage with instruction in English of students pursuing their International Baccalaureate at the first grade of their gymnasium. While the instruction at grades four and eight were along lines I was acquainted with, I encountered a décalage between my personal expectations and the ground realities I faced at the gymnasium. This experience led my search for pedagogical perspectives that were compatible with CHAT.

While my initial interest at the gymnasium was to study instructional discourse as it progressed through the academic year, I witnessed students working largely from their textbook loaded on their personal computers. The teacher was not steering instructional events as I had anticipated and it was students' computers that were the centre of instructional activity. While the teacher did provide individual guidance, such activity included free access to the internet and chat sessions with friends. The students were adolescents and treated as adults besides. Having obtained consent for research, I thus changed tact in two ways. *First* and making good of the time I spent therein, I interviewed students and provisionally reported my findings at a mathematics

© KONINKLIJKE BRILL NV, LEIDEN, 2022 | DOI:10.1163/9789004512160_006

education conference (Gade, 2012). *Second* I began searching in earnest for theoretical frameworks which would help me greater grasp the kind of scenario I was experiencing. In terms of the difference between educational climates I encountered in Sweden and India with respect to students' learning at these grades, I found students in India hard pressed for time, placed in highly competitive situations and having to negotiate schooling in a *buyer's market*. In contrast, students in Sweden seemed to have time and opportunity to follow their interests, while negotiating a *seller's market*. This latter called on them to make prudent choices amongst many alternatives that were available. Presently I provide excerpts from interviews with two gymnasium students. I first cite Erin who on being asked, articulated the negative experience students tended to have with learning mathematics as follows,

> a pain in the arse frankly ... I believe that some feel that they have these gaps and that the pace is too high, and they, you know, feel that they are *not stupid but unsmart*, because they don't know things they are supposed to know and that makes it negative and makes them feel, no, I don't like math ... because that's how it made me feel then .... (Gade, 2012, p. 270, emphasis in original)

On asking another student Sofia if she wished for anything, Sofia seemed to articulate the problem I thought these students had of having to make career defining choices on their own. She said and I quote,

> It's a hard question, do you wish for anything. I wish for, my God I don't know, *I don't know what to wish for* ... when I chose this program for school I just went *ole dole doff, kinkel ane koff* and said ok I'll take 1B, and it will be exactly the same next year ... I wish I had something to target, a goal, because it would be really important for me, something to work ahead for ... *that is what I wish for, something I can work for, something that I want to do.* (Gade, 2010, p. 272, emphasis in original)

As researcher the above study led me to two thoughts in relation to perspectives of CHAT that I was keen on deploying. *First* and at a methodological level and if I had opportunity, I wondered what manner of intervention I could conduct to transform the instructional scenario I observed. *Second* and from the point of view of human development, I wondered what instruction was best suited to *lead* the development of students who were adolescents. It was such a background that made me look out for insights from humanistic and social sciences which I could assimilate with CHAT, so as to intervene in instructional

PEDAGOGICAL PERSPECTIVES

scenarios which seemed to lie outside the predicated norm. Such thoughts led me to Danish educator Knud Illeris' (2007) book titled *How we learn: Learning and non-learning in school and beyond*.

Speaking from his specialisation in lifelong learning, Illeris' arguments helped me step back from the grades of schooling I was engaged with and reflect on four misunderstandings he argues are widespread in relation to education at large. Their very complexity prevents us from attending to them in our lives. These were (1) *The ideological misunderstanding* – one which assumes that there is a broad agreement between the objectives formulated for an educational program and the design of courses being offered. Formulated by the same authorities, rarely are such curricula designed towards the objectives of schooling. (2) *The technological misunderstanding* – one that considers education as a production process wherein meeting syllabi laid down in considerable detail, proclaims that the outcomes would be the same for all individuals. What is disregarded is that individuals express interests, have preferences and dispositions, besides aversions and dislikes. (3) *The psychological misunderstanding* – which is most widespread of the four and pretends that there is a direct correspondence between what is taught and what is learned, even as only some aspects of what is taught are actually learnt, and that what each student learns is different in addition. Not only is there a great deal of mislearning, students also learn something other than what is taught. (4) *The utopian misunderstanding* – not as tangible as the others this refers to the notion that education can solve all problems, even when we are up against societal forces that we have little power to deal with. Education cannot, he argues, produce both conformity and independence just as we cannot ignore social realities we are born into. Illeris thus argues,

> But if education is to be targeted and play a part in developing independence, responsibility, creativity, flexibility and all the other 'soft qualifications,' we must take seriously that this requires education programmes where such characteristics are practised and related to the academic content one is working with – and that conditions will be bad for them if the participants are more or less forced to attend the courses, *or if the programmes are not designed to include activity and reflection and the individual participant being able to see his or her interests in what is taking place*. (Illeris, 2007, p. 238, emphasis added)

Asking for academic content and instructional activity to be of interest to students, or meaningful to students in terms of CHAT perspectives, Illeris highlights the central question articulated at one time or another by most students in any ossified educational system – what is in all this for *me*? And the *me* in this question is in all probability, in singer and songwriter Bob Dylan's words – *Knock, knock, knockin' on heaven's door!*

2 Contexts for Local Change

The schools at which I collaborated with teachers and their students were all located in different parts of Umeå. My work here began concurrently with Lotta's grade four whose school housed grades from pre primary to grade six, and the gymnasium which housed grades from ten to twelve. I approached Tomas after my visits to the gymnasium gave over. Tomas' grade eight school housed grades seven to nine and like Lotta's school was a neighbourhood school, drawing students from close by. By the time I approached Tomas' school for my work, Lotta's students whom I knew fairly well had just enrolled there. I thought I might continue to work with them at their grade seven. My meeting the Rektor at Tomas' school however resulted in my working with students at grade eight led by another teacher whom I call Greta. The Rektor went on to explain that most students at her school came from families working at an automobile factory close by. The worldwide economic downturn of year 2008 was a reality back then and many parents of students she explained, might be questioning the kind of schooling their children were obtaining. Was the education they were receiving adequate, for an uncertain labour market and their economic future? The Rektor asked if I was willing to work with Greta, who could do with additional instructional support against the backdrop just described. My working with Greta in turn led me to work with Tomas as well. As with my visits to the gymnasium, my association with Greta and Tomas' school led me to search for literature which had potential to complement my ongoing CHAT based interests.

My search for frameworks which could help me grasp the contextual reality in which Greta and Tomas were teaching, was a composite of two trajectories. *First* was my personal need to understand schooling within industrial societies as different from those I had myself experienced in India, which was much more agrarian and quasi-industrial. *Second* was a need to draw on pedagogical and sociological perspectives in a manner that would enable me better grasp, design and carry out CHAT driven instructional interventions. Such efforts led to broadening my horizons from being a teacher-researcher to becoming an educator, envisaging how societal aspects nuanced pedagogical practices in classroom scenarios. With paucity of time in relation to conducting instructional interventions in Greta and Tomas' classrooms, I engaged with literature

PEDAGOGICAL PERSPECTIVES

that came my way in my library search. I proceed to dwell on *three* such writings in this section and *first* draw on the distinction Sharon Beder, Wendy Varney and Richard Gasden (2009) make between *enterprise education* and *citizen education*. The first lays focus on understanding business, was contract based, geared towards students taking risks, taking advantage of opportunities that came by and instilled skills of negotiation. The latter lay focus upon understanding the world, was ethics based, encouraged students to utilise creative and analytical skills for problems that they would formulate in collaboration with one another. Given my study of cooperative learning in my doctoral study and observing how the rights of the child were being discussed by students in Lotta's school, I found Beder's citizen education as being pertinent to Greta and Tomas' school and instruction. I had also found a socially responsible stance emphasised during our beginners course for learning Swedish as well.

During my initial days in Sweden there was palpable concern with the results of students in two tests – the Third International Mathematics and Science Study or TIMSS and the Program for International Student Assessment or PISA. The results of these were being discussed widely in newspapers as well as on television. I encountered a teacher at Tomas' school express concern about the results of these tests, saying that with Sweden not faring well in them, his students who had earlier grown up in a carefree environment, now felt demotivated as they knew they might not fare well after all. Apart from jokes by fellow researchers about their simple objective of bettering students' scores in comparison to their Scandinavian neighbours, the Swedish government invested substantially to address concerns generated by the public debate. It is for some grasp on issues such as these that I turned *next* to observations made by David Baker and Gerald LeTendre (2005) in their book *National differences, global similarities: World culture and the future of schooling*. Even as public or mass schooling was recognised in most nations as basis for positive economic change, Baker and LeTendre point out that a unique model of schooling did not exist in reality. While the kind of social behaviour schools foster were similar and recognisable worldwide, they mentioned three changes worthy of note (1) mass schooling had been able to achieve mass literacy in the last hundred years and there was no alternative model to its functioning in sight, (2) mass schooling had brought about wide acceptability for ideas that were considered unique not too long ago – that all children should be educated and that education was for the collective good, so that governments must fund these efforts and that the tradition of statutes like race, gender and language should not be barriers for students to attend them, and (3) that educational change was institutional change, one propelled by those present both inside and outside schools. While countries like Sweden and Iceland reported no gender difference, mass schooling had flattened gender differences world wide, and schooling had become a major medium for a growing ideology of gender equality. Despite school reform becoming commonplace and curriculum development now having to reckon with national politics, Baker and LeTendre observed that unlike families which are organised in an informal way, the organisation of stakeholders in schools is formal. From a sociological point of view they thus pointed out that,

> As an organisation, a school behaves more as the people within it think a school should behave than it does according to some unique rationalised plan of action. ...
>
> As sociologists have long pointed out, when institutions reach their height of power and influence on human behaviour they organise meanings and norms that are highly resistant to change. However, constant educational reform seems to move in the opposite direction. The powerful institution of mass schooling appears entirely open to change. (Baker & LeTendre, 2005, pp. 165–167)

Suggesting what can be done in light of their findings, they argue,

> Considerable public funds spent on narrow reforms that might boost national achievement scores in one subject by only a few points at one time can come at the cost of not improving other school factors that may in the long run hurt a nation's competitiveness. Nations would be better served by reforms that improve access to quality education for all students, including access to rigorous teaching, best curricula, and similar resources. (Baker & LeTendre, 2005, p. 174)

Baker and LeTendre's arguments about the dependency of education on the people that make up schools, the openness of schools to change, as well as the need to work towards the access of education for all students, preceded my accepting Greta's request of speaking at a forthcoming parent teacher meeting. Hard pressed for time I set aside any reading for later and drew on my prior experiences of meeting with parents. I set out to create mutual trust and greater transparency about my research. I spoke in English and requested Greta to offer clarifications in Swedish where needed. Though from the University, I mentioned my being a teacher at middle school grades in another democracy just like theirs. I also cited the billboard most would have seen in Stockholm's Arlanda airport – In every country the game is the same, but the

PEDAGOGICAL PERSPECTIVES

rules are different. I went on to explain in lay person's terms the mechanics of creating a zpd and the need for CHAT based research. The Rektor had sought their consent for my research and if published I assured them that their children would be anonymised. In addition it was Greta who would assess the performance of students, even as I would help her and them. One of them asked if her son would have opportunity to pick up more English and another if her daughter could get personal attention. While some welcomed my efforts with facial gestures, for reasons best known to them a few remained silent throughout our brief yet important interaction.

A search subsequent to my above meeting at our library, led me *third* to Gill Crozier's (2000) *Parents and schools: Partners or protagonists?* Based on her study with secondary schools in the UK, Crozier found parental partnership to be more complex and multifaceted than just being a good thing for schooling. While parents came from different social classes and differed in gender, teachers too were known to stress about responding to forces external to their own schools. On one hand, students were thought as unmotivated when their parents were working class. On the other, middle class mothers were expected to utilise every moment of their time for pedagogical purposes. Ironically parents from the working class trusted teachers to do their job. Crozier argues,

> Parent-teacher relationships are not therefore a given but are characterised by *a struggle for control and definition*. From their own perspective, teachers are seeking to assert control and maintain it in their interactions with parents. As we have seen, they have two broad sets of relationships to manage: with the assertive, demanding middle-class parents on the one hand, and with the seemingly passive, disengaged working-class parents on the other. In order to maintain their control, they need to establish, for the former, and maintain for the latter, an image of professional expertise. (Crozier, 2000, p. 123, emphasis added)

While pointing out that some parents, as might have been the case at Greta and Tomas' school, saw through the above manner of rehearsed interaction, Crozier also pointed out that while some parents keep up an appearance of being responsible, some are genuinely responsible for their children. It was also the case that even as my reading of arguments laid out by Beder et al. as well as Baker and LeTendre sensitised me to issues I was relatively unaware of earlier on, my reading of Crozier directed me to Willis' book on working class kids who refused to collude with their own suppression at school, an aspect I next turn to.

144   CHAPTER 6

3   Lads and Ear'oles

Paul Willis' many writings are instructive, both for his findings and for discussion on the constructs with which he arrives at them. In this section I begin with *Learning to labour*, whose opening lines are,

> The difficult thing to explain about how middle class kids get middle class jobs is why others let them. The difficult thing to explain about how working class kids get working class jobs is why they let themselves. (Willis, 1977, p. 1)

Allowing me to grasp the educational reality I was likely confronting on my regular visits to Tomas' school, Willis' study relates to working class boys he calls *lads*, in the industrial city of Hammertown in UK, in the 1970s. From a sociological point of view, Willis does many things (1) show how youth are far from dupes and actually active agents in the production and reproduction of the working class in society, (2) insist that what youth *do* in their everyday is important, besides (3) highlight school as a central location for youth to produce a culture that has the ability to oppose an upbringing being seemingly imposed on them. Describing their ability to both borrow and recycle elements of their working class culture, Willis singles out the importance for the lads in his study to be able to handle themselves and have a *laff*. He argues,

> The 'lads' resisted the mental and bodily inculcations of the school and rejected students who showed conformist attitudes to the school authorities. ... The lads deployed a particularly concrete and sharp way of speaking and were devoted to a certain kind of omnipresent humor – 'having a laff' – often directed cruelly against conformists and teachers. Their devotion to 'the laff' was central to the culture, and its deployment was a ubiquitous form capable of turning almost any situation into material for jokes and ribbing: 'It's the most important thing in life, even communists laff.' (Willis, 2003, pp. 392–393)

Willis' ability to single out students' laff was central to his understanding of the lads, besides how the lads in his study opposed the authority imposed by teachers and organised their lived culture. Wills continues,

> 'Who are they, tellin' us what to do when they're no better than us?' The central horizontal dynamic that organized and arranged their cultural assumptions and practices was a rejection of conformist pupils labeled

PEDAGOGICAL PERSPECTIVES   145

as 'ear'oles': 'They'm prats, they never get any fun do they?' This rejec-
tion was felt as a kind of distinction and superiority: 'We can make
them laff, they can't make us laff.' These positions and orientations were
enacted and embodied through a strong 'rough' masculine set of strategies, embellished in various ways through smoking, drinking, and stylish
dressing. (Willis, 2003, p. 393)

Willis clarifies the usage of *ear'oles* above, to be the slang used by lads for the
external ear of those who conformed to the expectations of school and seemed
to always listen, but never did anything. Willis goes on to note that while not all
working-class students failed at school, he found middle-class students were
about six times more likely to pursue higher education and not look for working class jobs.

For conducting the above insightful study Willis mentions his adopting an
interpretative, humanistic and ethnographic approach in line with the Bir-
mingham school of cultural studies, one different from a structural approach
dominant in sociological studies during his times. In relation to educational
contexts I was myself experiencing and wanting to change, Willis (2000) was
able to shed light on the commonly held meaning of three constructs. *First*,
Willis sought *ethnographic imagination*, wherein ethnography not only report
the reality of the everyday, but also deploy human imagination to transcend
that very everyday. This was needed, he argued, to grasp the sense social
agents made of situations in which they found themselves, an aspect often not
expressible in appropriate idiom. The conduct of ethnography thus required
a theorised relationship to the seemingly direct knowledge of reality, so as to
reflect and obtain some handle at the complexity and distinctions which social
categories like class, gender, ethnicity and identity brought about.

Second Willis viewed *culture* as an everyday phenomenon that was lived by
his participants. In *Profane culture*, which relates to the study of motor-cycle
boys and hippies, he points out,

The sheer surprise of a living culture is a slap to reverie. Real, bustling,
startling cultures move. They exist. They are something in the world.
They suddenly leave behind – empty, exposed, ugly – *ideas* of poverty,
deprivation, existence, and culture. Real events can save us much philosophy. (Willis, 1978, p. 1, emphasis in original)

Echoing the Marxian premise that philosophers have only interpreted the
world and the point was to change the same, Willis viewed everyday culture
and the formation of human subjectivity in culture, as not trickling down from

an overarching social order but in terms of how individuals interacted with their everyday. He argued,

> Culture, then, is not simply about a relationship with what is called 'art,' or with 'the best which has been thought and said,' or with the restricted or the refined. I see cultural experience essentially as shared material experience. ... It is in relation to the commonplace, to trivia and the slow accumulation of concrete lessons that individuals *in groups*, come to recognise their subjectivity. The determinations of the wider social system are borne in upon the social individual in a thousand different and variable ways. Tastes, feelings, likes and dislike are developed in minute articulation with the concrete world. (Willis, 1978, p. 2)

In arguing for a more unified notion of what he called *common culture*, one experienced in the concrete everyday by all of us, Willis identifies a dialectical mechanism at work. Incessant in its back and forth between human experience on one hand and theoretical conceptualisation on the other. It is this common culture which Willis views as giving shape to old world social structures that are identified with great ease, such as the middle or working classes. Such a view informs Willis' *final* construct of relevance to my work – the notion of *schooling*.

Willis viewed schooling as a site in which students responded to the material culture, in the midst of which their everyday lives played out. In the case of adolescents and young adults, these material aspects could be for example, genres of popular music, streaming smartphone and gaming apps, electronic messaging, headphones, brands of shoes, allegiance to clubs of various sport, hairstyles, T shirts, dressing codes and so on which wrest the educational landscape. This last is especially the case, Willis argues, if the space of schooling is vacated by a curriculum that holds little meaning for the daily lives of students. While working with students at grade eight, I became acutely aware of these aspects at play, besides the enormous power everyday manifestations of culture had in contrast to traditional perceptions sought such as spelling, reading, writing, debating history, becoming scientific or even learning mathematics say. Cognisant of issues such as these, Willis has the following advice to offer,

> Pedagogic voices can be shockingly quiet about issues of social context, as if the four walls of the classroom, sanctuary-making as they can be, contain all that is necessary to understand and direct what goes on within them. Educators and researchers should utilize the cultural experiences and embedded bodily knowledge of their students as starting points, not

for bemoaning the failures and inadequacies of their charges, *but to render more conscious for them what is unconsciously rendered in their cultural practices.* (Willis, 2003, p. 413, emphasis added)

Reminding me of the way in which Daiute was able to look beyond such walls in her study of narratives offered by youth in former Yugoslavia, Willis highlights the importance of starting points such as those he singles out above. Cultural experiences, students' bodily knowledge and their becoming more conscious of what is unconsciously rendered, he argues, could help teachers allow their students to understand their place and individual development in modern societies. Taken together Willis' insights made a twofold contribution to my ongoing, demanding work in Greta and Tomas' school. On one hand his penetrating grasp of student life, mirrored and helped me understand the many micro events I was witnessing – students' use of headphones in their classroom, slogans on their T shirts and their personal choice of music. On the other was the insight of his arguments in relation to culture as that which played out in students' material everyday. In line with CHAT perspectives, it was the relationships of students with this latter that guided my efforts and enabled me to ascend to the concrete in my studies.

4 Socio-Institutional Pedagogy

In this section and the two that follow, I examine school pedagogy from three different perspectives. Neo-Vygotskian in flavour each informs the manner in which we could reconceptualise the way in which students are taught in everyday classrooms. With rich potential for further research by practitioners in contexts of their individual work, each writing extends the basic Vygotskian assertion, that good instruction *leads* the development of students in their zpd. Willis' suggestion that we attend to the common culture that students are experiencing, would be a vital addition.

I begin with writings of Harry Daniels who guided my post-doctoral at the University of Oxford. As doctoral student of Basil Bernstein, Daniels enriches Vygotskian perspectives from a sociological point of view and draws attention to socio-institutional aspects of pedagogy. I admit that as erstwhile teacher, my initial reading of Daniels was demanding in that I had to broaden my unit of analysis from the micro level functioning of pedagogy limited to the confines of a classroom and envision a macro level functioning that took institutional ways of pedagogical production into account. Laying emphasis on the social nature of relations which Vygotsky argued as primary to cultural-historical development, Daniels draws attention to the ways in which pedagogical discourse is structured. A shift in focus is thus demanded from the psychological function of pedagogical discourse, to institutional processes and mechanisms which regulate its functioning within schools. There is opportunity here to grasp and alter mechanisms by means of which social relations enable educationally worthwhile cultures to be produced, reproduced as well as be acquired. With potential to examine ways in which the ideological misunderstanding that Illeris pointed to may be in place, such relations are known to result in actions of people with accommodating as well as competing interests within any institution. The contentious policy debate around the use and/or implementation of any one language as medium of instruction, when schools are located amongst a sociologically diverse and multilingual population, is a case in point.

Examining the sociology of pedagogy, Daniels at first demarcates three primary message systems which Bernstein identified as follows,

> curriculum, pedagogy (practice) and evaluation. Curriculum referred to what counted as legitimate knowledge and the latter was a function of the organisation of subjects (fields) modules or other units to be acquired. Pedagogy (practice) referred to the local pedagogical context of teacher and taught, and regulated what counted as a legitimised transmission of knowledge. Evaluation referred to what counted as a valid realisation of the knowledge on the part of the acquirer. (Daniels, 2001, p. 136)

Daniels allows me to clarify three aspects central to school instruction – legitimate knowledge essential for teaching, the pedagogical context for its transmission and what counts as valid realisation of knowledge for the assessment of students. Even as I examine curriculum studies as an area of scientific inquiry in Chapter 8, I presently turn to two key concepts – classification and framing, with which Bernstein and colleagues analyse socio-institutional pedagogy. Daniels clarifies that for Bernstein,

> Curriculum was analysed not in terms of contents but in terms of relation *between* its categories (subjects and units). Pedagogic practice again was not to be analysed in terms of its contents but in terms of the control over the selection, sequencing, pacing and criteria of communication in the transmitter/acquirer relation. It is apparent that the curriculum is regarded as an example of a social division of labour and pedagogic practice as its constituent social relations through which the specialisation of that social division (subjects, units of the curriculum) are transmitted and expected to be acquired. (Daniels, 2001, p. 136, emphasis in original)

PEDAGOGICAL PERSPECTIVES

Daniels' assertion above assists in carrying out pedagogical analysis by practitioners in two ways. *First* he allows for a focus on aspects other than the commonly held notion that content knowledge of teachers alone is cause for disappointing outcomes of teaching. What is suggested is an examination of the relations between subjects like politics and history say, or science and mathematics. *Second* he draws attention to teachers having control on the criteria that constitute successful delivery of any curriculum in terms of answers to questions like the what, when, how and why of any pedagogical practice. This allows teaching of any curriculum to be conceptualised in terms of the agency teachers could have. Grasping curricular relations and practitioner agency thus becomes grounds for bringing about pedagogical and institutional change.

Daniels goes on to elaborate on the two notions that enabled Bernstein to shed light and move the above discussion forward. By *classification* Bernstein refers to the manner in which various categories within a curricular subject are insulated or not from one another. For example is the teaching of geometry and trigonometry sharply distinguished from each other or taught as an inter-related cohesive whole. If distinguished in rigid terms the classification would be termed as strong and if not, the classification would be termed as weak. By *framing* Bernstein refers to the manner in which communication between teachers and students or parents and children, is regulated in pedagogical relations. When framing is strong, the teacher explicitly delineates various features of pedagogical communication, like when and who could speak during instruction. When framing is weak, students are given more control in relation to what is said and done, as encouraged in recent times. Framing thus defines what counts as legitimate discourse in any pedagogical practice.

A study of classification and framing is both feasible and revealing of discourses within institutions that shape the pedagogical experiences of students, both across schools and within administrative boundaries like primary, middle and high school. These could be revealing equally of the many convictions strongly held by teachers in relation to the progression of teaching across subject curricula and school grades. Daniels himself makes the case for attention to the following areas,

> Thus the following issues may be regarded as points for development in contemporary post-Vygotskian theory and research (1) insufficient empirical study of socio-institutional effects, (2) tendency to under-theorise differences between schools in terms of institutional effects on the social formation of mind, (3) lack of theory of structure of discourse as a cultural artefact, (4) lack of theory of constitution and recontextualisation of the psychological tool / cultural artefact. (Daniels, 2001, p. 135)

In Daniels having drawn on Vygotsky and Bernstein, I find it pertinent to also examine how each of them conceptualised the notion of pedagogy. For Vygotsky any pedagogical approach was always subject to wider social, cultural and political influences,

> Pedagogics is never and was never politically indifferent, since, willingly or unwillingly, through its own work on the psyche, it has always adopted a particular social pattern, political line, in accordance with the dominant social class that has guided its interests. (Vygotsky, 1997, as in Daniels, 2007, p. 307)

On his part, Bernstein offered the following operational definition,

> Pedagogy is a sustained process whereby somebody(s) acquires new forms or develops existing forms of conduct, knowledge, practice and criteria, from somebody(s) or something deemed to be an appropriate provider and evaluator. Appropriate either from the point of view of the acquirer or by some other body(s) or both. (Bernstein, 1999, as in Daniels 2007, p. 308)

The issue of students interests often left unarticulated and implicit, which the dominant class in any society instil in the kind of pedagogy advocated in educational institutions, is thus key to changing the socio-institutional pedagogy that is prevalent and considered normative. One could thus interrogate if Willis' lads could have had the opportunity of experiencing a different kind of pedagogical practice. My anecdotal experience both in Sweden and India is that students see schools failing them in two key subjects, mathematics in both nations besides Swedish in Sweden and English in India. I find the socio-institutional aspects of pedagogy to thus deserve much greater attention. More recently Daniels argues,

> When we talk in institutions, history enters the flow of communication through the invisible or implicit mediation of the institutional structures. *There is therefore a need to analyse and codify the mediational structures as they deflect and direct attention of participants and as they are shaped through interactions which they also shape.* In this sense, combining the intellectual legacies of Bernstein and Vygotsky permits the development of cultural-historical analysis of the invisible or implicit mediational properties of institutional structures which themselves are transformed through the actions of those whose interactions are influenced by them. (Daniels, 2012, pp. 59–59, emphasis added)

Even as I draw upon Wertsch's notion of explicit and implicit mediation to conduct instructional interventions with teachers I collaborated with, I recognise the notion of mediation which Daniels engages with to be of an institutional grain size, beyond classroom instruction in analytical scope. It is possible such insight might have eluded educational research and needs rightful attention from us practitioners. Having pointed to the value and premise of such an approach, I now turn to classroom pedagogies whose categorisation may be another useful starting point.

5   Pedagogical Categories

It was Lotta's manner of conducting interventions in her classroom that drew my attention to various categories of pedagogy that may be utilised by practitioners. I found her own pedagogical practice neither rehearsed nor something we would discuss before hand. Based on the instructional objectives of each of our interventions, I would let her instincts guide the choices she made on how she and her students would together achieve the goals at hand. As with frameworks that nuanced how we collaborated as teacher and researcher and elaborated in Chapter 9, I had also been on the look out for frameworks that could allow for greater grasp of classroom pedagogy. Familiar with Roland Tharp's work discussed in Chapter 4, in due course I came to his writing with Stephanie Dalton titled *Standards for pedagogy: Research, theory and practice*. Building on their earlier premise that teaching is assisting the performance of students in their zpd Dalton and Tharp, as with Moll in Chapter 4, focus on the taking part by students in social and cultural activities and point out,

> The CHAT approach emphasizes that the learner's interaction with materials and activity occurs primarily in a social context of relationships. In fact, that social context is the major constituent of the activity itself. As people (adults and children) act and talk together, minds are under constant construction, particularly for the novice and the young. *The social processes by which minds are formed must be understood as the very stuff of education.* In teaching/learning interactions, development and learning proceed best when assistance is provided that permits a learner to perform at a level higher than would be possible alone. (Dalton & Tharp, 2002, p. 181, emphasis added)

Drawing on literature which demonstrates the key role of social contexts in leading development and allowing educational access for all students, Dalton and Tharp arrive at five principles that meet objectives outlined above. While acknowledging these to not necessarily draw upon CHAT perspectives, they use CHAT to summarise these principles in a cohesive and powerful manner. Dalton and Tharp view these principles to serve as guidelines for practitioners, besides facilitate individual reflection on the effects and outcomes of their use. These five principles are,

> (1) Joint Productive Activity (JPA): teachers and students producing together, (2) Developing Language and Literacy Across the Curriculum (LLD), (3) Making Meaning: connecting school to students' lives (MM), (4) Teaching Complex Thinking: Cognitive Challenge (CC), (5) Teaching Through Instructional Conversation (IC). (Dalton & Tharp, 2002, p. 182)

In discussing each of the above principles as pedagogical categories, I offer examples from five interventions I helped carry out. It goes without saying that neither does classroom pedagogy across various local contexts subscribe to these five principles alone, nor are these categories the only ways of grasping pedagogical contexts. In fact while analysing Olaf and Knut's conduct of *When together* and *How Heavy* as instructional tasks subsequent to doctoral work, I deployed Engeström's triangular activity as unit of analysis on one occasion (Gade, 2014) and Dalton and Tharp's category of joint productive activity on another (Gade, 2015). I presently extend such analysis by conceiving each of these tasks as exemplifying the categories of meaning making and cognitive challenge in discussion that follows. Such analytical repertoire is demonstrative of the potential these categories have in aiding practitioner reflection.

Dalton and Tharp's *first* category of *joint productive activity* (JPA) is organised by the teacher to accomplish a joint product within instruction, in collaboration with her students. Besides making room for both time and increased communication amongst students, organised in groupings she finds appropriate, the teacher also participates in the JPA to maximise her students' development. This social context allows for intersubjectivity and sustained discourse towards arriving at the joint product. Tomas' conduct of a five task formative intervention greater detailed in Chapter 9, echoed principles of JPA (Gade & Forsgren, 2019). By the time his students participated in the last three tasks, we had established a routine which enabled them to suggest, consult, guess and refute each other's suggestions. Tomas and me each guided such manner of discussion which emerged in respective groups in Task 3, allowing us opportunity to assist students' performance and lead their development. While such assistance brought forth mathematical thinking, their transformative identity as well as emotion was evidenced by the time we conducted Task 5.

The *second* category of *developing language and literacy across the curriculum* (LLD) allows the teacher to shift the attention of her students within instruction, to the manner in which academic language is different from language used in their everyday. Under watchful guidance and by means of eliciting, probing, questioning, praising and at times restating students' responses, the teacher lays emphasis on the social context in which oral and written language is used. Lotta's use of vocabulary from the mathematics textbook utilised in her classroom, besides words her students thought belonged to the subject of mathematics, were both basis for an intervention in which students were asked to pose mathematical problems. Greater detailed in Chapter 9, our problem posing intervention echoed principles of LLD (Gade & Blomqvist, 2015). Herein students posed questions in dyads with words that were handed to them on slips of paper. When each dyad read out the question they had posed, Lotta would rhetorically ask – Is this a question? The intervention began with students using words handed to them, but soon developed to their challenging one another about solutions to questions others had posed.

The *third* category of *making meaning: connecting school to students' lives* (MM) allows teachers to design instructional activities based upon what students already know from their home, community or school. Such activities can be tailored to suit impending pedagogical aims like students working alone at times or working in groups. Drawing upon what is prior known makes the activity meaningful to students who can learn or revisit that which may be academically new. Greater detailed in Chapter 3, Olaf and Knut's conduct of *How Heavy* can be seen as an example of MM (Gade, 2014). Its pedagogical design was prudent in two ways – *first*, it called on the experience of students with the process of weighing objects in their everyday and *second*, it was used by Olaf and Knut to introduce the topic of algebra within their instruction. The use of different kinds of weighing balances in various inscriptions offered by student groups while attempting the group-task, besides the use of algebra by some of them enabled Olaf and Knut to meet with both aims.

The fourth category of *teaching complex thinking: cognitive challenge* (CC) allows the teacher to design instructional activity in which students have opportunity to see the whole picture as basis for understanding the parts. This challenges students' performance in two ways – *first*, arriving at a solution to complex tasks demands more than from merely recalling their memory of routine facts, *second* and in line with CHAT, the level of cognitive challenge may be defined by the limit set for what is possible by students to achieve with other's assistance in their zpd. By utilising CC teachers can surmise the kind of prior learning students bring to tasks, which becomes valuable basis for them to design future activity as well. Greater detailed in Chapter 3, Olaf and Knut's conduct of *When together* echoes key principles of CC (again Gade, 2014). By utilising this task to initiate cooperation of students in respective groups, each of them had opportunity to gauge the prior cognitive abilities which students brought to this task. Not necessarily calling for mathematical reasoning, student groups went about solving this task by using black and white dots in some cases and lines drawn by pen and pencil in another. Demanding students to think out of the box as it were, one group even suggested that the given group-task was in fact a trick question.

The *final* category of *teaching through instructional conversation* (IC) allows the teacher to lay focus on students' classroom talk, in greater measure than her own. Guided by the content of a specific goal she has in mind, her role here lies in guiding students by listening to them, seeking clarification, praising if needed, restating students' responses in more appropriate forms and negotiating turn taking, all in a bid to pursue the particular goal she has. Apart from encouraging students to be thoughtful, account for their views and offer rationale, the teacher has opportunity to draw upon students' everyday knowledge. Greater detailed in Chapter 9, Lotta's conduct of an exploratory talk based intervention was in line with pedagogical principles of IC (Gade & Blomqvist, 2018). Paired in dyads, Lotta's students at first discussed their responses to improbable questions in relation to the topic of measurement and measures, before exploring their responses with the rest of their peers in a plenary. Lotta's role was key in facilitating students' use of talk to externalise their thoughts, gauge how they sounded and see what others made of them.

The potential of the five pedagogical categories to guide the conduct of interventions by practitioners and assist in *their* reflecting on outcomes realised, makes them and other categories which might be conceived worthy of CHAT driven developmental research. Dalton and Tharp view practitioner competence in pedagogy as key to quality teaching, which besides being socially productive for them and students, is also generative of pedagogical theory arising from everyday practice.

6 Leading Activity across Ages

I follow my dwelling upon socio-institutional pedagogy and pedagogical categories with a third aspect of equal significance, which is the kind of activity which has potential to *lead* the cultural-historical development of students. I have myself begun research into this aspect only recently and argue for its rich potential based on Yuriy Karpov's (2003) writing *Development through the lifespan: A neo-Vygotskian approach*. While in Chapter 4, I drew on Karpov to highlight differences between everyday and academic concepts and the role of the latter in creating a zpd, my present interest is to dwell upon development across a student's lifespan. Karpov's construct of *leading activity* draws attention to that kind of activity which when conducted has most potential to lead development at different ages of a child, from infancy to adolescence.

Understanding Karpov's notion of leading activity is well served by grasping the manner in which Vygotsky conceived human development of a child dialectically, in relation to one's environment. Vygotsky argued that commencing with a mother's uterus a child's immediate environment continues to be limited and circumscribed soon after birth. A wider world opens when (s)he visits the front of the house as well as the street where she lives, which enables the child to enter into new relationships with others. The child next encounters various kinds of environments at school. Vygotsky thus pointed to the way in which the environment for any child keeps changing, as the child passes from one stage to another. On the role of this environment Vygotsky pointed out,

> The greatest characteristic feature of child development is that this development is achieved under particular conditions of interaction with the environment, where this ideal and final form ... is not only already there in advance in the environment and from the vary start in contact with the child, but actually interacts and exerts a real influence on the primary form, on the first steps of the child's development. *Something which is only supposed to take shape at the very end of development, somehow influences the very first steps in this development.* (Vygotsky, 1994, p. 348, emphasis in original)

Vitally pointing out that any child's environment is also the very source of development for any child and not merely its setting, Vygotsky draws attention to an aspect often misunderstood – that given adequate time, the child will be able to do things which are expected of her, on her own. A child's ability to speak Spanish or Telugu or any other mother tongue, Vygotsky would argue, is because these languages are spoken in their ideal or final form in the environment in which these children grow up. The ability of a child to interact with a form that is expected of her at the end of development and present from the very start of the process is key, Vygotsky underscored, to cultural-historical development.

Of relevance to the above discussion is also the fact that in Vygotskian inquiry the child is positioned as subject of the environment in which she or he is being nurtured. Along with critical issues of equitable access to resources, besides the fact that children might get to have a say or not with regards to the manner in which they would like to be a subject in any nurturing activity, CHAT perspectives recognise that a child's personality is also under construction by the child. Vygotsky argues that the changes in any child's needs and motives over time are the least conscious and voluntary part of their growing personality, and that,

> in the transition from age level to age level, new incentives and new motives develop in the child; in other words the motive forces of his activity undergo a re-evaluation. That which was essentially important, controlling, for the child becomes relative and unimportant at the subsequent stage.
>
> *The restructuring of needs and motives and the revaluation are basic factors in the transition from age level to age level.* Other things begin to interest the child, he develops other activity, and his consciousness is restructured, if we understand consciousness as the relation of the child to the environment. (Vygotsky, 2004, p. 499, emphasis added)

Vygotsky's quotes above lay emphasis on two aspects, *first* that a child's environment is the source of his or her development and *second* that the manner in which he or she relates to that environment is the very basis for his or her individual consciousness.

Yet a third aspect is highlighted by Holbrook Mahn, who underscores the fact that Vygotskian development does not subscribe to a linear model of incremental growth and progression. Mahn argues,

> Vygotsky's dialectical approach contrasts with evolutionary, linear approaches that analyze incremental growth but do not explain the creation of the new psychological structures that define the age levels. ... the process of motion, change, and development. Vygotsky felt that this essence was more apparent in critical periods than in stable periods in which the growth is slower, more incremental, and beneath the surface and thus harder to analyse. Vygotsky paraphrases Marx to underscore the need to discover the inner logic of development: 'If the form of appearance and essence of things coincided directly, then all science would be superfluous.' (Vygotsky, 1998, p. 54, as in Mahn, 2003, pp. 121–122)

Mahn draws attention above to the presence of two kinds of periods in the Vygotskian model – *stable periods* in which a child's growth is slower, incremental and harder to analyse, besides *critical periods* wherein profound changes take place in a child's physical, mental and social development. While

PEDAGOGICAL PERSPECTIVES

there is observable calm when children pass through stable periods, the kinds of upheaval discernible when a child is going through critical periods is exemplified say when children begin to talk, walk, negotiate their first encounter with school, commence thinking in conceptual ways, besides exhibit turbulence alongside gaining self-awareness during adolescence. Unlike stable periods, periods of crisis are thus characterised by major changes, shifts and discontinuities in a relatively short time, so much so that the resulting basic traits of a child's personality undergo complete change.

Mahn highlights a few other aspects in addition. *First* and in line with Vygotsky's argument that a child's consciousness being her relation to the environment, Mahn points out that the formation of new structures during critical periods determine the nature of newer environments as well as her psychological relation to her own life. *Second,* pedagogical styles which previously seemed appropriate now appear unappealing and difficult, since these do not keep up with the kind of rapid changes which are taking place in a child's personality. *Third* and vitally that in school age children, critical periods might correspond to a drop in interest and performance in a student's schoolwork. *Finally* and seeking greater grasp and understanding both by practitioners and research, is the fact that while critical periods have stable periods on either side of them, neither of these were clearly cut off nor definable in precise ways.

My dwelling on stable and critical periods in a Vygotskian conception prepares ground for a vital question which Karpov raises, which is an explanation for *why* children transit from one period of development to the next. Here Karpov draws on other neo-Vygotskian scholars as well to argue that children's development occurs in the course of activities that are oriented to the external world, carried out jointly with adults and peers. In children making changes or modifying their situation as part of the problem and tools they encounter in these activities, as also argued by Cole and Scribner in Chapter 3, new motives develop or ripen in them. These motives result in propelling their taking part in newer activities. Karpov thus articulates his construct of *leading activity*,

> A certain activity is defined as *leading* for the given age period because mediation within this activity produces major developmental accomplishments in children, which provide the basis for their transition to the next period, to the next leading activity.
>
> ... In the course of mediation within this activity, children develop the new leading motive, and new mental processes and abilities, which outgrow their current leading activity. This creates the basis for their transition to the new leading activity, which is specific to the next period of development. (Karpov, 2003, pp. 140–141)

In my ongoing discussion on pedagogy, four aspects stand out in the arguments laid out thus far. *First* conceiving the role of the environment as a source of development. Speaking a certain language is vital to any child's speaking the very same language. *Second* being prepared to view development as a process inclusive of both stable and critical periods. That is, there can be times when the personality of a child changes quite rapidly or not at all for long periods of time. *Third*, paying attention to pedagogic activity that leads a child's development. What may interest a child as an infant may cease to interest a middle school student. *Finally*, recognising leading activities for specific age periods as being situated in local contexts and concrete cultures. The age by which children are seen as passing into adulthood, varies with both gender and culture. I consider each of these propositions in relation to cultural-historical development to be fertile ground for further research. A fledgling study conducted on these very lines helped me argue for greater understanding of the nature of crisis children routinely face as students, so that practitioners in turn can recognise and ameliorate their incidence for students within everyday schooling (Saran & Gade, 2016). In light of these arguments I now turn to Karpov's description of the kind of leading activity that has benefits for leading the development of children.

During *the first year of a child's life* when the child is biologically helpless, the relation of infants to both reality and themselves is via the mediation of others. Adults become the psychological centre of the infant and the activity of *emotional caregiving* by adults becomes their leading activity. Needs develop and the gratification of their psychological needs are supplanted by their ability to communicate with their caregivers via their emotions. Aided by a positive attitude towards them, infants become interested in the external world which is presented to them, also preparing them for joint object-centred activity.

In *the second and third years of life* the nonspecific manipulations of objects like shaking and banging decrease and children begin to use objects in accordance with their social meanings e.g. feeding themselves as well as their doll with a spoon. Under the guidance of adults children become capable of making object substitutions as well, like treating a cubical object as body soap say. Such separation of thought from objects becomes basis for development of their symbolic thought. *Object-centred joint activity with adults* thus becomes leading activity for toddlers. The need for communication in the course of such activity leads in addition to the development of children's speech. Resulting in their ability to acquire language, this last plays a major role in the development of all mental processes besides achieving self-regulation through one's private speech. A collective of these outcomes prepare children for socio-dramatic play, which is the leading activity that follows.

PEDAGOGICAL PERSPECTIVES

For *three to six year olds* the world of human relations becomes very attractive, one children want to become part of. Unable to do so, they begin to explore social relations under the guidance of adults in *socio-dramatic play*, which is now their leading activity. In socio-dramatic play adults have the opportunity to act out various role and familiarise children with what doctors or train drivers do say. Following rules implicit in such social roles, children develop (1) an ability to control their own besides one another's behaviour, (2) an ability to take another person's point of view into consideration, besides (3) be dissatisfied with not being able to take part in the real world. Able to take part in symbolic thought, six year olds develop the prerequisites for learning at middle school.

During *middle childhood, learning in educational settings* is leading activity in the way Vygotsky argued all along i.e. by good instruction leading or marching ahead of students' development. Such instruction allows them to importantly bridge their everyday concepts with academic concepts that are introduced. In being able to use academic concepts as psychological tools, students' thinking now has opportunity to become more independent from personal experience. As mentioned by Karpov in Chapter 4, students can now make the transition from being practitioners to becoming theorists, and begin to exercise formal-logical thought. This last allows students to take part in various interactions with various peers during the coming period of adolescence.

In exercising formal-logical thought during the *period of adolescence* students become capable of self-analysis, a feature which enables them to reflect on their feelings as well as their place in the wider world around them. By adolescence, children develop the ability to integrate cognitive, social, emotional and motivational aspects of their individual selves. By way of *interacting with peers* as leading activity, adolescent students use social norms, practical models and human relations to create their own selves, as well as the wider world they live in. The ability of adolescents to internalise social standards and use them for self-analysis leads the development of self awareness in adolescents and their personal identity, preparing them to transit to adulthood.

I hasten to add that while offering the above trajectory of leading activities, Karpov draws together arguments which are in need for greater empirical evidence and theoretical work. He is aware of shortcomings in his insightful construct and acknowledges the guidelines he provides to be far from cast in stone. My own attempts at understanding the potential of leading activity as a CHAT construct took place in two recent studies. *First* via the use of peer interaction by Tomas' grade eight adolescent students (Gade & Forsgren, 2019). Such interaction was basis for active participation in three of the five tasks we conducted. *Second* was a more recent study which viewed the activity of reading aloud with preschool students as their leading activity. Herein Pradita the teacher was able to promote language learning via socio-dramatic play (Nambiar & Gade, 2021). Either study examined the nature of activity which had potential to lead students' cultural-historical development. With respect to such development while Mahn draws attention to the existence of both stable and critical periods for children, Karpov highlights the kind of activity which needs to be carried out pedagogically. Yet the dynamics of leading activity in stable as well as critical periods of children's development, seems wide open for engrossing and rewarding research. I now draw on my own teaching experience with middle school students.

7 The Tone of Teaching: Coda

As a practicing teacher of mathematics I would conclude daily teaching by setting my students a few questions for homework, so that they would have occasion to work independently at techniques we had utilised during the day. Towards the end of reading these out to them one day, a student commented – And that will be the last question. On asking how he knew that was the case, he quipped – Tone teacher, your tone! Years later, I came upon and felt compelled to read Max van Manen's book *The tone of teaching*. Introducing me to phenomenology or a study of how human beings experience their world, van Manen articulated many an aspect I found relevant in relation to pedagogy and research writing.

Manen's text had the elusive quality of articulating aspects less spoken about in wider literature, like the relational demands on a teacher and of being tactful as a practitioner – the ability of knowing what to say and what not to say, besides what to mention and what not to with children. Manen views pedagogy to be both a complex and subtle affair in which general principles were difficult to formulate. Yet he argues,

> Some adults seem to strike just the right tone with children. Others constantly flounder in their dealings with them. The difference is not necessarily that some adults have read more about parenting or teaching than others. Reading educational literature can give us important external knowledge, but that knowledge is external. It does not necessarily make us more thoughtful or more tactful in our day-to-day relations with young people. ...
>
> *Pedagogical thoughtfulness is sustained by a certain kind of seeing, of listening, of responding.* Out of this basis of thoughtfulness, tact in our

PEDAGOGICAL PERSPECTIVES

relationship with children may grow. (van Manen, 1986, p. 12, emphasis added)

Besides drawing attention to the kind of tone one needs to utilise with children, by drawing upon one's pedagogical thoughtfulness, van Manen speaks also about the need children have of *being seen* by teachers. As with thoughtfulness, he goes on to explain,

> Being seen is more than being acknowledged. For a child it means *experiencing* being seen by the *teacher*. It means being confirmed as existing, as being a person and a learner. Not all seeing has this quality, of course. ...
>
> A real teacher *knows* how to see children – notices a shyness, a certain mood, a feeling of expectation. Real seeing in this sense uses more than eyes. ... So to really *see* a child at the beginning and completion of each day is to give that child his or her place in specific time and space. (van Manen, 1986, p. 21, emphasis in original)

In addition to speaking about pedagogical thoughtfulness and the need for children to be seen by their teacher, van Manen argues classrooms to be lived spaces in which children explore aspects of the human world via, *atmosphere* – the way in which a space is lived and experienced, besides *mood* – as set by bodily gesture and tone of voice. Van Manen makes his point with a moving example,

> When the teacher reads Oscar Wilde's story *The Happy Prince*, a mood of spiritual beauty and sensitivity interweaves with the mood of storytelling itself. The teacher's voice breaks a little toward the end, and it deepens the catharsis for quite a few of the children. How can love sacrifice itself so beautifully, and yet so sadly for the little swallow?
>
> When the teacher slowly closes the book, there is silence in the room. Even those children who were not really touched by the story refrain from talking for a moment. This silence has mood as well. (van Manen, 1986, pp. 36–37)

Located at some distance in time from my own teaching experiences, I felt great kinship with van Manen above and soon turned to his other title *Researching lived experience*. This book introduced me to the practice of hermeneutic phenomenology as a human science – helping me recognise too that interpretive phenomenological research and theorising could not be separated from the textual practice of writing. This view challenged my own research writing from then on.

162   CHAPTER 6

While van Manen's earlier drew my attention to tone, thoughtfulness, tact, being seen, atmosphere and mood, he now argued the process of writing as central to cultivating *a critical pedagogical competence*. As different from pursuing a natural science, van Manen argued,

> The end of human science research for educators is a critical pedagogical competence: knowing how to act tactfully in pedagogic situations on the basis of a carefully edified thoughtfulness. To that end hermeneutic phenomenological research reintegrates part and whole, the contingent and the essential, value and desire. ... It makes us thoughtfully aware of the consequential in the inconsequential, the significant in the taken-for-granted. Phenomenological descriptions, if done well, are compelling and insightful. The eloquence of the texts may contrast sharply with the toil, messiness, and difficulties involved in the research/writing process. (van Manen, 1990, p. 8)

Van Manen goes on to elaborate the above manner of dialectic between research and writing to be an interplay between many a feature including (1) attending to experiences that interest us, (2) investigating those that are lived, (3) reflecting on aspects which characterise the phenomena, (4) describing them through writing and rewriting, besides (5) balancing parts and whole of any research context. On taking action full of thought and thought full of action, van Manen considers our ability to write in a reflective manner about our practice of living as practitioners, to allow us to be engaged in a more *reflective praxis*. He concludes,

> Writing tends to orient us away from contextual particulars toward a more universal sphere. As we try to capture the meaning of some lived experience in written text, the text in turn assumes a life of its own. Thus writing places us at a distance from the practical immediacy of lived life by being forgetful of its context. ... But as we are able to gain in this manner a deeper sense of the meanings embedded in some isolated aspect of practice, we are also being prepared to become more discerning of the meaning of new life experiences. (van Manen, 1990, p. 128)

Since encountering van Manen's writings, thanks to my student's quip, I have become conscious of walking the thoughtful path van Manen sheds light upon both in conducting research and its subsequent reporting. With regards to my present writing I have in particular placed focus on the relationships I come to

PEDAGOGICAL PERSPECTIVES

perceive between part and whole of any research context, a principle shared with ascending to the concrete in CHAT perspectives, besides the exercise of reflecting on my prior praxis towards its thoughtful realisation in the future as well.

References

Baker, D. P., & LeTendre, G. K. (2005). *National differences global similarities: World culture and the future of schooling.* Stanford University Press.

Beder, S., Varney, W., & Gosden, R. (2009). *This little kiddy went to market: the corporate capture of childhood.* Pluto Press.

Bernstein, B. (1999). Official knowledge and pedagogic identities. In F. Christie (Ed.), *Pedagogy and the shaping of consciousness: Linguistic and social processes.* Cassell.

Crozier, G. (2000). *Parents and schools: Partners or protagonists?* Trentham Books.

Dalton, S., & Tharp, R. (2002). Standards for pedagogy, research and practice. In G. Wells & G. Claxton (Eds.), *Learning for life in the 21st century: Sociocultural Perspectives on the future of education* (pp. 181–194). Blackwell Publishers.

Daniels, H. (2001). *Vygotsky and pedagogy.* RoutledgeFalmer.

Daniels, H. (2007). Pedagogy. In H. Daniels, M. Cole, & J. V. Wertsch (Eds.), *The Cambridge companion to Vygotsky* (pp. 307–331). Cambridge University Press.

Daniels, H. (2012). Vygotsky and Bernstein. In H. Daniels (Ed.) *Vygotsky and sociology.* Routledge.

Gade, S. (2012). To choose or not to choose mathematics: Voices of students schooling at a gymnasium. In G. H. Gunnarsdóttir, F. Hreinsdóttir, G. Pálsdóttir, M. Hannula, M. Hannula-Sormunen, E. Jablonka, U. T. Jankvist, A. Ryve, P. Valero, & K. Wæge (Eds.), *Proceedings of NORMA 11: The sixth Nordic conference on mathmatics education* (pp. 267–277). University of Iceland Press.

Gade, S. (2014). Analysing two group-tasks and a collaborative classroom practice with Engeström's activity theory. In P. Barmby (Ed.) *Proceedings of the British Society for Research into Learning Mathematics (BSRLM), 34*(1), 43–48.

Gade, S. (2015). Activity settings and pedagogical categories. *Research in Mathematics Education, 17*(2), 148–149.

Gade, S., & Blomqvist, C. (2015). From problem posing to posing problems by way of explicit mediation in Grades four and five. In F. M. Singer, N. Ellerton, & J. Cai (Eds.), *Mathematical problem posing: From research to effective practice* (pp. 195–213). Springer.

Gade, S., & Blomqvist, C. (2018). Investigating everyday measures through exploratory talk: Whole classroom intervention and landscape study at Grade four. *Cultural Studies of Science Education, 13*(1), 235–252.

Gade, S., & Forsgren, T. (2019). Realising transformative agency and student identity: Meaningful practical activity based formative intervention at grade eight. *Cultural Studies of Science Education, 14*(4), 897–914.

Illeris, K. (2007). *How we learn: Learning and non-learning in school and beyond.* Routledge.

Karpov, Y. (2003). Development through the lifespan: A neo-Vygotskian approach. In A. Kozulin, B. Gidnis, V. Agayev, & S. Miller (Eds.), *Vygotsky's educational theory in cultural context* (pp. 138–155). Cambridge University Press.

Mahn, H. (2003). Period's in child development: Vygotsky's perspective. In A. Kozulin, B. Gidnis, V. Agayev, & S. Miller (Eds.), *Vygotsky's educational theory in cultural context* (pp. 119–137). Cambridge University Press.

Nambiar, P., & Gade, S. (2021). Reading aloud as a leading activity with preschool students. *LEARNing Landscapes, 14*(1), 265–275.

Saran, R., & Gade, S. (2016). *Examining social situation of development, with two students of mathematics at grade four, in different national contexts* [Paper]. AERA 2016 annual meeting, AERA online paper repository.

van Manen, M. (1986). *The tone of teaching.* Heinemann.

van Manen, M. (1990). *Researching lived experience: Human science for an action sensitive pedagogy.* State University of New York Press.

Vygotsky, L. S. (1994). The problem of the environment. In R. van der Veer & J. Valsiner (Eds.), *The Vygotsky reader* (pp. 338–354). Blackwell.

Vygotsky, L. S. (1997). *Educational psychology.* St. Lucie Press.

Vygotsky, L. S. (1998). *The collected works of L. S. Vygotsky* (Vol. 5). *Child psychology.* Plenum.

Vygotsky, L. S. (2004). The crisis at age seven. In R. W. Rieber & D. K. Robinson (Eds.), *The essential Vygotsky* (pp. 491–499). Kluwer Academic/Plenum Publishers.

Willis, P. (1977). *Learning to labour: How working class kids get working class jobs.* Gower Publishing Company.

Willis, P. (1978). *Profane culture.* Routledge & Kegan Paul.

Willis, P. (2000). *The ethnographic imagination.* Polity Press.

Willis, P. (2003). Foot soldiers of modernity: The dialectics of cultural consumption and the 21st-century school. *Harvard Educational Review, 73*(3), 390–415.

CHAPTER 7

Critical Perspectives

Dialectical Inquiry

1 Preamble

Besides the need to be critical following my school visits as a researcher, the need for me to be critical was strewn along my life's journey as well. With my being a girl child at first and choosing to be a teacher later on I came to experience the deficit perspective held against both in society. There was also my training for a Master's in Physics on one hand and learning to become a teacher over time on the other. Acquainting myself with the ways of practicing a social and humanistic science in contrast to training in a natural science, needed me to be critical. It was also the case that before enrolling for a Bachelors in Science at college, I did not have to pay tuition fees as a girl student at a state run school in India. By this I benefited from government policy aimed at retaining girls at school in the 1970s. The many streams of knowledge we were getting acquainted with had in addition different status in society, both economic and social. Over the years, it was thus not difficult for me to become increasingly aware of the sheer complexity of educational realities which we students face, one that each of us practitioners have to contend with in our teaching.

Yet I have felt encouraged and been hopeful that meaningful change is possible. At the school I myself taught at, I witnessed first hand how the arts could be deployed to initiate lasting humanistic change. Realising change in concrete educational practices of teachers I later collaborated with, has also meant that I borrowed from social, educational, humanistic and practitioner genres of research, each with their own methodology. It thus came to pass that my attention to critical perspectives has been tempered by appreciating Bakhtin's wisdom that art and life are not one and do need to unite to answer our calling as practitioners.

As part of doctoral training, our methodology course was offered by Barbro Grevholm, an experienced mathematics teacher researcher, who introduced us to a volume edited by Steinar Kvale titled *Issues of validity in qualitative research*. Blown away by the title of Kvale's own chapter *To validate is to question*, I then had occasion to view methodological questions which I had during my professional trajectory, in the language and concepts of educational

© KONINKLIJKE BRILL NV, LEIDEN, 2022 | DOI:10.1163/9789004512160_007

166   CHAPTER 7

research. Helping me come to the realisation that it was a pragmatic approach that best suited my aims, Kvale lent greater clarity to the vital issue of validity in research that made one's methodological approach and claims which ensued, acceptable to the research community at large. Largely qualitative besides social and humanistic in scope, Kvale explained that contemporary conceptions of validity had replaced earlier notions which had emphasised measurement at first, testing for empirical correspondence later on and theoretical interpretation subsequently. I found my CHAT based research to meet with the later conceptions of validity that Kvale was pointing to. In a convincing manner he made me look beyond a central tenet I held while conducting experiments in Physics, wherein a correspondence between phenomena being studied and measurements being taken were adequate criteria for validity. Kvale pointed out,

> Within recent hermeneutical and pragmatic philosophy, the conception of truth as a correspondence between language descriptions and an independent objective reality has been undermined. Knowledge is not a mirror of an objective nature, consciousness is not a copy or a representation of an independent world. The distinction between a social reality and a language description of that reality is artificial; rather, *language is constitutive of the social reality, it defines what kind of reality it is.* (Kvale, 1989, p. 76, emphasis added)

In moving beyond criteria of correspondence to factor in aspects which constitute rather than measure reality, a stand that narrative inquiry also echoes, I found Kvale's criteria for validity to be in consonance with my own CHAT based interests. I found myself agreeing in particular with his notion of *pragmatic validity* which literally meant, to make true or to demonstrate effectiveness of research in terms of the actions practitioners take during its conduct. Allowing me to nuance the notion of educational action which I dwelt upon in Chapter 1, Kvale argued,

> *Knowledge is action rather than observation.* To pragmatists, truth is whatever assists us to take actions that produce the desired results. In his second thesis on Feuerbach, Marx stated that the question of whether human thought can lead to objective truth is not a theoretical but practical one. *Man must prove the truth, that is, the reality and power of his thinking in practice.* And the eleventh thesis is more pointed – the philosophers have only interpreted the world differently, what matter is changing the world. (Kvale, 1989, p. 86, emphasis added)

CRITICAL PERSPECTIVES

In sections that follow, I engage with writings that have allowed me to be critical in the Marxian and pragmatic sense that Kvale alluded to. I dwell also on the nature of dialectical inquiry which allowed me to take such action in the coda of this chapter. At the 12th *International Congress on Mathematics Education*, I argued this latter stance to enable collective discussion to move beyond research of classroom practice, to *researching* classroom practices via conduct of what Anne Edwards, Peter Gilroy and David Hartley term *close-to-practice research*,

> Close-to-practice research, which keeps its roots in robust theoretical frames can throw light on immediate pedagogical affordances, can highlight tensions and contradictions at the system level and can become integrated as informed problem-solving into professional practice. Additionally it can itself be open to questions from practice that can help disrupt the assumptions that support theory. (Edwards, Gilroy, & Hartley, 2002, p. 123)

In adopting a theory/practice CHAT stance underpinning the above, I had argued it possible for practitioners to have the opportunity to keep alive the vital relationship between two simultaneous aspects central to taking action (1) theory-which-informs with theory-being-built, and (2) existing-practice with steered-practice (Gade, 2012a).

Two other writings influenced my delving into critical perspectives for taking dialectical action outlined above, both of which relate to research conducted by two external opponents of my doctoral thesis. The *first* by Falk Seeger, spoke of how practitioners could grasp theory and practice in a complementary manner while conducting CHAT research. In line with another Marxian premise that the educator must herself be educated, Seeger viewed *practitioner reflexivity* in terms of,

> (1) *the complementarity of theory and praxis is an essential feature of meaning making in the social sciences* (2) the basis of this complementarity is reflexivity in a double sense: in the sense of self-application of theoretical/research results and in the sense of the necessity to take the reflexiveness of the subjects into account (3) praxis is guiding theory (e.g. through requiring that the totality of the situation be grasped in a theoretical/scientific analysis). (Seeger, 2001, p. 51, emphasis added)

I found my *second* though principal opponent Ole Skovsmose, to also speak in favour of his view on *critical mathematics education* at the 10th *International Congress on Mathematics Education,* as follows,

Critical mathematics education refers to concerns which have to do with both research and practice, and a concern for equity and social justice being one of them. Here I want to refer to the following challenges: (1) How do processes of globalisation and ghettoising frame mathematics education? (2) What does it mean to go beyond the assumptions of Modernity? (3) How should 'mathematics in action,' including a mixing of power and mathematics, be interpreted? (4) What forms of suppression can be exercised through mathematics education? (5) How could mathematics education provide empowerment? (Skovsmose, 2004, as in abstract)

Notwithstanding the wisdom of familiarising oneself with research conducted by one's doctoral opponents, my foray with adopting critical perspectives after doctoral research, came with co-teaching a course titled *Science Education* for students crediting their *Masters in Elementary Education* at TISS, Mumbai campus. Highlighting the manner in which masculinist perceptions could distort any scientific enterprise, herein I found Evelyn Fox Keller to argue,

> Feminism ... encourages the use of expertise that has traditionally belonged to women – not simply as a women's perspective but as a critical instrument for examining the roots of those dichotomies that isolate this perspective and deny its legitimacy. It seeks to enlarge our understanding of the history, philosophy, and sociology of science through the inclusion not only of women and their actual experiences but also of those domains of human experience that have been relegated to women, namely, the personal, the emotional and the sexual. (Keller, 1985, p. 9)

My journey with critical perspectives continued at The Graduate Centre, CUNY, where I had occasion to interact with Linda Tuhiwai Smith, who argued at the outset of her talk that while institutions don't remember, people don't forget. In particular, she drew attention to how Western methodological traditions colonised indigenous cultures such as the Maori in New Zealand. In her book titled *Decolonising methodologies: Research and indigenous people*, she thus sought to revitalise indigenous research by examining those themes that were intrinsic to their lives, like negotiating, protecting and celebrating survival. Smith also viewed *theory building* as a way to strategise and take greater control over resistances which people themselves felt and argued,

> *The language of a theory can also be used as a way of organising and determining action.* It helps us to interpret what is being told to us, and to

CRITICAL PERSPECTIVES 169

predict the consequences of what is being promised. Theory can also protect us because it contains within it a way of putting reality into perspective. If it is a good theory it also allows for new ideas and ways of looking at things to be incorporated constantly without the need to search constantly for new theories. (Smith, 1999, p. 38, emphasis added)

Echoing Kavle's view that knowledge was action rather than observation, both Keller and Smith's work was rich preparation for me to next read bell hooks. As a critical theorist, hooks combines her engagement with multiple issues related to race in the US, along with those raised by Paolo Freire whom I engage with in the next section, and the holistic approach which Buddhism forwards. In decided echo to Shanta, the founder of the school I taught at, hooks emphasised the need for learning to be fun, engaging student audiences in body, spirit as well as mind. On *theory building* hooks offers her perspective by saying,

I came to theory because I was hurting – the pain within me was so intense that I could not go on living. *I came to theory desperate, wanting to comprehend – to grasp what was happening around and within me.* Most importantly, I wanted to make the hurt go away. I saw in theory then a location of healing. ...

Theory is not inherently healing, liberatory, or revolutionary. It fulfils this function only when we ask that it do so and direct our theorising toward this end. (hooks, 1994, pp. 59–61, emphasis added)

It was my ability to take action as a teacher and my conducting CHAT informed instructional interventions in ongoing classrooms as researcher, that led me to study critical perspectives more closely. I have found a collective of these to speak forcefully for taking practitioner action in pragmatic and theoretical terms, besides realise as Greene argues in Chapter 1 a world that could be otherwise – more fun, more free, more just, more equal, more humane, more liveable, more reflexive and more democratic. It is towards these ends that I now turn to greater examine the kind of notions which critical inquiry indulges with.

2 Critical Consciousness

The allure of reading and grasping Paolo Freire is that his theorisation of *critical consciousness* draws on his own life's experiences. Dropping out of the middle class for reasons beyond his control, before returning to its fold of greater stability, Freire educated and was in turn educated by the poor he lived and worked with in the interim. His formulations drew on the fact that unlike animals who were submerged in surrounding reality, human beings could conceptualise an objective reality which they could know as well as transform. Arguing us human beings to not merely be *in* the world, but also *with* their world and fellow beings he proclaimed,

> Democracy and democratic education are founded on faith in men, on the belief that they not only can but should discuss the problems of their country, of their continent, their world, their work, the problems of democracy itself. *Education is an act of love, and thus an act of courage.* It cannot fear the analysis of reality or, under pain of revealing itself as a farce, avoid creative discussion. (Freire, 2005a, p. 33, emphasis added)

I found Freire's call for engagement with reality, even if such an effort needs courage and its outcomes disquieting at times, to be leitmotif of his larger efforts at educational theorisation. It is not surprising that Freire sought educators to ask questions, seek answers and take action, so that students could go beyond the very social conditions they felt conditioned by and actively determine themselves. Asking teachers to be ethically grounded and strive for such opportunities, he argued,

> to know how to teach is to create possibilities for the construction and production of knowledge rather than to be engaged simply in a game of transferring knowledge. When I enter a classroom I should be someone who is open to new ideas, open to questions, and open to the curiosities of the students as well as their inhibitions. In other words, I ought to be aware of being a critical and inquiring subject in regard to the task entrusted to me, the task of teaching and not that of transferring knowledge (Freire, 1998, p. 57)

Advocating a progressive outlook, wherein students were positioned as subjects in deciding what to make of their reality, as with Krishnamurti in Chapter 2 and with Stetsenko in Chapter 3, Freire recognised two aspects – *first*, that reality need not be a given but can be changed or transformed, and *second*, that to arrive at the newer objective reality desired, students have to inevitably struggle. Such struggle was conceived as a dialectic between two kinds of actions – denouncing processes of dehumanisation and announcing their new dream. In adopting such an ethico-political stance, one in which students

CRITICAL PERSPECTIVES 171

aspired for radical changes, Freire saw *education as act of intervention* in the world. He maintained,

> The world is not finished. It is always in the process of becoming. The subjectivity with which I dialectically relate to the world, my role in the world, is not restricted to a process of only observing what happens but it also involves my intervention as a subject of what happens in the world. My role in the world is not simply that of someone who registers what occurs but of someone who has an input into what happens. *I am equally subject and object in the historical process.* (Freire, 1998, pp. 72–73, emphasis added)

Recognising human beings to be both subject and object in their process of becoming, Freire clarified that the intense personal struggle and critical intervention he was advocating against poverty, exploitation or even market forces say, were central to students and teachers achieving their humanisation and personal identity as human beings at the same time. In redirecting one's lives to newer realities that one wished for and hoped, transgressing the status quo was thus inevitable.

First published in 1970, Freire's *Pedagogy of the oppressed* (2005b) offers key insights into his overall theorisation, of which I dwell on a selection of concepts in this section. Together, these serve to summarise his purpose in asking everyone especially the disenfranchised, *to name their world* and bring about transformation by means of their *praxis,*

> One of the gravest obstacles to the achievement of liberation is that oppressive reality absorbs those within it and thereby acts to submerge human beings' consciousness. Functionally, oppression is domesticating. To no longer be prey to its force, one must emerge from it and turn upon it. This can be done only by means of the praxis: reflection and action upon the world in order to transform it. (Freire, 2005b, p. 51)

In pursuit of humanisation and identity, for ourselves and fellow beings, Freire asked that we examine the reality in which our consciousness is submerged in, utilising which we could both reflect and take action. It is the culmination of these aspects that he terms as *praxis*, exercising which one can can realise the potential of transforming one's reality and world. Towards achieving such ends, Freire views *individual consciousness as prime mover and method* to bring about and initiate lasting change. In advocating such an introspective stance, he is quick to point out too that human consciousness neither precedes, nor follows the world.

It will thus come as no surprise that for Freire, there was no such thing as a neutral educational process. Teachers and students had the task of collaboratively unveiling, coming to know and re-creating reality. The knowledge they co-created for attaining their personal freedom was thus not pseudo-participation, but *committed involvement*. In adopting such a stance and realising that one's present way of life could be at odds with becoming fully human, Freire highlighted the importance of being and becoming, while posing problems in the world. He thus pointed to the futility of the *banking concept of education* and argued,

> In the banking concept of education, knowledge is a gift bestowed by those who consider themselves knowledgeable upon those whom they consider to know nothing. Projecting an absolute ignorance onto others, a characteristic of the ideology of oppression, negates education and knowledge as processes of inquiry. (Freire, 2005b, p. 72)

The need for *dialogue and communication* to be able to inquire and build knowledge was for Freire an existential necessity, one that eschewed the imposition and consumption of oppressive ideas, towards addressing how the world could be created together. Learning mathematics too in this view, was working in favour of becoming human. He argued,

> *Because dialogue is an encounter among women and men who name the world*, it must not be a situation where some name on behalf of others. It is an act of creation; it must not serve as a crafty instrument for the domination of one person by another. The domination implicit in dialogue is that of the world by the dialoguers; it is conquest of the world for the liberation of humankind. (Freire, 2005b, p. 89, emphasis added)

One can observe that the manner in which Freire conceived critical consciousness, he saw the activity of transforming one's reality and the world by practitioners as not only the dialectic between reflection and action, but also between theory and practice. In the absence of such a dynamic, Freire pointed to the risk of theory being empty verbalism and practice being merely activism. In fact Vianna and Stetsenko rightfully point out that perspectives of both Freire and CHAT,

> revolve around the idea that people produce history and culture while they are reciprocally produced by them. Both perspectives ground

development and learning in collaborative praxis and focus on theorizing consciousness that affords self-regulation and capacity for agentive action. Moreover, both place teaching-learning at the center of human development which crucially depends on a more knowledgeable other, as embodied in Vygotsky's concept of the zone of proximal development, and on the educator as an agent of social change who sets in motion a process of raising critical consciousness, which is at the core of Freire's pedagogy of the oppressed. (Vianna & Stetsenko, 2011, p. 318)

The above outlined synergy of CHAT perspectives and key premise of Freire, both reiterate and reinforce the many aspects which had made my own choice of CHAT attractive, to bring about the kind of transformation found necessary in ongoing instruction. What was aimed at was agentive action and praxis so that people and culture could dialectically produce one another, via collaborating with others – both for making our actions meaningful and developing our respective consciousness. Far from being ideologically neutral there was inbuilt emphasis herein on engaging with one's social reality, besides conceiving human development in those very terms. My reading of Freire thus opened the doors of how and to what end, we as practitioners could engage with the reality we and our students negotiate everyday, especially in the face of an overbearing focus on matters of epistemology in normative curricular documents. I thus turn to greater examine a critical ontology for teachers.

3 Critical Ontology for Teachers

I draw on writings of Joe Kincheloe to dwell on issues that teachers may encounter while adopting critical perspectives in their classrooms. I came to Kincheloe's writings while auditing Ken Tobin's course for doctoral students titled *Logics of inquiry* at The Graduate Centre, CUNY. Before Kincheloe's demise, he and Tobin collaborated with one another and I found their discussions familiar to many there. While I examine Tobin's writings on educational research as bricolage in the final section of this Chapter, I presently focus on the demands critical perspectives can make on teachers and their teaching. I do so by *first* discussing the kind of curriculum which teachers are likely given to teach and *next* discuss the importance of their *ontology* or *being* critical teachers.

Drawing upon Freire and other critical thinkers besides being a critical thinker himself, Kincheloe argues that as human beings we not only exist in interrelationships, but can also improve upon social circumstances we find ourselves in by being critical. He recognises that our consciousness and our

174 CHAPTER 7

mandated goals of education are influenced by dominant as well as sub-cultures that prevail. Kincheloe argues that far too often those well off in society are deemed as intelligent, while those who are poor and marginalised are deemed incapable. This last makes critical thinking an act of resistance in itself. With regards to teachers he adds,

> Teachers are induced by rationalistic management systems to think of curriculum outside of its social context. The people who create the curriculum and those who distribute it pretend that the knowledge it contains is politically neutral, a body of agreed-upon information being systematically passed on to students by an ever-evolving, but always impartial, instructional process. Complex critical thinkers are not seduced by the sirens of political neutrality. The curriculum is always a formal transmission of particular aspects of a culture's knowledge. (Kincheloe, 2004, p. 34)

Helping nuance Daniels' recognition in Chapter 6 that a curriculum refers to what counts as legitimate knowledge, Kincheloe directs attention to socio-political aspects which underpin its text. He highlights two salient aspects – *first* that school curricula and contemporary social order in any society constantly construct one another and *second*, that there is no objective political/social vision for curricula. While the first entails that practitioners need to examine both school curricula and the social order, the second endows them with responsibility of deciding the goals of education besides what constitutes good teaching. He argues,

> In this spirit I argue that the curriculum should be multilogical – that it should present a variety of perspectives on what should be taught in schools. A central feature of such a curriculum would involve understanding a variety of different viewpoints in a variety of academic domains and the ideologies, values, and world-views on which they are based. A classroom grounded on this multilogical curriculum would expose students to diverse interpretations of history, science, linguistics, literature and philosophy while encouraging them to support and defend their own interpretations in these areas. (Kincheloe, 2005a, p. 6)

Kincheloe above articulates *why* he views curricular documents as being far from politically neutral, besides *how* teachers and students could consider and together debate multiple viewpoints that might seem valid from one's individual perspective. With potential for bringing about intellectual and ethical maturity, Kincheloe views such an approach as essential grounding for teachers

CRITICAL PERSPECTIVES 175

and students to take part in any deliberative democracy. A *critical ontology* for him thus examines the relationship every individual has to the world, enabling each one to ponder about the nature of their being-in-the-world.

Advocating adoption of the above outlined stance, Kincheloe (2005b) addresses the nature of *alienation* that students as well as teachers face, if the mandated curriculum is dealing with truths that can be arrived at by deploying pre-prescribed seemingly correct methods. Identifying such a deterministic, infallible or positivist approach to arriving at knowledge to be the root cause for alienation in education, Kincheloe characterises the *detrimental features* of such a stance to proclaim for example that (1) Only scientific knowledge is true knowledge – with Western societies producing such knowledge, other cultures must give up their own ways of doing so. (2) All scientific knowledge is empirically verifiable – human emotions are often dismissed and human beings are treated as mere variables. (3) Mathematical language is best suited to express this knowledge – in having an underlying order, nature is thus uniform. (4) The best way to study the world is to isolate constituent parts and analyse them independent of their contexts – such quest thus focusses attention on trivial aspects which can be measured. (5) Since there is only one reality, this has to be conveyed to students in the best way possible – with teachers seen as passing on truths which experts give them, teachers are far from viewed as knowledge producing professionals who can interpret educational events as individuals themselves.

Kincheloe points out that the bane of adopting the above positivistic approach in education is a misplaced and inordinate focus on truths, and not on the well being of students and teachers. I am reminded here of Bronowski's viewing science as human progress in Chapter 1 and how a positivist approach far from achieves the progress that human beings strive to achieve. More specifically Kincheloe details how the adoption of a positivistic approach in education could result in some of the following outcomes (1) *abstract individualism* – viewing humans beings as set apart from the contexts that shape them, (2) *technilisation* – valuing technical over vital questions of human wellness and purpose, (3) *economism* – looking at human beings as cogs in the economy alone, rather than in terms of their ability to do human good, (4) *rationalism* – viewing humans as rational automatons, dismissing the importance of their intuition, emotion and compassion (5) *objectivism* – conceiving goals of education in terms of producing and consuming a neutral body of knowledge, that fails to acknowledge diverse ways of personal knowing. By adopting and propagating these aspects with little critique, classrooms become places where students merely learn how to survive for success and get by. As Kincheloe deftly points out,

Students in such a classroom are not simply learning 'what,' but they are also learning 'how.' In this case they are learning 'how to operate' in schools. Critical teachers want students to learn not only 'how to operate for success in schools' but also 'how schools might operate to produce a just, intelligent, and democratic society.' (Kincheloe, 2005b, p. 39)

My brief summary of Kincheloe's arguments laying emphasis on how schools could operate for students addresses a central problem that most students and teachers face – their respective inability to change a system of education forced on them by various levers of power in society, like parents, employment opportunities, national ambitions beyond school and district level administrations. In order to transform lives and bring about change that is desired, Kincheloe thus highlights the need for critical teachers to understand as well as expose the underpinnings that asks for thoughtless dissemination of reductionist truths which are generated elsewhere. Such teachers would, he argues,

understand that innovations in the production of knowledge rarely come from a linear accumulation of objective curricular data gleaned from knowledge of previous 'discoveries.' Major reconceptualisation comes out of a meta-analyses, a deeper study of the ideological and epistemological assumptions on which the framework supporting knowledge production and the academic curriculum is grounded. Complex insights and discipline-changing analyses are produced not so much by asking questions *within* the framework as they are by asking questions *about* the framework. (Kincheloe, 2005c, p. 94, emphasis in original)

In line with Kincheloe, my current writing draws on multidisciplinary sources as means of asking key questions not so much from within the confines of a classroom, as much as in terms of practical-theoretical frameworks by means of which classroom teaching and learning can be conceived and reflected upon. With reference to classroom instruction, Kincheloe offers a concrete example as well, pointing to how the topic of photosynthesis could be taught say – not as a disembodied concept equated to a dictionary type word or definition, but as a taken for granted process of nature which breathes life into one's own classroom, school, home, neighbourhood and our planet at large. It is at this point that Kincheloe's arguments in relation to a critical ontology *for* teachers come centre stage, for it is one thing to advocate that teachers need to adopt a critical stance and quite another for teachers to *be* critical in flesh and blood within their respective educational contexts.

With little attention within teacher preparation on the development of teachers' identity and consciousness, Kincheloe (2003) argues teachers' *critical*

CRITICAL PERSPECTIVES 177

ontology to involve a process of examining how their selves are connected to existing webs of social and physical reality. Some ways in which he sees such consciousness to materialise are (1) To understand the importance of ways in which one's self is constructed in socio-historical ways. This would include construction of one's gender say, or even the history of independence of one's country and present day outcomes of such movements. (2) To develop critical ontological agency so as to act upon one's own self and the world in a just and intelligent manner. As practitioners know too well, this could mean withholding action in the present and waiting for an opportune moment to do so in the near future. (3) To have schools as institutions examine the ontological realms of producing human selves with regards to particular milieu and the forces like national politics that affect its local functioning. Practitioners could discuss how what is being reported in the media say, does not speak for the views debated within the school one is working at. (4) To become detectives of difference between oneself and another, in search for new ways of being human. Such differences among views can be highlighted as not being a bad thing in itself. (5) To gain awareness of the ontological implications of studying things and events as they appear to be on the surface, as opposed to studying them in relationship to one another as well as their contexts. In line with this last argument, I have myself reflected on the kind of interactions I had with two students Sara and Eva in Lotta's school (Gade, 2016). While Sara drew me into her reality before releasing both of us from the same, Eva offered an interpretation of events that were political in nature, one which made me question what she may be asking of me as a researcher and educator. It was on the basis of these intimate, almost confessional personal interactions that I came to realise the potential of Kincheloe's arguments below,

> *a critical ontology pursues human agency* – the disposition and capacity to act on the world in ways that involve self-direction and the pursuit of democratic and egalitarian principles of community formation. A critical ontology insists that humans possess inalienable rights to knowledge and insight into knowledge production, to intellectual development, to empowerment, and to political agency in a democratic society. When teacher educators understand these ontological dynamics and work toward the political goals they portend, they have laid the foundation on which other aspects of professional education can be constructed. (Kincheloe, 2003, p. 53, emphasis added)

Having focused on many an issue that guides how we practitioners could realise a critical curriculum, critical thinking and bring about the critical construction of students selves besides one's own, I now turn to greater examine hidden

4 Hidden Curriculum of Work

I focus in this section on the work of Jean Anyon another critical theorist who like Kincheloe worked at The Graduate Centre, CUNY. Four aspects of Anyon's work display synergy with aspects I have dwelt upon thus far, the last of which examines the hidden curriculum of work being deployed in schools. *First* and in continued discussion about the nature of theory articulated by different scholars, Anyon speaks to the role that *critical theory* plays not just as a tool in establishing links across classrooms, schools, legislative dictates as well as social and political boundaries, but also as key means of emboldening youth. She argues,

> Theory allows us to plan research that connects the ways in which social actors and conditions inside of school buildings, districts, and legislative offices are shaped and changed by what happens outside the classrooms, offices, and official chambers they inhabit. Conversely, theory can point us to the larger political and social meanings of what occurs in educational institutions and systems. As well, theory can embolden youth and community participants from whom theoretical engagement in general has been withheld. (Anyon, 2009a, p. 3, emphasis added)

While Kincheloe had earlier recognised that the construction by teachers of curricular knowledge could be seen as an act of their resistance, Anyon views withholding opportunities for theoretical engagement by youth, to result in experiences of subordination and resistance. Even as Kincheloe focuses on teachers and Anyon on youth, both scholars dwell on issues that could be faced in one's *being* critical.

Recognising the experience of youth while taking part in political struggles and social movements to be key to influencing their continued participation, Anyon *next* examines ways in which such agency could be sustained. Some of her recommendations include (1) allowing youth to reimagine older social and political arrangements in a new light, waging struggle within which they see their efforts as leading to change, (2) knowing that youth do not become political and then participate in social movements, but do so by developing individual and collective identities as they take part, (3) facilitating participation in social struggles towards which they are predisposed to and likely to further

CRITICAL PERSPECTIVES

take part, (4) involving youth in movements wherein they are likely to develop skills and a sense of efficacy, affording them confidence to arrive at intended results, and (5) addressing issues which they themselves face as a starting point that can be studied, contributed to and changed. Taking a long term view in advocating these steps, Anyon concludes,

> My pedagogy builds on students' own insights into subordination and resistance. As I imagine is the case with other critical educators, I encourage students to become involved in the public contention that is a legitimate part of the political struggle for equity in democratic societies. I hope that my lessons will encourage them to become involved – if not not now, then later, when they are adults. (Anyon, 2009b, p. 389)

Anyon's writings *third* share synergy with critical perspectives in her utilising Marxian premise, as is also the case with neo-Vygotskian CHAT perspectives. I draw attention to two aspects she discusses in *Marx and education*. Herein Anyon (2011) *first* reiterates Marx's argument that economic inequality in capitalistic societies carry inherent contradictions with regards to human labour and corresponding wealth production. These contradictions are considered as sources of human development in CHAT. Anyon *second* points out that for Marx, human consciousness is produced by their social being and not vice versa, something Vygotsky adopted as founding premise as well. It is this latter which Anyon takes as point of departure in her class based empirical study of schools in the US. Herein she elicits ways in which a hidden curriculum is at play, one that corresponds to likely job requirements of children studying at particular schools. Alluding to curricular instruction in mathematics, Anyon outlines four categories which I proceed to summarise.

In her *first* category prevalent at *working-class schools*, Anyon found instruction to ask students to follow steps of procedure, besides call for rote learning. This was accompanied by very little choice and/or decision making on their part. Teachers also did little to explain why particular classwork was assigned, the ideas that underpinned their tasks or how any segment of work was connected with other assignments. There was thus little opportunity for students to arrive at greater coherence or personal meaning making. Their resistance was thus a dominant aspect of teacher-student interaction, displayed by their attempts to sabotage the attempts of teachers. One is reminded of students having to learn multiplication tables by rote say. Such experiences were similar to unrewarding tasks carried out by unskilled workers like those selling consumer items across the counter and/or clerical people. Forming a large percentage of jobs in the US, these schools seemed to be preparing students for such jobs.

Anyon's *second* category relates to instruction in *middle class schools* where the focus was on students getting the right answer. Herein students were expected to follow specific directions to arrive at the right answer, en route which they were expected to make appropriate choices towards arriving at the same. As example students needed to carry out two digit division by either the long or the short way, so that the answer arrived at would be the same as those found in solutions offered at the end of the book. Teachers followed rules and regulations which they used as criteria for justifying the answers that were being sought. Right answers or good grades could be accumulated by students, who could then exchange these for jobs. By laying emphasis on such skills, these schools were preparing students for low and middle level managerial jobs, besides those like public school teaching, police officers and fire fighters.

In her *third* category relating to *affluent professional schools*, Anyon found students being asked to work independently at creative activity. These students could express themselves, apply ideas and illustrate their thoughts with appropriate materials and methods. While fitting in with reality, students here had to show individuality besides making their work stand out and not be similar to those of their peers. In granting students freedom of expression, teachers offered hints and tips which would lead students to greater avenues of creativity. Students would in the process display their ability to work with the scale of a map say and demonstrate their grasp of concepts like agricultural produce in specific regions. By means of discovery, construction and meaning making, the work in these schools was conceptual. The kind of jobs being prepared for lay in media, arts or advertising. The ability of students to manipulate symbol systems prepared them for being medical doctors or highly paid academics.

In a *final* category at *executive elite schools*, Anyon found school work to stress on developing one's intellectual powers in preparation for life. Students were asked to reason through a problem and produce intellectual products that were logically sound and showed academic quality. They were expected to conceptualise how elements of a system fit together and use these to solve bigger problems. Having taught students how to arrive at a general formula for the area of rectangular figures, teachers could ask students if they could come up with one for perimeter say. Students were also treated as equals and were expected to define individual priorities, internalise control and conduct their work appropriately. Such training prepared students for being elected officials, leaders of large institutions, besides well paid top executives in corporations.

Alongside other critical scholars, Anyon's study outlined above shows how the experience of schooling has reproductive qualities not only for social class in society, but also for content in the curriculum. Located as these schools were in neighbourhoods where parents of children were largely from working class,

CRITICAL PERSPECTIVES   181

middle, professional or elite backgrounds, Anyon offers compelling reason to critically examine how the work we assign for students in schools can have a class derived basis. Maybe the patterns that Anyon found evident in the US are not found in other more egalitarian societies. If so, one could question what is the nature of such work and on what premise, explicit or implicit, is such work based upon. My intention of discussing Anyon at length, is to however sensitise us practitioners to the class based underpinnings the our instruction might have, even if our intentions could be otherwise. The importance of human consciousness being produced by their social being and not vice versa, which Marx and Vygotsky adopt as premise, thus demands the attention of practitioners in instructional actions we take. I now turn to wider issues practitioners could contend with in their praxis of research.

5   Research as Praxis

In line with Freire's notion of praxis as one's taking action and reflecting on the same in order to name and transform the world, I too reflected on the kinds of educational action I was able to steer in collaboration with Lotta (Gade, 2017). As mentioned in Chapter 5, such reflections took the form of a self-study about the CHAT methodology which underpinned the interventions I conducted with her. These deliberations referred to my (1) adopting a theory/practice stance (Edwards et al., 2002), (2) keep alive the relationship between theory-which-informs and theory-being-built, besides existing-practice and steered-practice (Gade, 2012a), (3) put into practice a tool and result methodology, by means of which I chose the object and tool best suited to each study (Newman & Holzman, 1997), and (4) enabled the complementarity between theory and praxis to inform my reflexivity as practitioner (Seeger, 2001). In line with Chaiklin in Chapter 3, my ability to grasp students' development in each study was a result in addition of having proactively intervened with instruction in ongoing, everyday, routine classrooms.

While I have greater dealt with each of the above aspects cited above in this as well as previous chapters, I turn to dwell on two methodological features worthy of note. *First* and as argued by Stetsenko (2010), my adopting a dialectical stance to theorise and understand the instructional practices I intervened with precluded my committing two common errors (1) of applying preconceived, ready-made, a priori categories towards grasping ongoing practices, and (2) of making empirical observations with facts that lay outside the context of my inquiry. Arguing researcher theorising to be part and parcel of any practice being studied, Stetsenko highlights three features characteristic

182 CHAPTER 7

of adopting such a stance (a) that any researcher's practical-political actions need to follow a practice-theory-practice cycle, (b) that conceptual categories utilised for making empirical observations need to be internal and not external to the practice being studied, and (c) that the taking of such actions leads researchers to ascertain contradictions which are embedded in those practices, whose resolution results in change and transformation. It was such manner of reasoning which led me recognise my taking political action in dialectic with CHAT perspectives being utilised (Gade, 2017).

The clarity of this last was *second* informed by what critical theorist Patti Lather terms *research as praxis*. In her paper with the same title, Lather engages with concerns that inform the very conduct of a critical social science. Her expressed objective is to dwell on what it means to do empirical research in an unjust world. In elaborating on her insightful view in this section, I begin with her notion of *praxis*,

> Praxis is, of course, a word with a history. In this essay, I use the term to mean *the dialectical tension, the interactive, reciprocal shaping of theory and practice which I see at the center of an emancipatory social science.* The essence of my argument, then, is that we who do empirical research in the name of emancipatory politics must discover ways to connect our research methodology to our theoretical concerns and commitments. At its simplest, this is a call for critical inquirers to practice in their empirical endeavours what they preach in their theoretical formulations. (Lather, 1986a, p. 258, emphasis added)

It was heartening for me to find Lather's notion of praxis resonate on many levels with the methodological conduct of CHAT based research I had drawn upon while conducting many a classroom intervention. *First* was the reciprocal and dialectical manner of letting theory and practice shape one another in each study, the intricacies of which I examine in the coda of this Chapter. Lather *second* lay emphasis on the manner in which researchers conduct studies in the name of emancipatory politics, in which theory building and personal commitments are far from neutral but inextricably woven with one another. Asking researchers to practice what they preach, Lather *third* situates her arguments in the human sciences. Here she draws on Donald Polkinghorne, alluded to in Chapter 5, whose views the enterprise of human sciences as being inclusive. This stance allows research to make use of multiple systems of inquiry and questions that pertain to the task at hand, which also inform the choice of methods to be used. Lather thus and *finally* argues for research as praxis, wherein researchers involve the researched in a democratic manner of inquiry that involves negotiation, reciprocity and mutual empowerment.

CRITICAL PERSPECTIVES

I also find distinct echo of many a CHAT construct discussed thus far in my writing, with Lather's notion of research as praxis. *First* is the use of a tool and result approach, instead of tool for result. As example, while attempting to rectify students' faulty use of the mathematical equal to sign in Lotta's Grade four, we devised four successive activities that were mediated explicitly by slips of paper with appropriate inscriptions. Each of these activities was tool which doubled as method and allowed us to devise the kind of activity we carried out subsequently (Gade, 2012b). In Tomas' Grade eight we drew on perspectives of situated learning of Lave, as well as meaningful practical activity forwarded by del Rio and Alvarez, in dialectic with the five stage formative intervention we carried out. Herein, the insightful theoretical perspectives we drew upon and the instructional practice we realised informed one another as the conduct of our intervention progressed (Gade & Forsgren, 2019). *Second* and in carrying out such research, we were able to practice in our empirical work, the theoretical formulations we subsequently reported, as argued by Lather. Following Kvale our efforts were pragmatic besides, in that the truth of our knowledge was not observational but realised in the actions we collaboratively took. As to the emancipatory nature of my actions as researcher, which Lather draws specific attention to, I can speak to two specific outcomes as my work with Lotta evolved. *First*, Lotta identified herself and become co-author in every subsequent reporting of our interventions since our initial conduct of action research (e.g. Gade & Blomqvist, 2015, 2016, 2018). *Second* and in right earnest I too began search for theoretical frameworks by means of which teacher-researcher collaboration could be understood – an aspect I reflected and reported upon as well (Gade, 2015).

Towards her quest for problematising the adoption by researchers of an emancipatory stance in their respective studies, Lather goes on to stress three specific aspects, (1) a reciprocity between those being researched and the researcher, as was the case with me and the students I interacted with, (2) how the mediation of researchers in their studies could be maximised without their actions becoming impositional, realised in terms of listening keenly to and acting upon what students had to say about our joint work, and (3) a pointed reconceptualisation of the notion of validity appropriate for research that is committed to a more just social order, realised in terms of the cultural-historical development of students in line with CHAT, besides empowerment in mathematics education in line with Skovsmose. While I greater dwell on the nature of reciprocity, along with frameworks that allowed me to explicate my own praxis with respect to my studies in Chapter 9, I turn to Lather (1986b) one last time to discuss her criteria for achieving empirical accountability. Suggesting that these criteria form part of research design itself, Lather argues in favour of (1) establishment of data trustworthiness by exercising *triangulation* of methods, data-sources and theoretical perspectives, (2) making a record of *reflexive subjectivity* by researchers, which documents how one's prior assumptions in a study were altered or affected by the logic of data being collected, (3) ensuring *face validity* that draws on responses of participants with regards to constructs being used to analyse any study, and (4) documentation of *catalytic validity* evidenced in the form of activism that the research process led to or provided opportunity for. In arguing for and advocating the above criteria, Lather draws not only upon Freire's arguments in relation to altering reality and empowering the oppressed, but also perspectives in neo-Marxist critical ethnography and feminist research. It is in this spirit that I now turn to discuss research as bricolage, allowing research methodology to realise the promise there lies in deploying multiple systems of inquiry in line with Kincheloe, besides arriving at Lather's criteria of accountability outlined above.

6 Research as Bricolage

In addition to auditing Tobin's doctoral course titled *Logics of Inquiry,* I had opportunity to take part in Saturday seminars he would organise once a month at The Graduate Centre. Open to students, teachers, researchers and faculty across CUNY, my attending these seminars held special significance for me since I experienced therein a milieu which I last encountered while teaching at my school in India. Many aspects of either institution seemed to be driven in similar ways, making me feel at home as a teacher in one place and a researcher at the other. One could make observations, contribute ideas, form new associations based on shared interests and stumble upon nuggets of wisdom that deserved further exploration. The underlying coherence steering both places seemed similar, even though one was a school for everyday instruction and the other a place for research examining the intricacies of the same. The free exchange of ideas that flowed in and out of either place, reminded me of Gandhi's oft cited quote which said that he did not want his house to be walled and windows stuffed, but have cultures of all lands pass through them, even as he refused to be blown off his own feet.

It is against such a backdrop that I examine research as bricolage, an approach that allows for realising multilogicality and critical ontology while conducting educational research. In discussing this interdisciplinary approach I once again take writings of Kincheloe as point of departure, who explains the French word *bricolage* to have been introduced by Norman Denzin and Yvonne Lincoln (2000) in their *Handbook of Qualitative Research.* As a practitioner, my own interest in research as bricolage arose from its potential to realise the kind of transformative action I found wanting in ongoing classrooms, as well

CRITICAL PERSPECTIVES   185

as being able to counter the many criticisms Kincheloe himself raised with regards to a positivist approach to generating knowledge and educating others.

Kincheloe (2001) describes the word bricolage to come from the French word *bricoleur* who is a handyman or handywoman who puts diverse tools to use in an imaginative manner to accomplish the job at hand. Since the bricoleur or knower besides what is possible to know are inseparable while grasping the totality of the human experience, *research as bricolage* refers to using diverse methods and theoretical frameworks of inquiry in the research act. In educational research this would mean drawing from across disciplinary confines to suit objectives of the study at hand. Allowing researchers to learn from the difference that underpin diverse frameworks herein presents researchers an opportunity for two aspects, (1) gain unique insights which might not be available when only one framework is used, and (2) address complexities which say social, cultural, psychological and educational domains can independently bring forth. Being dynamic, the process is not a straightforward application of a priori categories aiding analysis, but one in which relationships between diverse entities within ongoing reality are brought to careful unison and consideration. Such a process Kincheloe argues is cultivated life long and demands application, one that is never easy.

Elaborating on his initial thoughts on research as bricolage, Kincheloe (2005d) makes three notable extensions. *First*, he identifies the nature of complexity that could be embedded in educational scenarios. Some of these are (1) *polysemy* – the fact that different words and phrases have different meaning for different individuals in differing contexts, (2) *intersecting contextual fields* – recognising that multiple contextual fields may be at play simultaneously, (3) *multiple epistemologies* – the seeking of diverse epistemologies, which might bring sophisticated insights and unique modes of meaning making, (4) *intertextuality* – that narratives obtain meaning from material reality as well as relationships with other narratives, and (5) *power and knowledge* – the ability of power to limit and/or reward what constitutes a legitimate focus of research.

With bricoleurs taking the above dimensions and more into account, Kincheloe draws on Denzin and Lincoln (2000) *second* to delineate five dimensions of bricolage that can be adopted by such researchers (1) *methodological bricolage* – wherein numerous strategies are employed to gather data, (2) *theoretical bricolage* – where using diverse frameworks determine the purpose, meaning and uses of the research act, (3) *interpretive bricolage* – which values interpretations that emerge from differing perspectives and various participants, (4) *political bricolage* – which documents the effects of different forms of power at play, and (5) *narrative bricolage* – which recognises that research knowledge is shaped by the kind of stories researchers offer.

Kincheloe points *finally* to the goals which researchers adopt while conducting research as bricolage in their work to be,

> Understanding that research that fails to address the ontology of the human existential situation with all of its pain, suffering, joy, and desire is limited in its worth, bricoleurs search for better ways to connect with and illuminate this domain. In this context, much is possible. (Kincheloe, 2005d, p. 348)

My own journey with research as bricolage, was dictated by concrete particulars and demands made on my adopting a pragmatic approach to theory and practice, and drew instinctively over the years on narrative perspectives. Theoretically extensive in their breadth, these perspectives served my grasp of educational realities in three specific ways (1) the nature of small talk that students shared with me, (2) the narratives of teachers with whom I collaborated, and (3) ontological aspects in relation to my being a researcher practitioner. In line with Kincheloe's notion of methodological bricolage, I drew on narrative and CHAT perspectives in complementary ways for reporting upon each of these.

Exemplifying the *first*, was my attempt to grasp the narratives offered by three of Lotta's students, as they attempted mathematical tasks set for them on an individual basis. In narratives being simultaneously object, tool and result of students' cultural-historical development, I argued narratives to satisfy a key premise of activity theory as well (Gade, 2010). Another such effort was my attempt to understand what Bamberg and Georgakopoulou (2008) recognise as small stories or talk-in-interaction. Based on my interaction with two other students at Lotta's school, I was able to engage with their growing sense of self or identity. I argued such analysis to help grasp the sense students were making of their lived experience of educational scenarios in which they were taking part (Gade, 2012c). My *second* use of narratives not only shed light on actions me and my collaborating teachers took with respect to the interventions we conducted, but also about the nature of relationships we realised as we collaborated with one another. I greater elaborate on frameworks which enabled me to identify and nuance these relationships in Chapter 9.

Finally was the nature of my personal ontological experiences, about which I reflected and reported upon every now and then. Initially I spoke of deploying narratives as unit of analysis to grasp teaching-learning. Attention to narratives, I argued, had potential to empower the praxis of teachers, recognise their language of practice and allow research to access their personal, individual voice (Gade, 2011). With continued conduct of interventions and by calling on researcher reflexivity, I next engaged with theoretical underpinnings of the

CRITICAL PERSPECTIVES   187

two terms *praxis* and *phronesis*. In their ability to examine concrete educational practice I argued the use of these two notions to allow practitioners to pursue a social science that mattered to practitioners themselves (Gade, 2014). More recently and subsequent to teaching a Curriculum studies course to MA students and as greater discussed in the next Chapter, I reflected on my actions while addressing a gathering of students at their summer camp. I was here able to examine the notion of *poiesis*, alluding to the manner in which the meaning and significance of any performance by a practitioner subsisted in the work left behind, one intrinsic to its very completion (Gade, 2020).

I conclude this section by turning to Tobin (2014) summarising his own attempts at research as bricolage. Drawing on 40 years of experience Tobin argues in favour of conducting collaborative inquiry in classrooms, with co-teachers besides students. Allowing for the grasping of polysemy, multilogicality and difference, I elaborate on my own use of a framework he advocates, that of *cognerative dialogue* in Chapter 9. I find Tobin to also draw attention to four aspects which highlight what it may mean to carry out research as a bricoloeur. *First* is recognition of the very limits of our ability to express what we know in language, besides the limits of what we can know of social reality as we conduct research. *Second* is his attention to the individual/collective dialectic at play in the social world, of which even individual identity could be dialectical in nature. *Third* is the importance he assigns following Kincheloe to *radical listening*, which is the effort to understand the views of others without seeking to change them. *Finally* is his explicit attention to a vital ingredient of the research process in addition to ontology and epistemology – that of *axiology* or ethics and the value systems we come to exercise as practitioners. Such a multilectic in conducting research, enables one to honour the notion of difference in the social world as well as diversity in an epistemological sense, which he and Kincheloe have laid stress upon all along. I argue the aspects Tobin alludes to as vital for conducting sensitive, humane and nuanced educational research. I also find the depth of each of the issues to subtly underpin not only the conduct of one's research, but also the kind of research questions that are worthy of pursuit.

With regards to his attention to axiology for example, I allude to two cultural resources which may have contributed to notions of ethics and values that I might be bringing to research I myself conduct. By dwelling on these I draw attention to thought processes which each one of us could fall back upon either explicitly or implicitly, while carrying out besides re-storying the research we carry out and conduct. It goes without saying that readers from cultural backgrounds other than my own, have rightful recourse to value and belief systems in their own cultures as well.

Drawn from thought systems in India, the *first* of these is a Buddhist saying that was on display at the school I taught,

> Believe nothing
> Merely because you have been told it
> Or because it is traditional,
> Or because you yourselves imagined it.
> Do not believe what your teacher tells you,
> Merely out of respect for the teacher.
> But whatsoever, after due examination and analysis,
> You find to be conducive to the good,
> The benefit, the welfare of all beings,
> That doctrine believe and cling to,
> And take as your guide.
> (The Buddha)

The *second* is the *The hymn of creation* or *Nasadiya suktam*, which forms part of the *Rig Veda* in ancient Indian Sanskrit literature. After raising the question of where life came from, the hymn ends with wondering who really knows or who can even offer an answer to this question, since even God Almighty came after the moment of creation. The hymn goes on to say that maybe Almighty who surveys all reality from the highest heaven may know the answer to this question, or, maybe (s)he too does not know the answer to this question. It is possible that the Buddhist saying and the Vedic hymn may have contributed to my being skeptical of positivism in the enterprise of education and paved way to my eventually becoming a critical practitioner researcher. Having externalised premise lurking in my own axiology, I now turn to dwell upon dialectical inquiry.

7 Dialectical Inquiry: Coda

Way before embarking on a doctorate and as classroom teacher, I came across *Not all in the genes – Richard Lewontin: Evolutionary biologist*, in Lewis Wolpert and Alison Richards' (1997) *Passionate minds: The inner lives of scientists*. It was here that I had my first acquaintance with a dialectical manner of conceiving scientific problems. Even as I greater examine how human nature could have evolved in this manner at the end of this coda, I presently turn to the principle itself. Lewontin argues,

> I don't think the world is made up of natural bits and pieces that fit together in some natural way and bring to whole objects their own properties.

CRITICAL PERSPECTIVES

> I think the properties of the bits and pieces we divide the world into are properties they acquire in actually being part of wholes. ...
>
> ... So it's a dialectical principle, if you like, that both the rules and the objects about which the rules are made have to be simultaneously tried, and fit. (Lewontin, 1997, pp. 103–109)

Realising that much of the science that was being taught in schools was likely bits and pieces or reductionist in outlook, I had since been on the lookout for knowing more about this approach. This was possible only during my post-doctoral at Umeå where I could read Richard Levins and Richard Lewontin's (1985) *The dialectical biologist*. In consonance with CHAT and critical perspectives, which I discuss all along, I found Levins and Lewontin point to how science is being practiced in society,

> Cartesian analysis in science, alienates science from society, making scientific fact and method 'objective' and beyond social influence. Our view is different. We believe that science, in *all* its senses, is a social process that both causes and is caused by social organisation. To do science is to be a social actor engaged, whether one likes it or not, in political activity. The denial of the interpenetration of the scientific and the social is itself a political act, giving support to social structures that hide behind scientific objectivity to perpetuate dependency, exploitation, racism, elitism, colonialism. (Levins & Lewontin, 1985, p. 4)

While I found Lewontin's earlier quote to echo the principle of ascending to the concrete within CHAT, the later seemed to echo the problems with positivist science that critical theorists argue against. It was in these terms that I thus came to appreciate dialectical inquiry.

I also encountered a dialectical view in Clandinin's (1985) construct of *personal practical knowledge* as in Chapter 2, wherein any practitioner's theory and practice are deemed inseparable. In fact a teacher's practice is viewed as theory in action. Embedded in Clandinin's paper is reference to Richard McKeon's (1952) paper titled *Philosophy and action*, which opened my inquiry into this notion once again. McKeon's writing draws attention to the fact that the conception of the practical in any sphere of activity was in turn determined by the kind of scientific method that was being deployed. McKeon identified four, (1) *The dialectical method* – which treats theory and practice as inseparable. Action here relates to reconciling contradictions that arise in dynamic, organic wholes. (2) *The logistic method* – which constructs formal systems of science based on models in mathematics. The practical here is application of a science of action, that one needs to take. (3) *The problematic method* – a method of resolving problems that is geared to solving specific problems. With such attempts differing across problem areas, action here depended on mutual agreement communication and on the collective route going forward. (4) *The operational method* – a way of taking action by translating ideas into processes that could be verified with discernible results. Theoretical discussions are avoided and ideas borrowed from each of the other methods as well. In my attempts at grasping dialectical inquiry, McKeon provided two insights, (1) the manner in which the dialectical approach to solving problems was different from the three others he outlined, and (2) that the dialectical method was deployed differently by various scholars in history to solve issues encountered in their own times. It is thus that I presently turn to Bertell Ollman's (2003) *Dance of the dialectic: Steps in Marx's method*, since Marxian premise underpin both CHAT research following Vygotsky and critical research following Freire.

My reading of Ollman's arguments reinforced what Lewontin pointed out earlier on, that dialectics was a way of thinking that lay focus not on bits and pieces that went into making the whole, but on the manner of changes and interactions that transpired between them, to bring about the whole and constitute reality. Ollman cites Marx's retelling of the Roman myth of Cacus to ably illustrate this issue,

> Half-man, half-demon Cacus lived in a cave and came out only at night to steal oxen. Wishing to mislead his pursuers, Cacus forced the oxen to walk backwards into his den so that their footprints made it appear that they had gone out from there. The next morning, when people came looking for their oxen, all they found were footprints. Based on the evidence of the footprints, they concluded that, starting from the cave, their oxen had gone into the middle of the field and disappeared. (Ollman, 2003, pp. 12–13)

Ollman's rendering of Cacus asks practitioners to question the empirical evidence they collect in any study, as such data may indeed lead them to draw erroneous conclusions, many a time to the contrary as well. Causing nothing to happen and proving nothing, Ollman thus argues dialectics as a means of altering our thinking about reality in three specific ways (1) replacing the notion of *thing,* such as footprints in the quote above, with notions of *process,* (2) an attention to *history,* like those of creating the footprints would rightfully deserve, and (3) the notion of *relation,* like the conclusion which the observed footprints would have us draw, contrary to the reality that existed. Ollman finds Marx's approach to thus be critical of any exclusive focus on appearances that are separated from history and the system within which empirical observations are being made. Echoing Lewontin, Ollman reiterates dialectical research

CRITICAL PERSPECTIVES   191

to in addition begin with understanding the whole as much as is possible and only later proceed to examine how its parts function and fit together. Such an attempt could assist arriving at a fuller grasp of the initial whole, which was conceived as the initial problematic to be understood.

If positivist research is critiqued for focusing on the trees instead of the forest, a dialectical approach is at times critiqued for the opposite. Even as I greater address this issue in Chapter 9, I presently turn to two areas in which a dialectical approach offers unique insights – *educational theory* and *human nature*. It was in Lather's writings on research as praxis that I came across Brian Fay, who sought to view the relationship between theory and practice in terms of an *educative model*, one opposed to an *instrumental model* whose use may be currently dominant. Fay explained the latter to view knowledge in terms of its ability to guide actions not only in the natural world, but also say in medical practices, political institutions and psychological matters. Dedicated to controlling both natural and social processes, the risk in this latter view was in finding knowledge useful only if its outcomes offered the ability to manipulate existing state of affairs, to produce another desired state. On the other hand Fay viewed knowledge in the educative model as,

> useful to the extent that it informs people what their needs are and how a particular way of living is frustrating these needs, thereby causing them to suffer; its goal is to enlighten people about how they can change their lives so that, having arrived at a new self-understanding, they may reduce their suffering by creating another way of life that is more fulfilling. ... in the educative model, social theories are the means by which people can liberate themselves from the particular causal processes that victimise them precisely because they are ignorant of who they are. (Fay, 1977, p. 204)

Focusing upon self-understanding, Fay thus seeks knowledge creation to take place in a dialectical manner, one in which theoretical formulations enable people to relate to the very social and material conditions in which they find themselves. Leading to critical self-awareness such approach, he argues, allows one's thinking to be the cause of one's actions and also the means to one's own autonomy. In line with this model, individuals have the potential of achieving *self-determination* by becoming active subjects and transforming themselves. Fay's educative model of relating theory and practice echo two aspects which Lewontin argued earlier on. *First* in line with the dialectical principle, it is people who became aware of the part they are playing in the societal whole in which they currently take part. *Second* in line with the nature of science or knowledge being created, the social and political aspects of lives of individuals are brought to light, guiding *their* understanding of actions which *they* would likely take, besides *their* realisation of self-determination.

I return finally to my quest of understanding evolution, specifically of human beings in dialectical terms. In *Human nature: The Marxian view,* Vernon Venable (1945) explains that for Marx and Engels there was no single human nature and that this nature changed dialectically. In line with them, Venable points out that the pre-eminent mode of development for human beings was their production and reproduction of life and its material requirements. Thus and encountered as key premise in writings of both Vygotsky and Freire, it is the social being that determined their consciousness. Human beings are thereby conceived as products of their labour, upbringing and circumstances. Venable in turn reiterates that in Marxian thought, the underlying mechanism at work is one of human beings changing history and in the process, changing themselves as well. In other words and as also argued by Stetsenko earlier on, human beings change their ontology and the nature of the reality in which they take part. Venable in addition goes on to argue that unlike instinctive work by animals, human labour is always social,

> 'All production,' says Marx, 'is appropriation of nature by the individual *within and through a definite form of society.'* Human labour is social because man is social. 'Man is in the most literal sense of the word,' says Marx, 'a *zoon politikon*, not only a social animal, but an animal which can develop into an individual only in society .... (Venable, 1945, p. 50, emphasis in original)

Venable highlights few other points with respect to the dialectic at play between human beings and the reality they bring about, by way of labour they carry out in society. With labour being a necessary condition of human existence, Marxian thought reiterates that labour created human beings themselves. Vitally such kind of labour is a conscious one, which imagines and plans the reality which is desired before the same is also realised. In such manner of constructing reality human beings do not merely use external nature, but master the same through labour. It follows that unlike animals, human beings are capable of making their history.

The decisive step towards this last in evolution, Venable argues, is the freeing of the human hand while transiting from ape to human beings. Labour was responsible, Venable points out, for the human hand to not only be an organ of labour but also a product of human labour itself. Venable next directs attention to the manner of production which human beings carry out. Such

CRITICAL PERSPECTIVES

193

production is not only carried out for modifying natural substances to human needs and wants, but also the character of the social environment in which these needs are satisfied. Echoing many a premise that Leont'ev utilised in formulating his theory of activity, Venable argues labour and social organisation to constitute the subjective side of human beings in the course of their transformation. With requisite grasp of the nature of dialectal inquiry, I turn next to discuss aspects of a curriculum studies course I taught my MA students at TISS, Hyderabad campus, before bringing my writing of this book to completion.

References

Anyon, J. (2009a). Introduction: Critical social theory, educational research and intellectual agency. In J. Anyon (Ed.), *Theory and educational research: Toward critical social explanation* (pp. 1–23). Routledge.

Anyon, J. (2009b). Critical theory is not enough: Social justice education, political participation, and the politicization of students. In M. Apple, W. Au, & L. Gandin (Eds.), *The Routledge international handbook of critical education* (pp. 389–395). Routledge.

Anyon, J. (2011). *Marx and education.* Routledge.

Bamberg, M., & Georgakopoulou, A. (2008). Small stories as a new perspective in narrative and identity analysis. *Text and Talk, 28*(3), 377–396.

Chaiklin, S. (2011). The role of practice in cultural-historical science. In M. Kontopodis, C. Wul, & B. Fichtner (Eds.), *Children, development and education: Cultural, historical, anthropological perspectives* (pp. 227–246). Springer.

Clandinin, D. J. (1985). Personal practical knowledge: A study of teachers' classroom images. *Curriculum Inquiry, 15*(4), 361–385.

Denzin, N., & Lincoln, Y. (2000). *Handbook of qualitative research* (2nd ed.). Sage.

Edwards, A., Gilroy, P., & Hartley, D. (2002). *Rethinking teacher education: Collaborative responses to uncertainty.* RoutledgeFalmer.

Fay, B. (1977). How people change themselves: The relationship between critical theory and its audience. In T. Ball (Ed.), *Political theory and praxis: New perspectives* (pp. 200–233). University of Minnesota Press.

Freire, P. (1998). *Pedagogy of freedom: Ethics, democracy and civic courage.* Rowman & Littlefield.

Freire, P. (2005a). *Education for critical consciousness.* Continuum.

Freire, P. (2005b). *Pedagogy of the oppressed* (30th anniversary ed.). Penguin. (Original work published 1970)

Gade, S. (2010). Narratives of students learning mathematics: Plurality of strategies and a strategy for practice? In C. Bergsten, E. Jablonka, & T. Wedege (Eds.), *Mathematics *and mathematics education: Cultural and social dimensions. Proceedings of the seventh mathematics education research seminar MADIF7* (pp. 102–112). Stockholm University.

Gade, S. (2011). Narrative as unit of analysis for teaching-learning praxis and action: Tracing the personal growth of a professional voice. *Reflective Practice, 12*(1), 35–45.

Gade, S. (2012a). Close-to-practice classroom research by way of Vygotskian units of analysis. In *Proceedings of the 12th international congress on mathematics education (ICME)* (pp. 4312–4321). ICME.

Gade, S. (2012b). Teacher researcher collaboration at a grade four mathematics classroom: Restoring equality to students usage of the '=' sign. *Educational Action Research, 20*(4), 553–570.

Gade, S. (2012c). Two small stories about self and world at grades four and five Informing close-to-practice research of mathematics classrooms In P. Salo (Ed.), *Responsible research papers from the fourth qualitative research conference* (pp. 34–42). The Faculty of Education, Åbo Akademi University.

Gade, S. (2014). Praxis and phronesis as units of analysis: Realising a social science that matters in practitioner inquiry. *Reflective Practice, 15*(6), 718–729.

Gade, S. (2015). Unpacking teacher-researcher collaboration with three theoretical frameworks – A case of expansive learning activity? *Cultural Studies of Science Education, 10*(3), 603–619.

Gade, S. (2016). Oneself in practitioner research, with Vygotsky and Bakhtin. *Reflective Practice, 17*(4), 403–414.

Gade, S. (2017). Research as praxis, en route theory/practice teacher-researcher collaboration: A self-study. *Nordic Studies in Mathematics Education, 22*(3), 5–23.

Gade, S. (2020). Performance, the arts, and curricular change. *LEARNing Landscapes, 13*(1), 129–136.

Gade, S., & Blomqvist, C. (2015). From problem posing to posing problems by way of explicit mediation in Grades four and five. In F. M. Singer, N. Ellerton, & J. Cai (Eds.), *Mathematical problem posing: From research to effective practice* (pp. 195–213). Springer.

Gade, S., & Blomqvist, C. (2016). Shared object and stakeholdership in teacher-researcher expansive activity. In C. Csíkos, A. Rausch, & J. Szitányi (Eds.), *Proceedings of the 40th annual conference of the International Group for the Psychology of Mathematics Education (PME)* (pp. 2-267–2-274). PME.

Gade, S., & Blomqvist, C. (2018). Investigating everyday measures through exploratory talk: Whole classroom intervention and landscape study at Grade four. *Cultural Studies of Science Education, 13*(1), 235–252.

Gade, S., & Forsgren, T. (2019). Realising transformative agency and student identity: Meaningful practical activity based formative intervention at grade eight. *Cultural Studies of Science Education, 14*(4), 897–914.

hooks, b. (1994). *Teaching to transgress: Education as the practice of freedom.* Routledge.

CRITICAL PERSPECTIVES 195

Keller, E. F. (1985). *Reflections on gender and science.* Yale University Press.

Kincheloe, J. (2001). Describing the bricolage: Conceptualizing a new rigor in qualitative research. *Qualitative Inquiry, 7*(6), 679–692.

Kincheloe, J. (2003). Critical ontology: Visions of selfhood and curriculum. *Journal of Curriculum Theorizing, 19*(1), 47–64.

Kincheloe, J. (2004). Into the great wide open: Introducing critical thinking In J. Kincheloe & D. Weil (Eds.), *Critical thinking and learning: An encyclopaedia for parents and teachers* (pp. 1–52). Greenwood Press.

Kincheloe, J. (2005a). What are we doing here. In J. Kincheloe (Ed.), *Classroom teaching: An introduction* (pp. 1–24). Peter Lang.

Kincheloe, J. (2005b). Issues of power, questions of purpose, In J. Kincheloe (Ed.), *Classroom teaching: An introduction* (pp. 25–51). Peter Lang.

Kincheloe, J. (2005c). The curriculum and the classroom. In J. Kincheloe (Ed.), *Classroom teaching: An introduction* (pp. 85–103). Peter Lang.

Kincheloe, J. (2005d). On to the next level: Continuing the conceptualization of the bricolage. *Qualitative Inquiry, 11*(3), 323–350.

Kvale, S. (1989). To validate is to question. In S. Kvale (Ed.), *Issues of validity in qualitative research* (pp. 73–92). Chartwell-Bratt.

Lather, P. (1986a). Research as praxis. *Harvard Educational Review, 56*(3), 257–277.

Lather, P. (1986b). Issues of validity in openly ideological research: Between a rock and a soft place, *Interchange, 17*(4), 63–84.

Levins, R., & Lewontin, R. (1985). *The dialectical biologist.* Harvard University Press.

Lewontin, R. (1997). Not all in the genes. In L. Wolpert & A. Richards (Eds.), *Passionate minds. The inner world of scientists* (pp. 102–110). Oxford University Press.

McKeon, R. (1952). Philosophy and action. *Ethics, 62*(2), 79–100.

Newman, F., & Holzman, L. (1997). *End of knowing: New developmental way of learning.* Routledge.

Ollman, B. (2003). *Dance of the dialectic: Steps in Marx's method.* University of Illinois Press.

Seeger, F. (2001). The complementarity of theory and praxis in the cultural-historical approach: From self-application to self-regulation. In S. Chaiklin (Ed.), *The theory and practice of cultural-historical psychology* (pp. 35–55). Aarhus University Press.

Skovsmose, O. (2004). *Critical mathematics education for the future* [Paper presentation]. 10th International Congress on Mathematics Education. Retrieved September 24, 2020, from https://www.researchgate.net/publication/252205485_Critical_Mathematics_Education_for_the_Future

Smith, L. T. (1999). *Decolonising methodologies: Research and Indigenous peoples.* Zed Books.

Stetsenko, A. (2010). Standing on the shoulders of giants: a balancing act of dialectically theorizing conceptual understanding on the grounds of Vygotsky's project.

In W. M. Roth (Ed.), *Re/structuring science education: Reuniting psychological and sociological perspectives* (pp. 69–88). Springer.

Tobin, K. (2014). Using collaborative inquiry to better understand teaching and learning. In L. Bencze & S. Alsop (Eds.), *Activist science and technology education* (pp. 127–147). Springer.

Venable, V. (1945). *Human nature: The Marxian view*. Meridian Books.

Vianna, E., & Stetsenko, A. (2011). Connecting learning and identity development through a transformative activist stance: Application in adolescent development in a child welfare program. *Human Development, 54*(5), 313–338.

CHAPTER 8

Curriculum Studies

Schooling Is a Bold and Risky Means

1   Preamble

Upon returning to my hometown in India, I had opportunity of teaching students pursuing their Masters in Education and Bachelors in Social Sciences at the TISS, Hyderabad campus. I found this experience to be like none other. More than two decades ago in this very city, I was teaching middle school students who were full of aspirations and came largely from middle class backgrounds. This time I faced students from diverse socioeconomic backgrounds, not only from across the country but also from remote corners teeming with diverse geopolitical realities. The aspirations of these students were just as noteworthy, in terms of the future they saw for themselves as well as our society at large. While some spoke languages belonging to the twenty odd official ones recognised by the Indian Government, a good many spoke dialects. While many an Indian language has a unique script, some languages are merely oral, having no script at all. For students speaking quite a few oral languages and dialects, their experience of education in any one of the official languages while schooling is quite often a hegemonic one. Yet I found many of these students to also come with hauntingly unique stories and personalities, accents and viewpoints, besides a fierce and earnest need of wanting to speak, be heard and articulate themselves in English, the language in which our courses were offered at TISS.

It is against this backdrop that I examine aspects of curriculum studies, an area dealing primarily with legitimate knowledge that is to be taught and evaluated at schools. Brought forth by competent national authorities the scope of such knowledge in a country as vast as ours, risks making an assumption which simplifies complexity in terms of recognising students and teachers as being similar everywhere. Recognising the pitfalls and lack of success that such a view has brought forth in its implementation, there is presently much debate, awareness and visible effort in India by many a government and non-governmental organisation to understand the societal intricacies in which quality education needs to be realised. Before I left for my doctoral program in 2003 such efforts were restricted largely to experimental schools like the one I taught at. I now find the spirit to be widespread. It is encouraging to find an

© KONINKLIJKE BRILL NV, LEIDEN, 2022 | DOI:10.1163/9789004512160_008

earnest sense of activism almost everywhere. While I guess we have still some distance to cover, it goes without saying that an appreciation of such collective efforts is very much deserving of a detailed study and possibly another writing on my part. I thus limit my scope in this chapter to bring together aspects I came across in my post-doctoral journey, which might nonetheless be relevant to the scenario I allude to above. Towards these ends and in this section I draw upon three specific writings. I turn *first* to those of sociologist C Wright Mills who speaks to the importance of becoming a self-conscious thinker and of intellectual craftsmanship. I turn *next* to snippets of life histories offered by my MA students in assignments I had set in relation to their selves, one that spoke about their diverse ontologies. I found such insight into their lives to enrich my ongoing teaching immensely. I turn *finally* to philosopher John Dewey's writing titled *My pedagogical creed*, which outlines the scope of what could be taught at schools.

I found arguments made by Wright Mills (1959a) in *The sociological imagination* to direct my conduct of research in two ways. *First* is his focus on the manner in which to grasp problematic areas that are also worthy of transformation. In particular Mills views *method* as allowing us to ask and answer questions with some assurance, that these might be durable. His notion of *theory* is also one that offers clarity of concepts, economy of procedure, alongside a degree of generality and logical relations. The aims of either are to emphatically release and not restrict our sociological imagination. This leads Mills to view a *self-conscious thinker* in terms of being a researcher who knows the difference between mastering and not being mastered by any method and argues,

> To have mastered 'method' and 'theory' is to have become a self-conscious thinker, a man at work and aware of the assumptions and the implications of whatever he is about. To be mastered by 'method' or 'theory' is simply to be kept from working, from trying, that is, to find out about something that is going on in the world. Without insight into the way the craft is carried on, the results of study are infirm; without a determination that study shall come to significant results, all method is meaningless pretense. (Mills, 1959a, p. 121)

Echoing how Vygotsky and Freire went about their path-breaking work, Mills argues in favour of every practitioner becoming his or her own methodologist at their work – aware of the assumptions and implications of the work they are carrying out. To be a sociologist, for Mills, was thus to address human variety and call upon one's sociological imagination to engage with the myriad social worlds that people lived in the past, were living currently and might also live

CURRICULUM STUDIES

going ahead. Towards this Mills *second* offers practical advice worth following – to maintain a journal and keep notes of important ideas, both vague and more finished, from the writings of other scholars – something I have myself benefitted from and put into practice. The filing, classification, reorganisation and playfulness exercised towards these ideas, Mills argues, helps loosen and enrich one's *intellectual craftsmanship*. Mills concludes,

> Know that the human meaning of public issues must be revealed by relating them to personal troubles – and to the problems of the individual life. Know that the problems of social science, when adequately formulated, must include both troubles and issues, both biography and history, and the range of their intricate relations. Within that range the life of the individual and the making of societies occur; and within that range the sociological imagination has its chance to make a difference in the quality of human life in our time. (Mills, 1959b, p. 226)

It might come as no surprise that my present writing draws on Mills' advice, both in terms of the means I have come to deploy and the aims to which my efforts are directed – of making a thoughtful effort that draws on many a relevant scholar, towards making a difference to the quality of human life. I have explored the dialectic between these two aspects in two directions (1) between my troubles as a practitioner and those issues which hold meaning in educational research at large, and (2) the range of relations brought forth by biography and history in the personal lives of students, whose public persona we are trusted with so as to in turn make a difference in their lives. It is with the later objective, besides CHAT and critical perspectives in tow, that for half weightage of assessment each semester I would ask my students at TISS to draw on their personal selves. Being adults who could cast votes in our democracy, I considered them able to essay a topic of their choice that would likely be a starting point for them to transform their immediate reality.

With Bachelor students whom I taught *Appreciation of Mathematics* the essay expected was on any topic of interest to them in mathematics, which would be followed by an oral presentation they would make to all their classmates. The result of this effort was that almost all sixty students in my class made an effort to interest their peers in topics ranging from Fibonacci numbers, the Archimedes' principle or how playing tennis say would vary on courts with different surfaces. The Monty Hall and Dido's problem, besides contemporary issues like the effects of demonetisation of our currency or the dynamics of participation in our general elections were also discussed. In their ability to choose content of interest to them and have opportunity to convince their peers of their personal interest, we witnessed aspects of human activity at large and the many ways in which mathematics was deftly at work. Gödel's incompleteness theorem was the showstopper one year, which most were fascinated with and endeared to. It was in this manner that I was able to realise in some small measure, the humanistic philosophy which Hersh spoke about in Chapter 1.

For Master students, with whom I led a course on *Human development and learning*, I asked them to essay some aspect of their individual life's developmental journey, so that in line with Freire they could begin to name their world. Our prior discussion of Lindsay Huber's (2008) writing about *critical race testimonios*, was particularly useful in facilitating such attempts. Highly relevant to issues students were facing with regards to living in one's caste, tribe, gender and/or social strata, Huber's writing encouraged them to articulate personal struggles as well as view their development as human beings in relation to social justice, the presence of dominant ideologies and/or their subordination to pervasive social forces at play. The result of this exercise was the ability for many to enter and make use of what Kris Gutierrez, Betsy Rymes and Joanne Larson (1995) identify as a *third space*, wherein prevalent social and personal scripts in the lives lived by students could surface and interact in a meaningful and authentic manner. I found this collective space to be filled for example, with the personal struggles faced by the eldest of four daughters of a subsistence farmer, as she attempted to finish her graduation by living in the city with her uncle and aunt who were far from generous; the son of a *sarpanch* or head of a village committee who wanted those who were landless to also form part of the committee; yet another who wished to take part in village festivities from which families belonging to his caste were traditionally barred. There were in addition young men who found their fathers to be weak, needlessly bending to family or societal dictates; while those aspiring to be the first person from their village and tribe to pursue doctoral studies. There was a young women who was dismayed that her mother would not speak openly about gynaecological problems. Yet the draft essay of another found fault with her mother to not stand up for her to complete her studies and go on to arrange her marriage against her will. By the time of making her final submission, I noted her to have however forgiven her mother and moved on with resolve.

While the process of writing and engaging with such complex realities translated into stirring emotions and memories of family histories that could have been otherwise for many a student, their final essays also served as a source of motivation for sharing their lives and bringing about personal change and self-determination in line with Fay, as in Chapter 8. The naming of their own world in the third space of our classroom was a decisive first step for many.

CURRICULUM STUDIES   201

In terms of how curricular documents were designed, one could not help but surmise that the oft found emphasis on abstract content instead of lives lived by students was misplaced.

Some guidance on the way forward with many an issue just raised is found *third* in John Dewey's (1897) essay titled *My pedagogical creed*. Herein Dewey recognises education as principal means for students to participate in the social consciousness of humankind, whose storehouse they each had every right to inherit. Dewey argues,

> I believe that the only true education comes through the stimulation of the child's powers by the demands of the social situations in which he finds himself. Through these demands he is stimulated to act as a member of a unity, to emerge from his original narrowness of action and feeling, and to conceive of himself from the standpoint of the welfare of the group to which he belongs. Through the responses which others make to his own activities he comes to know what these mean in social terms. The value which they have is reflected back into them. (Dewey, 1897/1998, p. 77)

Dewey's recognition of education being a social process for individuals to inherit the storehouse of humankind, echos key psychological premise of CHAT and ontological premise of critical perspectives. Recognising education to be both psychological and sociological in spirit and deed, Dewey in turn conceives schools as social institutions, enabling them to form a community life which initiates students into processes of living in the here and now and not some abstract preparation for future living. In examining life being presently lived, Dewey thus asks students' activities be those that simplify reality, yet also establish continuity with aspects they would be familiar with at their home. Dewey also asks the content of different curricular subjects to not be isolated from reality but bear immediate relation to children's social life. The teacher's role is here seen as a facilitator, who helps contextualise the larger experience and wisdom in life that children need to examine. Dewey brings his articles of faith in his *Creed* to conclusion, by viewing education as a fundamental means of achieving social progress as well as social reform. It is by means of participation in educational activity herein, that children find basis for developing their individual as well as social consciousness.

While the oeuvre of Dewey's writings is extensive, I take his *Creed* as point of departure for arguments I examine in this Chapter in relation to the ends and means which need to be addressed in curriculum studies. As with purposeful writings of Mills and the kind of riveting testimonios my own students gave, my view of the role of teachers and researchers to be rightful curriculum makers in this enterprise gains credence. Offering an overview of the history of curricular theorising, Cheryl Craig and Vicki Ross' (2008) *Cultivating the image of teachers as curriculum makers*, recognises the importance of the interventional research I have been able to conduct in collaboration with teachers. They observe,

> In order to capture the nuances of the particular – the essences of the practical, future inquiries at the intersections of curriculum and teaching will need to unfold with researchers working alongside teachers, honouring practice, awake to diversity, and inviting participation and insights. Such a positioning will ensure that researchers pose relevant questions of social significance and follow where education inquiry leads. (Craig & Ross, 2008, p. 296)

Craig and Ross' quote above helps me identify the niche in educational research that I have attempted to carry out in collaboration with Lotta and Tomas. It is also a niche towards which I have geared all my arguments in a cumulative manner in this book. Even as I empirically substantiate my intent and conduct of this niche in the next chapter, I presently turn to insightful arguments put forward by many a curricular theorist.

2   Teacher as Artist Is Researcher

My foray into curriculum studies was via Lawrence Stenhouse's oft cited quote – It is teachers who, in the end, will change the world of the school by understanding it. I had wondered how Stenhouse came about making a claim that made much personal sense to me as practitioner and was also curious to know the specific stance he envisioned for teachers to bring about wider change. I shall dwell on both issues. Stenhouse's pioneering work, in the Humanities Curriculum Project or HCP, was conducted in the late 1960s, early 1970s, when students in the UK were to remain in school for a year longer, till they were sixteen. Stenhouse and teachers in the HCP examined how controversial human issues could be taught to students and whether teachers could remain neutral in such a process. Controversial issues were recognised by the HCP as those which divided students, teachers and parents in terms of the course of action that could be taken to resolve them. As example, these included topics such as war and society, relation between sexes, law and order or poverty. Society had collectively yet to find solutions to the way these issues had played out in their time. Stenhouse's view of curriculum research was in terms of building educational theory and an attack on its separation from practice. He thus viewed curriculum studies to concern itself with the difference between two ways in which curricula were viewed in his time, intention and reality or of aspirations and attempts to operationalise these in the classroom. His efforts in the HCP were to grasp how to promote and not frustrate the desire for learning by students. He argued,

> It seemed that the basic classroom pattern should be one of discussion. Instruction inevitably implies that the teacher cannot maintain a neutral position. In the discussion the teacher should be neutral on the issues which form the agenda of the group, but he should accept responsibility for the rigor and quality of the work. Accordingly, the teacher is seen as a neutral and relatively recessive chairman, though not a passive one, since it would be his job to develop quality in the students' work by shrewd, though sparing, questioning. (Stenhouse, 1971, p. 157)

Based on observations of the kind made above, I find Stenhouse's work to change the field of curriculum studies in UK in three specific ways. (1) Stenhouse worked against the objectives model dominant in his times, which assumed that if the ends of what is to be taught were specified with sufficient care, then the best means to attain them could be via controlled interventions that were scientifically evaluated. Such means were in turn thought appropriate for dissemination to teachers, for them to in turn implement in their own classrooms. (2) He adopted an anti-authoritarian epistemological stance, one which conceived and acknowledged that knowledge was provisional, revisable and connected to practice. He viewed classrooms as laboratories where educational theory was under continuous test by teachers as researchers. (3) In reflecting on his legacy, John Elliott and Nigel Norris (2012a) point out that Stenhouse placed the development of pedagogy at the heart of the HCP and this created some concern within the Project's sponsoring agency. While the agency was expecting high-quality curriculum materials, the expertise which the HCP staff brought to bear were in relation to questions like – what is worthwhile curriculum content?, what materials best exemplify/illustrate it?, rather than how precisely any content was to be taught by using any prepared material. This latter, the HCP staff pointed out, fell within the discretionary power of classroom teachers to decide. Prescribing methods of teaching, they went on to argue, amounted to unwarranted interference in teaching which was the professional domain of teachers.

While I shortly discuss Stenhouse's thoughts in relation to teachers as researchers, I presently turn to three constructs which form the backbone to his work. *First*, Stenhouse clarified what any *curriculum* meant,

> A curriculum is the means by which the experience of attempting to put an educational proposal into practice is made publicly available. It involves both content and method, and in its widest application takes account of the problem of implementation in the institutions of the educational system. (Stenhouse, 1975, p. 5)

Laying emphasis on making the results of any study public and in agreement with Mills' asking that we make public our biography and history, Stenhouse *second* clarified his vision of *research* as follows,

> Research may be broadly defined as systematic inquiry made public. The inquiry should, I think, be rooted in acutely felt curiosity, and research suffers when it is not. Such inquiry becomes systematic when it is structured over time by continuities lodged in the intellectual biography of the researcher and coordinated with the work of others through the cumulative capacity of the organisation of the discipline or the subject. (Stenhouse, 1979/2012, p. 128)

In line with Stenhouse above and in line with my CHAT and narrative based methodological journey in this book, I have attempted to locate my emerging thoughts with those proposed by others. *Finally* on the *role of the teacher in curriculum development*, Elliott and Norris argue,

> The teacher was at the heart of Stenhouse's theory of curriculum development because it was the teacher who held the keys to the laboratory, it was the teacher who could mount educational experiments in the classroom, it was the teacher who would, maybe with the help of others, marshal and interpret the evidence, and it was the teacher who had to learn from the experience of classroom action research if genuine and sustainable educational improvement were to be possible. Accordingly, *to develop a curriculum is to mount a series of educational experiments.* (Elliott & Norris, 2012b, pp. 2–3, emphasis added)

Stressing the need for teachers to be researchers, Stenhouse (1975) had been emphatic in pointing out that it was not enough that others studied the work of teachers, but that teachers studied their work themselves. With classrooms

CURRICULUM STUDIES

and school as key laboratories for such work, Stenhouse suggested researchers and teachers collaborate and come upon a common vocabulary that could be shared and utilised by both.

I now turn to the manner in which Stenhouse envisioned teachers to study their classrooms and decide for themselves, as Elliott and Norris pointed out, aspects like what might be worthwhile content to teach or what materials would best exemplify any contents' significance. In fact, it is towards these ends that he outlined the centrality of the *curriculum as a powerful medium*. Stenhouse argued,

> Curriculum is the medium through which the teacher can learn his art. Curriculum is the medium through which the teacher can learn knowledge. Curriculum is the medium through which the teacher can learn about the nature of education. Curriculum is the medium through which the teacher can learn about the nature of knowledge. And curriculum is the best medium through which the teacher can learn about these because it enables him to test ideas by practice and hence to rely on his judgment rather than on the judgment of others. (Stenhouse, 1980, p. 43)

I find Stenhouse to tie together three key aspects – the teacher as artist, the curriculum as medium through which the teacher could learn her art, and the opportunity any teacher has to develop professional judgement in the process of trying out and testing her ideas in practice. Stenhouse also viewed the *teacher as artist* in terms of the interpersonal transactions of knowledge she carried out with students. Such art could not be gleaned or improved upon by reading books but attained from critical practice and exercising the art in the first place. Inbuilt in his approach was the fact that there was no stasis – as an artist a teacher was constantly dealing with change both in the ideas she used and in the way she used ideas to intended effect in classroom practice. This last Stenhouse argued, meant that a teacher not only learnt her art but also learnt through her art. School improvement through curriculum study, Stenhouse emphasised, was thus about improving the art of the teacher and not improving students' learning outcomes without also improving the art of teaching.

Yet Stenhouse was very cognisant of ground realities in which teachers could exercise their becoming artists and conduct research in addition. Towards his earlier suggestion that teachers and researchers collaborate, he recognised teachers may lack confidence and argued,

> Researchers sometimes regard teachers as theoretically innocent. But much professional research drawing on, if not feeding, the disciplines

is also theoretically innocent. This is true of most surveys, field experiments and evaluations. You can partly detect them by the sign that all the theoretical work of their authors is methodological. On the other hand, some teachers are theorists, hot from PhDs or having informally developed theoretical interests. What teachers most often lack is confidence and experience in relating theory to design and in the conduct of research work. (Stenhouse, 1981, pp. 110–111)

Stenhouse above touches on an aspect I have myself observed in research that does not follow CHAT perspectives, wherein key attention to the cultural-historical development of children is found wanting. Stenhouse's point about teachers needing confidence and experience with relating theory to their conduct of research is also well taken, an aspect I intend to greater illustrate in the next Chapter, where my collaborative work with teachers is in line with his direction that research needs to be in service of concrete practice and not the other way around.

In *Artistry and teaching: The teacher as focus of research and development*, Stenhouse (1988) expands on his notion of teacher as artist by clarifying that by art he means an exercise expressive of meaning or the very *performance* by teachers so that students understand the nature and content of what is currently being learnt. Stenhouse goes on to add that all good art is inquiry, an experiment, by virtue of which the teacher becomes a researcher. The teacher as artist is thus a researcher par excellence. Stenhouse also recognised that for conducting any manner of curriculum inquiry training teachers is thus a non-starter, as teachers must themselves want to change and carry out the performance via which the subject content in question is conveyed. He concludes,

> For there is in education no absolute and unperformed knowledge. In educational research and scholarship the ivory towers where the truth is neglected are so many – theatres without players, galleries without pictures, music without musicians. *Educational knowledge exists in, and is verified or falsified in, its performance.* (Stenhouse, 1988, p. 51, emphasis added)

Having taken a focused view on Stenhouse's curriculum research efforts in the UK, one that since evolved into the conduct of action research as exemplified by arguments of John Elliot in previous chapters, I now turn to curriculum theorising led by Joseph Schwab in the US.

CURRICULUM STUDIES

3   Deliberating the Practical

My discussion of writings by Connelly and Eisner thus far, would prepare readers to work conducted by the descendants of Joseph Schwab. Even as I greater dwell on Eisner's work once again in the next section, I discuss those of Lee Shulman another of Schwab's descendants in the section that follows. It is also the case that in Schwab's life and work being tied to the city of Chicago, it was not surprising to find Schwab to have worked alongside McKeon, whom I discuss in the previous chapter. In John Dewey being one of two doctoral supervisors McKeon had, it is again not surprising that Dewey's thinking percolates in the work of all the scholars I just mention. One will find Dewey's thoughts to echo again when I discuss writings of Gert Biesta in the final section of this Chapter. Yet, in the immediate my drawing upon writings of Schwab, Eisner and Shulman offer a ring side view of the fruits of arguments made against the abstract in curriculum studies and in favour of the practical.

Schwab essayed four papers each titled *The Practical* with subtitles as – *A language for curriculum, Arts of eclectic, Translation into curriculum* and *Something for curriculum professors to do.* In this section I take the first of these as point of departure since its arguments shed light on Schwab's attention to what he called the practical, in terms of realities of curricular instruction and the kind of issues he was unhappy with in his time. Schwab (1970) argued that the methods and principles being used in his time were (1) unable to significantly contribute to the advancement of education, (2) that the field has reached this state by unexamined and mistaken reliance on theory developed outside the field of education, and (3) that a capacity to do so would be possible if curricular energies were diverted from theoretic pursuits to the concrete practical, whose methods and subject matter were different in character and kind. It is possible that Schwab was unaware of the theoretical-practical perspectives of CHAT, since the publication of Vygotsky's *Mind in Society* in English took place only in 1978. The potential of these perspectives have also been greater engaged with by scholars worldwide only in contemporary times. While I intend to examine any common ground that lies between Vygotsky's notion of practice and Schwab's practical in a separate writing, there is much to be learnt from the contrast Schwab himself drew between abstract theory and practical issues faced by practitioners and how these informed his view of curriculum studies.

To begin with Schwab argued the outcome of *a theoretic stance* was knowledge, one offered as general statements whose truths were durable, extensive in scope and confidence inspiring. The outcome of *the practical* on the other hand was a decision, taken by the practitioner as a guide to possible action while choosing from among the many alternatives that existed. Taking such decisions were never true but judged in comparison to existing alternatives after the action was taken. While the subject matter of abstract theory was impervious to change, he added, those of the practical were susceptible to circumstance and liable to unexpected change. It followed that the problems of the theoretic were recognised as being problematic beforehand, whereas practical problems arose from contexts only after one began to engage with them. Finally theoretic problems were controlled by some manner of principle, one which eluded practical problems till they were encountered and acted upon.

Given the attention being given to the kind of action practitioners take, I argue Schwab's expressed concern was in favour of grasping real events in concrete particulars or the practical taken as a whole, one that would decidedly differ from one concrete particular to another. For Schwab any *study of the curriculum* needed to be,

> brought to bear, not in some archetypical classroom, but in a particular locus in time and space with smells, shadows, seats, and conditions outside its walls which may have much to do with what is achieved inside. Above all, the supposed beneficiary is not the generic child, not even a class or kind of child out of the psychological or sociological literature pertaining to the child. The beneficiary will consist of very local kinds of children and, within the local kinds, individual children. The same diversity holds with respect to teachers and what they do. (Schwab, 1970/2013, p. 611)

Unlike Stenhouse's view of curriculum as the medium through which teachers learnt their art, Schwab's vision of curriculum studies directed emphasis on real events, real contexts inclusive of smells, shadows and conditions outside the four walls of the classroom, real children and not their generic conception. This rationale applied to teachers as well. I need to mention that I found Schwab's focus on the concrete particular as well as the practical and not the theoretic abstract, to be useful in determining the kind of approach I myself took with each MA student of mine, given their linguistic diversity, socioeconomic and geopolitical backgrounds besides geographic spread. It was not only the personal, sociological or psychological aspects that they went on to share in our third space that helped me decide upon my actions, but also those cues I surmised from interactions I individually had with each of them over time. Far from adopting a uniform approach to students' participation and evaluation, my approach was tailor made to each student's aspirations, abilities, lives

CURRICULUM STUDIES

being lived, besides wider societal circumstances they were negotiating as a whole. In my doing so I engaged with what Schwab recognised as *deliberation* about which he argued,

> Deliberation is complex and arduous. It treats both ends and means and must treat them as mutually determining one another. It must try to identify, with respect to both, what facts may be relevant. ... It must try to identify the desiderata in the case. It must generate alternative solutions. It must make every effort to trace the branching pathways of consequences which may flow from each alternative and affect desiderata. It must then weigh alternatives and their costs and consequences against one another, and choose, not the right alternative, for there is no such thing, but the *best* one. (Schwab, 1970/2013, p. 618)

By forgoing the notion of one right alternative and be thoughtful about the dialectic between ends and means prevalent, Schwab directed me to choose between alternatives available in the present.

I find Schwab's focusing on real people, attending to the concrete practical and directing attention to the taking of deliberative action, to be rooted conceptually in Dewey's pragmatic approach to education. I thus turn to Schwab's (1959) text titled, *The 'impossible' role of the teacher in progressive education.* In relation to *learning by doing* Schwab clarifies that for Dewey, any theory of doing or practice found its full meaning only when that theory was put into practice. The only means of testing the theory was thus by means of its verification within that practice. Any theory of practice was thus good to the extent its approach took into account various aspects that lead to the taking of action in the first place and which resolved the problem found in the concrete to the satisfaction of those caught up in its existence. A good pragmatic theory would thus do more than merely suggest means for solving problems and point also to what the solution might also be like at the same time. This in turn led to the possibility of reflection and arriving at flexible ways of acting by practitioners who could take steps that could be modified as well. One could consider alternative options of taking action, so that one could meet with scenarios yet to be encountered. Schwab thus argued,

> To 'learn by doing' was neither to learn only by doing nor to learn only how to do. Doing was to go hand in hand with reading, reflecting, and remembering. And these intelligent activities were to eventuate in something more than efficient coping with the bread-and-butter problems of existence. They were to yield the capacity for rewarding experience,

a doing and undergoing not merely for the sake of material outcome: often, not for that outcome at all, but for the satisfaction of the work itself. (Schwab, 1959/1978, p. 182)

Three aspects follow from arguments Schwab lays out above. *First,* in line with Dewey, a good theory in education allowed practitioners to take action, following which both practitioners and students were satisfied with the outcomes of actions jointly taken. Such a theory/practice stance in CHAT parlance, is valuable yardstick with which to gauge theoretical frameworks from across academic disciplines. *Second,* Schwab's learning by doing was not a specific method of learning, but a methodology by which one came to both learn and know. *Finally,* Schwab considered the primary ethic of teachers to be learners. This meant that in relation to any problem in classroom instruction, practitioners were to aim at achieving mastery of the problem situation, reflect upon actions they could take keeping related consequences in mind, besides reflect on the conduct of and knowledge from discovering both. It is at this point that Schwab was able to highlight who *a progressive teacher* was and argued,

> Only as the teacher uses the classroom as the occasion and the means to reflect upon education as a whole (ends as well as means), as the laboratory in which to translate into actions and thus to test reflections, actions, and outcomes against many criteria, is he a good 'progressive' teacher. (Schwab, 1959/1978, pp. 182–183)

Schwab recognised the existence of a progressive teacher to also be quite impossible in reality, since such a teacher had to be an everyday teacher as well. Yet it is of significance to note that Schwab lay emphasis on the dynamic between ends and means while describing the notions of both deliberation and the progressive teacher – in the *first* the dialectic was between alternatives available in one's own classrooms and in the *latter* the dialectic was between practitioner action and reflection against the backdrop of societal education at large. I find this last to echo concerns which Cochran-Smith and colleagues raise in Chapter 5, in terms of their notion of inquiry as stance which takes an expansive view of teaching and learning in terms of practitioner action.

4 Arts in Education

In discussing Elliott Eisner's extensive theorisation of arts in education, I draw on the opportunity I myself had to teach like an artist. By this I mean

CURRICULUM STUDIES

a fortunate realisation of three aspects he highlights. *First*, that the school I taught at had a climate in which it was possible for me to take pride in my efforts and obtain acknowledgement from students that their lives had been touched. This manner of satisfaction is what Eisner *second* recognises as being aesthetic and intrinsic,

> By art in education I am not talking about the visual arts, or music, or dance, but rather about the fact that activities motivated by the aesthetic satisfactions they provide – those that are intrinsic – are among the few that have any durability. ... Despite longer vacation periods and sabbaticals, professional opportunities and satisfaction for teachers are limited largely to the lives they lead in their classrooms. ...
> ... The aesthetic in teaching is the experience secured from being able *to put your own signature on your own work – to look at it and say it was good.* (Eisner, 1983, p. 12, emphasis added)

Drawing attention above to achieving the artistic and intrinsic in the time one spends in one's own classroom, Eisner *third* distinguishes the art of teaching from its craft. A skilled craftsperson, he argues, while managing her performance quite well does not create anything new as a performer. On the other hand, performances of artists while not being so plentiful do require ingenuity, one displayed in inventing new skills during the very process of performing. Making demands that one's teaching does not fall flat, I have argued such efforts to respond to the expectations of students who, as Sarason argues, are far from passive observers and come to see themselves and a slice of life differently (Gade, 2020).

Craig and Ross whom I cite in the preamble explain Eisner's emphasis on arts in education to emerge from him being introduced by Schwab to Aristotle, who argued that some things exist by nature and some by culture. This lead Eisner to realise that science had no monopoly on knowledge, leading him to reimagine schooling in artistic terms. On Schwab's need to be eclectic, in utilising multiple theories to constantly exercise deliberation in one's concrete practical, Eisner argues,

> The curriculum is first a process, one that requires above all the exercise of a practical rationality. It is a process that has standard features – the commonplaces of education – but not common activities or 'uniform solutions.' The aim of the curricularist is not to know, but to do; that is, the curricularist's task is to get a job done rather than to be a seeker of dispassionate truth (whatever that might mean). Both as an entity – a

212   CHAPTER 8

> body of material – and as a process – curricular activity is an artifact,
> a construction, the fruit of human and therefore fallible deliberation.
> (Eisner, 1984a, p. 202)

By viewing curriculum as a situated process as above, Eisner emphasises the need for practitioners to explore, develop besides refine humanistic modes of educational inquiry, however fallible these attempts may also be. It is to greater examine this line of thought that I now turn to dwell upon five arguments Eisner in turn makes about (1) what education can learn from the arts, (2) the role of arts in cognition and curriculum, (3) the role of art in transforming conscious-ness, (4) the kind of schools we need, besides (5) arts based educational research.

Delivering a lecture on *What education can learn from the arts*, Eisner (2009) highlights what may be missing in the commonly followed pursuit of efficiency, certainty, prediction and control, via a positivist approach to edu-cational theory and practice. For Eisner, helping students treat their work at school as a work of art, is an abiding concern even in their study of the sci-ences. His approach identifies that (1) form and content cannot be separated – how something is taught, besides how curricula and schools are organised may be the real and not side effects of practice, (2) everything interacts i.e. there can be no form without content and vice versa – in human experience the idea of large or small, hard or soft, fast or slow all engender educational contexts, (3) nuance matters – how words are spoken or gestures made affect the char-acter of the whole, (4) surprise is part of the rewards one reaps in the process of artistic inquiry – far from resisting surprise and creating conditions for its occurrence helps bring about one of the most powerful sources of intrinsic sat-isfaction, (5) the slowing down of perception is the most promising way to see what is there – unlike recognition, labelling and/or classification of any object or event, perception entails exploring a complex of qualities that constitutes its wholeness, (6) the limits of language are not the limits of cognition – we know more than we can tell, so that our being multi-literate allows for multiple forms of being as well as experiencing the world, (7) somatic experience is one of the most important indicators that one has gotten things right – somatic experience is body knowledge which allows for a sense of rightness of fit and an intuitive ability to discriminate without being able to articulate the condi-tions involved, (8) open ended tasks permit the exercise of imagination – as human virtue and aptitude this is the source of new possibilities by means of which students discover new seas in which they can set sail. Eisner thus argues that all the time spent at school should be devoted to the arts.

In *The role of arts in cognition and curriculum*, Eisner expands on some of the points he makes above. On the need for us to slow down cognitive processes so as to perceive the diverse qualities that make up any object or event, Eisner

CURRICULUM STUDIES

directs attention to the importance of our senses in arriving at our understanding of concepts. He argues,

> The importance of the senses in concept formation is that: 1) no concepts can be formed without sensory information, 2) the degree to which the particular senses are differentiated has a large effect on the kind and subtlety of the concepts formed, and 3) without concepts as images (whether these images are visual, auditory, or in some other sensory form) image surrogates – words, for example – are meaningless.
>
> *... The forms concepts take are as diverse as our sensory capacities and the abilities we have developed to use them.* (Eisner, 1981a, p. 49, emphasis added)

In what I consider needs to become a major focus in education at most levels of schooling, Eisner above underscores for me that the meaning of concepts symbolised by words are as diverse as our sensory capacities. The development of our multiple sensory capacities, he argues, is vital to both grasping and understanding of various concepts. I argue this last to have instructional significance in that just as words like flower and/or rainbow are made richer by how we slow down our cognitive processes to perceive their holistic existence, so also are concepts like justice and/or infinity say. These latter need to be somatically experienced just as the former, by slowing down one's own cognitive processes.

In *The role of art in transforming consciousness*, Eisner next argues that the way schools are organised, what is taught in them and the nature of relationships that are fostered among students, teachers and parents all matter, as these shape the many experiences students have. Each of these has every potential besides to influence the kind of individuals, students are likely to themselves become. Eisner explains,

> Experience is central to growth because experience is the medium of education.
>
> Education, in turn, is the process of learning to create ourselves, and it is what the arts, both as a process and as the fruits of that process, promote. Work in the arts is not only a way of creating performances and products; it is a way of creating our lives by expanding our consciousness, shaping our dispositions, satisfying our quest for meaning, establishing contact with others, and sharing a culture. (Eisner, 2002a, p. 3)

Of the many processes Eisner highlights that are implicitly involved in creating ourselves through the experiences we encounter, I highlight four in particular. (1) That in both arts and sciences, a primary process at work is the transforming of the private into the public. (2) An important role of education would thus be to organise instruction that facilitates young children to make this personal transformation as a way of knowing. (3) The arts has the ability in particular to liberate us from the literal, allowing students to vicariously experience aspects of our human life by stepping into others' shoes. This aspect would be key to sharing our common culture with others in its ability to genuinely move us in terms of the range of human emotions from grief to mirth and more. (4) The arts thus becomes a means of exploring our interior landscape. The possibility exists of seeing what we have not yet taken notice of or utilising forms of thinking to sort out experiences that are of consequence, for it is via these processes that our very selves are made and remade.

In *The kind of schools we need*, Eisner (2002b) seeks public debate on what its many stakeholders may want to collectively achieve. Eisner thus recommends that teaching become a professionally public process, where teachers have various opportunities to observe other teachers and provide feedback. Preventing isolated teachers to themselves figure out what went on while they were teaching, Eisner argues for the ability to overcome two kinds of ignorance, primary and secondary. In *primary ignorance*, he says, an individual recognises that one does not know and that if one wanted to, one could find out. In *secondary ignorance* an individual not only does not know something, but also does not know that she does not know. It is here that colleagues could step in with anecdotes and wisdom from their experiences which could lend vicarious support to the teaching of others. Echoing the significance of many a framework in Chapter 5, such efforts provide relief in cases where one's personal reflection alone may be unhelpful. In line with the kind of emphasis I have quoted Eisner to lay on the working of the human mind, the above argued manner of collective work can enable schools to recognise that for both teachers and students, their personal signature or distinctive way of learning besides of making public their current knowing, is to be respected and developed. Recognising that there are multiple forms in terms of which individuals can externalise knowing, in turn enables us to not be bound by number and text alone and use what is known outside school as well.

The above summary of Eisner's extensive writing, however brief and partial, brings me to the *kind of educational research* which allows us to attend to the artistic in human knowing. Two aspects worth highlighting here include – *first* and in line with Schwab's notion of deliberation in curricular practice, Eisner argues that we practitioners need to construct our own methods and conceptual apparatus which do not prescribe rules, but provide heuristic frameworks that allow each of us to make real time decisions. Such manner of research in turn asks that we have intimate acquaintance with ongoing life in classrooms. Eisner reiterates,

CURRICULUM STUDIES   215

What I believe we need if educational research is truly to inform educational practice is the construction of our own unique conceptual apparatus and research methods. The best way I know of for doing this is to become familiar with the richness and uniqueness of educational life. If we are sufficiently imaginative, out of such familiarity can come ideas, concepts, and theories of educational practice. Out of these theories can come methods of inquiry *that do not try to achieve levels of precision better suited to fields other than our own.* (Eisner, 1984b, p. 451, emphasis added)

Clarifying aims of research for the educational concrete, Eisner *second* argues in favour of *methodological pluralism* as a way of knowing,

Artistic approaches to research are less concerned with the discovery of truth than with the creation of meaning. What art seeks is not the discovery of the laws of nature about which true statements or explanations can be given, but rather the creation of images that people will find meaningful and from which their fallible and tentative views of the world can be altered, rejected, or made more secure. Truth implies singularity and monopoly. ... The field of education in particular needs to avoid methodological monism. *Our problems need to be addressed in as many ways as will bear fruit.* (Eisner, 1981b, p. 9, emphasis added)

Not denying the value that comes from a search for truth, by identifying artistic approaches in research with the creation of meaning and diversity, Eisner underscores the need for the latter to not be uni-dimensional but multi-dimensional is scope. In distinct echo to Kincheloe in Chapter 7, this last would follow Eisner's recognition that educational experiences are key to the formation of human minds of students as well as teachers. In spanning the oeuvre of Eisner's writings that ring true with my own experiences of classroom teaching, I am taken up by the scope of an artistic approach to cognition, curriculum, schooling, education and research, whose problems while identified by critical perspectives might need arts based solutions to navigate them creatively.

5   Cases – Portfolios – Tasks

In tracing Schwab's legacy in promoting teachers as curriculum makers, Craig and Ross (2008) identify four major ways in which Lee Shulman's work relates to the practical – pedagogical content knowledge in relation to teaching school subjects, wisdom of practice which led to advocating teaching standards, institutional based research of teaching, besides case studies in teaching/ teacher education focusing on a narrative of inquiry. From such a wide canvass, in this section I take Shulman's case studies on teaching/teacher education as point of departure. There is possibility here for me to synergise across research genres like practitioner research and research in mathematics education, allowing me to shed light on one fruitful way for practitioners to contribute to curriculum studies.

Shulman's *Towards a pedagogy of cases* draws attention to how *cases* can be utilised by practitioners to study content, context, tools, purposes or any of the multiple dilemmas and complexities that entail teaching in a wholistic manner. The benefits of case studies to grasp curricular action extend beyond their being a record of actions carried out. Shulman points in particular to their ability to offer concrete images of what is possible, unpack moral and ethical issues that could arise, display dispositions and habits of mind of teachers at work, besides the work of specific principles that are of value in concrete practice. As precedents of teaching practice, cases offer multiple benefits to practitioners both in terms of individual teacher learning and in the forming of communities in which one could think like a teacher and reflect on the teaching profession as a whole. Ideal for understanding teaching in a variety of contexts, there is also opportunity to witness the exercise of deliberation in line with Schwab. Being messy and found to cross disciplinary boundaries, cases thus have no single story to convey and have the potential of being viewed from multiple perspectives addressing diverse educational concerns. Arguing that *the* case method does not exist Shulman argues,

> *To call something a case is to make a theoretical claim.* It argues that the story, event, or text is an instance of a larger class, an example of a broader category. In a word, it is a 'case-of-something' and therefore merits more serious consideration than a simple anecdote or vignette. ... To call something a case, therefore, is to treat it as a member of a class of events and to call our attention to its value in helping us appreciate more than the particularities of the case narrative itself. (Shulman, 1992, p. 17, emphasis added)

I find Shulman's emphasis on identifying what any case is representative of, vital for two reasons (1) their study enables practitioners to articulate what *they* thought any case meant to them personally, besides (2) what category of teaching *they* think the case being examined best exemplifies. In every case having potential of being identified as a case-of-something, there is opportunity for case learning to be transformative as well. This last is possible when

CURRICULUM STUDIES

practitioners are able to connect propositional ideas and convey their learning in terms of practitioner narratives, motivating others. For Shulman, cases offer practitioners vital opportunity to theorise about curricular actions being taken. Such attempts at theorisation could then be tried out in newer scenarios and tested via new case studies in which contextual circumstances could change, conditions found altered and purposes of instruction remodelled.

Shulman also characterises *case narratives* as having a plot with a beginning, middle and end, while dealing with an educational tension that is relieved. Embedded in time, concrete materials besides social contexts, the process of practitioner inquiry through case narratives could reveal human agency in myriad forms – motives, misconceptions, frustrations, needs and human hands at work. He also distinguishes *case reports* – first person accounts reporting one's own activities and experiences, from *case studies* – third person accounts which portray events that can enable the carrying out of further examination. In addition *teaching cases* are those original accounts which are written or edited for teaching purposes. Extending Shulman's line of thought, Anna Richert focuses on dilemmas which novice teachers face while writing about their teaching experience, articulating problematic issues and discussing suggestions for potential solutions. In Shulman's terms this would mean helping teachers make the transition from case reports to other kinds, in the process of which they realise professional growth. Richert argues,

> My work is motivated by a belief that *teaching is fundamentally an intellectual task.* Helping teachers acknowledge what they know about it, writing about it, and sharing it with one another moves not only the individual teacher forward but the profession forward into the domain where it is defined and owned by people who do it. (Richert, 1992, p. 158, emphasis added)

The value of learning to examine teaching and realising professional development via cases, Pamela Grossman (1992) adds, lies in their ability to represent the messy world of practice and to stimulate problem solving in a realm where neither the problem nor the solution is clear. She thus suggests contexts in which teachers can discuss case studies or teaching cases to need a climate in which practitioners can express their views honestly. Besides reading up teaching cases and noting down personal observations prior to discussion, Grossman suggests cases could also be viewed from more than one perspective to elicit the multidimensionality of teaching that is inherent in real life. The brief summary I just present, about the grounds on which Shulman's argued for a pedagogy of cases, allows me to turn to arguments made in favour of practitioner portfolios, which is the *first* of two ways by which cases can be put to an educative beyond instrumental use in line with Fay as in Chapter 7.

Creating a *portfolio* could be a transformative experience for teachers, argues Nona Lyons (1999), who views the many documents and thought processes that go into making a portfolio as empowering teachers and validating their professional authority. Vitally the very construction of portfolios can shape their emerging practice as practitioners. The process of choosing ends and means in line with Schwab and creating a portfolio helps practitioners articulate their teaching philosophy, besides develop their technique as well. Following Shulman's need for cases to make a theoretical claim, Lyons views portfolio construction as a theoretical activity in which teachers are guided by their personal theory of teaching and learning. Lyons cites Shulman as follows,

> A teaching portfolio is the structured documentary history of a (carefully selected) set of coached or mentored accomplishments substantiated by samples of student work and fully realised only through reflective writing, deliberation and serious conversation (Shulman, 1994, p. 37, as in Lyons, 1999, p. 64)

In her oeuvre of writing on portfolio construction, Lyons also lays special emphasis on their ability to enable practitioner reflection and inquiry. Yet she is aware too that portfolios are utilised for assessment of teachers, an aspect which poses both promise and threat to them. In this regard Lyons cites Linda Darling-Hammond who makes a useful distinction between *bureaucratic* and *professional conception* of portfolios,

> In a pure bureaucratic conception, teachers do not plan or inspect their work: they merely perform it. ... In a more professional conception of teaching, teachers plan, conduct and evaluate their work both individually and collectively. Teachers analyse the needs of their students, assess the resources available, take the school district's goals into account, and decide on their instructional strategies ... Evaluation of teaching is conducted to ensure that proper standards of practice are being employed. (Darling-Hammond, 1986, p. 532, as cited in Lyons, 1998, p. 13)

It will come as no surprise that in line with his long standing arguments Shulman himself recognises portfolio construction as a theoretical act,

> By this I mean that every time you design, organise or create in your teacher education program a template, a framework, or a model for a

CURRICULUM STUDIES

> teaching portfolio, you are engaged in an act of theory. Your theory of teaching will determine a reasonable portfolio entry. What is declared worth documenting, worth reflecting on, what is deemed to be portfolio-worthy, is a theoretical act. (Shulman, 1998, p. 24)

Echoing some of the concerns Lyons spoke to earlier on, Shulman is wary of the fact that teacher portfolios can become basis for classroom intervention by others, as aspect that echos the very concerns Goodson raised in Chapter 5, that studying a teacher's practice is also studying an aspect within which she could feel most vulnerable. Yet, I ague teacher portfolios can become teaching cases, when deployed with care.

I find the use of case studies to *second* parallel what Edward Silver (2009) in mathematics education research terms as *professional learning tasks* or PLTs. Silver explains PLTs to be activities which are carried out within ongoing instructional practice. Built around artifacts of classroom practice such as textbooks, measuring instruments, curriculum materials, narrative or video records of teaching as well as students inscriptions, the documentation of any PLT makes the work of teaching available for investigation. Enabling the construction of a teaching case that can in Shulman's words make a theoretical claim, the very conduct and analysis of PLTs allows for wider discussion amongst practitioners on the aims, design, preparation and enactment of teaching. The contextualised nature of these tasks, Silver argues, allows for two worthwhile outcomes, (1) for teachers to move back and forth on one hand, between past and current teaching practices, besides (2) realise their *practice based professional development* experience or PBPD on the other. Similar to the manner in which Shulman's case studies and portfolios provide insight into the complex world of teaching, by examining the conduct of PLTs it is possible for teachers' PBPD to treat mathematics content, mathematics pedagogy, teacher thinking and student thinking in a wholistic as well as integrated manner. Such manner of knowledge has potential to be both nuanced and useful for their teaching of mathematics.

6   Taking Intelligent Action

I consider attempts by Shulman, Lyons and Silver in advancing practice as well as theory via cases, portfolios and tasks in previous sections, to be pragmatic in spirit, as argued by Kvale in Chapter 7. By this I mean that the activity of gaining knowledge or theory building in each was gained by taking practitioner action and reflecting on actions taken to produce desired results. The methodology adopted in each was dialectical as well, in that the theoretical perspectives being built were inseparable from actions taken in instructional practice, as argued by McKeon also in Chapter 7. What was under examination related to the manner in which such efforts resulted explicitly in a case-of-something, teaching portfolio or practice based professional development. There was opportunity to reflect on these wholistic constructs which had overcome contradictions that arose within ongoing instruction, and have occasion to contribute towards living in society at large in line with Dewey. Yet, it was my intention to greater grasp and understand the adoption of a pragmatic stance and its implications for education that my literature search led me to Gert Biesta and Nicholas Burbules' *Pragmatism and educational research*. Highly readable and able to shed nuanced light on Dewey's philosophical thought there was opportunity here to grasp the underlying connection between practitioner research and action. Importantly, Biesta and Burbules argue educational research to not be about education, but *for* education. The raison d'etre of such activity was for practitioners to collaborate with others and *take intelligent action*. They explained,

> not only does Dewey provide us with a new way to think about knowing and acting, but his philosophical account is ultimately motivated by an attempt to restore rationality, agency and responsibility to the sphere of human action. We believe this perspective is of crucial importance for education and educational research today, because education is also not simply a technical enterprise where educators simply 'apply' the findings of educational research. *Education is a thoroughly human practice in which questions about 'how' are inseparable from questions about 'why' and 'what for.'* (Biesta & Burbules, 2003, p. 22, emphasis added)

Echoing Stetsenko's view of our ability to become human via education in Chapter 1, Biesta and Burbules view education as a thoroughly human practice and highlight three aspects in addition, (1) they shift the very aim of educational research to the realm of taking action, (2) they point out that our very process of knowing is an activity, literally something we do, and (3) in rejecting knowledge as stemming from observing a passive reality and recognising human action as constitutive of our coming to know, they argue that the notion of the practical as against theory no longer has a secondary status and becomes a domain for potential inquiry and taking action to generate knowledge. Biesta and Burbules thereby conclude that a pragmatist understanding of educational research is not one in which the search is on for a more efficient, a more sophisticated or a more effective means of achieving preconceived goals,

CURRICULUM STUDIES

but rather of making the aims, the ends and the purposes of education form an integral part of the research act itself. This means that these aspects also form an integral part of the taking of practitioner action. They thus underscore educational research to not only be about finding out what might be possible to achieve, but also whether what is being achieved through practitioner action is *desirable* from an educational point of view. It is in this sense that Dewey characterised human action as *being more intelligent.*

An emphasis on taking action that I have been discussing all along, either via a theory/practice manner within CHAT, or towards articulating individual voice in practitioner research, or achieving instructional aims in pedagogical perspectives, or factoring lived social reality with critical perspectives, or even attending to the practical in curriculum studies, can thus be viewed as offering practitioners the opportunity to know and be and become more intelligent in line with Dewey. It is to greater grasp the significance of adopting such a stance that I draw upon subsequent writings of Biesta and examine what it may mean to keep the purpose of education front and centre, to achieve what is desirable. In line with arguments made with Burbules that educational research was not about but *for* education, in *What is education for?* Biesta (2015a) forwards what he considers are three main domains of purpose, (1) *qualification*, which enables students to do things, by them acquiring the ability to utilise knowledge, skills and dispositions, (2) *socialisation*, which initiates them into ways of being and doing that are found prevailing in cultural and professional traditions, and (3) *subjectification*, which relates to how students exist and take responsibility as acting subjects, as against being treated as objects of actions taken by others.

Drawing on scholars besides Dewey, Biesta highlights four additional aspects that have implications for education. In the *first*, Biesta argues that the three domains of purpose or reasons which underpin the societal practice of education, not only vary in everyday concrete practices but are also multi-dimensional in nature. As example and in line with the three criteria he elaborates upon above, a particular student's need to gain qualifications could impinge on the time needed for her to acquire adequate socialisation. Similarly a student's subjectification may come under stress when the need to qualify may be an overriding need.

Biesta (2012) *second* argues that teachers need to have the ability to exercise judgement in lieu of concrete realities they steer, so as to enable students to arrive at some measure of achievement in each of the three domains he singles out above. Speaking in favour of practitioners taking action and/or *giving teaching back to education*, Biesta argues against efforts that categorise teaching or reduce teacher education to a check list of preconceived criteria. He argues,

The existence of such lists can result in a situation where teacher education turns into a tick box exercise focused on establishing whether students have managed to achieve everything on the list. This not only can lead easily to a disjointed curriculum and an instrumental approach to the education of teachers, but also runs the risk of turning teacher education from a collective experience to a plethora of individual learning trajectories where students are just working towards the achievement of their 'own' competencies, without a need to interact with or be exposed to fellow students. (Biesta, 2015b, pp. 3–4)

In working towards the Aristotelian greater good in society Biesta argues, as I also have (Gade, 2014), that practitioners need to have the sanction to exercise practical wisdom or *phronesis* while teaching. In relating their acting upon such wisdom to their ontology, as Kincheloe does in Chapter 7, Biesta recognises practical wisdom to be a quality or excellence that is related to a practitioner's *being*. Such an emphasis does not relate to how teachers can go about acquiring practical wisdom, but relates to how they can become a practically and educationally wise person, associated with being a good or virtuous teacher or one with character. It is following the above that Biesta is also against the present emphasis on what he terms as *learninfication*, a societal discourse which conceives all aspects including schools and lifelong education in terms of of learning. Such a view, he argues, relegates teaching to mere facilitation of students' learning. He is similarly not in favour of what are called *competence based approaches* to teacher preparation geared towards teachers having specific attributes. This last sidesteps a focus on their ability to take intelligent action based on practical wisdom teachers acquire via teaching over time.

The need for practitioner judgement in teaching is the *third* aspect of significance I wish to highlight. Biesta (2015b) argues such judgement to enable teachers to, (1) articulate what *their* purpose of any educational activity is, (2) decide in what form *they* intend to take action that is educationally appropriate, (3) resolve contradictions and tensions that arise in *them* attempting synergy between the domains of purpose, and (4) envision whether the educational actions *they* intended might bring about what is desired. Biesta thus argues that any decision with regards to education being flexible, personalised, curriculum-led, transparent, strict or otherwise cannot be decided in the abstract, but by practitioners in the many actions they take which constitute *their* teaching.

I turn *finally* to Biesta's (2013) arguments in relation to what he views as the *beautiful risk of education*. By drawing on Arendt and others, he takes his stand

CURRICULUM STUDIES   223

against learnification and competence based approaches further and argues against a risk averse approach to education which has come to proliferate in modern day educational discourse, one that speaks in deterministic specifics of evidence and outcomes. Instead he views education as a risk, one not connected to the likelihood of teachers failing because they are not sufficiently qualified, or that there is not enough scientific evidence, or even that students may not be working hard enough or lacking motivation. Biesta argues instead,

> The risk is there because, as W. B. Yeats has put it, education is not about filling a bucket but about lighting a fire. The risk is there because education is not an interaction between robots but an encounter between human beings. The risk is there because students are not to be seen as objects to be molded and disciplined, but as subjects of action and responsibility. (Biesta, 2013, p. 1)

Echoing Freire's arguments against the banking concept of education as in Chapter 7 though in a philosophical manner, Biesta seeks attention to what works for students as human subjects in education. The educational way which he recognises as being slow, difficult, frustrating and weakly deterministic while not popular in present times, may in the long run be the only *sustainable* way of educating students. Towards this he seeks a pedagogy that is willing to engage with the beautiful risk inherent in all education worthy of its name. He clarifies this pedagogy to be an event in which the subjectivity of students comes into being in the world they live in, as recognised in neo-Vygotskian CHAT perspectives. Herein there is opportunity for students to be addressed, questioned and not be edited out or immunised by calls and actions of others. If education were hundred percent risk free, Biesta argues, education would become fundamentally uneducational. That is why he conceives education as a beautiful risk, one in which students are called to action in line with Arendt as in Chapter 1, one in which they are not determined in any way but actively determine themselves in response to the actions of others. I now turn to examine two other notions of risk within education.

7   Schooling Is a Bold and Risky Means: Coda

Arguing a theory of education to lie at the intersect between questions about the nature of mind and that of culture, in *The culture of education* Bruner (1996) forwards ten tenets that could anchor such a conception. Culture, Bruner argues, inducts young into canonical ways, shapes mind and provides the toolkit by which we construct conceptions of ourselves and our world. Close on the heels of Biesta arguing in favour of the beautiful risk of education, in this coda I juxtapose his arguments with those of Bruner who also views education as risky though in cultural terms. Recognising that education is institutionalised in most instances, Bruner's *institutional tenet* characterises educational institutions as those which prepare young to take part in other institutions of culture. Yet institutions are also situated and practitioners in them draw on their own value systems to cope with the kind of contemporary crisis they face in culture, like poverty or racism say, in their own way. Bruner thus views schools to not be free standing but forming part of the main where improving education requires teachers to be committed to improvements envisioned, for they are the ones who will take educational action. While offering his cultural-psychological perspective, Bruner recognises the extent his tenets lay emphasis on the powers of human consciousness, reflection, dialogue, and negotiation. He is wary too of the failure to act in favour of these in a cultural sense, and argues,

> In all systems that depend on authority, even duly constituted and representative authority, all these factors seem to pose risks by opening discussion of currently institutionalised authority. And they are risky. Education *is* risky, for it fuels the sense of the possibility. But a failure to equip minds with the skills for understanding and feeling and acting in the cultural world is not simply scoring a pedagogical zero. It risks creating alienation, defiance, and practical incompetence. And all of these undermine the viability of a culture. (Bruner, 1996, pp. 42–43, emphasis in original)

My intention of discussing Bruner's institutional tenet, is to examine the normative dimension which schooling could impose in the practice of education in society, one paralleled by those with regards to any subject curricula as well. I thus turn next to David Olson's (2003) *Psychological theory and educational reform: How school remakes mind and society*, wherein he dwells on the manner in which we may have neglected the institutional aspects of schooling, at the expense of attending to the functioning of human psychology in designing subject curricula. Olson elaborates on Bruner's institutional tenet considerably and puts forward his arguments in terms of three aspects (1) intentional states of students, (2) schools as bureaucratic institutions and (3) the need for teachers and students to establish joint intentionality.

To begin with Olson articulates *the intentional states of students* in terms of their beliefs, desires and/or intentions as learners, even if these remain largely implicit in their speech and actions initially and become conscious

CURRICULUM STUDIES

with age, experience and education. He then recognises the ability of students to act intentionally in two ways, (1) their ability to take responsibility and feel accountable for praise or blame, as well as those of achievement or dissatisfaction, and (2) their ability to act intentionally and grant to themselves freedom and autonomy as doers, by means of which they form their unique identity or selves.

Bureaucracies on the other hand, Olson points out, are rule governed institutions not characterised by rules as much as created by the rules specified in establishing them in the first place, like law courts or state hospitals. By participating in *school bureaucracies*, students thus learn to follow rules that apply particularly to them, the reporting structure they need to adhere, the manner of accountability prescribed for them as well as their own entitlements. Olson thus reiterates that while human feelings and personal morality are important, the goal of the school is much more limited – that of teaching students at large to participate in bureaucratic institutions of wider society. In this sense schools provide a meeting ground between the subjectivity of students as learners, the local culture and institutional normativity. In the décalage that could prevail between students' intentional states and their bureaucratic manner of functioning Olson too views schooling as risky,

> *Schooling is a bold and risky means of pursuing education.* It preempts in a major way the intentionality and responsibility of the learners themselves by turning over those responsibilities to an institution. But schools are successful to the extent that they, through their teachers and programs, return these responsibilities to the learners by negotiating goals acceptable to both and by allowing students to recruit the resources and energy to achieve them. (Olson, 2003, pp. 288–289, emphasis added)

Understanding how students, teachers, parents and institutions negotiate these responsibilities for learning, Olson argues, is the first step that can explain what schools are, what they do, why they are universal and why they are resistant to change. Olson however does provide a way out of the impasse he articulates by making two viable suggestions. *First*, he argues that each and every level of school bureaucracy needs to articulate the many responsibilities its functioning has taken on, especially those that concern teachers as well as their students. Such clarity would, he says, be an important step in arriving at an educational theory that is viable in the concrete. In the *second*, he suggests the formation of what he calls *a pedagogy of joint intentionality* between teachers and students. By this he means an explicit agreement between teachers and students on the criterion of pedagogical exchange, besides choosing the means by which the criteria agreed upon will be reached. This manner of pedagogy seeks explicit articulation of educational purpose, in line with Biesta earlier on, of pedagogical actions that will be likely taken instead of allowing such transactions to take place as a matter of faith and tradition. In giving reasons and/or rationalising respective actions, such manner of pedagogy would display explicitness. In arriving at joint intentions, Olson argues, both teachers and students have the possibility to contribute to and accept responsibility, for their individual as well as collective roles.

It is interesting to see how the notion of risk is articulated by all three scholars I refer to. In seeking the beautiful risk of education for students, Biesta envisions their learning, personal views and actions to be called into question by other students, else their educational experiences would be uneducational. In students becoming alienated, defiant and practically incompetent, Bruner sees the risk of institutions in terms of failing to make culture at large viable for them. Olson's notion of risk focuses attention on the intentional states of students and teachers being met by bureaucratic routines in terms of which schools function. I argue each of the risks articulated by Biesta, Bruner and Olson to demand the attention of practitioners, educators and society at large.

References

Biesta, G. J. J. (2012). Giving teaching back to education: Responding to the disappearance of the teacher. *Phenomenology & Practice, 6*(2), 35–49.

Biesta, G. J. J. (2013). *The beautiful risk of education*. Paradigm.

Biesta, G. J. J. (2015a). What is education for? On good education, teacher judgement, and educational professionalism. *European Journal of Education, 50*(1), 75–87.

Biesta, G. J. J. (2015b). How does a competent teacher become a good teacher? On judgement, wisdom and virtuosity in teaching and teacher education. In R. Heilbronn & L. Foreman-Peck (Eds.), *Philosophical perspectives on teacher education* (pp. 3–22). Wiley Blackwell.

Biesta, G. J. J., & Burbules, N. C. (2003). *Pragmatism and educational research*. Rowman & Littlefield Publishers

Bruner, J. (1996). *The culture of education*. Harvard University Press.

Craig, V. J., & Ross, V. (2008). Cultivating the image of teachers as curriculum makers. In M. F. Connelly, M. F. He, & J. Phillion (Eds.), *The Sage handbook of curriculum and instruction* (pp. 282–305). Sage Publications.

Darling-Hammond, L. (1986). A proposal for evaluation in the teaching profession. *The Elementary School Journal, 86*(4), 531–551.

CURRICULUM STUDIES

Dewey, J. (1998). My pedagogic creed. *The School Journal, 14*(3), 77–80. Retrieved September 23, 2020, from http://infed.org/mobi/john-dewey-my-pedagogical-creed/ (Original work published 1897)

Eisner, E. (1981a). The role of the arts in cognition and curriculum. *The Phi Delta Kappan, 63*(1), 48–52.

Eisner, E. (1981b). On the differences between scientific and artistic approaches to qualitative research. *Educational Researcher, 10*(4), 5–9.

Eisner, E. (1983). The art and craft of teaching. *Educational Leadership, 40*(4), 4–13.

Eisner, E. (1984a). No easy answers: Joseph Schwab's contributions to curriculum. *Curriculum Inquiry, 14*(2), 201–210.

Eisner, E. (1984b). Can educational research inform educational practice? *The Phi Delta Kappan, 65*(7), 447–452.

Eisner, E. (2002a). The role of art in transforming consciousness. In E. Eisner (Ed.), *The arts and the creation of mind* (pp. 1–24). Yale University Press.

Eisner, E. (2002b). The kind of schools we need. *The Phi Delta Kappan, 83*(8), 576–583.

Eisner, E. (2009). The Lowenfeld Lecture 2008: What education can learn from the arts. *Art Education, 62*(2), 6–9.

Elliott, J., & Norris, N. (2012a). The Stenhouse legacy. In J. Elliott & N. Norris (Eds.), *Curriculum, pedagogy and educational research: The work of Lawrence Stenhouse* (pp. 137–152). Routledge.

Elliott, J., & Norris, N. (2012b). Introduction. In J. Elliott & N. Norris (Eds.), *Curriculum, pedagogy and educational research: the work of Lawrence Stenhouse* (pp. 1–6). Routledge.

Gade, S. (2014). Praxis and phronesis as units of analysis: Realising a social science that matters in practitioner inquiry. *Reflective Practice, 15*(6), 718–729.

Gade, S. (2020). Performance, the arts, and curricular change. *LEARNing Landscapes, 13*(1), 129–136.

Grossman, P. (1992). Teaching and learning with cases: some unanswered questions. In J. H. Shulman (Ed.), *Case methods in teacher education* (pp. 227–239). Teachers College Press.

Gutierrez, R., Rymes, B., & Larson, J. (1995). Script, counterscript and underlife in the classroom: James Brown versus Brown v. Board of Education. *Harvard Educational Review, 65*(3), 445–471.

Huber, L. P. (2008). Building critical race methodologies in educational research: A research note on critical race testimonio. *FIU Law Review, 4*(1), 159–173.

Lyons, N. (1998). Portfolio possibilities: Validating a new teacher professionalism. In N. Lyons (Ed.), *With portfolio in hand: Validating a new teacher professionalism* (pp. 11–22). Teachers College Press.

Lyons, N. (1999). How portfolios can shape emerging practice. *Educational Leadership, 56*(8), 63–65.

Mills, C. W. (1959a). Philosophies of science. In C. W. Mills (Ed.), *The sociological imagination* (pp. 119–131). Grove Press.

Mills, C. W. (1959b). Appendix: On intellectual craftsmanship. In C. W. Mills (Ed.), *The sociological imagination* (pp. 195–226). Grove Press.

Olson, D. R. (2003). *Psychological theory and educational reform: How school remakes mind and society.* Cambridge University Press.

Richert, A. (1992). Writing cases: A vehicle for inquiry into the writing process In J. H. Shulman (Ed.), *Case methods in teacher education* (pp. 155–174). Teachers College Press.

Schwab, J. J. (1978). The 'impossible' role of the teacher in progressive education. In I. Westbury & N. J. Wilkof (Eds.), *Science, curriculum and liberal education* (pp. 167–183). The University of Chicago Press. (Original work published 1959)

Schwab, J. J. (2013). The practical: A language for curriculum. *Journal of Curriculum Studies, 45*(5), 591–621. (Original work published 1970)

Shulman, L. S. (1992). Toward a pedagogy of cases. In J. H. Shulman (Ed.), *Case methods in teacher education* (pp. 1–30). Teachers College Press.

Shulman, L. S. (1994, January). *Portfolios in historical perspective* [Paper presentation]. Portfolio Conference.

Shulman, L. S. (1998). Teaching portfolios: A theoretical activity. In N. Lyons (Ed.), *With portfolio in hand: Validating a new teacher professionalism* (pp. 23–37). Teachers College Press.

Silver, E. A. (2009). Toward a more complete understanding of practice-based professional development for mathematics teachers. In R. Even & D. L. Ball (Eds.), *The professional education and development of teachers of mathematics* (pp. 245–247). Springer.

Stenhouse, L. (1971). The humanities curriculum project: The rationale. *Theory in Practice, 10*(3), 154–162.

Stenhouse, L. (1975). *An introduction to curriculum research and development.* Heinemann Educational Books.

Stenhouse, L. (1980). Curriculum research and the art of the teacher. *Curriculum, 1*(1), 40–44.

Stenhouse, L. (1981). What counts as research? *British Journal of Educational Studies, 29*(2), 103–114.

Stenhouse, L. (1988). Artistry and teaching: the teacher as focus of research and development. *Journal of Curriculum and Supervision, 4*(1), 43–51.

Stenhouse, L. (2012). Research as a basis for teaching. In J. Elliott & N. Norris (Eds.), *Curriculum, pedagogy and educational research: The work of Lawrence Stenhouse* (pp. 122–136). Routledge. (Original work published 1979)

CHAPTER 9

Taking Transformative Action

Gaining from Triangulation

1   **Preamble**

By the time of writing this penultimate chapter, I am not only in my home-stretch but also home. I have come back to my desk under the shade of the fig tree outside my window, which has known many a spring and fall during my extended travels. During these years many a fruit eating bat and birds ranging from the red vented bulbul, golden oriole, crow pheasant, the tailor bird and its nests have found respite. And watching the drama is my daughter who has returned from her own journeys which began as a teenager and culminated in her becoming the spunky, loving and mature woman I see before me today. We have made room for her tabby cat who stands beside her peering out of the same window, playing mind games with the many pigeons who dare to roost outside. In recent times we have made some more room for her indie puppy as well, who displays ample eagerness to discover the many spaces in our lives. Their presence makes this world worth living in and striving for.

Even as I have come back to gentle neighbours who help make me call this southern Indian city of Hyderabad my home, included in this midst are my green grocer, milk man, home chef, house keeper and watch man, well wishers all. In addition to my old friends strewn across the world, it is my good fortune to have gained enduring friendships in places I have had occasion to visit recently as well. For me nothing summarises this experience better than the one so many come to have while walking down the walkways of New York's Central Park. Watching the benches lining them and being able to enjoy moments of personal quiet amongst the brisk movements of familiar yet unknown visitors, I have often hummed Paul Simon and Art Garfunkel's soulful rendition of *Old friends*,

> Old friends
> Old friends
> Sat on their park bench
> Like bookends
> A newspaper blown through the grass
> Falls on the round toes

230 CHAPTER 9

On the high shoes
Of the old friends

Nourished, I return to my writing and am reminded of another chapter in Lewis Wolpert and Alison Richards' *Passionate minds: The inner lives of scientists*, by David Pilbeam (1997) titled *A very tidy desk*. Pilbeam explains his field of palaeoanthropology to be more of a question than a science, where one makes judgements with available data akin to solving a thousand piece jigsaw puzzle with half of its pieces missing. To begin with and in parallel to Pilbeam's question of what happened in human evolution and why?, I see my own attempts as examining what happens in K-12 school education and why? In articulating a lengthy response via this writing, two nuggets from Pilbeam's approach have remained with me. *First* and given the lack of order in a field as interdisciplinary, vast and consuming as education, I have like Pilbeam maintained a very, very tidy desk. This has involved organising and trying to fit various jigsaw pieces together, striving for greater understanding. In doing so, I have tried to bring order to a subject where one might not get as much order as one might like, but where some order is certainly possible. *Second,* acknowledging that education like palaeoanthropology as a field, would probably always remain incomplete, I attempt to capture its features in a manner Pilbeam himself elaborates as follows,

> It's very like impressionist paintings. You can't afford to get too close to them because they dissolve into meaningless blobs. You have to stand back, and then you'll get an impression. And I think a good evolutionary biologist, the good paleoanthropologist, is someone who's a good impressionist; who's going to be able to paint, sketch, a quick picture that's got the essence, that captures the critical features. (Pilbeam, 1997, p. 212)

Pilbeam's writing never quite left me as I embarked on my journey into educational research. In responding to the question I articulate above, I too attempt to render impressions of aspects I have considered valuable. In doing so I am aware of having left out aspects other practitioners would view as valuable to their educational journeys, for which I look forward to their impressionist renderings as well.

In proceeding to draw my writing to a close I am reminded too of the attention Connelly (2013) draws to Schwab's manner of reading any text with his students, in terms of what any author of a text was *doing* beyond what (s) he was saying. Connelly points out that what Schwab was saying in the four papers titled *Practical,* was that the field of curriculum studies was not yielding relevant results. Yet what Schwab was doing through his efforts was to look at epistemological ways of relating theory and practice based on actual phenomena and experience. It is against such a backdrop that in four sections that follow I dwell on the classroom interventions we did or were able to carry out, three in collaboration with Lotta at grade four and one in collaboration with Tomas at his grade eight classroom. In a final section *Forests and trees – a multilectic*, I gather constructs found useful in grasping teacher-researcher collaboration, those which led our instructional interventions, before reflecting on the relationship between student cohorts and individual students in terms of a multilectic between forests and trees. In a coda titled *Gaining from triangulation* I dwell on salient features of programs led by two CHAT scholars in triangulation with mine and argue the CHAT agenda to remain fertile and open.

I find it pertinent to mention here that the four interventions I discuss in this Chapter have been reported in journal articles, beginning with the conduct of action research and ending with the conduct of what is known in CHAT as *Formative interventions*. Developmental in aims and scope and as argued by Engeström (2011), the conduct of this last lays emphasis on human agency, one very much at play for Lotta, Tomas, their students, besides me as researcher-collaborator. In viewing each intervention via this framework I evidence the dialectic between (1) *how* we practitioners collaborated to conceive and realise our interventions, besides (2) *what* each intervention was about. The titles of the four sections that follow thus indicate the nature of collaboration realised, alongside the aims of each of intervention. Yet before discussing these, I presently turn to the scope and grammar of CHAT based formative interventions. Doubling up as summary of perspectives introduced in Chapter 3, I find Cole and Engeström (2007) to outline six principles which underpin interventions that promote students' cultural-historical development:

1. *Mediation through artifacts*, which help to radically alter the condition of human existence. Artefacts change our psychic condition and allow us to regulate the way we act or behave from the outside.
2. *Activity as unit of analysis*, which means one analyses psychological functions that take part in historically accumulated forms of human activity like pottery say or writing. Embedded in both material conditions and social relations such activities are realised as joint production proceeds, in which people are collectively engaged.
3. *Cultural organisation of human life*, which alludes to various practices we come to participate in our lives. Implied in the notion of mediation, this refers to the material aspects of culture that are both acted upon and assist the bringing about of meaningful human action.

4. *Adoption of a genetic perspective*, or our grasping phenomena observed by understanding the history of their occurrence spread over considerable periods of study. This last provides basis for leading the development of individuals in any sociocultural group.

5. *Social origins of higher psychological functions*, which recognises the social in cultural behaviour. This traces the interpsychological between people becoming their intrapsychological attribute.

6. *The ethical and strategic contradictions of intervention research*, which gives due attention to the social circumstances conducive to developmental change, one requiring practitioner action to become intrinsic not only to interventions conducted but also of the analysis that follows.

As brought rightful attention to by Tobin in terms of researcher axiology in Chapter 7, Cole and Engeström are careful to point out that the nature of researcher engagement with the host community is just as vital to the ethics of its conduct,

> The values of intervention researchers, by virtue of their infusion into those activities, become a part of the ensuing developmental process. ...
>
> In short the relationship between researchers and other intervention participants needs to be a part of the analysis. ... The 'formative process' is itself a form of joint mediated activity in which critical analysis of the notion of 'more capable peer' should be part of the analysis. ...
>
> ... In addition it is also necessary to attend to the quality of that practice, as it is evaluated by the community that plays host to the intervention. (Cole & Engeström, 2007, p. 488)

In proceeding to discuss salient features of formative interventions, I begin with two arguments made by Bronfenbrenner in Chapter 4. *First* is his seeking the very conduct of transforming experiments. In realising these, educational ecologies are radically restructured so that for those taking part in them, their unrealised psychological activity is brought forward to life. *Second* is our recognising that it is one thing to study the development of educational systems with elements already present and quite another to restructure established norms and practices that exist. In highlighting the above, Yrjö Engeström, Annalisa Sannino and Jaakko Virkkunen (2014) clarify that what Bronfenbrenner called transforming experiments, they sharpen and call formative interventions. In discussing the grammar of such interventions they point to three sets of arguments as deserving of our attention (1) the principle of double stimulation, (2) the manner in which these differ from the conduct of design experiments, and (3) the distinctive features of their conduct.

The key methodological principle underlying the conduct of formative interventions, Engeström (2011) explains, is the Vygotskian principle of *double stimulation*. Herein students are placed in a structured situation in relation to a well designed problem, and provided a set of stimulus-means by the experimenter who facilitates but does not produce, the construction of new psychological phenomena by students. It is by using stimulus-means introduced by the experimenter that students in any instructional activity mediate their actions and govern their behaviour from outside. In so doing they utilise the stimulus-means to serve their aims and purpose, and subject the structured environment and their own behaviour to their own authority. As example in Lotta's class we utilised slips of paper with inscriptions on them as stimulus-means and in Tomas' class we made use of group-tasks designed with different stimulus-means in five successive tasks. Our use of these enabled students to act is ways not anticipated beforehand. For example a student Nelly, in Lotta's grade four broke down in tears while reflecting on her perceived abilities at learning the mathematics expected of her. Similarly a student in Tomas' grade eight broke into a song, one that seemed to express his ongoing adolescent sentiments. Such behaviour evidences Engeström's contention that unlike a linear trajectory in design experiments, formative interventions are contested terrains throwing up unanticipated surprises as their conduct progresses. Engeström thus highlights the following in favour of *carrying out formative interventions*, (1) that their *starting points* are not pre determined but found embedded in the life activity engaged with, (2) in resolving particular problematics, individuals involved gain agency and take charge of the *process* that is unfolding, (3) the *outcome* of using pedagogical ideas, offers the potential for these to be utilised later on as well, and (4) the *researcher's role* in such conduct, is of provoking and sustaining the growth of interventions as these evolve over time.

Based on their ability to realise double-stimulation, Engeström outlines four *analytical features of formative interventions*:

1. *Collective activity systems as unit of analysis*, which means that the intervention conducted by researchers and participated in by students is a conceptual tool for both of them, wherein numerous individual actions of either contribute to qualitative transformations that are brought about. As example Tomas' students overcame individual disinterest and continued to take part in the tasks we set.

2. *Contradictions as a source of change and development*, meaning that unlike dealing with personal conflicts, these interventions have the ability to deal with structural tensions that address systemic and individual aspects. Lotta's coming upon the faulty use of the equal to sign by one student was recognised by her and treated in our intervention as a classroom wide systemic issue.

3. *Agency as a crucial layer of causality,* by which any intervention transforms any meaningless situation into a meaningful one, changing the psychological field in which students act. In rectifying their faulty use, Lotta's students exhibited such agency in offering statements that were numerically equal on both sides of many an equal to sign.

4. *Transformation of practice as a form of expansive concept formation,* which means that the pattern of activity that endured in one cycle of the intervention became a germ cell that gave rise to new uses which could be put to in prospective interventions. In students being able to externalise their thinking in using slips of paper with inscriptions on them, in line with Wertsch's construct of explicit mediation, we found the classroom wide practice of explicit mediation to be germ cell that we tailored to appropriate use in subsequent interventions as well.

Taken together the sets of ideas which Engeström lays down above for carrying out as well as grasping the conduct of formative interventions, guides my discussion of the four formative interventions conducted with Lotta and Tomas, whose individual details I now turn to.

2   Relational Knowing | The Equal to Sign

My extended collaboration with Lotta, with whom I conducted the first of three interventions I report in this section, lasted one and a half academic years of schooling in Sweden. While we continued to meet when needed later on as well, we had agreed upon and stuck to a routine of my visiting her classroom once every week. I was lucky to have been introduced to Lotta by a colleague at Umeå University who thought we might get along despite my not knowing Swedish. The primary school Lotta taught at was within walking distance from my home and university, making my visits convenient despite the snow and dark winter nights. At the time of these visits I was pursuing my two year postdoctoral, before signing up for the six year Assistant Professorship that followed. My initial visits coincided with Lotta teaching about thirty, grade six students and I was myself exploring narrative perspectives as worthy extension to those of CHAT. Wanting to experience the workings of a classroom in Sweden, for which I had just one spring semester of time and intending to use narrative perspectives, I asked if I could interact with students and examine their narratives in relation to their learning mathematics. Lotta took permission from the parents of students for my work and her students readily agreed to my observing their day-to-day instruction when she introduced me to them.

TAKING TRANSFORMATIVE ACTION

They trusted Lotta and in time I was able to earn their trust, besides that of Lotta as well. I would sit myself on a chair at the rear end of the classroom with a desk nearby, and for most part observe and make notes of instructional events like the lessons being taught, the textbook being followed, the norms with which Lotta addressed her students and the way in which they in turn addressed and related with her.

Lotta and me would exchange notes after most lessons gave over and in time I took on the role of a second and silent teacher in her classroom. I would assist with passing out workbooks or help in any manner that did not replace her central authority. In time our exchange led to longer conversations about teaching mathematics besides pertinent aspects like a particular student's family circumstances or performance as a student. While Lotta's instruction was in Swedish, her students learnt English as well and some chatted with me about mathematics and shared personal aspects of their lives, like having freshly baked cinnamon buns at home the previous evening. As Lotta and me grew conversant with one another and as she found my rapport with her students to grow, she would send a student or two to work with me at my desk. Having finished the work she had set for them during her teaching routine for any particular day, they would work at additional problems I always took with me, which I would borrow from the mathematics competition for students in Sweden known as the Kängaru.[1]

A couple of aspects resulted from the above changes I describe. *First*, some of Lotta's students attempted the Känguru problems I had with me, graded as these were according to grade levels. In this I had opportunity to record narratives about their attempts of working at their mathematics. On observing our rapport Lotta asked if I would work with a particular student who she thought could do with greater personal attention than she could herself provide in her teaching. Having collected enough narratives of students who worked at the problems I took, I went on to report on a selection of these at a conference in which I anonymised Lotta as well as her students. I also showed Lotta a draft of my writing for her to make changes if she so wished (Gade, 2010). *Second* and as the academic year came to a close I asked and Lotta consented to my working with her class the following year as well, which would be grade four students. Looking ahead and over summer vacation, Lotta took me for granted and applied for and obtained project funding from the Swedish National Agency for Education.[2] Lotta wished to study the role of students' communication while learning mathematics, for which I began to look out for activities that we could utilise. These events nurtured our collaboration further as practitioners. While our explicit mediation based activity that I soon discuss was a direct result of such collaboration, two parallel outcomes ensued. *First* was the advent in my own research of teacher-researcher collaboration, for our joint conduct of CHAT based interventions. *Second* was my look out for theoretical frameworks that would treat teacher-researcher collaboration as an additional object of my study. Before discussing the first intervention Lotta and me were able to conduct, I now turn to one such framework that encapsulates and nuances the nature of my collaboration with Lotta at this point of time.

Attending not only to classroom instruction but also our own selves as practitioners, the construct of *relational knowing* focuses on teaching as well as learning to teach, by drawing on extended conversations that we practitioners come to have with one another alongside routine teaching. I draw herein on two writings by Sandra Hollingsworth who reports her experience of regularly meeting with a group of teachers in relation to literacy education. The extended conversations they went on to have resulted in Hollingsworth and her fellow teachers to free these from a focus on reading alone and over time talk about insights they each had in relation to their teaching, classroom relationships, schooling, community values, engagement with grandparents, display of power in its many forms and the development of one's professional voice. Fraught with risks of dwelling on experiences one might feel uncomfortable to share for fear of being judged, such manner of exchange however held promise for these teachers to be changed as practitioners by the very process of research. The abstract of her first paper reads as follows,

> From the social, collaborative, and non-evaluative conversations, personally and contextually relevant issues in learning to teach emerged, as did the processes of identifying and understanding them. The result was not only a clarification of important relational and political issues that seem prerequisite to issues of academic learning, but also the emergence of feminist consciousness – in both teachers and researcher. The method of studying the group's learning, then, became an example of feminist praxis: a willingness to risk and examine personal experiences as women and to be changed by the research process itself. (Hollingsworth, 1992, p. 373)

Some issues which Hollingsworth cites as aspects of feminist praxis are

1. *A commitment to relational processes*, essential to developing trust as well as one's professional voice.
2. *Valuing experiences and emotions as knowledge*, by raising context bound concerns to publicly validated knowledge so that teachers could see themselves as knowledgeable.
3. *Valuing biographical differences*, whereby there was opportunity to appreciate and celebrate similarities and differences, preparing ground for working with diverse student populations.

TAKING TRANSFORMATIVE ACTION

4. *Developing a supported critical perspective*, one valuable for investigating efforts of fellow practitioners that would not be possible in an apprenticeship model.
5. *Reinforcing learning to teach as a process*, by way of an epistemology which recognises a wider range of relationships than those recognised by traditional curricula, supported by schools or universities.

Hollingsworth points out that in the course of conversations had, she found a knowing voice to not necessarily be a loud one, but one that was clear, structured as a narrative and oriented towards practitioner action.

In her writing with Mary Dybdahl and Leslie Minarik, Hollingsworth elaborates how the construct of relational knowing lies at the intersection of three aspects (1) Theories of the social construction of knowledge (2) Theories of self and other relationships, and (3) Theories of feminist epistemologies. Each of these contributes to recognising a practitioner's ability to grasp existential reality as being central to one's ability to teach, besides placing the child at the centre of one's learning. It thus becomes possible to articulate educational processes in terms of care and love, one not distorted and merely attentive to evaluation and control. The stories offered in turn illustrate the nature of passion involved in learning to teach and the need for developing personal, political and relational ways of knowing. Critical of teacher preparation programs they argue,

> The stories will suggest that these teachers' general mode of teacher preparation, growing out of research that emphasised apolitical, objective and distanced knowing, left them somewhat surprised, confused, and unprepared. Worse, trying to implement a curriculum based primarily on cognitive and technical knowledge of teaching in classrooms, where the experience of joyous learning often occurred through social and relational interaction, set up both teachers and children for failure. *They lacked an explication of and support for the very ways of knowing that would give them the freedom to teach and learn successfully.* (Hollingsworth, Dybdahl & Minarik, 1993, p. 6, emphasis added)

The vital point Hollingsworth, Dybdahl and Minarik make above is that relational knowing contributes to practitioners having their own personal freedom to both teach besides learn to teach successfully, something a normative cognitive based curriculum is unable to adequately prepare teachers for. This latter also risks denying teachers vital ways of knowing which are ubiquitous to teachers as practitioners.

My exchanging notes and having extended conversations with Lotta exemplified the construct of relational knowing, primarily in not denying ourselves the kind of relationships Hollingsworth and her collaborating teachers drew specific attention to. In this we made room for individual histories as well as the professional lives we were currently living. One day Lotta would tell me how she did not notice her son's cell phone in the trousers she had placed in her washing machine and on another I would tell her of my experience with the frozen snow outside. Then there was a worried parent who wanted to know if I would have a say in the way Lotta graded her son's progress on one hand and on the other Lotta kept me informed about the demise of the mother of a pair of twins who were in her class. A great many conversations dealt with her students ability or inability to satisfy the expectations that she would have of them as their mathematics teacher. In line with the aims of Lotta's project I suggested she conduct the game of *Yes or No* in relation to numbers students would have to guess, inscribed on slips or paper or *lappar* in Swedish. In what turned out to be a pilot study of our project related work, this game about guessing the inscribed number, which I would visibly had out became highly popular, one played at home by some with younger siblings as well. With only yes or no as valid responses to questions students would ask, their need to listen attentively to questions asked by their peers in guessing the number was an exciting adventure for many of them. Lotta encouraged her students to conduct the game themselves in due course. Yet as Lotta continued with her curricular teaching, one day she sent me an email, as detailed in Chapter 5, about the problematic issue she faced in relation to the faulty use of the equal to sign by her students. It was on receipt of the email that I led the conduct of a CHAT based intervention reported in the journal *Educational Action Research*. Herein I describe how I came to greater understand the issue Lotta was facing,

> Curious to find out how it was that Lea came upon the problem, I arranged to meet Lea before my weekly visit. With a body language that many primary teachers effectively use, Lea recreated for me the events that prompted her email. Lea narrated how she had asked one of her students, Jan, to attempt a particular question on the whiteboard. While I detail Jan's usage of the equality sign in the next section, Lea's narrative expressed dismay in finding that none of her other students objected to Jan's faulty usage. (Gade, 2012, p. 557)

Subsequent to the above I examined Jan's usage of the equal to sign, that prompted Lotta to write to me. Jan showed me his response to a question which asked how long 20 eggs would last a family of four, if each of them ate one every morning as follows: $20 - 4 - 4 - 4 - 4 - 4 = 5$. Jan, who spoke English fluently, pointed to the number 20 and said that there were 20 eggs to begin with. Pointing to the first '$- 4$' he said that took away four eggs for the first

TAKING TRANSFORMATIVE ACTION 239

morning, leaving behind 16 eggs. Counting down 12, 8 and 4 eggs for each successive morning, he arrived at 0 eggs after the fifth day. His answer or *svar* in Swedish was thus '= 5.'

Jan's usage detailed above led us to conduct an action cycle that would have students make both sides of a given equal to sign numerically equal, in consultation with their peers. Yet before detailing the intervention we conducted in consultation with one another I mention three aspects. *First*, since it was early days in my extended collaboration with Lotta, I had at the time of reporting still anonymised her as Lea, even as I recognised the centrality of teacher-researcher collaboration in my reporting. *Second* and given the immediacy of addressing the problem Lotta brought to my notice, I decided to resort to the straightforward rules of action research. Having conducted this cycle in 2009, greater clarity on its developmental aspects became clear only later with Engeström's (2011) paper. Similarly and *third*, we came to draw on Wertsch's concept of explicit mediation when reporting our work for a teacher's journal in Sweden (Blomqvist & Gade, 2013). I argue such retrospective instances in the timeline of one's reporting of research is not unusual and in fact enriches one's research, especially while engaging with perspectives like those of CHAT that are evolving and maturing in contemporary times.

Even as we drew on Wertsch's notion of explicit mediation for the conduct of our intervention, we drew also on Cole and Scribner's notion of mediation, both of which I elaborate upon in Chapter 3. Briefly, in Lotta's students working explicitly with *lappar* provided to them, they actively modified the mathematical expressions inscribed upon them as stimulus-means. This provided ample opportunity for students to develop their higher psychological functions in collaboration with their peers. The specific psychological functions we had planned to realise, was in having Lotta's students use the equal to sign in line with its conventional usage and meaning. By conducting a four-stage action cycle, at the end of which Lotta as teacher was satisfied with her students' usage we were able to make explicit and evident for correction by students what was incorrect and implicit as was the case with Jan's usage.

As reported in Gade (2012) our action cycle was conducted in four stages, providing successive opportunities for students to make both sides of the given equal to sign, numerically equal. Giving students opportunity to attempt more than one question and as evidenced in Figure 8, students offered their solutions on sheets of paper we had handed out. One will notice the use by Swedish students of the '·' sign for multiplication, in their solutions. The four stage cycle asked students to fill in missing blanks in the following sequence,

(1) using the equal to sign along with signs for addition and subtraction, e.g. 200 = __+__ and __ – __ = 40

200 − 150 + 50

200 = 1 + 1 + 1 + 1 + 1 + 1 + 1 + 1 + 1 + 1 + 190

200 = 190 + 10

200 = 8 + 192

$\frac{15}{3} = 5$	3·5 = 15	10·1 = 8+2	25 + 25 = 50
$\frac{3}{3} = 1$	5·1 = 5	11 − 2 = 27 ÷ 3	60 − 10 = 50
$\frac{60}{3} = 20$	5·20 = 60	20 − 11 = 27 ÷ 3	30·3 = 90
$\frac{99}{3} = 99$	99·1 = 99	25·1 = 20+5 = 30−5	100 − 10 = 90
		25·1 = 15+10 = 40−15	90 + 0 = 90
		5·5 = 20+5 = 50−25	100 − 20 = 80
		3·5 = 10+5	80·1 = 80
		3·5 = 3+12	50 + 30 = 80
		3·5 = 7+8	

FIGURE 8 Students' inscriptions in the four-stage action cycle as in Gade (2012)

(2) using the equal to sign with those for addition, subtraction and multiplication, e.g. 16 = __+__, 16 = __ − __ and 16 = __ × __
(3) using the equal to sign along with those for multiplication and division, e.g. 40 = __ × __ and 40 = __ ÷ __ and finally
(4) using signs for any of the four operations on both sides of the equal to sign, e.g. 6 + 4 = __ ÷ __ and 30 ÷ 10 = __ − __.

Many features of the action cycle were in line with those of conducting formative interventions in line with Engeström. *First* the starting point of the above outlined action cycle was certainly embedded in the ongoing life of Lotta's everyday instruction, one she at first recognised, brought to my notice and stopped her everyday instruction to intervene and rectify with my assistance. *Second*, both of us as practitioners and her students gained agency as the cycle unfolded, in students filling in the blanks and our designing the next stage of the cycle based on responses we obtained in the previous stage of the cycle. *Third* and based on the manner in which we successfully had students realise the behaviour we wanted from them, our use of *lappars* as stimulus-means became the fertile germ cell we went on to use in subsequent interventions as well. *Finally*, my role as researcher relied on sustaining the entire action cycle, for which I drew on CHAT perspectives throughout. Lotta and me drew on our relational knowing besides, especially when we had students attempt the second stage of the cycle not in pairs but individually. In line with Vygotsky,

TAKING TRANSFORMATIVE ACTION

this last allowed students' learning in their interpsychological experience *lead* their intrapsychological development.

Conducted as a classroom wide social practice involving all students, one could argue that within the formative intervention, the action cycle we had designed was unit of analysis not only for Lotta and me, but also for her students. By this is meant that by taking part in the intervention her students were able to gauge their individual ability of bringing about numerical equality in a graded manner, starting from simpler arithmetical operations of addition and subtraction, to utilising different arithmetical operations on both sides of the equal to sign in inscriptions handed out. The initial contradiction of students faulty use of the equal to sign which prompted Lotta to initiate the action cycle, was also one which motivated her students to come up with a resolution that was acceptable to her as their teacher as the action-cycle lived its course. Her agency as teacher, mine as researcher, besides those of her students was key to transforming our actions in ways that were meaningful to each of us.

The germ cell of using lappars as stimulus-means which while being beneficial to all of us, also enabled Nelly to rebuild her confidence as a student. As reported in Gade (2011) it was possible for me to draw on my reflexivity as researcher to help deconstruct Nelly's breaking down into tears in relation to her perceived inability to perform as well as she would have wanted to, at a paper and pencil test that Lotta administered during the action cycle. Participating in the cycle enabled her to regain her lost confidence. This last exemplifies the kind of detours Engeström argued could be expected when human agency is at play and can be leveraged in the conduct of formative interventions. The transforming nature of our joint conduct and first reporting, in addition resulted in Lotta becoming my coauthor in reporting the interventions that followed. In our conduct of these I had opportunity to study two other constructs that encapsulated the evolving nature of our teacher-researcher collaboration.

3   Relational Agency | Problem Posing

Unlike relational knowing which recognises the ability of practitioners to realise and validate their knowledge about relationships they enter into with one another for teaching, I presently discuss the notion of *relational agency*. As forwarded by Anne Edwards (2010), this notion recognises the agency of practitioners to collaborate across institutional boundaries like schools and universities in taking mutually supportive action. Lotta and me were able to exercise relational agency in the process of reporting the second intervention we jointly conducted. Even as we continued to realise relational knowing, by drawing on conversations we had time and again, my appreciation of the notion of relational agency was due to changes in professional circumstances that Lotta and I faced. Soon after conducting our third intervention which I report in the next section, Lotta's experience in obtaining funding and conducting project driven research, was basis for the Swedish National Agency for Education to ask her to work for them at Stockholm. Our eventual reporting thus drew on her experiences as a teacher, besides those she gained while working at a policy making and governing agency. As example she was able to gather an overview of the kind of work that was expected of and negotiated by other mathematics teachers at schools across Sweden. Yet working there left Lotta disconcerted at times as well, in the absence she felt of her own professional voice as a teacher besides that of teachers in general, in the kind of work such national agencies mandate teachers to carry out in their classrooms. Our combined reflections and reporting thus drew on such manner of conflicting personal experiences, which emboldened and led to Lotta becoming my co-author in reporting our research.

Before elaborating on the theoretical notion of relational agency I shed light on how we came to design and conduct an instructional activity related to students' problem posing in mathematics, as the second of three interventions we jointly conducted. Three separate aspects influenced this decision. *First* was the fact that Lotta and me had recently concluded our use of *lappar* as stimulus-means in our first intervention with reasonable success. Easy to make as teaching progressed, such lappar we found could be deployed towards other instructional purposes as well. *Second* was the aims of Lotta's project of studying students' communication in mathematics, for which she had obtained funding. I thus gave thought to how these aspects could be studied with another lappar based activity. *Finally* I had came across writing within mathematics education research which drew attention to the emerging area of problem posing. It was in this topic that I sensed a contradiction of the kind Lotta faced in her students' faulty use of the equal to sign. Widespread in routine instruction of mathematics the contradiction identified this time in terms of CHAT perspectives, was the ubiquitous fact of students learning mathematics largely in terms of answering questions others had set for them. There was very little occasion for them to conceive a world in which they could pose problems. I thus considered it fruitful to examine how students went about posing problems within mathematics, given the opportunity. It was against this backdrop that we selected vocabulary from the textbook Lotta and her students were using and inscribed them on lappars. As with our previous intervention we let students to pick these from the blue wicker basket we passed around the classroom. In posing problems with the words and numbers we provided, we were able to observe and identify the kind of agency students developed this time around.

TAKING TRANSFORMATIVE ACTION

Before discussing the CHAT based notion of relational agency, I find it pertinent to mention our making use of the notion of *mediated agency* as forwarded by Wertsch et al. in Chapter 3, as unit of analysis. Extending the Vygotskian notion that the use of mediational means, like lappars, alters the entire flow and structure of psychological activity, Wertsch et al. viewed actions of individuals with stimulus-means as an aggregate of *individuals-acting-with-mediational-means*. Lotta and me found this unit useful to understand the actions her students took as our problem posing intervention progressed. From initially taking part in problem posing in pairs at their desks, which they wrote down on sheets of paper handed out to them, towards the final stages of the intervention we found students to physically pose problems and challenge one another. This involved their making use of the whiteboard to explain their rationale for arriving at solutions and making use of calculators to ratify the numerical accuracy of their answers. We recognised such a display of agency by students as *students-acting-with-lappar-as-mediational-means*.

Edwards (2010) traces the origins of relational agency as a notion, to efforts made by Vygotsky in identifying the cultural formation of the human mind, besides later contributions made by Leont'ev as well as Engeström in contemporary times. The latter two help shift the analytical focus of agency, she argues, from the manner in which psychological activity of individuals is mediated by stimulus-means, to the kind of activity which mediates pursuit of specific goals by human collectives. While the object, motive or purpose of such activity could be an ideal for which different kinds of stimulus means are put to use, the analytical focus also recognises the nature of collective efforts involved. I had demonstrated the use of activity as analytical unit in Chapter 3, with the first forwarded by Leont'ev and the second by Engeström. It is by deploying the latter, that Lotta and me argued at a mathematics education conference, that my conducting research with its focus on disciplined inquiry and her classroom teaching which took into account her praxis and phronesis were aspects of respective collective activities (Gade & Blomqvist, 2016). This latter recognised my working with the research community at large and her being able to work with students and other teacher colleagues. In our conduct of three successive interventions over time we were able to thus create a shared object of two units of activity, whose pursuit not only evolved dynamically but was also able to realise two distinct outcomes, (1) both of us became stakeholders in each others professional practice, and (2) we collectively overcame the contradictions faced in Lotta's classroom teaching-learning, to bring about instructional change. It is in drawing attention to our working alongside one another, that Edwards nuances the kind of relational agency our work demanded, as we jointly conceived and realised a shared object and went on to report our second intervention. Edwards recognises such form of practitioner agency, displayed by both Lotta and me, as a more powerful form of agency than realised when working individually on our own,

> *Relational agency, as a joint and more powerful form of agency, will be presented as an alternative to the idea of professionals as heroic individuals who are given status through their ability to work autonomously.* Instead, the argument will be made that the relational turn in professional practice offers the opportunity for an enhanced form of practice, which is potentially more beneficial to professionals than claims to individual autonomy might be. (Edwards, 2010, p. 61, emphasis added)

In drawing attention to the enhanced agency professionals can arrive at by working across respective institutional confines, Edwards offers a way out of a problem recognised by Sarason in Chapter 2 – that of teachers feeling lonely and isolated one one hand, yet having to appear competent at their ability to solve any or all problems that arose while teaching on the other. The ideal of heroism attributed to the ability of teachers to work autonomously is thus I argue, rightly called to question by Edwards. In terms of relational agency she thus visualises an enhanced version of professionalism wherein, both Lotta and me as example, could treat each other as resourceful to help interpret issues that arose in pursuance of our respective principal professional activities of teaching and research. Via exercise of relational agency we could offer support and also ask for each other's support with regards to our focused engagement with the world so as to take mutually supportive joint action. Edwards maintains,

> *Relational agency can, I suggest, underpin an enhanced version of professionalism.* Professional learning should not be simply a matter of induction into established practices; though induction into values and key skills is important. It also needs to include a capacity for interpreting and approaching problems, for contesting interpretations, for reading the environment, for drawing on the resources there, for being a resource for others, for focusing on the core objects of the professions whether it is children's learning or social inclusion. (Edwards, 2005, p. 179, emphasis added)

I argue it was the resource seeking, enhanced professionalism which Edwards draws attention to via relational agency that led me to suggest the problem posing intervention I had conceived of to Lotta, in response to which she readily accepted and drew the attention of her students in turn to *matteord* or words often used in the subject of mathematics, in Swedish. As detailed in Gade and Blomqvist (2015) it was these words along with those found in the textbook that

TAKING TRANSFORMATIVE ACTION   245

we offered to Lotta's students on their lappars in two colours. Designed for them to work in dyads, each dyad had two lappars to work with, one with a blue word and a green number and the other with a green word and a blue number. This enabled students to offer blue questions and green questions.

Denoting the *first* of three distinct stages in this intervention, the above instructions led Lotta's students to come up with and offer problems like the following, depending on the words and numbers handed out,

> What is the sum of the digits in 2673? (siffarsum in Swedish)
> How much is needed for 2196 to become 2200?

While these problems reflected topics discussed in Lotta's teaching, a few students posed problems in relation to their societal experiences,

> If there are only 4831 football players in Umeå how many teams are there?

> If I get 6574 kronor as weekly allowance and 10000 kronor for monthly allowance how much money do I get in a month? (Answer: 36296 kronor)

With the constraint of posing blue and green questions lifted in the *second* stage, Lotta's students who had become familiar with what was expected of them, began to pose problems *as* dyads. By this is meant that while they articulated the question together, one of them took on the role of a scribe. Some of the problems posed as dyads were,

> Berta and Bert want a monocycle that costs 3265 and they have 3200. How much are they short of (missing)? (Answer: They are short of 65 kronor)

> In Australia the temperature is 830 degrees Fahrenheit hot. In America it is 110 Fahrenheit degrees. What is the difference? (Answer: 720)

In Lotta filling in for a student who had swimming lessons to attend, one reflecting the year in which the problem was posed read,

> 1000 people voted for president Noel but 600 voted for President Blomqvist. How many more voted for president Noel than President Blomqvist? (Answer: 400).

Two girls sitting at desks right behind Noel and Lotta, did not leave the above go unchallenged and offered the following problem,

> There is a presidential election in the United States for the President. Noel was dismissed. President Ulla received 320 votes, and President Sara 165 votes. How many people voted?

The range of problems outlined above evidence the increasing range of everyday situations in relation to which Lotta's students were able to satisfy the task of problem posing set to them when they were at Grade 4. Yet by the time the same instructional activity was carried out at Grade 5, the agency displayed by students was remarkably transformative and a joy to watch. Seated as I was beside the teacher's table at the head of the classroom, I witnessed students stand up at their desks and physically pose problems and challenge one another. Some had their calculators in hand to ratify the numerical accuracy of the solutions that were being offered. Two problems are representative of this *third* round. Without specific instructions from me, these were discussed at the whiteboard by students. The first was offered by Nelly, who I had mentioned as having broken down in tears earlier on, as below,

> Pelle's little sister has 500 horses. 7/10 of the horses are Icelandic horses. How many horses are Icelandic horses?

The other was offered by Jan, whose use of the equal to sign led Lotta to conduct the four-stage action cycle, as follows,

> Pelle's hot dog is thirteen thirty seven kilometers long in reality. How long is his hot dog on a scale of 1:1000? [Talking about a ridiculously long hot dog, perhaps tongue in cheek]

The manner in which students physically posed problems to one another at this stage evidenced Wertsch et al.'s notion of mediated agency in terms of *students-acting-with-lappar-as-mediational-means.*

Taken together and as reported in Gade and Blomqvist (2015), the above description allows me to reflect on the formative intervention Lotta and me were able to conduct. Four aspects deserve particular mention. *First* the starting point of this intervention while grounded in the lappar based activity we had used as germ cell with reasonable success in our previous intervention, was now remodelled to address a contradiction perceived at the systemic level of wider mathematics education research. *Second*, my role as researcher was challenged in finding theoretical constructs in addition to explicit mediation, with which to understand the nature of mediated agency which Lotta's students now exhibited. *Third*, our ability to realise Lotta's enhanced agency and mine as described above, demanded that we in turn conceive our practices of

TAKING TRANSFORMATIVE ACTION

TABLE 5   Comparison of the practices of teaching and research, conceived as activity systems, in the study of teacher-researcher collaboration as in Gade and Blomqvist (2016)

Activity system	Practice of teaching	Practice of research
Instruments	Of classroom	Of research
Subject	Teacher	Researcher
Object	Conduct of project related instructional interventions	
Outcome	Sharing of object and stakeholdership	
Rules	Of praxis, phronesis	Of disciplined inquiry
Community	School students	Students and their teacher
Division of labour	Primarily of teaching	Primarily of research

teaching and research as two separate yet collaborative activity systems. As tabulated in Table 5, such manner of joint agency worked towards a shared object between our activity systems of teaching and research, as a result of which we were able to conduct and report our intervention.

Finally, in sharing of the object of respective activity systems and our stakeholdership, we certainly utilised the resource seeking and enhanced professionalism attributed to professionals working across respective institutional confines. While such professionalism enabled us to take joint action in pursuance of goals that emerged in Lotta's concrete practical, we drew on the ability of Lotta and myself to utilise relational agency across our respective institutions of school and university.

4   Cogenerative Dialogue | Making Measurements

Unlike conducting our first and second intervention whenever Lotta had a few minutes to spare during everyday instruction, the first spanning a few months at grade four and the second spanning almost a year across grades four and five, we conducted our final intervention during one teaching session of forty minutes at Grade four. Geared towards Lotta's project aims of students' communication in learning mathematics, I had at this point been thinking about how her students might use *exploratory talk*, a kind of talk which British educator Douglas Barnes argued was different from what he termed as *presentational talk*. Barnes argued,

> Exploratory talk is hesitant and incomplete because it enables the speaker to try out ideas, to hear how they sound, to see what others make of them, to arrange information and ideas into different patterns. The

difference between the two functions of talk is that in presentational talk the speaker's attention is primarily focused on adjusting the language, content and manner to the needs of an audience, and in exploratory talk the speaker is more concerned with sorting out his or her own thoughts. (Barnes, 2008, p. 5)

The opportunity for having Lotta's students use exploratory talk came by coincidence. During routine exchange of emails in run up to my regular visits, Lotta informed me that she was onto the topic of measurements. She had by that time asked students to make concrete measurements in the classroom and on their sports field outside. They had also worked at exercises in their textbook aimed at metric conversions of length and weight, besides those of time. She had one teaching session remaining, enabling me to plan an activity I might consider pertinent. As reported in Gade and Blomqvist (2018) we were able to have students pairs explore improbable scenarios in relation to various measures utilised in their everyday, besides various acts of measurements. In order to personalise the issue at hand for her students we asked for example

Can Eva and Anton measure the length of Sweden on foot? or Can Lars and Iris measure their age in decimetres?

Apart from the fun, shock and surprise that was in store for all of us, our conduct and its reporting had three aspects worthy of special note, (1) Lotta had to guide and encourage her students' use of exploratory talk, (2) the plenary session she led into the notion of measurement had vital elements of surprise as the intervention progressed, and (3) our analysis of the exploratory talk based session, saw Lotta and me benefit from Tobin's construct of cogenerative dialogue mentioned in Chapter 7. I presently turn to discuss each of these aspects.

While my initial interest in using exploratory talk drew on writings of Barnes, such thoughts were extended by those of Neil Mercer who drew attention to how children can use language as a tool for thinking and how others must help them do so as well. Mercer argued,

I want to argue two main points: first, that the prime aim of education ought to be to help children learn how to use language effectively as a tool for thinking collectively; and secondly that *classroom-based involvement in culturally-based ways of thinking collectively can make a significant contribution to the development of individual children's intellectual ability*. Drawing mainly on classroom-based research, I describe classroom-based education as a dialogic process, in which both talk between

TAKING TRANSFORMATIVE ACTION 249

teachers and learners and talk among learners have important roles to play. (Mercer, 2002, p. 141, emphasis added)

Mercer's arguments explicitly echo Vygotsky's conception of cultural-historical development in terms of the interpsychological becoming the intrapsychological, as in Chapter 3. Yet Mercer also points out that in any study of how the above takes place in local classrooms, the role which the teacher plays in having students consolidate what they are learning is critical. Offering implementable guidelines, he and Lyn Dawes also argue that just placing students in small groups and leaving them to solve problems set for them by themselves is not enough to reap the benefits of cooperating with one another in dialogue. Viewing whole-class, teacher-led and group-based discussion activities as complementing one another, they offer concrete ways to realise the promise of exploratory talk,

First, they should take an *active role, guiding their pupils' use of language and modelling the ways it can be used for thinking collectively.* ...

Second, teachers should *establish an appropriate set of ground rules for talk in class*, building on children's own raised awareness of how language can be used. ...

Third, a teacher needs to ensure that *group activities are well designed to elicit debate and joint reasoning.* ... Activities should draw on children's existing common knowledge, but should also draw them beyond it into a consideration of new ideas and the search for more useful information. (Mercer & Dawes, 2008, pp. 70–71, emphasis in original)

As reported in Gade and Blomqvist (2018) the plenary of exploratory talk which Lotta conducted in Swedish and one we went on to transcribe into English, evidenced the wisdom of Mercer and Dawes' guidelines above. In terms of the formative intervention we designed and conducted, Lotta's students had to draw upon existing knowledge and also explore their thinking in avenues that lay conceptually beyond what was being currently explored by them. Lotta's guidance began with asking her students to discuss questions we had handed out on *lappar* as before, in pairs at their own tables, before they read these aloud to their peers and offered their arguments, by standing beside her. For example in relation to Eva and Anton discussing *Can Eva and Anton measure the length of Sweden on foot?* the discussion ran as follows,

Lotta   Once more
Eva   Can Eva and Anton measure Sweden's length with/on foot

Many	Nooo ... @@ [Laughter]
Lotta	No, no, not now ... Eva and Anton will attempt this question ... only them first
[??]	It works (*Det går*)
Liam	You have to go straight ahead
Ulla	What if you go into a building
[??]	Then you go over the house
Lotta	Noel! Do you have anything good to say
Noel	And you can go through the house ... and you can go inside the house and jump off the balcony
Leon	And what if it is a high building
Nils	If you have a map, you can take that, you can look how much a foot is and use the scale of the map

One can observe above how Lotta established ground rules by insisting, that Eva and Anton read the question once more, telling others students that it only them who would respond to the question. Cautioning Noel who was making made fun of suggestions that others made, she wanted to know if he could contribute positively as well. Subsequent to the above and as suggested by Nils, Lotta pulled down a map from the ceiling and discussed how its scale could be used and concluded.

Lotta	Good, so you could measure Sweden's length on/with foot/feet
Noel	It is possible to measure Sweden's length with feet, but it's a lot of work
Lotta	At first even I did not think it was possible
Lotta	Maria and Nelly it is now your turn, you must listen

In a manner outlined above Lotta took active part in fostering the ability of her students to think collectively, for which she set ground rules for participation as well as promoted ongoing debate.

It was also the case that with our intervention designed for students to explore improbable scenarios of measurement, one that countered normal practices encountered in students' everyday lives, Lotta's plenary threw up rebellion and surprise which either of us did not foresee. For example Noel who felt at odds with the proceedings was heard protesting,

> Vad? Jag fattar ingenting! or What? I don't understand anything!
> And Du är inte klok! or You are insane!

TAKING TRANSFORMATIVE ACTION 251

One response that took both Lotta and me by surprise in particular was Leon's response to the question

Can Mikael and Elsa measure daytime in/with kilograms?

Where on one hand Noel said he did not grasp what was going on, we found Leon to share his knowledge about radioactivity by saying,

Leon   I know a difficult way to advance this answer ... how to measure time in kilograms ... the whole time the particles change and we can measure the weight of the particles count how many particles there are ... over time.

Lotta's plenary ended with students discussing the question,

Can Lena and Noel measure milk in/with minutes?

Nils who by this time expressed to Lotta that he thought the plenary to be a surreal space in which anything could happen, now suggested that one go back to normal life and argued that it was the volume of milk and not time that was to be measured, adding,

Nils   Som vanligt! or As is common!

For reasons mentioned in the previous section, the transcription and analysis of Lotta's plenary had to wait for her to return from the Swedish National Agency for Education. We soon collaborated once again and struggled with how best to report about findings of our promising plenary intervention. Unlike relational knowing where we drew on our extended conversations, and relational agency which drew on our ability to work across institutional confines, we drew this time on our own experience of how Lotta's students used exploratory talk. Deploying our first person approach we found it useful to utilise Tobin's notion of *cogenerative dialogue*. As a conceptual twin of *coteaching* which asks researchers to coparticipate in teaching in order to understand its ongoing progress, cogenerative dialogue is ongoing discourse between participants which enables them to generate theory about what had transpired. As explained in Wolff-Michael Roth and Kenneth Tobin's (2002) *At the elbow of another: learning to teach by coteaching*, the processes involved in such theory-oriented work takes place at two levels,

> *First, we cogenerate theory together with teachers and students*, with whom we have already shared classroom experiences, for the purpose of improving the practices of teaching and learning. ... this is 'open theory,' a democratic process of generating understanding and explanation. *Second, we simultaneously theorise the activity systems of teaching/learning and researching at a meta-level* .... Because of the particularities of human practices (e.g. meaningful and mediated subject-object relations) only first-person (subject-centered) perspectives allow us to recognise salient meanings and motivations that subjects (teachers, students) deliberately use to ground their actions. (Roth & Tobin, 2002, p. 245, emphasis added)

Exemplifying the two levels of analysis that Roth and Tobin point to, it will come as no surprise that while transcribing and analysing Lotta's plenary, both she and me were able to relive the fun and jest we had during our first person co-participation on one hand and the theoretical aspects that were emerging in our analysis. As detailed in Gade (2015a) and far from applying theory to practice, such an effort enabled Lotta to reflect and reason about her own praxis. Raising her hand in a manner her students would, Lotta understood her students' actions as their wanting to search an explanation for questions we had set, even if the whole exercise seemed crazy. She thought too that it was good enough if her students took part in the plenary, even if they did not have the right answers. Another aspect she offered rationale for, was how she ended her plenary with asking students to respond to each of the ten questions they had just explored with a *yes* or *no*. Conducted at the spur of the moment one not planned for at all, Lotta explained that she wanted to bring closure to that day's lesson and convey to her students that they had done important work and not indulged in something fancy. She also said that next time she worked with such manner of questions, she would convey the goals of such a lesson to students beforehand.

Lotta's experience of sharing how talk based lessons worked with her colleagues, is also worthy of note. Such lessons were hard for teachers to carry out on their own she said, as there was no way for them to assess how such lessons progressed. Yet, such lessons were helpful she argued, in teachers coming to know the kind of knowledge students themselves had. Lotta recognised too the issue of teachers not letting researchers assist them as knowledgable partners by using the phrase *they often close the door on themselves anyway*. My own presence she thought was an advantage as I had been in her class for a long time concluding,

> The children are comfortable with you and that is really important. I have had many researchers who came to my class, sit for an hour at the back and leave thereafter. (Gade, 2015a, p. 614)

TAKING TRANSFORMATIVE ACTION

I find this last to speak to the promise of professional development via coteaching, one we had achieved by way of conducting our intervention. Arguing such manner of change in teaching to be more lasting than what teacher workshops set out to achieve, Roth and Tobin argue,

> The success of our coteaching experience has probably come from the support that any one of us experienced as part of collaboration. *Coteaching and cogenerative dialoguing constitute a practice and mechanism that mediate the insecurity that comes with change and even with prospects of change.* Other possibilities arise because the move from individual teaching to coteaching constitutes a radical change in the conditions of teaching, which open up a space for continuous teacher development to occur in a context that participants experience as safe because the responsibilities are both collective and shared. (Roth & Tobin, 2004, p. 176, emphasis added)

Many aspects of Lotta's plenary viewed as formative Intervention are worthy of note. *First,* is the starting point that emerged in our continued exchange as teacher and researcher who were taking part in extended collaboration, and our ability to swiftly make use of classroom time we found ourselves at hand. To Lotta's credit she ably guided her students' exploration of their thoughts till the very end, even conveying to them towards the end that the plenary session participated in was educationally valuable and not something trivial. *Second,* was our ability to question normative ideas of classroom instruction by having students explore the improbable scenarios we presented to them. Such an exercise was not only rich for students' learning experience, but also for open theorisation of the same as practitioners. *Third* and for either of these outcomes and as with our rectifying the faulty use of the equal to sign by her students, we drew on CHAT perspectives to not only provoke but also sustain the growth of the interventions we conducted over time. *Finally* in either intervention our unit of analysis focused upon contradictions that were situated within Lotta's everyday instruction, one we capitalised on in the conduct of our intervention to realise students' development. The manner of agency displayed by Lotta, her students and me had a dynamic quality, one whose expansive features I now turn to discuss.

5   Expansive Learning | Meaningful Activities

My extended efforts with Lotta, brought to light three frameworks with which to grasp the nature of our collaboration as teacher and researcher – relational

254 CHAPTER 9

knowing, relational agency and cogenerative dialogue. While I shed light on the manner in which they played out in three interventions in previous sections, producing different outcomes at different times, my reflecting on these in Gade (2015a) led me to a fourth framework which focused on the new, emerging and unforeseen aspects of our work in terms of *expansive learning activity*. As recognised by Engeström (2011) in relation to Formative Interventions, the focus here is on those patterns of activity which act like a germ cell, that evolve, expand and give rise to new uses in prospective interventions. Taken as a whole the outcomes of the three interventions I conducted with Lotta were new, emerging and unforeseen by either of us when I initiated my narrative based study of her students' learning mathematics expected of them (Gade, 2010). One could argue that Wertsch's concept of explicit mediation was the germ cell that we tailored to meet ongoing educational exigencies arising in Lotta's teaching. As such in line with Engeström's notion of expansive learning activity soon discussed, via conducting each of the interventions we collectively learnt something that was not yet there.

The many salient features which Engeström (2010) highlights with regards to his notion of *expansive learning activity* are worth examining. *First* while traditional instruction is a subject-producing activity and traditional science an instrument-producing activity, Engeström argues expansive learning to be an activity-producing activity, like with the three successive interventions Lotta and me were able to conduct and realise. As such expansive learning is a movement from individual actions to the collective activity of collaborating participants, which in our case was both Lotta, me and her students as well. None of the interventions was a solo act driven by any one person alone. *Second* it follows, Engeström argues, that expansive learning is multi-voiced in the Bakhtinain sense, one that takes into account continued debate and negotiation leading to the production of new outcomes. This last is evidence of a kind of agency that all participants have opportunity for and utilise. Students working with the equal to sign, Noel's declaring himself as President, Nils' asking for the use of a map or Leon's alluding to radioactivity, all exemplify students' agency in the expansive learning we realised. As teacher and researcher our realisation of what we were able to realise was not only in terms of the subject matter content we had in mind, but one in which each of these students developed in ways for which the activity afforded them agency. As I argue in Gade (2015b) while responding to contradictions in Lotta's instructional concrete we were able to materially transform the nature of vital relations that were prior and preexisted in their classroom. Of the dynamic and synchronous nature of such manner of collective activity based transformation, Engeström argues,

The basic argument is that traditional modes of learning deal with tasks in which the contents to be learned are well known ahead of time by those who design, manage and implement various programs of learning. When whole collective activity systems, such as work processes and organizations, need to redefine themselves, traditional modes of learning are not enough. *Nobody knows exactly what needs to be learned. The design of the new activity (externalization) and the acquisition of the knowledge and skills it requires (internalization) are increasingly intertwined. In expansive learning activity, they merge.* (Engeström, 2010, p. 75, emphasis added)

Engeström's notion of expansive learning detailed with respect to my work with Lotta, highlights a noteworthy feature – that in attempting to overcome contradictions in a collective manner, participants in expansive learning do not know what has to be learned as the activity progresses. As evidenced in the previous sections, new avenues of development arise for students, teacher and researcher. That each activity participated in led to another activity in the above, is a key feature that helps me to portray the kind of intervention Tomas and I were able to conduct at his Grade eight mathematics classroom at another school in Umeå. On his part, I found Tomas to teach students who wished to avail of his personal assistance, for which they collected twice a week from many grade eight sections at his school. Unlike their mainstream peers following routine instruction, his students were those who felt less confident in their ability to learn the mathematics expected of them and had opportunity to work in a less competitive and stressful environment. Few in number, they could ask for individual assistance from him with little hesitation.

Yet my visiting his class once a week and upon exchanging notes with Tomas when lessons gave over, I was able to observe the disinterest his students had for mathematics, evidenced by their unwillingness to engage with their textbooks which seemed burdensome to them, one they could be seen pushing away at their tables. On developing a reasonable degree of familiarity with them and on my suggestion, Tomas became willing to ask them to work in pairs at Kängaru problems that were appropriate for their grade. After they had worked in pairs, we asked them to share their thinking and solution at the blackboard for all their peers to see. This task or activity became the first of five tasks we went on to conduct, which culminated in one in which his students displayed their sense of identity in unique ways. As detailed in Gade and Forsgren (2019) we drew on our analysis of each prior activity to design and conduct the next.

Four aspects are noteworthy in our ability to successfully carry out and realise cultural-historical development of Tomas' students in our five-task intervention. *First,* we designed and conducted each successive task by drawing on results obtained from our conduct of each previous task. *Second*, our realisation of students' development and unique identities was lead by their participation in tasks or activities that were practical and meaningful to them, in line with del Rio and Alvarez as in Chapter 4. *Third*, the identity which some of Tomas' students exhibited in the fifth task, exemplified the notion of *Transformative Activist Stance* in line with Stetsenko, alluded to in Chapter 1. This last enabled viewing students as coming to know themselves, their world, and their becoming human in and through processes of collaboratively transforming the world in light of individual goals. *Finally* our conduct of the five-task intervention, enabled us to empirically substantiate Engeström's notion of expansive learning activity. I now turn to discuss each of the five tasks.

Our *first* task of having Tomas' students to work at Kängaru problems was to invite them to work at problems that could be solved by drawing on their common sense, without specific mathematical knowledge. Their working in pairs was to allow opportunity for their interpsychological to become their intrapsychological. With students able to meet with Tomas' expectations and mine, from the next task onwards I set problems in the topic Tomas was dealing with in everyday instruction. Since this topic was area and perimeter of geometrical figures, for the *second* task I selected textbook problems involving rectangles and circles, for which students would need to make a calculation after being able to recognise which formulae was to be applied. Our conduct of this task met with resentment, since students now seemed to face the kind of mathematics they were up against and one they tacitly rejected. Since it was obvious that I had designed the tasks, they even came up to me to express their disappointment. It was then that I decided to design problems that were practical and meaningful to them.

With scale being the next topic in Tomas' instruction, I resorted to maps downloaded from the internet and asked students to find the scale utilised in their *third* task. By this time Tomas organised his students into two groups which he and me led separately. The scale of each map was in some way familiar in an intuitive manner to them as one traced the route from their city centre to their school, the other from Umeå to a nearby town they all knew and the last from Umeå to Stockholm, the capital city of Sweden. Since Tomas' students could relate to each of the scenarios presented, the interest they displayed in their attempts was evidenced by using their earphone wires to measure the route marked and asking if they could measure distances as-the-crow-flies (*fågelvägen*) while arriving at the scale of each map, even if this was in approximate terms.

With the efficacy of deploying meaningful practical activity evident in the kind of excitement with which Tomas' students took part in pursuing the goals

TAKING TRANSFORMATIVE ACTION

of the task, our design and conduct of the next two tasks was also based on aspects which del Rio and Alvarez highlighted. In pursuing these tasks the object and purpose of each activity was apparent to the students, the results of their efforts was contingent to the kind of actions they took and the feedback they received from their peers was immediate. Such attempts strengthened students' sense of self-efficacy and identity. Relating to the topic of volume, the *fourth* task asked students to guess and calculate the volume of household objects whose volume measure was not marked on them, like an iPod box, biscuit tin and shoe box say. With Tomas tabulating their guesses on the board and on inquiring how one could ascertain the accuracy of their guesses, on my suggestion one student searched his textbook for the appropriate formula. He then used the same to ratify his guess. While such agency was not surprising given the way we designed the task, our conduct of the *fifth* and final task had far more developmental aspects in store. In line with the topic of statistics which Tomas and his students were working on, in this task we asked his students to (1) work in groups of two or three, (2) decide on a question of their choice, (3) collect data from peers in the classroom and (4) display their results in a column or pie graph. While the excitement of students taking part in this task was palpable, it was in line with instructions given to them that the externalisation of personal identity by some of them was visible and noteworthy, something I now turn to.

In response to our instructions in the fifth task, the majority of student groups set questions like *What is the brand of your car?* or *How much do you get as monthly pocket money?* leading to column graphs as in Figure 9. While indicative of the cultural-historical development for each, the participation of two students stood out. First was the response of a student I named Hans-Erik, who along and his partner offered a graph in response to the question *Are you 15 years (of age)*? I had observed Hans-Erik to have a mercurial nature, someone who appeared quite able at mathematics, yet also display unease with being who he was as a student. Tomas too mentioned the concerns Hans-Erik's mother had about his doing well at mathematics and learning personal discipline. Yet it was Hans-Erik's breaking into Adam Lambert's song, one audible to all of us, that was striking. Revealing of his emotions and complexity filled phase of being an adolescent and becoming an adult, the lyrics of this song which seemed to voice his self were as follows,

> Hey! slow down, what do you want from me!
> What do you want from me!
> There might have been a time when I would give myself away
> What do you want from me!

Oh, once upon a time, I wouldn't give a damn,
But now, here we are.
What do you want from me!
Just don't give up, I'm working it out,
Please don't give in, I won't let you down!
What do you want from me!

In line with Wertsch's concept of mediated agency, one can argue that Hans-Erik-spoke-with-his-song. Yet in line with Stetsenko's construct of transformative activist stance or TAS, Hans-Erik's emotions were not in addition to his learning and knowing mathematics, but intrinsic to his *becoming* the self he was then able to, while taking part in the fifth task. As Stetsenko points out, in his spontaneous rendition of Lambert's song, Hans-Erik was not only participating in the collaborative educational task we had set but also becoming human in that very process, by creating his identity and finding a place among his peers.

A similar *becoming*, was evidenced by Alba who created her identity, when along with her partner she collected data for the question *Har du testad röka?* or Have you tried smoking? The significance of this question lies in the kind of displeasure Alba faced from her teachers in relation to her smoking, one not allowed by children of her age under Swedish law. One can argue Alba resented the caution she was receiving from her teachers and wanted to speak up and show that she was not the only one among her peers who was smoking. Hence her question, for which the data she collected evidenced that 77 percent of her classmates had tried smoking as well. In a manner similar to Hans-Erik, Alba was not just learning and coming to know mathematics in the task but vitally becoming human at the same time, as argued by Stetsenko in terms of TAS and as evidenced by her graph included in Figure 9.

In relation to the five-task intervention detailed above, I turn finally to greater dwell on the notions of formative intervention and expansive learning. My extended collaboration with Tomas, as with Lotta, lasted close to an academic year. As detailed in Gade and Forsgren (2019) it was Tomas' whole class that was unit of analysis for his students as well as for us practitioners, enabling us to conduct and report on our five-task intervention. In doing so we utilised a contradiction that arose in events that transpired within Tomas' everyday instruction as starting point and designed each successive task in our intervention as the conduct and our reflections on the same progressed in their entirety. Two aspects however stand out in the collective actions we took in this regard. *First* is the notion of human agency which Engeström argues as representative of adopting a dialectical approach to initiating change and transforming reality. Herein Tomas and me adopted a stance that altered the

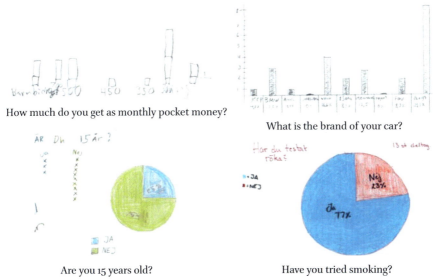
FIGURE 9   Students graphs as in Gade and Forsgren (2019)

prior and preexisting status quo. As also argued by Stetsenko, the responses of Tomas' students to the tasks we designed and conducted, brought forward their agency, towards learning and knowing mathematics and becoming human, evidenced by externalising their personal identities. *Second*, we realised Engeström's notion of expansive learning, not only in terms of each task producing a subsequent new task as activity, but also in terms of the kind of new learning that each task demanded from his students, as well as Tomas as teacher and myself as researcher. Only a transformative notion of agency as forwarded by Stetsenko was also able to explain the seemingly ubiquitous adolescent actions we are given to see in everyday classrooms like their singing and/or protesting. These aspects evidence that we were able to merge the design and conduct of every new activity alongside the acquiring of knowledge which led to such realisation.

6   Forests and Trees | A Multilectic

Having provided an overview of the interventions I was able to conduct, albeit separately with Lotta and Tomas, I find it appropriate to gather my thoughts on the potential of the integrative and interdisciplinary CHAT stance I have argued for and come to adopt. Towards this I *first* highlight constructs found useful to grasp teacher-researcher collaboration, *second* highlight those which enabled us to conduct instructional interventions, before reflecting *finally* on the relationship between student cohorts and individual students in terms of a multilectic between forests and trees. My use of this metaphor as alluded to in Chapter 7 is deliberate, symbolising the struggle practitioners face in ensuring the development of individual students, even as we remain in-charge of a classroom full of cohorts. I will argue that the individual and cohort issue faced by us is not at odds with one another but strung in a multilectic composed of many a dialectic that could be developmental, sociological, pedagogical, critical, curricular and/or practitioner focused in orientation. Personally I remain moved in knowing that while unaware of these conceptual categories which serve as insightful analytical lenses, caring and sincere practitioners call upon intuitive common sense and commit vast amounts of time to the cause of raising our young despite innumerable odds, with aplomb. In a world that is increasingly chaotic and often unforgiving, the intrinsic satisfaction they derive in carrying out localised instruction, day in day out, is most deserving of our appreciation, gratitude and applause.

I *begin* with pointing to the immense potential and promise there lies when we practitioners collaborate, as teachers and researchers, or when novice teachers and the more experienced do. I have in previous sections exemplified ways of realising these with four constructs (1) *relational knowing* – which recognises the knowledge that could be externalised in conversations we practitioners are known to often have with one another, (2) *relational agency* – which highlights how practitioners could move beyond a solo conception of teaching and work with others practitioners across institutional confines to utilise resources that might be brought to bear for ongoing instruction, (3) *cogenerative dialogue* – which promotes first person ways by which practitioners can engage with students and fellow teachers to generate theory with regards to ongoing teaching, and (4) *expansive learning* – which recognises human agency and allows for the unexpected that classroom teaching can bring forth in its realisation, so that the new, unforeseen and the unexpected is learnt as any activity unfolds. With either of these collaborative modes underpinning the four interventions I discuss in previous sections, I mention too that by and large an understanding of the kind of intersubjective relationships which practitioners enter into while collaborating with one another for concrete practice or educational research, is not only scarce but also inadequately understood. There is thus much scope for research in this regard, one that could yield empirical evidence and theoretical rationale about how and towards what ends practitioners collaborate and respond to instructional issues deserving greater attention in their concrete practical.

Two arguments augur well for the collaborative efforts of practitioners I argue in favour of. The *first* is found in writings of Leont'ev, whose explanation of *human consciousness* is as follows,

TAKING TRANSFORMATIVE ACTION

> Consciousness is co-*knowing*, but only in the sense that individual consciousness may exist only in the presence of social consciousness and of language that is its real substrate. In the process of material production, people also produce language, and this serves not only as a means of information but also as a carrier of the socially developed meanings fixed in it.
>
> ... Consciousness is originated in society; it is produced. For this reason consciousness is not a postulate and is not a condition of psychology but its problem, a subject for concrete scientific psychological investigation. (Leont'ev, 1978, p. 60)

Leont'ev's articulation of human consciousness in terms of co-knowing in material activity within society is both profound and practical. While on one hand our knowing is viewed in terms of what we might come to agree with or disagree with our follow human beings, on the other he draws attention to our use of language to exchange what we know, so as to gather meanings that underpin its conventional and historical usage in society. The very formation of human consciousness as co-knowing thus needs investigation in various concrete instances.

My *second* argument draws on Vera John-Steiner's study of the way in which scientists, artists and women are found to collaborate. Drawing on Vygotskian and Bakhtinian ideas on how individual and social thought processes are interdependent, John-Steiner argues,

> We have come to a new understanding of the life of the mind. The notion of the solitary thinker still appeals to those molded by the Western belief in individualism. However, a careful scrutiny of how knowledge is constructed and artistic forms are shaped reveals a different reality. Generative ideas emerge from joint thinking, from significant conversations, and from sustained, shared struggles to achieve new insights by partners in thought.
>
> ... *Solo practices are insufficient to meet the challenges and the new complexities of classrooms, parenting, and the changing workplace.* (John-Steiner, 2000, pp. 3–4, emphasis added)

By recognising the dynamics of sustained and shared struggles in human collaboration, to be relevant not just for artists, scientists and women but educational practitioners at large, I find John-Steiner to echo Leont'ev. Of relevance too is the attention she draws to the changes that accompany the manner in which places of work are themselves evolving. For both John-Steiner and

Leont'ev, human consciousness is co-knowing, besides a reflection by human subjects upon their own reality, their own activity and their own selves as individuals.

I *second* dwell in this section on five theoretical constructs that have enabled me to lead the conduct of formative interventions I outline (1) *leading activity* – which asks that we factor the developmental stage of students in the design of our instructional interventions (Karpov in Chapter 6), (2) *explicit mediation* – whose thoughtful use in various material activity with specific instructional aims, enables students to externalise their individual or group thinking (Wertsch in Chapter 3), (3) *meaningful practical activity* – which recognises the ability of students to draw upon directive functions in their pursuit of goals in any practical task at hand (del Rio & Alvarez in Chapter 4), (4) *pedagogical categories* – that point to the diverse ways in which teachers realise specific social arrangements geared towards attaining instructional goals within their classroom at the spur of the moment in an effortless manner (Dalton & Tharp in Chapter 6), and (5) *personal practical knowledge* – which recognises the strengths of the knowledge teachers possess of theoretical and practical aspects, one blended with their personal background and externalised by them in *professional knowledge landscapes* they steer and sustain (Clandinin & Connelly in Chapter 2). I mention too that while the first four constructs summarised above are CHAT based, it was giving due credence to the final one which is more practitioner focused, that led Lotta and Tomas to realise each of our interventions.

In fact it was my being able to empirically recognise Lotta's personal practical knowledge in terms of the nature of pedagogy she deployed in the plenary of exploratory talk she led, that enabled me to conceptualise any instructional intervention more generally, in terms of *a landscape of teaching-learning* in Gade & Blomqvist (2018). By this construct I have argued it possible to examine and understand classroom instruction in terms of four interrelated dimensions (1) *the category of pedagogy* that teachers utilise as just mentioned above (Dalton & Tharp, 2002), (2) *the kind of talk* that each kind of pedagogy promotes (Pierce & Gilles, 2008), (3) *the manner of teaching* that teachers utilise to lead each instructional activity (Alexander, 2008), besides (4) *the nature of learning* that each instructional activity demands of most students (van Oers, 2009a). The ability of educational research to realise and substantiate such landscapes theoretically and empirically, I argue, could not only offer findings that are wholistic, but also allow for practitioners to reflect on the strengths and/or weaknesses of any instructional intervention. The importance of analysing instruction in terms of units and not elements in research, is what Vygotsky had been unequivocal about.

TAKING TRANSFORMATIVE ACTION

Having brought together constructs I found useful to jointly carry out CHAT based developmental agenda in instructional interventions, I turn *finally* to examine the relationship between a cohort of students and the individual child in classrooms at large, in terms of my chosen metaphor of forests and trees. I argue the kind of agency we were able to achieve classroom wide in Lotta and Tomas' classrooms, when viewed as forests, resulted in promoting the cultural-historical development of individual students, viewed as trees. In other words how we organise instruction for any cohort of students is what *leads* the cultural-historical development of individual students as well, allowing the interpsychological between students to become each student's intrapsychological, an aspect Mercer cited earlier in this very Chapter also recognises.

Within these forests and as argued by Stetsenko (2008) we were able to observe first hand how students viewed as individual trees had many an occasion to learn, know, do, be and become human. Jan's faulty use of the equal to sign when rectified by a classroom wide instructional practice, was able to realise cultural-historical development for him as well as his peers. Nelly broke down in tears, but also regained her composure while working in the same classroom wide intervention. On partnering with and defeating Lotta in an election, Noel conceived himself to be President. His two peers Ulla and Sara, seated not too far away, soon dismissed such an eventuality in a classroom wide problem posing intervention. Leon was able to share his nascent knowledge of radioactivity in a plenary which Lotta led with all her students, one Nils considered to be a space in which anything could happen. Just as Hans-Erik seemed to sing about his inner state of mind and self while learning mathematics, so did Alba show in quantitative terms that she was not the only one who had tried smoking amongst her peers, in the five-task intervention Tomas conducted. In the four instructional forests we were able to steer, we were able to visibly observe and single out the cultural-historical development of individual students as trees.

I argue each of the above incidents to also exemplify the mathematical development of students in the dialectic and/or multilectic between the cohort of students on one hand besides individual students on the other. In line with Stetsenko's arguments in Chapter 1, our joint ability to take *transformative action* in each intervention was evident in two ways, (1) in the way we were able to transform the status quo in Lotta and Tomas' existing classrooms by creating new instructional environments, and (2) the manner in which our instruction enabled students to not only know for the sake of knowing, but also allow for the creation of individual student identity and become human by way of contributing to historically evolving sociocultural practices, like classroom instruction and everyday local schooling in this case, of humanity itself. I contend the multilectic I speak about to play out in two specific ways as well, (1) in the multilectic of relationships which have potential to be realised between the kinds of talk, pedagogy, teaching and learning that go on to constitute a *landscape of teaching-learning* as proposed in Lotta's plenary intervention, (2) in the multilectic between the five insightful constructs with which we were able to conduct our interventions and realise productive relationships between teachers and researchers as practitioners. It goes without saying that the dialectic and/or multilectic between either in the interventions discussed, met with instructional aims in Lotta and Tomas' concrete practical. The potential to realise these towards aims that could arise in other concrete practical scenarios remains entirely open.

At this point I am reminded of an old proverb attributed to the people of Suriname, who recognise that their equatorial rainforests have answers to questions that haven't yet been asked. I find this saying to ring true with respect to ongoing instruction in everyday classrooms as well. We as teachers, educators, researchers and practitioners may have not yet asked questions of our everyday classrooms, whose answers while lying in plain sight, may have as yet remained unrealised and unarticulated for the benefit of education and educational research. It is in making such an assertion that I turn to triangulate my own efforts with those of two other CHAT scholars, Bert van Oers and Gordon Wells.

7   Gaining from Triangulation: Coda

In my efforts to learn from the process of triangulation, I begin with two notions as points of departure from van Oers writings, both of which informed the conduct of our problem posing intervention (1) his program called developmental education, and (2) the difference he points out between cultural meaning and personal sense. van Oers (2009) program of *Developmental Education*, builds on the central Vygotskian idea that instruction *leads* development. Such a stance places the responsibility of students' learning on *their* ability to make personal sense and cultural meaning in the kind of instructional activities their teachers organise – an idea easy to underestimate. Summarising his program of developmental education and highlighting its tenets for concrete instructional practice as well as teacher education at large, van Oers maintains,

> The basic idea of this approach is that pupils can only meaningfully learn in school when this learning is embedded in practices in which they participate with peers and teachers. The purpose of education should always

TAKING TRANSFORMATIVE ACTION

be to support *the broad identity development of pupils as well-informed participants in sociocultural activities.*

... Good education, as Vygotsky (1978) once pointed out, should always be one step ahead of pupils. It is supposed to promote human development through meaningful interactions with children, by offering them cultural tools for meaningful participation in the cultural life of their social communities. (van Oers, 2009, pp. 214–215, emphasis added)

Underscoring the importance of attending to the development of students' identity, an idea which Stetsenko in Chapter 1 views as central to human knowing and becoming, van Oers singles out four strategies that could enable students to become both autonomous and critical participants (1) reading and writing or dealing with textual information as core activity, (2) inculcating a positive attitude towards reflection on problem situations they encounter, for which they go on to take action, (3) mastering subject matter skills and understanding, one that leads to proficient participation, and (4) giving greater attention to an underdeveloped area in education – the arts or aesthetic thinking. Recognising the theory driven nature of the CHAT enterprise, van Oers and is also quick to point out that the design of instructional practices in line with the above arguments, is not geared towards finding one effective method alone but an ever-evolving program that is geared towards realising students' cultural-historical development. The manner in which Lotta and I came to utilise the germ cell of explicit mediation, besides Tomas and me utilised the conduct of successive tasks as germ cell van Oers argues, depended on the professionalism of Lotta, Tomas and myself – in other words teachers, teacher trainers, researchers and curriculum developers combined.

While our problem posing intervention *led* students to consciously use textbook vocabulary in consultation with their peers and Lotta, before these were encountered by students in a manner routine to their usage in classrooms, van Oers draws attention to another aspect of significance – the distinction Leont'ev makes between *cultural meaning* and *personal sense*. While the former is argued as represented in language and refers to generalised knowledge for dealing with the world, one built throughout our collective history, the latter is based on the value and significance which individual students attribute to their actions, goals and motives as they take part in cultural activities. An example of personal sense made during our problem posing intervention was our finding a student Mark to add and later remove the word *bönde* or farmer in Swedish to the list of words belonging to mathematics or *matteord* which Lotta had listed on the whiteboard in prior whole classroom discussion with her students (Gade & Blomqvist, 2015). Following Leont'ev and in light of his attention to students' development, van Oers draws attention to two aspects here, (1) that cultural meaning can be transformed to curriculum content one mandated as necessary to be taught, yet on the other hand (2) that personal sense cannot be taught directly and needs occasion for students to personally build the same by becoming involved in educative relationships or activities. Nonetheless, van Oers hastens to add that cultural meaning and personal sense should not be treated as independent phenomena and points out that,

> The attempt to transmit cultural meaning without allowing pupils to attach personal sense to it – as is often the case in traditional instruction – generally ends up in formal rote learning. According to Leont'ev, such learning actually results in dehumanizing the individual.
>
> ... Hence, the learning of mathematics as a meaningful activity refers both to the process of technically mastering mathematics as an historically developed activity and to the process of attaching personal meaning [sense] to the actions, methods, and results involved. Only then can this learning promote the personal and cultural development of the individual. (van Oers, 1996, p. 94)

In recognising good education to always be one step ahead of pupils in line with Vygotsky, via Leont'ev's caution above van Oers nuances the kind of dialectic that needs to be at play between cultural meaning and personal sense within a zpd that educational activities can bring about. Importantly he points to the ill effects and risks of the practice of rote learning of cultural meaning by students without opportunity for them to make personal sense, an aspect that dehumanises them. One can argue that in the process of posing problems acceptable to their peers and Lotta with the personal sense they made of words handed out, her students had occasion to make personal sense and grasp cultural meaning.

I turn next to Gordon Wells' (1999) *Dialogic Inquiry*, which we drew upon while reporting our exploratory talk based intervention in relation to students' making measurements (Gade & Blomqvist, 2018). In addition to van Oers' attention to the development of students' identity in Lotta's plenary and following Wells, we viewed her guidance of students use of exploratory talk as a dialogic *activity of knowing* – wherein the nature of their understanding was personal and immediate, besides holistic and intuitive. Drawing on his own experiences of building communities of dialogic inquiry, Wells (2002) puts forth two ideas found generative to his own thinking, (1) *improvable object*, which is a problem encountered in practical situations that is improved through collaborative action and dialogue. We came to consider students' understanding of measures

TAKING TRANSFORMATIVE ACTION

and measurement to be the improvable object for students in Lotta's plenary, (2) *spiral of knowing*, which traces the many roles that speaking, writing and other modes of communication are historically at play in thinking about and building collective knowledge around any improvable object. In having made measurements in the concrete and worked at textbook exercises, Lotta's plenary was opportunity for her students to reflect on their experiences in a spiral of knowing.

In continuation of the two constructs above, Wells draws attention to two insurmountable problems he finds within classroom instruction, (1) *commodification of knowledge*, or the failure of not being able to make a distinction between knowledge and knowing. While knowledge could be realised in activities of knowing such as Lotta's plenary, when such manner of acquisition is separated from its corresponding activity of knowing, Wells cautions that the knowledge objects alone could be used in school instruction for show, to compete or gain credits in assessment. (2) *intolerance of diversity*, or the unwillingness of school instruction to accept the diversity in learning trajectories of different students, an aspect related to their age, gender, social experience or economic background of families they come from. In students being far from alike even within the same family, a one-size-fits-all transmission and accreditation model in education as norm, Wells reiterates, fails to allow students to recognise and pursue their personal interests and strengths.

As different from van Oers' program of developmental education and Wells' program of building communities of dialogic inquiry, my efforts have led me to realise teacher-researcher collaboration, in dialectic with which we conducted instructional interventions. While such conduct was aimed at the cultural-historical development of students as they took part in classroom wide social practices, it is to grasp the kind of agency found embedded in these interventions, that I turn to Engeström et al.'s notion of *transformative agency*. Herein they argue,

> Transformative agency differs from conventional notions of agency in that it stems from encounters with and examinations of disturbances, conflicts, and contradictions in the collective activity. Transformative agency develops the participants' joint activity by explicating and envisioning new possibilities. Transformative agency goes beyond the individual as it seeks possibilities for collective change efforts. ... it underlines the crucial importance of expansive transitions from individual initiatives toward collective actions to accomplish systemic change. Transformative agency also goes beyond situational here-and-now actions as it emerges and evolves over time, often through complex debates and stepwise

crystallizations of a vision to be implemented (Engeström, Sannino & Virukkunen, 2014, p. 124)

I argue Lotta, Tomas and myself to have realised transformative agency in conducting our interventions, in that we collectively brought forward change, not only in terms of students' cultural-historical development but also in terms of transforming the instructional reality in which we took part in agentive ways as students, teacher and researcher. In collaborating with Lotta, such agency developed across a pilot we conducted and the three interventions that followed, whereas with Tomas such agency was realised as the five-task intervention itself evolved.

An offshoot of realising transformative agency in concrete classrooms is recognised by Engeström once again in terms of transforming what he calls the middle layer of school, one constituting its *hidden curriculum*. Lying between structures such as bureaucratic regulations and budgets on one hand, and means that structure teaching such as curricula, textbooks and study materials on the other, Engeström argues,

> This middle layer consists of relatively inconspicuous, recurrent and taken-for-granted aspects of school life. These include grading and testing practices, patterning and punctuation of time, uses (not contents) of textbooks, bounding and use of the physical space, grouping of students, patterns of discipline and control, connections to the world outside the school, interaction among teachers as well as between parents and teachers. (Engeström, 2008, p. 86)

I argue that by way of interventions we conducted in Lotta and Tomas' classrooms, it was taken-for-granted aspects of school life or the middle layer Engeström talks about that we were able to change in productive ways. We altered the hidden curriculum or prior status quo by grouping students and conducting appropriate instructional activities which were meaningful to students and ongoing curricular progress. In such conduct we were able to observe ways in which the development and identity of a few students at least was not only externalised but also found unique. It was in realising such conduct that me and my two collaborating teachers were able to carry out the nuanced nature of transformative action which Stetsenko has highlighted all along within *their* ongoing classrooms. By this is meant (1) our joint ability to transform the status quo in existing classrooms by creating new instructional environments, and (2) enabling students to not only know for the sake of knowing, but allow for the creation of their identity and become human

TAKING TRANSFORMATIVE ACTION   269

by contributing to the historically evolving practice of everyday instruction in mathematics. Before turning to bring the collective of thoughts in this writing to conclusion in the *Epilogue* that follows and based on this coda alone, I would like to argue in favour of greater research in all three CHAT based programs I have just discussed. I wish to thereby reiterate as well that the educational agenda of CHAT is far from finished and entirely open to newer, richer and more productive directions as well.

Notes

1   http://ncm.gu.se/kanguru
2   https://www.skolverket.se

References

Alexander, R. (2008). *Towards dialogic teaching: Rethinking classroom talk* (4th ed.). Dialogos.

Barnes, D. (2008). Exploring talk for learning. In N. Mercer & S. Hodgkinson (Eds.), *Exploring talk in school* (pp. 1–15). Sage.

Blomqvist, C., & Gade, S (2013). Att kommunicera om likamedtecknet [Communicating about the equal to sign]. *Nämnaren, 2013*(4), 39–42.

Cole, M., & Engeström, Y. (2007). Cultural-historical approaches to designing for development. In J. Valsiner & A. Rosa (Eds.), *The Cambridge handbook of sociocultural psychology* (pp. 484–507). Cambridge University Press.

Connelly, F. M. (2013). Joseph Schwab, curriculum, curriculum studies and educational reform. *Journal of Curriculum Studies, 45*(5), 622–639.

Dalton, S., & Tharp, R. (2002). Standards for pedagogy, research and practice. In G. Wells & G. Claxton (Eds.), *Learning for life in the 21st century: Sociocultural perspectives on the future of education* (pp. 181–194). Blackwell Publishers.

Edwards, A. (2005). Relational agency: Learning to be a resourceful practitioner. *International Journal of Educational Research, 43*(3), 168–182.

Edwards, A. (2010). *Being an expert professional practitioner: The relational turn in expertise.* Springer.

Engeström, Y. (2008). Crossing boundaries in teacher teams. In Y. Engeström (Ed.), *From teams to knots: Activity-theoretical studies of collaboration and learning at work* (pp. 86–107). Cambridge University Press.

Engeström, Y. (2010). Activity theory and learning at work. In M. Malloch, L. Cairns, K. Evans, & B. N. O'Connor (Eds.), *The Sage handbook of workplace learning* (pp. 86–104). Sage Publishers.

Engeström, Y. (2011). From design experiments to formative interventions. *Theory and Psychology, 21*(5), 598–628.

Engeström, Y., Sannino, A., & Virkkunen, J. (2014). On the methodological demands of formative interventions. *Mind, Culture and Activity, 21*(2), 118–128.

Gade, S. (2010). Narratives of students learning mathematics: Plurality of strategies and a strategy for practice? In C. Bergsten, E. Jablonka, & T. Wedege (Eds.), *Mathematics and mathematics education: Cultural and social dimensions. Proceedings of the seventh mathematics education research seminar (MADIF7)* (pp. 102–112). Stockholm University.

Gade, S. (2011, September 5–10). Researcher reflexivity leading to action research in a mathematics classroom – Enabling Nelly to multiply again through deconstruction and reconstruction. In *Abstract of papers presented at The International Society for Cultural-historical and Activity Research congress (ISCAR 2011)* (pp. 280–282). ISCAR.

Gade, S. (2012). Teacher researcher collaboration at a grade four mathematics classroom: Restoring equality to students usage of the '=' sign. *Educational Action Research, 20*(4), 553–570.

Gade, S. (2015a). Unpacking teacher-researcher collaboration with three theoretical frameworks – a case of expansive learning activity? *Cultural Studies of Science Education, 10*(3), 603–619.

Gade, S. (2015b). Teacher-researcher collaboration as formative intervention and expansive learning activity. In K. Krainer & N. Vondrova (Eds.), *Proceedings of the ninth Congress of European Research in Mathematics Education (CERME9)* (pp. 3029–3035). Charles University and ERME.

Gade, S., & Blomqvist, C. (2015). From problem posing to posing problems by way of explicit mediation in Grades four and five. In F. M. Singer, N. Ellerton, & J. Cai (Eds.), *Mathematical problem posing: From research to effective practice* (pp. 195–213). Springer.

Gade, S., & Blomqvist, C. (2016). Shared object and stakeholdership in teacher-researcher expansive activity. In C. Csíkos, A. Rausch, & J. Szitányi (Eds.), *Proceedings of the 40th annual conference of the International Group for the Psychology of Mathematics Education (PME)* (pp. 2-267–2-274). PME.

Gade, S., & Blomqvist, C. (2018). Investigating everyday measures through exploratory talk: Whole classroom intervention and landscape study at Grade four. *Cultural Studies of Science Education, 13*(1), 235–252.

Gade, S., & Forsgren, T. L. (2019). Realising transformative agency and student identity: Meaningful practical activity based formative intervention at grade eight. *Cultural Studies of Science Education, 14*(4), 897–914.

Hollingsworth, S. (1992). Learning to teach through collaborative conversation: A feminist approach. *American Educational Research Journal, 29*(2), 373–404.

TAKING TRANSFORMATIVE ACTION

Hollingsworth, S., Dybdahl, M., & Minarik, L. T. (1993). By chart and chance and passion: The importance of relational knowing in learning to teach. *Curriculum Inquiry*, *23*(1), 5–35.

John-Steiner, V. (2000). *Creative collaboration*. Oxford University Press.

Leont'ev, A. N. (1978). *Activity, consciousness, and personality*. Prentice-Hall.

Mercer, N. (2002). Developing dialogues. In G. Wells & G. Claxton (Eds.), *Learning for life in the 21st century* (pp. 141–153). Blackwell Publishers.

Mercer, N., & Dawes, L. (2008). The value of exploratory talk. In N. Mercer & S. Hodgkinson (Eds.), *Exploring talk in schools* (pp. 55–71). Sage.

Pierce, K., & Gilles, C. (2008). From exploratory talk to critical conversations. In N. Mercer & S. Hodgkinson (Eds.), *Exploring talk in school* (pp. 37–54). Sage.

Pilbeam, D. (1997). A very tidy desk. In L. Wolpert & A. Richards (Eds.), *Passionate minds: The inner world of scientists* (pp. 204–212). Oxford University Press.

Roth, W.-M., & Tobin, K. (2002). *At the elbow of another: Learning to teach by coteaching*. Peter Lang Publishing.

Roth, W.-M., & Tobin, K. (2004). Coteaching: From praxis to theory. *Teachers and Teaching: Theory and Practice, 10*(2), 161–179.

Stetsenko, A. (2008). From relational ontology to transformative activist stance on development and learning: Expanding Vygotsky's (CHAT) project. *Cultural Studies of Science Education, 3*(2), 471–491.

van Oers, B. (1996). Learning mathematics as a meaningful activity. In L. Steffe, P. Nesher, P. Cobb, G. Goldin, & B. Greer (Eds.), *Theories of mathematical learning* (pp. 91–113). Lawrence Erlbaum Associates.

van Oers, B. (2009a). Learning and learning theory from a cultural-historical point of view. In B. van Oers (Ed.), *The transformation of learning: Advances in cultural-historical activity theory* (pp. 3–12). Cambridge University Press.

van Oers, B. (2009b). Developmental education: Improving participation in cultural practices. In M. Fleer, M. Hedegaard, & J. Tudge (Eds.), *World yearbook of education 2009 – Childhood studies and the impact of globalization: Policies and practices at global and local levels* (pp. 213–229). Routledge.

Vygotsky, L. S. (1978). *Mind in society: The development of higher psychological processes*. Harvard University Press.

Wells, C. G. (1999). *Dialogic inquiry: Towards a sociocultural practice and theory of education*. Cambridge University Press.

Wells, C. G. (2002). Inquiry as an orientation for learning, teaching and teacher education. In G. Wells & G. Claxton (Eds.), *Learning for life in the 21st century* (pp. 197–210). Blackwell Publishers.

CHAPTER 10

Epilogue

Practitioner-as-Artist-and-Scientist

1 Preamble

While introducing this book I had explicitly asked, what collective of theoretical, concrete-practical and methodological perspectives inform a productive practice of school education and educational research. In an impressionist manner, I surmised such a quest to implicitly examine what happens in K-12 school education and why? While both my questions are broad in scope, my narrative in preceding chapters details, (1) various problematic issues I came across in the journey I made from classroom teacher to conducting classroom research, and (2) my empirical studies which were limited however to collaborating with teachers and students in mathematics classrooms at middle school grades. In rendering these I chose CHAT perspectives as my primary framework and borrowed from philosophical, social and humanistic fields as well.

In attempting to draw the above outlined efforts to conclusion I am reminded of two scholars, (1) Bruner in Chapter 5, who argued that any narrative that is autobiographical in never completed but only ended, by arriving at some version of coherence therein. In line with Bruner, the self and coherence I have attempted to portray in this writing is that of my becoming a researcher and carrying out independent research which appealed to my practitioner sensibilities. (2) Wells in Chapter 9, whose construct of activity of knowing encapsulates the travelogue I detail in the first eight chapters in this book. While I have dwelt on actions I took and outlined specific knowledge gained from such knowing in Chapter 9, it goes without saying that my quest began decades ago.

My acknowledging Bruner and Wells helps me put my present writing in perspective, one I bring close to in the following manner. In the section that follows I allude to areas in CHAT which I think hold promise for further study, but for whose pursuit I have not had adequate time. In the next section I provide a short summary of key findings in relation to my present study, followed by another where I qualify three key constructs that have appeared time and again throughout my writing – the nature of action, the nature of theory and the nature of dialectic at play in concrete-practical instances. My coda discusses a wholistic and conceptual unit I forward, namely practitioner-as-artist-and-scientist, one that recognises the continuum of aspects which

© KONINKLIJKE BRILL NV, LEIDEN, 2022 | DOI:10.1163/9789004512160_010

EPILOGUE

a practitioner negotiates and brings forth in relation to everyday teaching. I argue this construct to not only offer analytical insight but also have potential to be utilised with regards to educational practices of different grain size. The ability for practitioners to take CHAT based transformative action, besides realise the analytical potential of various theoretical lenses I discuss all along, is at the heart of the insight this unit could likely provide. I now turn to research areas in CHAT that hold promise and invite a closer examination.

2   Promising CHAT Avenues

The *first* of five avenues that seem to hold promise and offer engrossing challenge in CHAT, relates to the observation Vygotsky makes about the role of speech in solving practical problems. He argues,

> *Prior to mastering his own behaviour, the child begins to master his surroundings with the help of speech.* This produces new relations with the environment in addition to the new organization of behaviour itself. The creation of these uniquely human forms of behaviour later produce the intellect and become the basis of productive work: the specifically human form of the use of tools. (Vygotsky, 1978, p. 25, emphasis added)

While Vygotsky's pursuit of what is uniquely human in us was premise for the cultural-historical psychology he was laying foundations for, his quote above directs our attention to the use of speech by infants prior to their ability to organise their own behaviour. I have been curious to know the manner in which speech contributes to the intellect of infants, besides becomes basis for their practical work. My own interests in this direction were aroused during doctoral work while attempting to analyse students' problem solving in small group tasks. I had then surmised Luria's stage wise study of concrete processes of thinking (Luria, 1973; as in Gade, 2006, p. 25). Grasping the nature of intellect as a construct in examining the role of speech in its formation seems personally inviting.

The *second* construct relates to the conception of *real learning activity*, as forwarded by Vasily Davydov (1999). While revisiting data collected during doctoral work, in relation to a problem solving task attempted by a small-group of students, I examined how the task being attempted was real learning activity following Davydov (Gade, 2013). Recognising the task set for students to be a mediating process by which surrounding reality could be transformed by their creative effort and labour, I found Davydov to recognise that any such activity to *first* be object related and directed towards creating some material or spiritual product e.g. industrial workers creating machines or writers creating artistic work. Davydov *second* argued *school children's learning activity* to have object-related content, one that helped instruction distinguish learning activity from other kinds like games or cooking say. Davydov continued,

> *Third*, learning activity necessarily involves some creative or reforming elements. If the listed components are not present in actually observed lessons, then we can state that in such lessons the proper learning activity is not realised at all or realised quite imperfectly (a case which is not rare in school). ... Children can only appropriate knowledge and skills through learning activity *when they have an internal need and motivation to do so*. Learning activity involves transformation of the material to be appropriated and implies that some new mental product i.e. knowledge, is received. (Davydov, 1999, p. 125, emphasis added)

I find a rush of concepts bound together in Davydov's arguments above, (1) attention to the distinct purpose of any learning activity, (2) prior vision of what students are expected to create, (3) the need for students to work with or transform aspects of content that need to be appropriated by them, (4) the presence of components in instructional activity that could be creatively reformed by students, besides and vitally (5) the internal need and motivation for students to follow through with their creativity. As erstwhile teacher and researcher practitioner, I seek recognition of the significance of the aspects Davydov highlights, one that can be examined and nuanced in concrete-practical learning activities.

Nelly's breaking down in tears during the first intervention we led in Lotta's classroom leads me *third*, to two interrelated notions in CHAT – periods of crisis which children undergo as they transit from one age to another, and the wider social situation of their development. Vygotsky argued that periods of crisis which are in control of a child's behaviour at particular points of time, might even become unimportant at a later stage in their trajectory of development. He thus proposed that in *periods of crisis* a child's needs and motives are restructured,

> The restructuring of needs and motives and the re-evaluation of values are basic factors in the transition from age level to age level. *Here, the environment also changes, that is, the relation of the child to the environment.* Other things begin to interest the child, he develops other activity, and his consciousness is restructured, if we understand consciousness

EPILOGUE

as the relation of the child to the environment. (Vygotsky, 2004, p. 499, emphasis added)

Recognising a child's relationship with the environment to be unique, one that is restructured in periods of crisis, Vygotsky forwarded the related notion of *social situation of development* as follows,

> The social situation of development represents the initial moment for all dynamic changes that occur in development ... It determines wholly and completely the forms and the path along which the child will acquire ever newer personality characteristics, drawing them from the social reality as from the basic source of development, *the path along which the social becomes the individual.* ...
>
> ... The new structure of consciousness ... inevitably signifies a new character of perceptions of external reality and activity in it, a new character of the child's perceiving his own internal life and the internal activity of his mental functions. (Vygotsky, 1998, pp. 198–199, emphasis added)

I contend the need to greater grasp the intermittent periods of crisis which children go through, as a result of which their interests and personality also change. Their transition from one stage to another is far from routine and smooth and in some cases needs compassionate understanding by their teacher, parents as well as society at large. While my attention to theoretical aspects in relation to periods of crisis came by drawing on data from two national contexts (Saran & Gade, 2016), it is the ethical responsibilities of teachers in this regard that gives this research gravitas. The issue needing attention here is that students going through periods of crisis do so in environments not of their own choosing. The environments teachers provide, may also be those that are beyond their control as well. For me the key phrase directing attention to this aspect is – the path along which the social becomes the individual. I would like to greater grasp theoretically and in concrete-practical instances, this personality and interest forming facet of students' development.

A *fourth* avenue seeking study came from observing dramatic changes which adolescent students display, whose identities stood transformed as they took part in tasks that were practical and meaningful to them (Gade & Forsgren, 2019). To greater understand such changes in individual development, I have found Davydov and Markova (1982/1983) to conceive the content and structure of any educational activity in terms of the kind of changes that students display as *subjects* when taking part in them. Drawing upon D B Elkonin another of Vygotsky's collaborator, these scholars argue that an educational task is one whose results are not seen in terms of changes the subject make to the objects in the task, but in terms of changes that are brought to the acting subject herself.

Such changes, they point out, are accompanied by any student's assimilation of scientific concepts and are directed to the cultivation of thinking in a theoretical manner. As also argued by Karpov in Chapter 4, such manner of changes are observable in the way students display newer modes of action or capabilities with newer scientific concepts. Drawing attention to human agency which in turn gives rise to newer kinds of personality in students, Davydov and Markova argue,

> Learning is organized so that the individual characteristics of the pupil are taken into account – not on the basis of adaptation to them, but as the projection of new types of activity and new levels of development. Education cannot be reduced to the transmission of knowledge and the cultivation of acts and operations; rather, *it involves mainly the formation of the pupil's personality and the development of those qualities that determine his behavior (values, motives, goals, etc.).* The developmental and educational effect is not achieved through just any activity, but only through formative educational activity. (Davydov & Markova, 1982/1983, p. 71, emphasis added)

Even as the formative aspects of developmental activity have been drawn attention to by Bronfenbrenner in Chapter 4, and Engeström et al. in the previous Chapter, Davydov and Markova draw attention above to the changes which students themselves undergo and exhibit. Greater dwelling on this analytical construct I contend, might shed light on why and how Nelly, Jan, Noel, Mark, Leon, Hans-Erik or Alba were able to stride the dialectic between the object of instructional activity that they took part in and the nature of their behaviour or personality as subjects, which they externalised while making their individual attempts.

My interest of greater understanding the student as subject in activity brings me *finally* to the notion of personhood in contemporary CHAT. To shed greater light on this issue I turn once again to Stetsenko (2013) who makes many an insightful observation. Stetsenko finds existing models of personhood to fall short of explicating what constitutes humanness and what is unique about each one of us. These models, she says, view human beings either as solitary individuals or completely at the whim of external forces, conceiving of no other way out for them than to adapt to existing status quo. She thus finds it

EPILOGUE

necessary to incorporate the notions of social change and activism, as not only central but vitally *formative* in any developmental model of personhood. Such a model could then conceive persons as being able to address not just *who they are* in any human practice, but importantly *who they could be*. Such a stance shifts attention from what presently is to what could possibly be. Incorporating this last would expect persons to take a stand about their selves and the kind of world they would like to live in. Such a model of personhood would thus also be political, moral, scientific and critical.

In line with the above, Stetsenko conceives Vygotskian cultural-historical and/or CHAT psychology to look far beyond human agency and incorporate a central concern of creating a better society for all persons. Such impetus also helps lay the foundation for developing a dialectical framework that conceives individuals as interdependent – both on one another and the world around them. Human development is herein seen as grounded in collaborative, purposeful and answerable activist deeds, committed to projects of social transformation. As discussed in Chapter 1, one's knowing, being, doing and becoming in order to change the world in such pursuits thus forms the very path for any individual's *personhood*. Vitally Stetsenko points out,

> From a transformative activist stance, persons are agents not only for whom 'things matter' but *who themselves matter* in history, culture and society and, moreover, who come into Being as unique individuals exactly through their own activism, that is, through and to the extent that they take a stand on matters of social significance and find ways to make a difference in these processes by contributing to them. (Stetsenko, 2013, p. 187, emphasis in original)

In underscoring the role of any individual's ontology and activism above, Stetsenko highlights the Vygotskian tenet of a relational conception of human development, one that connects individuals and their world and also undermines the dualism between any subject and object. Two points follow through from such a conception, (1) that the process of being and becoming human and of knowing oneself and the world, lies in unity within wider collaborative transformative practices being engaged with, and (2) that such a view is a forward looking one, which engages with the future of human development and personhood as well.

This last aspect which was very noticeable in my study with Tomas' adolescent students, Stetsenko argues, is somewhat under-theorised in CHAT. With regards to practitioners, Stetsenko's arguments decidedly recognise the importance of our collaborating with one another and our students in pursuit of much needed human and social transformation in the wider societal practice of education at large. Importantly such an activist agenda relates to our individual selves as practitioners and our very own personhood. In line with Stetsenko, my erstwhile self as teacher and present self as researcher very much *mattered* to my personhood and my own manner of activism and quest for educational transformation and a better society for all as a practitioner.

3   Short Summary of Key Findings

The following is a summary of key findings in relation to educational contexts I have had occasion to engage with:

1.   Theoretical, concrete-practical and methodological perspectives of CHAT have every potential to inform a productive practice of classroom instruction, school education and educational research. In fact the Vygotskian contention that practice is supreme judge of theory and acts as its truth criterion, necessitates researchers to be thinking practitioners who engage with ongoing realities and intervene in the same as a means of understanding, transforming and realising those which are more democratic and socially just.

2.   Realisation of the cultural-historical development of students is possible, in ways that make them more agentive and human, one that facilitates realisation of their personal identity as well. In fact the element of surprise which is externalised by students in the conduct of CHAT based instruction as well as interventions seems a worthy outcome that can even be anticipated.

3.   Productive collaboration between teachers and researchers as practitioners is possible and may even be necessary if we are to face and productively resolve the many issues that continue to arise in any concrete practical. Such a stand counters arguments that recognise the loneliness and isolation which teachers face on one hand, besides help arrive at the goal of deprivatising everyday teaching on the other.

4.   Such an outlook both necessitates and benefits from integrating research perspectives in situated use across institutions like primary, middle and high schools, besides teacher colleges and universities. Such attempts make the CHAT enterprise both integrative and interdisciplinary in its ability to draw upon and be enriched by multiple kinds of perspectives.

5.   In presenting the above outlined sketch I am also presenting my version of science-in-flux, one very much in the making with respect to the

overall CHAT enterprise. In drawing upon strengths which the arts offer in addition to those offered by the sciences, my case of arts-and-science-in-the-making along with those of many prospective others has potential to yield a more robust and public version of CHAT in the forthcoming future.

6. Such a case is premised by my having been a teacher-practitioner, who has traversed the journey to now become a researcher-practitioner. While I had occasion to travel and interact with many a scholar, my writing throughout this book clearly emerged from empowering myself as a practitioner. In doing so my intention has been to persuade other practitioners with regards the fruitfulness of the CHAT approach I have come to adopt.

7. Taking practitioner action and pursuing the cultural-historical development of both students and teachers is possible and goes on to contribute to the ecological validity and the viability of educational theory and practice in local concrete practicals. Such an approach is also geared to pursuing human agency and societal transformation in an activist manner.

8. The adoption of a tool-and-result methodological stance is possible and allows practitioners to draw on their reflexivity towards drawing on the results of actions taken in the recent past towards steering future action. The exercise of such manner of dialectical inquiry enables practitioners to exercise their imagination and master specific methods being deployed and not the other way round.

9. The intention of ascending to the concrete in CHAT based research, makes it possible to deal with educational phenomena conceptualised as a whole and not in a fragmentary or reductionist manner. By this is meant that the pursuit of such a non-classical or romantic science accommodates the coming upon and grasping the numerous ways in which the integrated whole is interconnected.

10. And finally, viewing education as the becoming human of students, teachers and researchers via the conduct of ongoing instruction in mathematics makes the strongest case for realising a humanistic philosophy of mathematics. Such a stance recognises that human beings intentionally mediate activities they take part in and take advantage of different kinds of activities in their developmental journey as well, making it possible for *them* to construct their identity and voice. There is every opportunity here for making instructional efforts taken to be educational, democratic and socially just.

Two philosophical ideas of Bakhtin underpin the above outlined effort. The *first* addresses how individuals come to create themselves by way of being in dialogue with the multitude of human beings interacted with in one's journey of life. In distinct echo to Leont'ev in Chapter 9, Bakhtin also recognises human conscious as co-knowing or co-consciousness and our very being as co-being. About the creation of ourselves in line with this stand, Katerina Clark and Holquist paraphrase Bakhtin as saying,

> The way in which I create myself is by means of a quest: I go out to the others in order to come back with a self. I 'live into' an other's consciousness; I see the world through the other's eyes. But I must never completely meld with that version of things, for the more successfully I do so, the more I will fall prey to the limitations of the other's horizon. A complete fusion (a dialectical *Aufhebung*), even were it possible, would preclude the difference required by dialogue. (Clark & Holquist, 1984, p. 78)

While Bakhtin offers a dialogic rationale above for the manner in which my researcher personhood evolved, he also helps me explain the choice I made in my writing to cite from writings of other scholars. While such a stance is to some extant necessitated in contemporary CHAT for which the original writings of Vygotsky and his colleagues, besides primary interpretations of these are central to my arts-and-science-in-the-making, I also wanted my students in India to have the opportunity to hear, read and enunciate the words of scholars I was engaging with. As alluded to in Chapter 8, for many of them access to a good library is limited, even non-existent at times, and their use of a wi-fi service at a bus/railway station very much a strenuous and demanding reality.

Bakhtin *second* helps me draw attention to the notion of *taste* of words that scholars in various disciplines come to offer. He argues,

> For any individual consciousness living in it, language is not an abstract system of normative forms, but rather a concrete heteroglot conception of the world. *All words have the 'taste' of a profession, a genre, a tendency, a party, a particular work, a particular person, a generation, an age group, the day and hour.* Each word tastes of the context and contexts in which it has lived it socially charged life; all words and forms are populated by intentions. Contextual overtones (generic, tendentious, individualistic) are inevitable in the word. (Bakhtin, 1981, p. 293, emphasis added)

While Bakhtin's notion of taste nuances his construct of heteroglossia, alluded to in Chapter 5, I argue that in an enterprise as integrative and interdisciplinary

EPILOGUE   281

as my case study has turned out to be, I have been keen to showcase via Bakhtin's notion of taste that each area of research drawn upon has much to offer. Such an effort is intentional, allowing my readers to decipher the polysemy of words, the multilogicality across academic fields which are rich in concepts and the difference between the premise and approach that each use, in line with Tobin in Chapter 7. And then there is sound advise from the field of arts by Eisner, also in Chapter 7. Eisner's urging our use of methodological pluralism that could stem from attention to a wide range of approaches which diverse fields bring to bear, is a prudent way for practitioners to address and gain knowledge about what bears fruit in relation to instructional realities.

In presenting my case of arts-and-science-in-the-making by drawing on CHAT, I finally acknowledge having to sift through English translations of writings originally in the Russian to grasp both history and intent which underpinned the original approach seeded by Vygotsky, Luria and Leont'ev. While English translations of their writings may be few, it is nonetheless encouraging to find a fair amount of material that both draws and expands on their vision. Yet the greatest appreciation of the potential of CHAT perspectives in my experience has been gained while drawing on the personal sense I made while deploying constructs of relevance in instructional practices. As my writing demonstrates, my adopting such a strategy has led my efforts to be integrative and interdisciplinary. It is to highlight the significance of such a feature, that I turn to quote Bernard Weissbourd who mentions how work at the Centre for Psychological Studies at The University of Chicago, drew on Vygotsky to construct an integrated account of social and psychological processes, bringing together disciplines like philosophy, anthropology and semiotics to study human consciousness and its formation. In his foreword to a volume edited by Wertsch on Vygotskian perspectives, he argues,

> A major virtue of Vygotsky's sociohistorical approach to consciousness is that it provides an overarching theoretical framework in which these and other issues can be examined and interrelated. ... The fact that a diversity of issues can be addressed and integrated within a single theoretical perspective reflects a strength that is all too often missing in today's academic world of fragmented disciplines and sub-disciplines. (Weissbourd, 1985, pp. VII–VIII)

With practitioners, both teachers and researchers as readers in mind, I argue my findings to evidence the interrelatedness Weissbourd draws our attention to. While acknowledging that the CHAT based project I have invested myself in is far from finished, I presently turn to qualify three constructs whose reference has arisen time and again throughout this writing – the nature of action,

282   CHAPTER 10

nature of theory and nature of dialectic at play in the concrete-practical engaged with by practitioners.

4   Nature of Action, Theory and Dialectic at Play

In recognising the nature of polysemy or signs that words with different taste direct our attention to, I qualify three notions that inform the taking of transformative action by us practitioners. My intention of bringing together references to these notions below is to come closer to arriving at a meta-vocabulary with which to grasp and address various issues that have potential to arise in one's concrete practical. In CHAT parlance such an effort is very much in line with ascending from the conceptual abstract to various concrete practical we might encounter.

I have found the *nature of action* alluded to in the following ways in my writing, that

1. action is plural by definition because we are human and different from one another in the lives and times we live (Arendt in Chapter 1),
2. human action is political in nature, taken to distinguish ourselves from others and achieve our identity (Arendt in Chapter 1),
3. taking non-violent action is imperative, since social realities in which human action is taken, can only be known in a partial and incomplete manner (Gandhi in Chapter 1),
4. unlike the conduct of research on education, educational research views classrooms from the perspective of taking and developing a substantive theory of action to bring about change (Elliott in Chapter 1),
5. human perception of concrete situations needs to be geared towards one's ability to single out what may be relevant for thought and action (Nussbaum in Chapter 1),
6. language enables children to plan solutions to problems prior to execution and mastery of one's behaviour to overcome impulsive action (Vygotsky in Chapter 1),
7. theory and practice are inseparable in actions practitioners take in terms of personal practical knowledge, wherein practice is seen as theory in action (Clandinin & Connelly in Chapter 2),
8. cultural tools can be seen as templates of human action or objects-that-can-be-used-for-a-certain-purpose in respective social practices (Stetsenko in Chapter 3),
9. a practice can be viewed as a historically developed tradition of action organised to produce products that satisfy collective needs (Chaiklin in Chapter 3),

EPILOGUE

10. the unity of human perception, speech and action, constitutes the central subject matter for analysing the origin of uniquely human forms of behaviour (Vygotsky in Chapter 3),

11. mediated action is characterized by an irreducible tension between any agent and the mediational means encountered (Wertsch in Chapter 3),

12. all human actions, including acts of thought, involve the mediation of material and symbolic objects which are culturally constructed, historical in origin and social in content and essence (Scribner in Chapter 4),

13. in meaningful practical activities, the object and purpose of the activity are apparent, the result of the action is contingent and feedback is immediate (del Rio & Alvarez in Chapter 4),

14. the ability to exercise a diachronic view in narrative research is a result of actions taken by researchers as a practice over time (Polkinghorne in Chapter 5),

15. action research may be viewed as the study of a social situation with a view to improving the quality of action within it (Elliott in Chapter 5),

16. the notion of inquiry as stance is a powerful means of affirmative action and educational transformation (Cochran-Smith & Lytle in Chapter 5),

17. our ability to write in a reflective manner about our practice of living as practitioners, allows for engaged reflective praxis i.e. by means of taking action full of thought and thought full of action (van Manen in Chapter 6),

18. for pragmatists, truth is whatever assists us practitioners to take actions that produce desired results, knowledge here is action rather than observation (Kvale in Chapter 7),

19. praxis is reflection and action upon the world in order to transform it (Freire in Chapter 7),

20. the outcome of a theoretic stance in education is knowledge, while that of the practical is a decision guiding practitioner action (Schwab in Chapter 8),

21. educational research is not only about finding out what might be possible to achieve, but also whether what is achieved through practitioner action is desirable from an educational point of view – one Dewey would argue as being more intelligent (Biesta & Burbules in Chapter 8),

22. transformative action alludes to the ability of practitioners to change the status quo and create new social environments, besides students and teachers achieving identity and becoming human while contributing to historically evolving sociocultural practices of humanity (Stetsenko in Chapter 9).

The *notion of theory* was also alluded to in the following manner, that

1. unlike developing formal theory with a priori concepts in research on education, educational research develops a substantive theory of action by using a posteriori concepts (Elliott in Chapter 1),

2. Kurt Lewin's expression that there is nothing more practical than a good theory can be expanded with CHAT perspectives, by its mirror expression that there is nothing more theoretically rich than good practice (Stetsenko & Arievitch in Chapter 1),

3. the construction of theory is an attempt to go beyond what we know or to correct what we think are the erroneous explanations of others (Sarason in Chapter 2),

4. practice sets the task and serves as the supreme judge of theory, as its truth criterion (Vygotsky in Chapter 3),

5. grey is every theory, but evergreen is the tree of life (Luria quoting Goethe in Chapter 3),

6. in Vygotsky's enterprise in the beginning was the word and the word is theory or science in embryonic form (Veer & Valsiner in Chapter 4),

7. Vygotsky's texts do not illustrate or propound his method and theory, they are his method and his theory (Sinha in Chapter 4),

8. practitioner judgment paving way to one's theorising, is based on what action at any time, place and situation with students, helped accomplish specific goals (Polkinghorne in Chapter 5),

9. in action research theories are validated through practice (Elliott in Chapter 5),

10. practitioner theorising within action research includes three key dimensions – the professional, the personal and the political (Noffke in Chapter 5),

11. there is lack of adequate theorisation in relation to differences between schools in terms of institutional effects on the social formation of mind and the structure of discourse as a cultural artefact (Daniels in Chapter 6),

12. the language of a theory can be used as a way of organising and determining action, besides putting one's reality into perspective (Smith in Chapter 7),

13. close-to-practice research can itself be open to questions from practice that can disrupt the assumptions that support theory (Edwards, Gilroy & Hartley in Chapter 7),

14. in line with CHAT perspectives, practitioners have the opportunity to keep alive the dynamic relationship between theory-which-informs and theory-being-built, besides existing-practice and steered-practice (Gade in Chapter 8),

EPILOGUE

15. the ability to view theory and praxis in complementarity ways is essential to meaning making in the social sciences (Seeger in Chapter 7),

16. any theory is not inherently healing, liberatory, or revolutionary, but fulfils this function only when theorising is directed toward this end (hooks in Chapter 7),

17. theory can embolden youth and community participants from whom theoretical engagement has been withheld (Anyon in Chapter 7),

18. in an educative model of theory and practice social theories allow for self-understanding, liberating people from ignorance of who they are (Fay in Chapter 7),

19. to have mastered method and theory is to have become a self-conscious thinker – to be mastered by method or theory is simply to be kept from trying to find out about what is going on in the world (Mills in Chapter 8),

20. teachers were at the heart of Stenhouse's theory of curriculum development since it was they who could mount educational experiments in classrooms, learn from their experience and develop a curriculum (Elliott & Norris in Chapter 8),

21. to call something a case is to make a theoretical claim that the story, event, or text is an instance of a case-of-something, a member of a class of events that enables us to appreciate more than the particularities of the case itself (Shulman in Chapter 8),

22. one's theory of teaching determines a reasonable portfolio entry, one documented as worth reflecting upon in a theoretical manner (Shulman in Chapter 8).

The *notion of a dialectic at play* between two or multiple opposing positions or extremes was also alluded to as follows, that

1. the dialectic between means and ends in pursuing swaraj or self-governing autonomy, is end-creating as well (Bondurant in Chapter 1),

2. the relationship between knower and what is known is not independent but co-present in a dialectic, each modifying and shaping the other (Greene in Chapter 1),

3. the practical nature of good theory and the theoretical richness of good practice are viewed in a dialectic within CHAT perspectives (Stetsenko & Arievitch in Chapter 1),

4. any practitioner's professional knowledge landscape is composed of an incessant dialectic of relationships among people, places, and things, one that is an intellectual and moral landscape (Clandinin & Connelly in Chapter 2),

5. the dialectical approach, while admitting the influence of nature on man, asserts that man, in turn, affects nature and creates through his changes in nature new natural conditions for his existence (Vygotsky in Chapter 3),
6. the psychological theory of activity flows from a dialectical approach and is basis for studying the higher psychological activity of human beings (Vygotsky in Chapter 3),
7. Vygotsky's dialectical methodology amounts to deploying a tool-and-result approach rather than a tool-for-result approach, wherein tool and result come to existence in dialectical unity (Newman & Holzman in Chapter 4),
8. personal practical knowledge as a concept embodies a dialectical view of theory and practice, wherein theory and practice are viewed as inseparable (Clandinin in Chapter 5),
9. the term dialectic refers to the reciprocal, recursive, and symbiotic relationships of research and practice, analysis and action, inquiry and experience, theorizing and doing, conceptual and empirical scholarship, and our being researchers as well as practitioners (Cochran-Smith & Lytle in Chapter 5),
10. the dialectical mechanism at work in common culture refers to the incessant back and forth between human experience on one hand and theoretical conceptualisation by us of old world social structures like the middle or working classes (Willis in Chapter 6),
11. the dialectical method treats theory and practice as inseparable, action here reconciles contradictions that arise in dynamic, organic wholes (McKeon in Chapter 7),
12. praxis means the dialectical tension, the interactive, reciprocal shaping of theory and practice at the centre of any emancipatory social science (Lather in Chapter 7),
13. the struggle by students for a new transformed reality is a dialectic between actions which denounce processes of dehumanisation and announce a new dream, education is thus as act of intervention in the world (Freire in Chapter 7),
14. critical consciousness is the activity of transforming one's reality by means of the dialectic not only between reflection and action, but also theory and practice or else theory could become empty verbalism and practice merely activism (Freire in Chapter 7),
15. the properties of the bits and pieces we divide the world into are properties they acquire in actually being part of those wholes, so it is a dialectical principle that both the rules and the objects about which the rules are made, have to be simultaneously tried and fit (Lewontin in Chapter 7),

EPILOGUE

16. deliberation is complex and arduous, it must consider the dialectic between ends and means and treat them as mutually determining one another so as to choose not the right alternative, for there is no such thing, but the best one (Schwab in Chapter 8).

The above exercise of qualifying the nature of action, nature of theory and nature of dialectic at play in respective concrete-practicals, reminds me of points made by two scholars earlier on in my writing. The *first* is by Lave in Chapter 4 whose attempts at theorising the nature of situated learning were not in terms of maximum definition, but in articulating the same in relational terms. The *second* is by Nussbaum in Chapter 1 who drew attention to the importance of universal rules which have the ability to attend to concrete characteristics found similar across numerous cases. Following Lave and Nussbaum, the nature of action, the nature of theory and the nature of dialectic at play, I argue, are not only relational in scope but universal in outlook with potential to attend to relationships that are similar across numerous concrete practicals. Having dwelt on the scope of such rules I turn one last time to forward a construct which I consider to have potential for practitioners, teacher educators and policy makers to not only further concrete realities but also take the kind of transformative action *they* would consider as needed and germane.

5 Practitioner-as-Artist-and-Scientist: Coda

I begin my coda with the distinction Elkana makes in Chapter 1 between public science and personal science-in-the-making, with the latter best understood by means of case studies that dwell upon the historical and psychological aspects of an individual's efforts. Following my artistic instincts and scientific training combined, I had drawn on Eisner also in Chapter 1, to refashion Elkana's notion as one of arts-and-science-in-the-making. In line with this formulation I argue my current writing to be one such case, wherein I have pursued a practitioner oriented practical-theoretical approach to educational research in line with CHAT. While adopting such an approach has contributed to my responding at length to my research questions, besides wider educational interests, certain key aspects emerge as I write as a practitioner for practitioners.

The *first* is that in focusing on the notion of practice and attending to the concrete-practical in my studies, it was not the notion of practice per se but the nature of action, theory and dialectic at play which became key to taking transformative action. I contend a triangulation of these notions, which are themselves polysemic and unsaturated, to allow for realisation of three other aspects, (1) dwell upon what it might mean to do empirical research in an unjust world, besides view such efforts in coherence with what our reporting preaches in theory (Lather in Chapter 7), (2) be able to exercise deliberation with respect to means and ends, so that particular children in particular classrooms benefit from the best possible alternative that is available to carry out (Schwab in Chapter 8), besides (3) take intelligent action in line with Dewey, by which one examines not only the *how*, but also the *why* and *what for* questions which are pertinent to any educational practice (Biesta & Burbules in Chapter 8).

Second, in arriving at the three notions dwelt in the previous section, in addition to the construct of practitioner-as-artist-and-scientist I shall soon present, my very writing with regards my study has played a central role. By this I mean that towards my intention to be of service to the concrete practical, my writing has been able to (1) engage with issues encountered along my extended journey, making my writing both means and material for my personal investigation, something Vygotsky himself practiced (Sinha in Chapter 4), (2) record various actions I took over time, so that in being diachronic my writing allows readers to appreciate the why of various actions I took along the way (Polkinghorne in Chapter 5), and (3) benefit from capturing meaning of the work I did at a reflective distance from my lived experience, so that I could become more discerning of the personal sense I made of events as well as language, so as to appreciate the implications they in turn connote (van Manen in Chapter 6).

Third and finally I forward the analytical construct of *practitioner-as-artist-and-scientist.* Alluding to both teachers and researchers working in concrete practicals which are educational and geared to teaching-learning, I intend this construct to be wholistic in line with the romantic and non classical science which CHAT perspectives aspire (Luria in Chapter 3). I also view the intent of this construct to emerge from two lines of thought, (1) that any teacher or researcher as practitioner is embodiment of many an aspect in incessant dialectic in terms of being a doer, actor, performer, care giver, friend, pedagogue, knower, knowledge producer, researcher and storehouse of wisdom – in short constantly striving and exercising his or her role as both artist and scientist combined, and (2) that, the practice of arts and the practice of science are themselves unsaturated and abound with creativity if social and material conditions allow them to so flourish. The practitioner-as-artist-and-scientist as construct is thus unsaturated as well and recognises the plurality of its empirical manifestation as a given. Far from conceiving the construct as a mentalistic one, that can be in turn used as a box to tick in the hands of teacher educators, policy makers besides members of the educational bureaucracy, I argue for the potential of this holistic construct to (1) be a together-system in the developmental sense, whereby practitioners are viewed as unified individuals who

EPILOGUE

draw on their combined symbolic, affective, practical, social, motor as well as intellectual processes (Stetsenko in Chapter 3), and (2) form a central, pivotal, critical and very much a living unit of analysis with respect to instruction, schooling and education (Zinchenko in Chapter 3). Such a unit can be used to conceptualise the teacher in far richer terms than is probably the present case and be deployed in three different grain size, in turn shedding light on the individual teacher, everyday schooling and the societal practices of education at large in tandem.

With respect to *the individual teacher*, the practitioner-as-artist-and-scientist as unit could ascertain say, (1) if any practitioner is exercising her personal self as an artist, scientist and the dialectic in-between. Is the curriculum mandated expecting conformity on her part or allowing her to exercise her personal experience with the subject matter. In other words is the practitioner's world making including or excluding the making of her self in the process of teaching (Britzman in Chapter 5), (2) if any practitioner is achieving her self-determination through teaching. In other words is the underlying relationship between existing theory and practice useful only to achieve predetermined outcomes or is the relationship enabling her to become critically self-aware and work in an autonomous manner (Fay in Chapter 7), and/or (3) if the practitioner is not only able to address who she presently is but who she could possibly become in addition. Making demands on moral and political stands that might also position her against the grain, is she viewing herself as mattering or not to history, culture as well as society at large (Stetsenko this Chapter).

With respect to *everyday schooling*, the practitioner-as-artist-and-scientist as unit could ascertain, (1) if any practitioner is finding school to be an institution which is facilitating her learning to teach. Is it the case that even though she is feeling isolated and lonely, she feels the pressure of having to appear competent in addressing any and all problems that tend to arise in its functioning (Sarason in Chapter 2), (2) if a practitioner is finding her school to be an institution that is a context for her teaching. In other words is there opportunity for her to work with her students and colleagues in a collaborative manner in activity settings where a zpd can be formed and knowledgable others can assist the performance of novice learners (Tharp & Gallimore in Chapter 4), and/or (3) if any practitioner is only dealing with the reality she finds currently existing in her school, or is she able to deploy her imagination to transcend that very everyday. Is the material culture engaged with by students bemoaned for its failures, or is there opportunity for her to make students conscious of the many unconscious aspects of their culture (Willis in Chapter 6).

With respect to *the societal practice of education*, the practitioner-as-artist-and-scientist as unit could ascertain, (1) if any practitioner is feeling locked into circumstances defined by others or is she able to move past the taken-for-granted and summon alternative ways for living and being in the world. Is her imagination given free play, so that she could look at existing situations as if they could be otherwise (Greene in Chapter 1), (2) if any practitioner is creating opportunities for the co-construction and production of knowledge rather than simply transferring knowledge. In other words is she allowing herself and her students to be equally subject and object in naming their world, or allowing some others to name the world on their behalf (Freire in Chapter 7), and/or (3) if any practitioner is using artistic concepts and research methods that serve the richness and uniqueness of educational life. For methods of inquiry and theories are of relevance only if they achieve levels of precision suited to the concrete practical within ongoing education (Eisner in Chapter 8).

I hope the above arguments have as example, helped me demonstrate some of the ways in which the practitioner-as-artist-and-scientist as a unit can provide insight while examining educational practices in reality with regards to individual teachers, everyday schooling and societal practices of education at large. I contend such insight to be invaluable in aiding the ability of practitioners to take CHAT based transformative action, besides also draw upon numerous analytical lenses this writing has highlighted. It is in allowing such realisation that reform efforts can promote and not rein in the human development of both practitioners and students in their charge. Of no small significance is the manner in which attending to the human in CHAT, can become basis for realising mathematics education and its research in human terms so as to bring a humanistic philosophy of mathematics to life. In drawing my arguments favouring a CHAT based practice of education and educational research to a final conclusion, I revisit the emphasis Vygotsky's collaborator Luria articulated in terms of ascending from the abstract to the concrete. Herein Luria in turn alludes to Goethe's succinct dictum that grey is any theory, evergreen is the tree of life. In pursing a romantic and non-classical approach in line with both scholars and the strengths of an implementable analytical unit in terms of practitioner-as-artist-and-scientist, I argue it very possible for education and educational research to ascend from the grey to the green.

References

Bakhtin, M. M. (1981). *The dialogic imagination: Four essays.* University of Texas Press.
Clark, K., & Holquist, M. (1984). *Mikhail Bakhtin.* The Belknap Press of Harvard University Press.

EPILOGUE

Davydov, V. V. (1999). What is real learning activity? In M. Hedegaard & J. Lompscher (Eds.), *Learning activity and development* (pp. 123–138). Aarhus University Press.

Davydov, V. V., & Markova, A. K. (1982/1983). A concept of educational activity for school children. *Soviet Psychology*, *21*(2), 50–76.

Gade, S. (2006). *The micro-culture of a mathematics classroom: Artefacts and activity in meaning making and problem solving* [Doctoral dissertation]. Agder University College.

Gade, S. (2013). Surface area to volume ratio and metabolism: Analysing small group-task as Vygotskian activity. In C. Smith (Ed.), *Proceedings of the British Society for Research into Learning Mathematics (BSRLM)*, *33*(3), 25–30.

Gade, S., & Forsgren, T. L. (2019). Realising transformative agency and student identity: Meaningful practical activity based formative intervention at grade eight. *Cultural Studies of Science Education*, *14*(4), 897–914.

Luria, A. R. (1973). *The working brain: An introduction to neuropsychology*. Allen Lane, The Penguin Press.

Saran, R., & Gade, S. (2016). *Examining social situation of development, with two students of mathematics at grade four, in different national contexts* [Paper]. AERA 2016 annual meeting, AERA Online Paper Repository.

Stetsenko, A. (2013). Theorizing personhood for the world in transition and change: Reflections from a transformative activist stance on human development. In J. Martin & M. H. Bickhard (Eds.), *The psychology of personhood: Philosophical, historical, social-developmental and narrative perspectives* (pp. 181–199). Cambridge University Press.

Vygotsky, L. S. (1978). *Mind in society: The development of higher psychological processes*. Harvard University Press.

Vygotsky, L. S. (1998). *The collected works of L S Vygotsky: Volume 5 – Child psychology*. Plenum Press.

Vygotsky, L. S. (2004). The crisis at age seven. In R. W. Rieber & D. K. Robinson (Eds.), *The essential Vygotsky* (pp. 491–499). Kluwer Academic/Plenum Publishers.

Weissbourd, B. (1985). Foreword. In J. V. Wertsch (Ed.), *Culture, communication and cognition: Vygotskian perspectives* (pp. vii–viii). Cambridge University Press.

Subject Index

action research 6, 11, 38, 105, 112–115, 121, 122, 126, 129, 130, 183, 204, 206, 231, 238, 239, 283, 284
activity as unit of analysis 42, 66–70, 102, 152, 231
activity of knowing 62, 266, 267, 272
activity settings 97, 98, 100, 130, 289
ahimsa 4, 5
alienation in education 175
analysis into units 60
answerability 134
artefacts 42, 51, 54, 57, 61–65, 68, 70, 149, 231, 284
artistic imagination 1, 12, 14, 16
arts-and-science-in-the-making 1, 18–20, 279–281, 287
ascending to the concrete 41, 42, 71–73, 83, 116, 163, 189, 279
authoritative discourse 131
axiology 187, 188, 232

child's development of the child 9, 155, 158, 206, 248
citizenship education 8, 141
classification 62, 63, 148, 149, 199, 212
close-to-practice research 167, 284
co-being 280
co-consciousness 280
cogenerative dialogue 247, 248, 251, 254, 260
co-knowing 261, 262, 280
collaborative classroom practice 42, 47, 48, 50–53, 64, 71, 98
commodification of knowledge 267
common culture 146, 147, 214, 286
consciousness as method 18, 37, 67, 101, 102, 156, 157, 171, 173, 261
cooperative learning 42, 43, 45–48, 50, 51, 141
critical consciousness 169, 172, 173, 286
critical mathematics education 167, 168
critical ontology 173, 175–177, 184
critical periods 156–158, 160
critical race testimonios 200
critical theory 31, 178
cultivating humanity 1, 6, 16
cultural meaning 264–266

cultural tools 9, 11, 42–45, 47, 54–59, 61, 96, 265, 282

deliberation 52, 58, 118, 181, 209–212, 214, 216, 218, 287, 288
developmental education 264, 267
diachronic research 111
dialectical methodology 35, 58, 61, 77, 286
dialogic inquiry 266, 267
dialogism 132
difference 39, 70, 120, 129, 138, 141, 142, 149, 155, 160, 177, 185, 187, 198, 199, 203, 236, 245, 248, 264, 277, 280, 281, 284
directive functions 101, 102, 262
double stimulation 65, 232, 233

ecological validity 79, 80, 279
educational research 1, 2, 5–7, 20, 27, 28, 32, 41, 76, 79, 89, 105, 113, 117, 126, 151, 173, 184, 185, 187, 199, 202, 206, 212, 214, 215, 220, 221, 230, 260, 262, 264, 273, 278, 282, 283, 284, 287, 290
enterprise education 141
ethnographic imagination 145
everyday concepts 37, 98, 99, 159
expansive learning activity 254–256
experimental genetic method 59, 62, 65
explicit mediation 112, 234, 235, 239, 246, 254, 262, 265
exploratory talk 154, 247–249, 251, 262, 266

feminism 168
flexible purposing 13
formative interventions 80, 152, 183, 231–234, 240, 241, 246, 249, 253, 254, 258, 262
framing 148, 149
functional approach to cognition 89
funds of knowledge 92–95

general rules 6, 7
genre 110, 119, 124, 133, 134, 146, 165, 216, 280

heteroglossia 131, 280
hermeneutic phenomenology 161
hidden curriculum 178, 179, 268

294 SUBJECT INDEX

higher psychological activity   10, 37, 59, 66,
 67, 69, 71, 73, 286
human action   1–4, 12, 16, 45, 64, 65, 95, 108,
 111, 220, 221, 231, 282, 283
human freedom   27, 28, 55, 57
human transformation   1, 9, 11, 12, 16
humanistic mathematics   1, 16

ideological misunderstanding   139, 148
implicit mediation   65, 150, 151
impossible role of the teacher   209
impressionist painting   230
improvable object   266, 267
indigenous research   168
inquiry as stance   117–120, 210, 283
integrated intelligence   27, 28, 37
intellectual craftsmanship   198, 199
internalisation   10, 44, 45, 54, 56, 96
internally persuasive discourse   131, 132
intolerance of diversity   267

knowledge artefacts   62, 63
knowledge as attribute   34
knowledge as narrative   34, 35

landscape of teaching-learning   262, 264
leading activity   154, 155, 157–160, 262
learning by doing   209, 210
lesson study framework   129, 130
liberal education   6, 8, 28
life history research   121–123

meaningful practical activity   87, 100, 102,
 183, 256, 262
mediated action   42, 61, 63, 64–66, 283
mediated agency   42, 61, 64–66, 243, 246, 258
mediation   64, 65, 93, 95, 112, 150, 151, 157,
 158, 183, 231, 234, 235, 239, 246, 254, 262,
 265, 283
methodological pluralism   215, 281
multilogical curriculum   174

narrative imagination   8, 12
narrative research   106, 107, 109, 111, 112, 283
nature of action   64, 272, 281, 282, 287
nature of dialectic at play   272, 282, 287
nature of theory   178, 272, 282, 287

objects-that-could-be-used-for-a-certain-
 purpose   47

pedagogical categories   151, 152, 154, 262
pedagogical thoughtfulness   160, 161
pedagogy of cases   216, 217
person centric research   125
personal practical knowledge   23, 32–35, 42,
 110, 130, 189, 262, 282, 286
personal sense   10, 202, 264–266, 281, 288
personhood   276–278, 280
phronesis   187, 222, 243, 247
poiesis   187
polysemy   185, 187, 281, 282
portfolio   215, 218–220, 285
positivistic approach in education   175
practical thinking   88, 90
practice based professional
 development   219, 220
practitioner as artist-and-scientist   272,
 287–290
practitioner judgement   111, 112, 222
practitioner reflexivity   127, 167
presentational talk   247, 248
primary ignorance   214
professional judgement   205
professional knowledge landscapes   34, 35,
 42, 262, 285
professional learning tasks   219
progressive teacher   210
psychological misunderstanding   139

qualification   139, 221

radical listening   187
reflective rationality   129
relational agency   241–244, 247, 251, 254, 260
relational knowing   234, 236, 237, 240–242,
 251, 260
research as bricolage   173, 184–187
research as praxis   181–183, 191
research on education   6, 17, 117, 219, 220,
 242, 246, 282, 284

Sarvodaya   4, 5
satyagraha   4, 5, 78
school children's learning activity   274
scientific concepts   99, 276
secondary ignorance   214
self-conscious thinker   198, 285
self study research   126
situated learning   82–85, 183, 287
socialisation   221

SUBJECT INDEX

social situation of development 275
socio-institutional aspects of pedagogy 147, 150
spiral of knowing 267
stable periods 156, 157
stimulus-means 233, 239–243
subjectification 53, 221
swaraj 4, 5, 285

taste of words 280
teacher as artist is researcher 202, 205, 206
teacher's voice 122, 161
teaching as assisting performance 97
teaching as school practice 109, 112
teaching is a lonely profession 38
technological misunderstanding 139
theory 2, 5, 6, 9–11, 16, 31, 35, 39, 41, 52, 61, 62, 66, 68, 71, 73, 76–78, 83, 85, 92, 93, 95, 96, 106, 110, 111, 114, 116, 118, 127, 149, 151, 154, 167–169, 172, 178, 181, 182, 186, 189, 191, 193, 198, 203, 204, 206–210, 212, 218–221, 223–225, 231, 251, 252, 260, 265, 272, 278, 279, 282, 284–290
third space 200, 208
together-systems 56, 106, 288
tool-and-result approach 77, 78, 286
transformative activist stance 12, 256, 258, 277
transformative agency 267, 268
transforming experiment 79–81, 232

universal rules 6, 7, 287
utopian misunderstanding 139

validity in qualitative research 165

working the dialectic 117, 118

zone of proximal development 42–44, 173

Author Index

Alvarez, Amelia   87, 100–102, 183, 256, 257, 262, 283
Anyon, J.   178–181
Arendt, Hannah   2–5, 12, 64, 125, 222, 223
Arievitch, Igor   11, 12, 20, 58, 116

Baker, David   141–143
Bakhtin, Mikhail   110, 130–134, 165, 254, 261, 280, 281
Barnes, Douglas   247, 248
Bernstein, Basil   147–150
Biesta, Gert   207, 220–224, 226
Britzman, Deborah   125, 126
Bronfenbrenner, Urie   79–82, 232, 276
Bronowski, Jacob   19, 175
Bruner, Jerome   107, 108, 112, 223, 224, 226, 272
Bullough, Robert   126, 127
Burbules, Nicholas   220, 221

Chaiklin, Seth   53, 54, 89, 181
Clandinin, Jean   33, 34, 42, 110, 111, 130, 189
Clark, Katerina   280
Cochran-Smith, Marilyn   116, 118–120, 210
Cole, Michael   59, 61, 62, 64, 87–89, 157, 231, 232, 239
Connelly, Michael   34, 42, 110, 130, 207, 230
Craig, Cheryl   202, 211, 215
Crozier, Gill   143

Dalton, Stephanie   151, 152, 154
Daniels, Harry   147–151, 174
Davydov, V.   273–276
del Rio, Pablo   87, 100–102, 183, 256, 257
Dewey, John   13, 14, 198, 201, 207, 209, 210, 220, 221, 283, 288

Edwards, Anne   167, 241, 243, 244
Eisner, Elliot   12–15, 207, 210–215, 281, 287
Elkana, Yehuda   19, 20, 287
Elkonin, D. B.   275
Elliott, J.   6, 7, 113, 117, 203–205
Engels, F.   66, 192

Freire, Paolo   169–173, 181, 184, 190, 192, 198, 200, 283

Gallimore, Ronald   38, 96–100
Gandhi   2, 4–6, 27, 78, 184
Goethe   71–73, 290
Goodson, Ivor   121–125, 133, 219
Greene, Maxine   12, 14–16, 105, 169

Hollingsworth, Sandra   236–238

Illeris, Knud   139, 148

John-Steiner, Vera   261

Karpov, Yuriy   99, 100, 154, 155, 157–160, 276
Kincheloe, Joe   173–178, 184–187, 222
Krishnamurti, Jiddu   23, 26–28, 30, 33, 37, 102, 170

Lather, Patti   182–184, 191
Lave, Jean   82–88, 94, 183, 287
Leont'ev, Aleksei   9, 66–71, 78, 80, 81, 193, 243, 260–262, 265, 266, 280, 281
LeTendre, Gerald   141–143
Levins, Richard   189
Lewin, Kurt   11, 38, 115, 116, 284
Lewontin, Richard   188–191
Luria, Alexander   9, 71–73, 76, 78, 106, 116, 273, 281, 290

Mahn, Holbrook   156, 157, 160
Marx, K.   18, 43, 53, 62, 66, 68, 72, 73, 106, 145, 156, 166, 167, 179, 181, 184, 190, 192
McKeon, Richard   189, 190, 207, 220
McNiff, Jean   114, 115
Mercer, Neil   248, 249, 263
Mills, C Wright   198, 199, 201, 204
Moll, Luis   92–96, 151

Nias, Jennifer   127–130
Noffke, Susan   115, 117
Norris, Nigel   203–205
Nussbaum, Martha   6–8, 12, 14, 15, 24, 28, 106, 287

Ollman, Bertell   190
Olson, David   224–226

AUTHOR INDEX

Pilbeam, David   230
Pinnegar, Stephanie   126, 127
Polkinghorne, Donald   111, 182

Radford, Luis   18, 71
Roth, Wolff-Michael   18, 71, 251–253
Ross, Vicki   202, 211, 215

Sarason, Seymour   23, 38, 39, 96, 102, 127, 128, 211, 244
Schwab, Joseph   206–211, 214–216, 218, 230, 231
Scribner, Sylvia   59, 64, 87–91, 95, 157, 239
Seeger, Falk   167
Shulman, Lee   207, 215–219
Skovsmose, Ole   167, 183
Stenhouse, Lawrence   202–206, 208
Stetsenko, Anna   11, 12, 16, 18, 20, 44, 45, 47, 55–58, 102, 106, 116, 170, 172, 181, 192, 220, 256, 258, 259, 263, 265, 268, 276–278

Tagore, Rabindranath   23–27
Tharp, Roland   38, 96–100, 151, 152, 154
Tobin, K.   2, 173, 184, 187, 232, 248, 251, 253, 281

van Manen, Max   160–162
van Oers, Bert   264–267
Venable, Vernon   192, 193
Vygotsky, Lev   9–12, 18, 23, 32, 35–38, 41–44, 47, 48, 52–63, 65–67, 69, 71–73, 76–78, 82, 85, 89, 91, 95, 101, 102, 106, 107, 147, 150, 155–157, 159, 173, 179, 181, 190, 192, 198, 207, 240, 243, 249, 262, 265, 266, 273–275, 280, 281, 284, 286, 288, 290

Wartofsky   62, 63
Wells, Gordon   62, 63, 264, 266, 267, 272
Wertsch, James   64–67, 112, 151, 239, 243, 246, 254, 258, 262, 281
Willis, Paul   143–147, 150

Zinchenko, Vladimir   61

Printed in the United States
by Baker & Taylor Publisher Services